Le chant intime

Le chant intime

The Interpretation of French Mélodie

FRANÇOIS LE ROUX
ROMAIN RAYNALDY

English Translation by
SYLVIA KAHAN

OXFORD
UNIVERSITY PRESS

OXFORD
UNIVERSITY PRESS

Oxford University Press is a department of the University of Oxford. It furthers
the University's objective of excellence in research, scholarship, and education
by publishing worldwide. Oxford is a registered trade mark of Oxford University
Press in the UK and certain other countries.

Published in the United States of America by Oxford University Press
198 Madison Avenue, New York, NY 10016, United States of America.

Library of Congress Cataloging-in-Publication Data
Names: Le Roux, François, author. | Raynaldy, Romain, author.
Title: Le chant intime : the interpretation of French mélodie /
François Le Roux, Romain Raynaldy.
Other titles: Chant intime. English
Description: New York : Oxford University Press, 2021. |
Includes bibliographical references and index.
Identifiers: LCCN 2020042106 (print) | LCCN 2020042107 (ebook) |
ISBN 9780190884178 (hardback) | ISBN 9780190884185 (paperback) |
ISBN 9780197552278 (updf) | ISBN 9780197564516 (oso) | ISBN 9780197552285 (epub)
Subjects: LCSH: Songs, French—France—History and criticism. |
Songs, French—Interpretation (Phrasing, dynamics, etc.)
Classification: LCC ML2827 .L3913 2021 (print) | LCC ML2827 (ebook) |
DDC 782.421680944—dc23
LC record available at https://lccn.loc.gov/2020042106
LC ebook record available at https://lccn.loc.gov/2020042107

DOI: 10.1093/oso/9780190884178.001.0001

1 3 5 7 9 8 6 4 2

Paperback printed by Marquis, Canada
Hardback printed by Bridgeport National Bindery, Inc., United States of America

Contents

Foreword   ix

Introduction   1

PART I: LISTENING TO AND UNDERSTANDING
FRENCH MÉLODIE

1. To Listen   5

2. To Know   13

3. To Perform   28

PART II: ANALYSIS AND INTERPRETATION
OF FRENCH MÉLODIES

4. Georges Auric   49
   Le petit bois   49

5. Hector Berlioz   53
   Au cimetière   53

6. Charles Bordes   59
   Sur un vieil air   59

7. Lili Boulanger   63
   Reflets   63
   Le retour   66

8. Emmanuel Chabrier   70
   Pastorale des cochons roses   70
   Tes yeux bleus   73

9. Cécile Chaminade   75
   Malgré nous   75
   Mignonne   77

10. Ernest Chausson   81
    La chanson bien douce   81
    Le chevalier Malheur   87

11. Claude Debussy   91
    NUITS BLANCHES   91
       I. *Nuit sans fin*   92
      II. *Lorsqu'elle est entrée*   96
    Apparition   101

TROIS POÈMES DE STÉPHANE MALLARMÉ 103
  I. *Soupir* 104
  II. *Placet futile* 105
  III. *Éventail* 106

12. Henri Duparc 108
Sérénade 108
Romance de Mignon 114
Le galop 117

13. Louis Durey 122
TROIS POÈMES DE PÉTRONE 122
  I. *La boule de neige* 123
  II. *La métempsycose* 124
  III. *La grenade* 125

14. Henri Dutilleux 127
San Francisco Night 127

15. Gabriel Fauré 131
L'absent 131
Puisque j'ai mis ma lèvre 135
Tristesse d'Olympio 138
Cygne sur l'eau 141

16. Charles Gounod 149
Ô ma belle rebelle 149
Ma belle amie est morte (Lamento) 153

17. Reynaldo Hahn 157
En sourdine 157
Au pays musulman 162

18. Philippe Hersant 167
Paroles peintes 167

19. Augusta Holmès 174
Rondel 174

20. Arthur Honegger 179
TROIS POÈMES DE PAUL FORT 179
  I. *Le chasseur perdu en forêt* 180
  II. *Cloche du soir* 181
  III. *Chanson de fol* 184

21. Vincent d'Indy 186
L'amour et le crâne 186

22. Marie Jaëll 190
Larmes 190

23. Thierry Lancino 194
L'amour par terre 194

24. Jules Massenet 201
    Le poète et le fantôme 201

25. Olivier Messiaen 206
    TROIS MÉLODIES 206
        I. *Pourquoi?* 206
        II. *Le sourire* 208
        III. *La fiancée perdue* 209

26. Darius Milhaud 211
    L'innocence 211

27. Francis Poulenc 214
    Poète et ténor 214
    Pierrot 218

28. Ravel 221
    Les grands vents venus d'outre-mer 221
    Sainte 224
    DEUX ÉPIGRAMMES DE CLÉMENT MAROT 226
        I. *D'Anne, qui me jecta de la neige* 227
        II. *D'Anne jouant de l'espinette* 228

29. Albert Roussel 230
    La menace 230

30. Camille Saint-Saëns 237
    Au cimetière 237
    Si vous n'avez rien à me dire 242
    Grasselette et maigrelette 244

31. Déodat de Séverac 250
    Paysages tristes: Soleils couchants 250
    Les hiboux 252

32. Germaine Tailleferre 255
    Vrai Dieu, qui m'y confortera 255

33. Pauline Viardot 259
    Lamento 259
    Ici-bas tous les lilas meurent 262

Glossary of Poetic Forms and Terms 267
Bibliography 269
Credits 277
Index 279

Foreword

This book on French song was born one morning in January 1999 in the backstage area of the Opéra-Comique in Paris. That morning, I met François Le Roux for the first time, on the occasion of the revival of *Pelléas et Mélisande*, directed by Pierre Médecin. It was in this production that François undertook the role of Golaud, after having shone for many years in the role of Pelléas. Our meeting gave me the material for a portrait for *Le journal de l'Opéra-Comique*: the interview covered many subjects. François was gracious during this exercise. And it was in the course of this conversation—much longer than anticipated—that, after a side discussion on the subject of French song, he told me, jokingly, "I would have much to say on the subject of song, but an article wouldn't be long enough. It would need an entire book!" The phrase ran around in my head. So much so that, one week later, I wrote François to suggest him that we do this book together. After one more meeting, he trusted me with the project—something for which I thank him deeply—and he agreed to get started.

My position was neither that of a learned person nor of a scholar, but that of a journalist, music lover, and "honest man." I suggested that François not take a musicological approach to French art song, but rather to write the kind of work that would allow his readers to discover and expand their understanding in a lively and accessible language. The same pedagogical concern carried over to the analysis of the songs. Singers will find here enough to satisfy their curiosity and to accompany their apprenticeship, while music lovers will have at their disposal a valuable listening guide.

In its first version, *Le chant intime* was presented as a series of interviews, in which I undertook the role of Candide. If the final edition did not retain this form, it preserved the spontaneity and the generosity of numerous discussions on wide-ranging subjects.

Romain Raynaldy

My thanks go first to Romain Raynaldy, who came up with the idea of writing a piece "in two voices." To Sophie Debouverie, director of the music department at Fayard Publications, who permitted the publication of this book. To Jean-Pierre Angremy (1937–2010), for having imagined and sparked off the exploration of the French song repertoire "in concerts" at the Bibliothèque nationale de France, over five fruitful years, from 1997 to 2002. Then to all those—musicologists, composers, poets, conductors, pianists, and singers—who pushed me further and further in the study and interpretation of French song. They are very numerous, and as they will appear in the course of the text, I will mention only my longtime accomplices: Marie-Claude Arbaretaz, Nicole Aubert-Cazalet, Erik Berchot, Thierry Bodin, my aunt Marta Bracchi-Le Roux (1932–2000), Philippe Cassard, Nicolas Chevereau, Myriam Chimènes, Jeff Cohen, Gérard Condé, Irwin Gage (1939–2018), Elizabeth Giuliani, Olivier Godin, Mikhail Hallak, Denis Herlin, Cyril Huvé, David Hunter, Christian Ivaldi, Graham Johnson, Hervé Lacombe, Alexandra Laederich, Louis Langrée, Noël Lee (1924–2013), Felicity Lott, Catherine Massip, Mady Mesplé (1931–2020), Jason Nedecky, Philippa Neuteboom, Pascal Rogé, Craig Rutenberg, David Selig, Madame Rosine Seringe (1918–2017), Rena Sharon, Nicolas Southon, Erika Switzer, Alexandre Tharaud, Roger Vignoles, and Vincent Vivès. A special mention goes to the irreplaceable François Lesure (1923–2001), who left us too soon, and who, in a certain way, "entrusted" me with Debussy's NUITS BLANCHES, and eternally inoculated me with the "bug" of collecting manuscripts—handwritten and unpublished documents. This book, on an art form that he so loved, is dedicated to him.

Of course, and her name could easily have been cited earlier with the other musicians and partners mentioned above, my gratitude and admiration goes to Sylvia Kahan, who offered and provided the translation in English of the original book in French, and contributed to its updating in many ways. Her contribution is priceless, as is the collaboration of all OUP people with whom Romain and I have worked, notably Suzanne Ryan and Sean Decker. The English *Chant intime* could not have existed without them.

Finally, Romain and I thank Isabelle Cortès, François Lesens, Sara Ceberio and Dan Siegelstein for their helpful remarks.

François Le Roux

Introduction

This book is born of an observation as obvious as it is astonishing: since the 1978 publication of Pierre Bernac's work, *The Interpretation of French Song*, almost nothing has been written on the interpretation of French art song by a recognized singer in this specialized domain of the art of singing. And that which was published was not in French, but in English, since it was published in the United States and the United Kingdom. Closer to us in France, the great recitalist (among other things) Gérard Souzay (1918–2004) penned several works, but these are books of recollections. From time to time, of course, some interpretive suggestions can be found in there, but not in a way that is significant, and, consequently, not in a way that can be efficiently helpful to the singer wishing to learn. Additionally, while indeed there exist essays and musicological studies on French art song, as well as guides to repertoire, they approach only in an incomplete or a biased manner the subjects of style and interpretation. These subjects determine, however, the specificity of the genre. For the most recent work on French song, one should consult the books by my friend, the incomparable collaborative pianist Graham Johnson. He has written on the entire recital repertoire of lied and mélodie; on French song in particular, Johnson has written, with Richard Stokes, the indispensable *A French Song Companion* (Oxford University Press, 2000).

I will also cite Marie-Claire Rohinsky's *The Singer's Debussy* (1987), which also discusses phonetics, and Robert Gartside's *Interpreting the Songs of Maurice Ravel* (1992). Jane Bathori's *Sur l'interpretation des mélodies de Claude Debussy* (1953) has been published in English under the title *On the Interpretation of the Mélodies of Claude Debussy* (Pendragon Press, 1998). Obviously, these last works do not include the numerous songs by the composer of *Pelléas* discovered—or rediscovered—in the second half of the twentieth century. There are also *50 mélodies françaises* by Charles Panzéra (1896–1976), written in French and English (1964), but if you want to find it, you'd better try your luck by visiting the used-book sellers along the river Seine in Paris, known as the "bouquinistes." In sum, the books on interpretation are few and far between. Finding them is no easy task.

However, it seems that a new generation of singers wants to seize this enormous span of French music, which also serves poetry in all its musicality. You can tell by the number of recent recordings, recital programs, and the crowds at specialized performance classes. As for interpretation itself, it has evolved quite a bit in the last several decades, and certain principles mandated by Pierre Bernac deserve to be

Le Chant Intime. François Le Roux and Romain Raynaldy, Oxford University Press. © Oxford University Press 2021.
DOI: 10.1093/oso/9780190884178.003.0001

nuanced, others reaffirmed. For all these reasons, it seems to me to be as necessary as it is interesting to write a book on this theme.

In Part I, Listening To and Understanding French Mélodie, I will endeavor to sensitize the reader (and the singer!) to French mélodie, in taking a path that goes from listening to interpretation, while building understanding of the song genre. For we must not put the cart before the horse: I find that, in musical training, the "doing" is usually put before the "learning," which I see as a fundamental error. This division begins not with vocal technique, but with "reception" of the song. I think that this is a good way to proceed when wanting to get involved with interpretation—and even more so with the teaching of interpretation. For it is hoped that this book will interest both singers and teachers of singing—the two categories more or less overlapping, sooner or later.

In Part II, Analysis and Interpretation of French Mélodies, I will discuss sixty mélodies, from Berlioz to the present day, each time bringing together analysis (poetic and musical) and interpretation. It seems to me impossible to approach interpretation by limiting the discussion to vocal technique and the printed phrase. Musical and poetic analyses are indispensable.

As for the choice of songs, given the immensity of the repertoire (between 1870 and 1920 alone, around 30,000 mélodies or related materials were catalogued at the Bibliothèque nationale de France!), I had to arbitrate. In a way, I tried to supplement what Bernac had already done, in choosing works that he had not discussed, or composers that he had rejected—notably a number of women composers, whose important contribution to the art of song has rarely been brought to light by my predecessors, and to whom we have given the place that they deserve. Additionally, I thought it was important to write about and study the work of contemporary composers. I am proud to include an unpublished song by Thierry Lancino, who is among those whose works are analyzed. Generally speaking, I have chosen only songs that I know well. And even with this enormous restriction, the repertoire is so vast (and that's a good thing!) that I had to leave much out. But I would like to think that this book will inspire the publication of others, in such a way that new songs by "great oldies" will be discovered—but also, I hope, a body of contemporary songs will be developed, and, as a result, the singers of the young generation will be "bitten by the bug" of song.

PART I
LISTENING TO AND UNDERSTANDING FRENCH MÉLODIE

1

To Listen

The French language is already, as a consequence of its unique sonority, intrinsically musical. And the French language that is at the source of French art song is poetic language, wedded as much to harmony (consonant or dissonant) and rhythm (regular or irregular) as to image and meaning. Additionally, a simple poetic phrase, by virtue of all the meanings that it contains, whether overt or hidden, can open multiple doors. It's for that reason that working on an art song—and, by extension, on the French language—involves the ear more than the voice, at least the first time around. A professor should first give young singers the appetite to listen to very subtle things in order to then try to get them to reproduce—to savor—the sounds. We cannot start with the assertion "on the basis of what I know, my technique, and my sound, I am immediately going to find the colors." That discovery can be done only as a second step. The first step is to listen—and to listen first to the text, to become impregnated by it.

So, reading a poem out loud is the first step. However, the student is warned against "adding in the notes"—or of interpreting too fast the intentions or nuances that can be discerned. At the same time, written punctuation is done more for a visual reading than for sonic rhythm; it doesn't indicate where to breathe. To sum up, one should strive for a "neutral" reading. I will explain in the following section.

From Sound to Word

The attitude of the future performer, at this stage as in those that follow, should be as dual as that of a puppetmaster and a puppet: the puppetmaster acts (here, speaks); the puppet follows (listens) and memorizes. This double task should be performed, ideally, on all poetic phrases. In consequence, one discovers a succession of sonorities that the poet desires. It's even more clear that the work of poetry chosen by musicians is written to be spoken, and thus, of necessity, possesses a vocal quality, even before being set to music by the composer. I repeat, what I mean by "working the ear" is the acute yet passive attention to the multiple sonic propositions that could be given to a simple phrase. Ideally, one should be able to read a poetic text while listening objectively, without "explanation of preconceived meaning," to its sonorous result. It's a little like reading through a new score, and listening to the music that one has read only in one's head. It's not an easy exercise, but everything is a question of learning. It's better to begin with poetry in verse than

Le Chant Intime. François Le Roux and Romain Raynaldy, Oxford University Press. © Oxford University Press 2021.
DOI: 10.1093/oso/9780190884178.003.0002

with prose—it's much easier. With prose, you have to make your own divisions and find the poet's intentions—but, generally, there's nothing obvious to help you!

And, then, the professor should be there to guide the student. The goal of instruction, in my view, is to show that each phrase, each word has a musical emission, an aesthetic value inherent to the French language, something that gives it its flavor. Let's take a simple example: the word "amour" (love). It's a key word of poetry. The equivalent in Italian is *amore* and in Spanish *amor*. In pronouncing these words within the same Romance languages family as French, we see that the [a] and the [o] are very close in terms of vocalization and the [m] is barely hinted at, in a sort of pout; however, the shape formed in the oral tract changes very little from one language to another. Now let's pronounce "amour." Passing from an open and relatively full vowel like [a] to a vowel pronounced in the back of the vocal tract, the [u]—the farthest back of the whole sonic palate—via a consonant to which one puts sound, the [m] (in French, this pronunciation is possible only with [z], [ʒ], [n], [m], and [v]) requires the singer to give a precise weight and the right amount of emphasis to the consonant. One cannot half-swallow the [m] or get around it—that's impossible. This connection or passage between two vowels that absolutely can't be gotten around is typically French. The only thing that can be done is to give equal weight—some would say the same accent—to the two vowels and to insert between them a fully sonorous [m], produced with the lips. This effect cannot be found in either the Italian *amore*, in which the upper jaw is relaxed, or the German *Liebe* (the German equivalent) or the English *love*, in which the flicking of the tongue in [l] is essential. This process is how a word translated from another language gives a different image and physical perception to the same emotion.

The French verb *approfondir* (to deepen) is equally interesting to analyze from a sonic point of view. We find the word, for example, in the verse "Et dont l'unique soin était d'approfondir" (And whose sole task it was to fathom) from Charles Baudelaire's poem *La vie antérieure* (Past life), which has been set to music many times. Here is an example of how a word phonetically evokes its meaning: if we take the vowels in their order, we begin with [a], then [o] and [õ]. One has only to pronounce the vowels in order to realize that the sound gets darker as the word goes from the front to the back of the vocal tract. If the language had followed this sonic logic right to the end, the last vowel of the word would have been "ou" [u], which is even more muffled than "on" [õ]. Now, there is an *i* [i], brighter, more horizontal and especially farther forward (in French, it's the vowel closest to the teeth). And Henri Duparc, who set *La vie antérieure* to music, "heard" this: in his mélodie, all the syllables from "soin" to "ap-pro-fon" are sung on the same pitch, repeated six times, but, going from "fon" [fõ] to "-dir" [dir], the performer sings an ascending half step, thus doubling the linguistic contrast with a musical surprise. So, we can see how a composer can reinforce the musical intuition of a poet by creating coloration with an ordinary interval. This approach is, I think, typically French: this alertness to the infinitesimally tiniest detail, giving the result of the marriage between language and music a special sound. To give further credence to the idea, we may note that Poulenc used the same device in *Hôtel*, the second song in the cycle BANALITÉS (on five poems by Guillaume Apollinaire), on the line "Je veux fumer": the three syllables of "Je veux fu-" [ʒevəfy], are all set on the same pitch, and the final syllable, "-mer" [me], is a half step higher than the "fu-."

Poetic language can be so strong, from a sonic point of view, that sometimes it can even bother composers. Take, for example, the case of Gabriel Fauré's setting of Paul Verlaine's lines "Cela ressemble au cri doux / Que l'herbe agitée expire" ("It resembles the soft scream / That waving grass exhales") in the last song of the CINQ MÉLODIES DE VENISE. The poet intentionally places the word "cri," which has a hard sound, in opposition with the adjective "doux," a word meaning "soft" that also has a soft sound (this device is called an "oxymoron"). In writing "cri," Verlaine presents the idea of a noise, giving the word a sort of iconic meaning, and he humanizes the weeds rustled by the wind. Fauré didn't like this sound (did he find it too dry?). Whatever the reason, he replaced "cri" with "bruit," which gives us "Cela ressemble au bruit doux" ("It resembles the soft noise"). But to associate "bruit" (noise) and "doux" (soft) is banal, poetically speaking, while "cri doux" (soft cry) a typically Verlainian antagonism, is a real treasure. That said, it seems to me that if performers are conscious of these variants, they have the right to decide to go back to the original poetic text—if it's musically feasible, of course. We will come back to this subject later.

From the Word to Music

Returning to the connections between the sound of a poetic text and its musical setting, I don't think that the sound of the text—or, more exactly, the sound of the word—leads to any specific kind of music; it's more an ensemble of parameters, a phrasing. As an example, the *Fables* of Jean de La Fontaine, so intrinsically rhythmic, so "musical," have rarely been set to music, and rather in the form of musical skits than songs. In Fauré, and in the melodic school considered "classic," it's rather the atmosphere and the general meaning of a poem that induces the harmonies and the color of the mélodie (whence springs, perhaps, the desire not to take into account too much preexisting music, as we have just seen). The Symbolist poets figured as well that a poem forms a whole, a *Gestalt*, and that a phrase, in its ensemble, has more importance than an isolated word. In any case, even a "complete" poetic phrase cannot, in and of itself, inspire a melodic phrase. Claude Debussy well understood this wholeness, to the point that many say that his music is not "melodic"; it is so wedded to the text that his songs are, ultimately, conversations, musical speeches, elocutions. It is obvious that everything always begins with the spoken emission of the poem and with the diction. It's only then that the inflections of the language become, in a slightly amplified manner, a melisma. Just as the melisma is an ornament in which several notes are sung on the same syllable, in the poems themselves it is not the sound of the word itself that creates the song, but rather a "combination of inflections." Debussy's compositions result from a stupefying working of the *ear*, which shines through, as well as in his own poems. One example: in his poem *De fleurs*, which he set to music and made the third of his PROSES LYRIQUES, a line like "Dans l'ennui si désolément vert de la serre de douleur" ("In the desolate green hot-house of pain's boredom") with its five [d], and the [e], [ɛ], [ə], [ø], and the long sounds of the end, we distinctly hear the searching and the playing of one who is impassioned by the French language and its sound.

Listening to Others

Since we are speaking about listening, I would like to bring up here the issue of listening to other performers, whether illustrious forebears or others, whether in concert or in recordings. I do recommend it (especially listening to concerts), but one must pay attention: admiration can be a bad guide and might introduce idiosyncrasies, effects, or imitations close to caricature. From the start, young performers all have the same problem: they want to do things like everybody else—or rather, like those who are successful; they're thinking, no doubt, that the same recipes will produce the same results, and that's only human. A tenor who wants to sing like Luciano Pavarotti doesn't think that he can simply *be* himself— it's the unique individuality of his personality that will make him a noted per-former. And to be oneself, since we are performers and not composers, we must trust the composers, whose works will enlighten our own interior personalities. But it is not so easy to figure out which works and which composers will help singers to look deeply within themselves. There, again, the role of the singing teacher should be determinant: the teacher should not just impose, but open up the young performer to new horizons. It is most informative to listen to the performances of other artists, especially early recordings, whether or not we like them. Moreover, to understand why we do or don't like them is in itself quite beneficial. It's through this experience that singers are inevitably able to ask them-selves how to sing such-and-such a passage, if they wish to hear it and make it sound different. That experience is what happened to me when I started listening to Pierre Bernac's recordings. At first, I was bothered by what I perceived to be his pompous, precious way of singing. Today this is no longer the case, because I think that I've come to understand why and how he sang in this manner. And I must confess that, taken in their historical and social context, his interpretations are extraordinary by virtue of their perfect diction and the singer's understanding of the works. Nonetheless, that being said, I don't think that mélodies can be sung today the way they were back then. It is not by borrowing from Bernac's perfor-mance practices that this repertoire is brought to life; imitating Bernac will not create larger audiences, nor will it inspire them to listen to and love the art-song repertoire. On the contrary, it is his books that, to this day, have an unparalleled value as instructional materials.

Being Understood Today

I think that audiences today can experience French mélodie only as part of a living repertoire if the genre embodies modern French and is embraced by today's performers. If these songs continue to be performed by singers who treat them like museum objects and sing them in the style of our grandparents, we might as well just let them go, as they will be merely "historical songs." So, I beg to differ with the "Gallic" interpretation of seventeenth-century French religious music, which asks us to pronounce the Latin *u* [y] as a closed vowel and not "ou" [u]. Doing so might add a little historical polish, but the Latin—already a language incomprehensible to the general public—will seem even further away from us. This musicological posture is not going to revive early music. On the contrary, it will bury it a little more deeply, by rendering its perception more "elitist" and thus making it trendy. As Jean Cocteau said so well, "What's trendy now is already outdated." We have to know our audience. It might be said that certain contemporary composers seem, intentionally or not, to have forgotten that generally music is created to reach an audience. Whether these are large audiences or not is another story. If singers want to sing to themselves in the bathroom, they are free to do so; if composers write music to satisfy their egos, they may do what they wish. But if performing and creative artists want to communicate with others, they would be wise to use a "comprehensible"—or at least perceptible—language, for is Stéphane Mallarmé "comprehensible" to everyone? The language used by the French poets set to music (in general) is, as we have seen, poetic language: it obeys rules, which take into account elements such as etymology and assonance. When performers are confronted with the question of whether or not to use liaisons between words, they have to know the rules governing liaisons. These rules should not, however, render the text incomprehensible; on the contrary, it's in respecting the essence of a work that one respects the public. And basic "politeness" dictates that the text should be well articulated—or, rather, as Charles Panzéra said so well, the text should be clearly enunciated.

Since we are speaking of pronunciation, let us address the typical question of the *r*: should it be rolled? In "classic" singing, up until the 1970s, *r*'s were supposed to be rolled, in the name of sacrosanct traditions, based on the practices of both classical and popular or cabaret singers before World War II. As far as I'm concerned, I have no particular "religious" stance. Anyway, I believe that truth and art shouldn't have much in common. That being said, today, in daily life, practically no one rolls *r*'s— and neither do pop singers. In any case, I don't see that the *r* spoken with a guttural pronunciation ([r]), aka "*Parisian r*," would pose any particular obstacle, especially since it's spoken every day with no one paying attention. I always tease my students who find this difficult, by telling them that if they find that pronouncing an *r* "normally" is a technical obstacle, they had better worry about their careers. Not that I'm saying that this *r* is as easy to sing as the rolled *r*; it is more "blocked," and therefore less projected and less sonorous. Although . . .

Although this problem with *r* is true only if we take the Italian language as the absolute reference for vocalism. Considering that the only valuable reference is the language for which the music was written puts every technical problem into perspective. To be faithful to a language, one would needs to abandon their technique. Unfortunately, singers go often to the easiest solution, doing what they already know how to do. They have a technique, and according to what they are more or less capable of doing in such-and-such a language, they work with that, often with the consent of the voice teacher. As far as the native language is concerned, this choice comes in addition to imprecisions and weakening of sonorities that have become common practice in everyday language and that may sometimes lead to misunderstandings.

Fine Diction . . .

Singing a language so that it is understood doesn't impede good diction in any way. On the contrary, I am certain that audiences can comprehend and understand the subtlety of the French language, if one is brought to it little by little. A performer must start by engaging and interesting the listener so that, then, they can orally perceive the difference, for example, between the future tense "j'irai" (I will go) [ʒire] and the conditional "j'irais" (I would go) [ʒirɛ]. Because of these subtleties, diction should be very meticulous. I've sometimes been reproached for being "sophisticated" in my interpretation of French repertoire, but I think that this approach is an obligation somehow, especially when one is singing French mélodie, based on a language whose rules are the same as those of poetry. One must cultivate together refinement both in vocal and textual emission. Contrary to what many people say, diction is not an obstacle to vocalism. Besides, as far as the German lied is concerned, no one has ever said that the texts of Wilhelm Müller were an obstacle to the music of Schubert's *Die Winterreise* or *Die Schöne Müllerin*. A result of speaking French poorly is that one ends up removing all that is dimensional in the language. Consequently, French loses its edge. It's a bit as if someone had wanted all mortals to resemble one another, and no longer let anything show up from their personality. The asperities of a language don't prevent its fluidity when it is sung. One only has to look again at German: it's been said that German is an arid, rough language, but when we hear lieder beautifully sung, no one complains anymore that it's hard on the ears. For, if "music hath charms to soothe the savage breast," it also softens the edges. If French is planed down too much, its richness will be lost—and so will its difficulty, as some may say.

But then again, it's a question of perspective. For many singers who have made a career in opera—and, obviously, sing lots of Italian repertoire—French doesn't seem vocal, in that it doesn't favor the homogeneity of sound that allows the performer to move from one vowel to the next effortlessly. The "music" of the French language is specific, certainly because it is much richer and more varied in sounds than the majority of Romance languages, especially Spanish and Italian; in that aspect, it is closer to German, which remains nonetheless more sharply contrasted, more abrupt. French is one of the European languages that has the greatest variety of vowels: we have not only [a] [ɑ] [e] [ɛ] [i] [ɔ] [o] [y] and [u], but also [é] [ø] [œ] and the nasals, [õ] [ã] [ɛ̃] and [œ̃]. Instead of having, like in Italian, only one [a] by way of a basic vowel—a rather round [a] that slides easily between the [o], the [i], and the [u], French has a much more extended vocal palette. On the other hand, the problem of a singer is not the vowels as much as the consonants that are between them.

It is also said that the French language is not very musical. There again, Italian is used as the point of reference. What those who find that French is not musical mean by that opinion is, I think, that it is not musical in the *vocal* sense like Italian— and, so, setting aside "pure music." But if one speaks of vocalism, we need to know what is meant by that term. If the objective, for a performer, is only to make pretty sounds, anyone can come up with something, starting with any computer owner. But French mélodie is not that. It's unfortunately also because of this sad truth that there are so few opera singers who are interested in the French art-song repertoire. A lack of curiosity, or of culture (or sometimes both!), go together with the disdain that a certain number of musicologists have for the French song repertoire, thought to be elitist and outdated. The mélodie is, in its essence, an art form that is, alas, a little confidential. But that confidentiality is a mark of trust and intimacy. Italian song is about enjoyment, the pleasure of beautiful sound. The French mélodie is something else: it's the pleasure of encountering intelligence, the poetic image and the special sonority; it addresses itself globally to our entire being: the head, the heart, the ear, the senses. We are far from the simple glorification of the physical (athletic), raw aspect of song. Everything is a question of posture: if we put our-selves in an exclusively vocal perspective—and that's a singer's right—we might as well just sing songs without words!

. . . That Helps Perception

For it is indeed the perception of the poetry, composed according to the intrinsic music of the French language, that makes a prize of French mélodie. And it's cer-tainly because of that perception that the French language, which has created so much poetry, is seen as more intellectual and less sensual than Italian—this that the English call the "language of love"! But to be preoccupied exclusively with making round sounds, to forget the consonants and, as a result, to forget the intelligibility of the text in order to favor the "emotion," is this truly the goal of a work that melds poetry and music, whether it's an opera or a song? I'm not so sure. We live in a time that favors emotion—not to mention the sentimental. Debussy countered that point with a credo: "Music should humbly seek to *please*" ("La musique doit humblement chercher à *faire plaisir*").[1] This statement is not the same thing as saying that music

---

[1] In *L'état actuel de la musique française*, interview by Paul Landormy in *La revue bleue*, April 2, 1904, reprinted in *Monsieur Croche et autres écrits*, ed. François Lesure (Paris: "L'Imaginaire" Collection, Gallimard, 1987), p. 279.

should seek to "move someone." To move someone, it's to create vibrations that could be ordinary, even vulgar, appealing to what is already known. To please is to enrich, to lead elsewhere. Hector Berlioz had already reproached the romance (as opposed to the mélodie) for its sentimentality.

But these notions of emotion or sentiment are already in the domain of interpretation, and we're not there yet. I repeat: for me, everything begins with listening, the work of the ear on sonority. It would be idiotic for singers to deprive themselves of the immense repertoire of the French mélodie solely on the pretext that French is a difficult language. It is difficult only in that one sees it merely as a vehicle for meaning, and not a fantastic sonorous object. To rediscover this original aspect of our language is just a question of learning, of practice, even if I agree that one has to be motivated and ready to make the effort solo. For, generally speaking, instruction—in schools and conservatories—does nothing to awaken and develop the ear to the sonorities of the French language. Personally, I never took a class that put poetry and music in contact with each other. But fortunately, at least in elementary school, students learned and recited poetry by heart, developing both the ear and the memory. Is it still done today? I hope so. The whole pedagogy of learning languages should be reexamined for its great weaknesses, since currently theory and grammar—written language, in fact—are favored, to the detriment of their sensorial perception. In addition, the basic disciplines should be taught together in one class, which would correspond to making all students practice what was called comparative literature—a fascinating discipline, which, at the university level, associates all the arts. The teaching of each discipline is much too compartmentalized; the schools should open all the doors, create bridges, not set out to create—much too early—a population of specialists. In music, in any case, one should never, in my opinion, specialize too much and remain in a little box—even if it's a little box as beautiful as that as the French language. I think that the public will become aware, little by little, of the dangers of specialization, and the ever-increasing free time will again create a thirst for knowledge. So, we might as well start early, since learning is always faster when we start young.

And thus, to young singers who want to begin exploration of the French mélodie, I will first say bravo! Then, I will tell them that they should listen to a good voice teacher, and not hesitate to plunge headfirst into the repertoire: read as many scores as books, sight-read, try to understand why it's written, musically, in such-and-such a way. Those students who are sufficiently bold will look for the original texts of the poems to see the differences and the modifications that were made by the composer and try to understand the reasons that they are there. And as soon as singers start to ask "why?" it means that they have caught the "bug" of mélodie. It will become a passion, like playing. It is, as well, the same passion that inspires the lieder singers, the recitalists! No need to deceive them: all the concise musical forms lead to this fascination: look at how a composer can become the master of their art with forms that rarely exceed two or three minutes. It's extraordinary. It's as exciting or intriguing as a drawing by Leonardo da Vinci or a sanguine by Watteau.

2

To Know

The birth of the mélodie is considered to date from the composition of Berlioz's LES NUITS D'ÉTÉ (1840–1841), even if this opinion is a bit arbitrary. It is true that Berlioz, as we mentioned earlier, deplored the artistic level of the romance, which was, at that time, the contemporary song style that wedded text (often poetic) and music. It seems that the use of the term mélodie was inspired by the book title *Irish Melodies* by the Irish poet Thomas Moore (1779–1852). Several excerpts from this book were set to music. To make a long story short, matters evolved when the composers of romances wanted to give more independence to the melodic line in relationship to the poetic text. Their goal was to stick to the poetic suggestions as much as possible, and not to be too constrained by a form that was completely closed, cyclic, or "blocked," as a succession of couplets interspersed by a refrain could be. Calling LES NUITS D'ÉTÉ the first cycle of mélodies is not completely accurate, since the first song of the cycle, *Villanelle*, is still a romance, like the fourth song, *Absence*. On the other hand, in *Sur les lagunes*, we notice a change, even if there is a sort of refrain: "Que mon sort est amer! / Ah! Sans amour s'en aller sur la mer!" (How bitter is my fate! Ah! Without love, to go to sea!).

Another element makes LES NUITS D'ÉTÉ an important marker: the cycle is the fruit of a direct collaboration between two artists, Hector Berlioz and Théophile Gautier, who knew each other personally.[1] It even seems, if we look at the dates of composition, that Gautier gave the poems to Berlioz even before their publication; one can also imagine that Gautier wrote his poems with the idea that music could accompany them. It is also interesting to note that *La comédie de la mort*, the collection poems LES NUITS D'ÉTÉ come from, include many more pieces than just the six in the cycle. Gautier probably gave more texts to Berlioz, who chose only six. Whatever the case, if we take Berlioz's cycle as a point of departure, we might consider that the result represents a kind of "coexistence" between genres. Among the mélodies of Charles Gounod, for example, many are still in the form of a romance, because, in that period, nothing was fixed. The only thing that seemed clear was that a mélodie was a work in which there existed a strong relationship between music and poem. But composers still hesitated in the terms: as proof, there is often a strong denomination—"chanson," "romance," "mélodie," "ballade," "scène"—after the title of the work.

---

[1] Note, however, that a precedent exists in the romance: the poet Marceline Desbordes-Valmore (1786–1869) and the guitarist and composer Pauline Duchambge (1778–1858) wrote together more than thirty published romances.

Le Chant Intime. François Le Roux and Romain Raynaldy, Oxford University Press. © Oxford University Press 2021. DOI: 10.1093/oso/9780190884178.003.0003

Let's be careful, though: there are pieces entitled "mélodie" that, in reality, are only a vocal part accompanied by a piano, without any real connection in terms of musical development and poetic meaning. It bears repeating: when Berlioz wrote his *NUITS D'ÉTÉ*, nothing was fixed yet. The mélodie as we define it was still embryonic.

Certain scholars place the birth of the mélodie at a later date. Vincent Vivès, co-author with Michel Faure of the remarkable *Histoire et poétique de la mélodie française* (CNRS Editions, Paris, 2001), suggests (contestably, as are all things that one would like to date with that level of precision) that the first true mélodie was Fauré's *Lydia* (1870) on a poem by Charles-Marie-René Leconte de Lisle: first, the composer uses the Mixolydian mode in reference to Lydia—a lovely musical idea—and, second, the musical writing is completely parallel to the poetic form, with one note per syllable (to accomplish this, Fauré modified lines 2, 3, and 8 of the poem). However, prior to Fauré's song, there had already been multiple attempts of "absolute faithfulness" to the poetic text, by, for example, Camille Saint-Saëns with the mélodie *Rêverie* (1851) on a poem by Victor Hugo. As Saint-Saëns wrote prolifically and lived longer than Fauré, we always think that he came later, but that is not true: Saint-Saëns was Fauré's professor!

To show how long the ambiguity exists, we might also consider the first steps of Debussy. As we know his early mélodies well, we notice that he is also quite advanced: in his 1881 mélodie *L'archet*, on a poem by Charles Cros (a poet considered eccentric, but, however, quite prominent), Debussy makes some cuts, looks for a catch, and is absolutely no longer concerned with the line-by-line equivalencies of rhythm: he creates a "unique object." At the same time, he also writes romances—under the eponymous title *Romance*, which is used by the poet he often sets to music at the time, Paul Bourget.

From the Romance to the Mélodie

As for me, I think, quite simply, that the French mélodie was born when the composers wanted to set themselves apart from what, in their eyes, the romance symbolized—a fashionable, stereotyped object of musical consumption—in order to become more demanding about musical quality and to come closer to the accomplishment of the German lied. It was with this goal alone in mind that the word was chosen. And then came the moment when the terms "mélodie" and "romance" were no longer used as subtitles in scores. Let's return to two previous cited examples: Berlioz had already demonstrated a desire to create a more demanding music; later on, Debussy, who had begun as an accompanist when writing romances (complex works, but romances nonetheless) for Madame Vasnier, would follow the same path, inventing a new style that was faithful to the poetry and, in the process, having a long-term influence on an entire generation of composers. Conversely, some early-twentieth-century composers continued to write romances: we find them, for example, in the last mélodies of Jules Massenet, composed in the 1910s.

Curiously, these romances are rather close, formally speaking, to the German lied before Schumann. This similarity is probably due to experiments by Massenet and other French composers who had a keen interest in German music, specifically in the simplicity of means used by Schubert, for example. Later on, the term "romance" would reappear in the works of Maurice Delage and Jacques Ibert, probably with a desire to return to simplicity after a period of extreme compositional refinement as their hidden agenda.

It should also be observed that the birth of the mélodie is closely connected to evolutions in the French language and poetic style. Hardcore Romantic poetry of the nineteenth century—such as Victor Hugo's most famous poems, like *Odes et ballades* (musical terms) or *Les orientales*—could never give birth to the genre of mélodie for one simple reason: it had already given rise to the composition of romances and chansons. Thus, the "poetic object" that favored the development of this new musical form was still not born. It was only with the arrival of more open poetic forms—less strictly "classical," with vaguer content (Verlaine would say in his *Art poétique*, "where the indecisive joins the precise")—that musical creation would also truly evolve. The poetic revolution generated by Baudelaire, and then the advent of the Parnassian movement, were decisive in the appearance of the mélodie. It is interesting to note that Gautier, the great precursor, considered to be the "patron saint" of the Parnassians (since he extolled the reform of art for art's sake), played the role of scout in the poetry that would nourish mélodie: a poetry that made room for asymmetrical rhythms, adopting non-Western forms (*pantoum, haiku*, etc.). He was joined by Leconte de Lisle, Théodore de Banville, and—of course—Verlaine, the international record holder of poems set to music. In fact, the titles of Verlaine's works are already incitements: *Romances sans paroles, Ariettes oubliées*, and *La bonne chanson*, for example. Verlaine also inspired the composition of romances and chansons, written to his short poems in classical form: some of *La bonne chanson* and the *Poèmes saturniens*, among others. On the other hand, for the asymmetrical subtleties of *Fêtes galantes*, the great alexandrines of *Sagesse*, we had to wait for Ernest Chausson and Debussy to see them put to music. However, the honor of being the first composer to set Verlaine to music goes to Massenet, in 1871: his *Rêvons, c'est l'heure* (Let us dream; it is the hour) from *La bonne chanson* (unpublished for a long time) is a romance in two voices and three verses—so, it's not really a mélodie, despite Verlaine.

From the Parnassians to the Symbolists

One might say that the Golden Age of mélodie and its "definitive" establishment as a genre can be dated back to the moment when Parnassian poetry mutated into Symbolist poetry. When Mallarmé abandoned the "pure form" of absolutely unshakable poetic feet to go even further, poetic content would never again be applied to the telling of stories, but rather to allowing the reader to perceive ideas, sensations, and impressions—even if it meant using archaisms, like Maurice Maeterlinck and all the Belgian poets of his generation did. It was during this period, between 1885 and 1914, that mélodies were composed by great names of French music such as Fauré, Duparc, Massenet, Chausson, Debussy, and the young Maurice Ravel; and all the others, less famous or even forgotten: for example, Gabriel Fabre (1858–1921), a friend of Maeterlinck and his companion Georgette Leblanc; Léon Delafosse (1874–1955) and Reynaldo Hahn (1874–1947), friends of Proust. Hahn composed *Si mes vers avaient des ailes* from a poem of Victor Hugo at the age of fourteen and personally knew Verlaine, whom he visited when the poet was hospitalized.

Let's point out that this "Golden Age" took place much later than that of the German lied, whose origins were very different: if the mélodie wants to distance itself from the banality of the romance, the lied staked a claim to its popular and "national" origins (given that the German language did not yet emanate from a "nation" but from a federation of territories), which would be its point of reference more or less through the lifetime of Brahms. Although poetry was already there at the origins of the lied and throughout its evolution, it must be noted that, curiously, almost all the lieder composers chose poetry written prior to their generation: Schubert did not live during the generation of Schiller or Goethe; moreover, Goethe, as a result of his prestige, is the true instigator of the birth of the "scholarly" lied. There are many reasons for this difference: the concentration of intellectual circles in a sole location—Paris—favored interdisciplinary artistic contacts, while the multitude of little "provincial" centers in the Germany and Austria of Schubert, Schumann, and so forth didn't facilitate the development of the genre. It is only in the late nineteenth century, when Vienna became a true artistic capital and Symbolist poets like Richard Dehmel and Stefan George, as well as musicians like Richard Strauss and Arnold Schoenberg, stepped up, that a sense of adequacy was found and that collaborations among German artists of the same generation could be forged in a similar way to the French during la Belle Époque.

But that period of artistic interaction and collaboration in Germany and Austria did not produce the same quantity of masterpieces as the musical settings of Verlaine and Mallarmé did in France. This difference is undoubtedly due to the fact that the birth of a powerful empire gave rise to "imperious" works that were purely musical, like symphonies or operas—with Wagner as the towering figure. Wagner wrote only a few lieder and—rarities to discover—a few French mélodies, written during his stay in Paris. These were set on poems by, among others, Victor Hugo and . . . Pierre de Ronsard! Wagner's famous WESENDONCK LIEDER vastly exceed the customary lied form; they are also orchestrated. Hugo Wolf, recognized by many as the last great lieder composer, represents the culmination of the Wagnerian harmonic and prosodic experiments in this miniature form that is the lied; he, too, used poetry of early generations, while throwing out of his experimental sphere the German poets who were his contemporaries. Did this rejection correspond with an identity crisis for the German language? Actually, when Rilke—from a later generation—wrote poems in French, he felt (as he himself acknowledged it) freer than he did when writing in German! Another difference appeared at the turn of the century: if one of the inheritances of Wagnerism was the development of the lied with orchestra (as exemplified by Wolf and Strauss), in France the orchestrated mélodie remained marginal, despite (or because of) the fabulous craze for Wagner's music. However, a few French composers did write, happily, in this genre: for instance, Saint-Saëns and Duparc, along with Ravel, whose SHÉHÉRAZADE, a cycle of three mélodies on poems of Tristan Klingsor, was written in 1903. It was at the concerts of the Société Nationale de Musique that orchestrated mélodies were heard: with such programs, the organizers hoped to mix the symphonic and opera audiences.

What about Chanson?

To be thorough, we must equally address the genre of chanson in contrast with the mélodie. Like the romance, the chanson is written in cyclic form, with verses and chorus. The main difference between chanson and romance or, even more so, between chanson and mélodie is the stance of its performer: certain forms of chansons are crafted around a simple framework, which is nothing but an invitation to take liberties; it necessarily follows a foregrounding of the performer, who must completely take over the work. For the mélodie, it is the composer who is the "star"—and, in turn, the poet. The audience is also different: the romance was written for domestic use; it was sung in the salons, among members of well-born families—and the chanson was intended for the audiences of the cabarets, the theaters, or the street. As for the mélodie, it found its place between the two. Its destination was elitist, as Berlioz had already claimed; its audience was carefully chosen: connoisseurs and friends who were often artists themselves—poets, painters, musicians. These groups were brought together to share novelty, experimentation—to participate, as it were, in a laboratory of expression. The mélodie is, if one must label it, destined for what I would call "intimate use": not familial intimacy, but personal, from an "elected" creator to an "elected" listener. It was a fitting form to address oneself to a trusted circle, to tell them personal things in an individualized manner. The philosopher and semiologist Roland Barthes (1915–1980) writes of the mélodie as "the place for cultivated French language." It's a "cult object" for the initiated.

If we look closely at the three forms—chanson, romance, and mélodie—we will note that their musical roots are the same. We find dance rhythms like the minuet, the gavotte, and the waltz, as well as "foreign" (i.e., non-French) dance forms: the habanera, the seguidilla, the polonaise, and the tarantella. Graham Johnson, the great British pianist-accompanist who is an expert on French art song, declares that the quintessence of French music is the dance, that it all begins there. I think that he's right: a singer who performs a mélodie by Fauré, for example, must not forget about rhythmic rigor. The performer should almost be capable of marching or dancing while singing; the movement is corporeal. We find terms common to both music and poetry: ballade, villanelle, quatrain, sonnet, rondeau (or rondel).

This commonality is also true of the German lied, in which, broadly speaking, there are only two forms: the *volkslied*, which we can call popular song, with its square, steady rhythm to which one can march; and the *ländler*, a form with a triple meter that gave rise to the waltz (sung or not). As for the dramatic scene with recitatives, as exists in Schubert's work, it comes from the eighteenth-century cantata and is linked to a miniature opera. The first lieder singers were also opera singers, contrary to what will be the case for the mélodie. For me, the big difference in interpretation of the lied and the mélodie is that the attitude in the lied is more "naturalist," more embodied or personified: performers take the poetry on their own behalf; they sing in the first-person singular and act as if they were the poet—in a certain way, the poet and the performer are but one. On the other hand, in the French mélodie, performers remain the performer; they are, in the literal sense, the transmitter, the one who opens the door to the public. They are certainly not the incarnation of the poet or the composer, and one could see this, from that standpoint, as a kind of modesty. But French mélodie can't be "played": the performer cannot act as if there were a character to play. Many composers can't stand singers who overplay. And therein lies the entire difficulty for the performer of mélodie: you can't go past the limits; you can't put yourself at the forefront, or ham it up. And this challenge leads us to the difference between the mélodie and the chanson: when we listen to Joseph Kosma's[2] *Autumn Leaves* (set to a poem by Jacques Prévert) sung by Juliette Gréco[3] or Yves Montand[4] (or Nat King Cole or Frank Sinatra), it's not the same work from singer to singer—while a mélodie by Duparc, for example, whether it is sung in a medium key by a baritone or in a high key by a soprano *should* remain the same work: that of Duparc.

In France and Elsewhere

I speak of the German lied—but what about songs of the same genre in other countries? Naturally, countries under the musical influence of a great neighbor will see a similar form flourish in their own lands: in Holland, in the Nordic countries, the lied has a national equivalent. For France's neighbors, let's examine the question in

---

[2] Born in Budapest (Hungary) in 1905, in an artistic Jewish family, Kosma studied first with Béla Bartók, then with Hanns Eisler in Berlin. He wrote lieder and worked with Brecht. After the arrival to power of the Nazis in 1933, he fled to France, where he achieved great recognition through his collaboration with the poet Jacques Prévert and the filmmaker Marcel Carné. Acquiring French nationality in 1949, he died in 1969. His songs, and especially *Les feuilles mortes* (Autumn leaves) (composed on a poem by Prévert for Carné's movie *Les portes de la nuit*), remain popular to this day.

[3] Juliette Gréco (1927–2020) was the quintessential singer of Saint-Germain-des-Prés, center of post–WWII Paris culture. She made the musical works of Joseph Kosma, Léo Ferré, and Serge Gainsbourg (set to poems by Jacques Prévert, Jean-Paul Sartre, Robert Desnos, and Pierre Mac Orlan, respectively) famous throughout the world.

[4] Yves Montand (1921–1991), born Ivo Livi, was a movie star in both France and Hollywood (he played opposite Marilyn Monroe in George Cukor's 1960 film *Let's Make Love*); an exceptional entertainer, he had successes in music halls on both sides of the Atlantic. He popularized French ballads and protest songs from 1945 through the 1980s.

detail, starting with Spain: as we do in France, we find the song (*canción*) and the art song. This parallel is not surprising, since all the great Spanish composers who wrote art song came through Paris to study and find a publisher (which is fundamental). Moreover, their music is also based on the rhythm of popular dances, which enjoyed great success throughout Europe. Thus, we find ourselves in the same situation, although a bit later than in France. The great Spanish composers all wrote French art songs—that is to say, songs whose texts came from French poetry—before writing Spanish songs. Additionally, as most of these were twentieth-century composers, they wrote free verse as well: the poetry of Federico García Lorca, for example, is completely dreamlike. Thus, there is no strict accent.

In Italy, the case is a bit different: there are very few Italian art songs, for two apparent reasons: Italian composers have not found a generation of poets equivalent to the Parnassians in Paris, and the geographical situation was even more fragmented than in Germany. Almost all the Italian composers wrote only ballads or songs—unless they were influenced by Debussy, as were Alfredo Casella (1883–1947) and Ottorino Respighi (1879–1936). Additionally, opera remains the Italian vocal genre par excellence. And pure vocal enjoyment hardly takes anything from the genre of art song. Even the "French songs" of Francesco Paolo Tosti (1846–1916) are romances: his *Chanson de l'adieu* (Farewell song) (1899) on a poem by Edmond Haraucourt is a true romance, and a very beautiful one at that. It's thought of as an art song because the poem is well known ("Partir, c'est mourir un peu" [To depart is to die a little]), but, formally speaking, it's a romance. What's most curious is that when French composers like Gounod or Reynaldo Hahn write songs with Italian words, they "re-use" the romance form: whether it's the duo *Barcarola* (Gounod) or VENEZIA (a cycle by Hahn), these are romances. Or else, when Fauré composed songs based on works heard in Venice, he asked for the help of a voice professor at the Paris Conservatoire, Romain Bussine, so that the result could be as close as possible to the Italian *romanza*, as much on the vocal level as the prosodic level (see his *Sérénade toscane* or the well-known *Après un rêve*).

A Poetry in the Making

Let us return to linguistic evolution to highlight one thing: if mélodie develops while the poetic French language rediscovers itself not as a closed language, constructed *ad vitam aeternam*, but as one capable of evolution, openness, and mystery, we also see composers turning toward poets of the past or poetry inspired by the past. This trend is not contradictory: returning to poetry from the past entitles them to be freed from all too pervasively present rules. All the composers of French mélodie who really matter, at one moment or another, turned toward the past, sometimes by using what "modern" publications of earlier music allowed them to rediscover. Thus, Fauré set Molière to music (the *Sérénade* from *Le bourgeois gentilhomme*) and a *Hymn to Apollo*, according to a discovery made about ancient Greek music by an archeologist. Reynaldo Hahn also looked toward the past: he set to music poems by Ronsard, Charles d'Orléans, and Théophile de Viau. In his *ÉTUDES LATINES*, composed on some of Leconte de Lisle's *Poèmes antiques* (which are based on Latin and Greek poets such as Anacreon), Hahn was, for all intents and purposes, acting as a musicologist, employing the ancient musical modes and rhythms used during the Roman period. And then there's Debussy, who, in revisiting Charles d'Orléans, Tristan L'Hermite, and François Villon, is not placing himself in a perspective of early music, but rather in a perspective of new "linguistic" sonorities: his objective is to musically explore the language of yesteryear, which was fixed in neither meaning nor spelling, and thus offering means of escape. There were, of course, other reasons, but these are outside of the domain of mélodie. I think that one must not neglect the historical aspect: after the defeat of France in its war against Prussia in 1870–1871, viewed as a disaster by the majority of French, artists needed to rediscover the quintessential and most singular qualities of the French language; it was good to return to and rediscover a past seen as glorious as a way of reclaiming a bit of pride. We often have a tendency to see this rediscovery of the past as a reactionary reflex. But it was the poet René Char[5] who said that the really interesting historical figures are not those who invent but those who rediscover. And it seems to me, according to my own experience, that one builds further only in relation to that which has already been done. One doesn't make innovative work by throwing out the past and, hypothetically speaking, starting from scratch. For an example, just look at Debussy: he is a discoverer and an inventor, but he never rejects his masters. He is simply very resourceful; turning to poets of the past re-energizes him and allows him to enter even more deeply into the mysteries he has unveiled and explored with the Symbolist poetry of his time.

Moreover, in having a predilection for the poetry of the past, composers are not choosing at random! As a consequence, some illustrious ancient poets are left aside. Let's take La Fontaine (1621–1695), for example; for me, he is the Mozart of the French language, in that he incarnates, like the illustrious musician in his domain a century later, the epitome of French classical language, a perfection almost unsurpassable. It is because of that perfection that I believe La Fontaine's work to be extremely difficult to utilize: he starts from a rigorous form, which he understands completely, and overthrows the form when he wishes, by playing with it. It's fabulously free, but very arduous to put to notes: the language of La Fontaine is already so intrinsically musical that it's impossible to make an abstraction of it. With a simple versification of eight syllables or ten syllables, or pretty regular alexandrines, a poetic text can be carved up at will. But with La Fontaine, one can do nothing but follow it. Already, in his era, if his verses were set to music, it was not directly, but in paraphrases, reproducing a form more banal, with couplets or highly regular

---

[5] René Char (1907–1988) is first linked to Surrealism. His poetry was set to music by Pierre Boulez, among others, in *Le marteau sans maître* (1954), a piece for alto voice and six instruments of about thirty-five minutes.

verses. The Bibliothèque nationale de France in Paris owns the originals: they are but mere adaptations by obscure would-be lyricists of the original fables of La Fontaine that everyone already knew by heart. In the nineteenth century, it was operetta composers like Jacques Offenbach, Charles Lecocq, or Edmond Audran who, in transforming the fables into short sung plays, "helped themselves" to the great poet rather than helping him!

Not Every Poet Inspires Musicians

If La Fontaine barely inspired composers of mélodie (with the very notable exception of André Caplet, who created something of a masterwork with his 1919 *TROIS FABLES DE JEAN DE LA FONTAINE*), there are other equally indispensable poets who seem to have repelled musicians, even during the Golden Age of mélodie: Arthur Rimbaud (1854–1891), for example—undoubtedly because his poetry is too "awe-inspiring"—as well as Paul Claudel (1868–1955) or Saint-John Perse (1887–1975) later on. Their poetry was so intimidating that composers were afraid of falling into traps: becoming redundant or pompous, or remaining neutral or too subjugated. It's not by accident that most of those who set Rimbaud to music were not French, but foreigners who were in love with the French language—for example, Benjamin Britten and Paul Hindemith. These were composers who were less afraid of the "heaviness" or the revolutionary freedom of this poetry, who were less affected by the history of the language and its upheavals. I think as well that Rimbaud was not in sync with the French composers of his time. Unlike Verlaine, who had the time to carve his niche in society and who right away saw his poems set to music by important composers, Rimbaud passed through like a meteor. Very few knew him (and most of those who spent time with him found him unbearable), and it took several generations for his poetry to find its place. His poetry remains difficult; more than his poetry, it was his rebellious adolescent personality that made him a hit.

Let us not forget that the language that gave birth to and nurtured the mélodie left free spaces in thinking. It was neither too loaded with meaning nor too "dense," nor too strict in its formal structure; neither its content nor its form is seen as constraints. Closer to the present day, it's not by accident, in my opinion, that the poetry of Aragon inspired only two mélodies by Francis Poulenc and a few by Auric—although, on the other hand, it inspired a plethora of chansons and romances; for, from a rhythmic point of view, his poetic structure is strictly—and intentionally—classical, with a goal of accessibility for a popular audience. As for the mélodies inspired by the poetry of Claudel, they are often, in my opinion, disappointing, because they are already constrained by the very full sonorities of a language already swollen with richness and meaning. If I might make a rather daring comparison, it's as "busy" poetically as is, visually, a film by Cecil B. DeMille! This overly rich language is not well served by opera, either; it creates every difficulty in the production of a masterwork play like *Le soulier de satin* (The satin slipper)—and I'm not even talking about the length of the work. It is, additionally, more difficult to render musical justice to its poetry. Moreover, the composer is obliged to "submit": "First Claudel, then the music"!

In other words, Claudel's language doesn't allow itself to be heard—it imposes itself; the content aside, its very form doesn't allow the mind to wander. This is the reason I'm saying that language that lends itself to musical setting must be "airy"— not only from a formal standpoint but also in ideas; it should suggest rather than assert. Pierre Bernac and Francis Poulenc himself often spoke of these "interstices," between which musical inspiration could glide into the heart of a poem. Even when Poulenc sets to music the verses of Jean Moréas,[6] a poet whom he hardly likes, he never seems constrained in intentionally choosing a mocking form, almost caricatured in nature, which gives to the poetry a tonality that Moréas himself had certainly never foreseen. When Poulenc sets Ronsard to music, we see as well that in the search for a form, there is a freedom that is not a return to the past: the composer is not seeking a direct equivalency with the text, because the text is not speaking to him directly, but he manages quite well to adapt Ronsard's language in allowing the text (this is Poulenc's gift) to proceed simply. And the reason he is so successful is that he knows the poetry very well and he chooses only poets whom he likes (apart from the Moréas previously mentioned[7]). Poulenc's two preferred poets are Guillaume Apollinaire—a vagabond "playing hooky" with language—and Paul Éluard, whose Surrealist poetry opens a thousand doors merely by putting together two words. Debussy also chose only poets whom he liked and always refused to be commissioned. Considering himself as a poet (two of his poems that were included in his cycle of four PROSES LYRIQUES were published in a literary magazine, minus the music), he respects the poetry. It's because of that he never completed any opera other than *Pelléas et Mélisande*: even his incessant literary work on his unfinished project for *The Fall of the House of Usher*, using translations by Baudelaire or Mallarmé of Edgar Allan Poe's text, was, as far as what remains is concerned, more advanced than his musical sketches for this opera.

Great Poetry Equals Great Mélodie?

Up to this point, I have talked about many great poets, but let's not be fooled here: certain composers don't need a great poetic text to write an interesting mélodie. Fauré is often taken to task for not having cared more about poetic quality, setting to music a number of poems by Armand Silvestre, after having written his first song on a poem by Victor Hugo. No one would say that Silvestre is a poet on the level of

---

[6] A poet of Greek origin whose real name was Ioannis Papadiamantopoulos (1856–1910). He is the founder of the French "decadent school" of poetry, which tried to succeed to the former "Parnassian school."

[7] About these songs, Poulenc said, "I detest Moréas and I chose these poems precisely because I found them suitable for mutilation" (see Carl B. Schmidt, *Entrancing Muse: A Documented Biography of Francis Poulenc*, Hillsdale, NY: Pendragon Press, 2001, page 163).

Hugo—more still because Hugo was famous during his lifetime—but, without a doubt, Fauré *needed* the poetry of Silvestre in order to develop his own modes of expression, before going on to the poetry of Verlaine and Albert Samain and, then, Charles Van Lerberghe. Curiously, Debussy didn't encounter this type of criticism, as he began right away with Alfred de Musset,[8] and never chose minor poets: even Paul Bourget, forgotten today, was, at the time, a very famous poet. Through his poetic choices and his work with prosody, Debussy remains the most "literary" of French composers. As for Ravel, he had very eclectic tastes, and often wandered off the beaten paths of poetry, setting for himself a new problem of musical craftsmanship to solve each time. Saint-Saëns, another literary specialist (he published his own poems), seemed at ease with the poets of his generation. But when the style changed, even if indeed he attempted to follow it, he was not "in sync." For him, the height of his accomplishments in songwriting came in 1870 with Armand Renaud (in the cycle *MÉLODIES PERSANES*) or, earlier, Victor Hugo. But, in the end, whether composers are well informed in literary matters or not, they all work to their own benefit. To paraphrase Debussy, each composer should feel free to choose the poetry upon which he wishes to "transplant his own dream." I truly believe that the heart of mélodie is resonance, the placing of an image within oneself—not reality, not subjugation. This is the reason that, for example, I have trouble fully appreciating Lili Boulanger's cycle *CLAIRIÈRES DANS LE CIEL*, on thirteen poems by Francis Jammes. It certainly is harmonically rich, but one senses a kind of ever-present "glorification of suffering," a lack of distance. The choice of Francis Jammes, the poet of "return to the earth," certainly says something. In this cycle, we notice a sort of impasse for the mélodie—a little bit like Brahms's *Die Schöne Magelone*, in the lied repertoire: the literary work that inspired the cycle was originally a medieval fairy tale from southern France; Brahms turned the tale, based on the German translation, into a completely Romantic—and Germanic—piece by having the hero singing the story in the first-person singular. But then, I find that that approach doesn't work: while Brahms had a fantastic way of setting German poets to music, in these romances he's out of his element, because he transposes emotions and sensations of his own time to a story from the Middle Ages. At the end of the story, all that the hero feels and experiences with his lover (the Fair Magelone of the title) is mocked! After more than an hour of music, one asks, "So what?" All that remains is to admire Brahms's music in making an abstraction of the literary support—a result that is, all the same, quite ironic for one of the greatest of all lieder composers!

There are also some lieder by Schumann that I find, for similar reasons, a little difficult to defend: when the poems contain aspects reclaiming Germanism—in a word, "politics"—his musical settings are sometimes outrageous (or it seems so to French ears) and the poetry is downgraded. For example, the citation of *La marseillaise* in *The Two Grenadiers* (on a poem by Heine), although it was fairly bold to

---

[8] Debussy's first song setting (known to date) was a poem by Musset, *Madrid* (1879), written when he was seventeen years old.

do it, comes across as a little artificial.[9] It doesn't work with poetry as impregnated with irony as is Heine's. One can be more "delicate." When Debussy wrote a protest mélodie in 1917 (*Noël des enfants qui n'ont plus de maison*), he didn't choose a text by patriotic writers Maurice Barrès (1862–1923) or Charles Péguy (1873–1914)— he wrote his own text, choosing a form of chanson (which he called "Noël") and had it sung by children: "We don't have a home anymore." Despite the figure of compassion that he was looking for, he etched himself into it. I think that this attitude is typically French. No doubt one can speak here of fear of ridicule or of a "measured" approach. As Louis Jouvet[10] said in his course on theatrical interpretation, one shouldn't put "la flamme sur la flamme"—in other words, you don't have to add fuel to the fire. Erik Satie said it another way: "Watch out, a tree doesn't convulse because a character walks onstage." One does not play a scene literally, for the face value is so evident that there's nothing interesting about it. On top of that, the audience members would be under the impression that they are being taken for idiots. The same applies to interpretation of mélodie: one must always hold back. Moreover, the "patriotic" works become quickly out of date: does anyone still sing *Vive la France* of Saint-Saëns (on a text by Paul Fournier) or some rather vindictive mélodies such as Albéric Magnard's *Le Rhin allemand*, on a poem by Musset, which has been the source of many other compositions?

A Genre in Decline?

Having spoken of the birth of the mélodie, we must now approach the question of, if not its death, then at least of its end, which, according to certain commentators, has already occurred. I think that if there has been an end, and I would say, rather, a decline, it has happened alongside that of tonally based music. For, in the last century's musical experimentations (serialism, minimalism, dodecaphonic music, aleatory music), language was utilized like a raw sonic material and not as a vehicle for meaning, aesthetic values, and culture. Certain composers tried to apply to the French language the kinds of experiments that Schoenberg made with German in *Sprechgesang* (speech-singing), but that didn't work. Others have wanted to turn the voice into an instrument like any other instrument, so as not to depend on literary texts to convey meaning or an aesthetic sense. In the history of the mélodie there was, therefore, a sort of dry spell. This didn't prevent a certain form of continuity, as always. It is not because some refuted the genre of art song that others did not engage with it. But these others formed part of a minority considered regressive.

---

[9] Wagner set this poem to music as well, in 1839, but on a French translation by François-Adolphe Loève-Veimars (1801–1854).

[10] Louis Jouvet (1887–1951) was a renowned actor, in films and on stage, as well as a stage director and a teacher at the National Acting School in Paris. Jouvet wrote a series of books on acting that are still considered important nowadays in France, one especially: *Le comédien désincarné* (The disembodied actor), which has been published thirty-four times between 1954 and 2013.

Even so, I don't think that one can speak of "death." Besides, one only has to look at the genre of opera: in the 1980s, people were claiming its demise; today, not only is it alive and well, but all kinds of music are called "opera." It is, I believe, always simplistic to think that an artistic form is condemned: it's only so in *a certain manner*. In literature, the New Novel (*Le nouveau roman*) enjoyed only brief popularity, and it seems to me that we have returned to a more "traditional" narration. As far as mélodie is concerned, I assert that today the French language and, by extension, French poetry are back into favor; we see it in new publications and in the flowering of new songs. As to *Sprechgesang*—well, today we call it rap!

Consequently, conditions are propitious for a renaissance of mélodie, with the caveat that poets and musicians must work together again. Since Gautier and Berlioz, there have always been special contacts between these two types of artists: Gounod was a personal friend of Émile Augier, Saint-Saëns knew Victor Hugo, Fauré met Verlaine, Debussy was a constant guest of Mallarmé's, Poulenc corresponded regularly with Éluard, and so forth. But I find it equally interesting to see that earlier poetry is always capable of inspiring advances in language, and to see as well that some works are inspired by specific performers, an accord that has not been the case for some time. Since the end of World War II, there have been lots of contemporary works in which the performer was a simple instrumental object. Today, meaning seems to make sense again. It's rather reassuring. My secret hope is that, in amplifying poetry, the movement of song creation will bring back the writing of poetry that is meant to be spoken, for it is not only composers who are responsible for the demise of the art song: it is difficult to choose within modern poetry, which is not so concerned with the musicality of the language. Poetry borrowed, it seems to me, a "philosophically thinking" or "post-Mallarméan" path in the use of language—but without his finding a sonorous and physical enjoyment of it, which was characteristic of Mallarmé. There are some exceptions, like Francis Ponge and René Char, whose poems have been rarely set to music. Is it, perhaps, that current poets are afraid of music? Poets need to ask why composers don't call on them—for opera librettos, for example—and often prefer to write their texts themselves. My impression is that composers are afraid of finding themselves with a language that they don't understand, a language that is too complex in terms of syntax—in other words, a foreign language!

But if the golden age of mélodie is clearly behind us, there is still, on the other hand, much to discover in what already exists. The mélodie is a genre that still holds a large number of little-known works of outstanding quality, which are not necessarily unknown pieces by famous composers; certain forgotten or unrecognized musicians wrote mélodies of the highest order. I myself have sung and recorded mélodies by Louis Durey, whose music is never performed. It's absurd, because, frankly, within the Groupe des Six, it is his mélodies that have, for me, the most value alongside those of Poulenc. It's a body of song repertoire that speaks to me. First of all, Durey always chooses interesting poems—a choice that denotes perfect literary taste—and, second, he has an immediately recognizable personal style; if one listens carefully, that style is identifiable at the very first hearing. Durey has a natural, straightforward side. It is quite close to what Cocteau demanded in his manifesto *Le coq et l'arlequin*, namely, an immediacy that has nothing to do with impressionism. I don't mean to imply, however, that none of his works are impressionist: his TROIS POÈMES DE VERLAINE, for example, are very Debussyste. But that is his first piece in the domain of song. In LE BESTIAIRE (Apollinaire), the IMAGES À CRUSOÉ (Saint-John Perse), and the TROIS POÈMES DE PÉTRONE, he perfectly accomplishes this objective: these are mélodies that are so obvious, clear, and limpid that they are almost transparent. Durey never seeks to complicate things—unlike Auric, whom I confess not to have sung much, but who seems to have embraced the cult of the "wrong note." It's been said that Poulenc invented his own folklore. Auric looks in this direction as well, but, at the same time, he seems to have wanted to demonstrate that he could also be "intellectual," so he adds dissonance, even bitonality. Poulenc never adds superfluous difficulties, and neither does Durey. Both of them write "straight-arrow" music. And, since Durey's total song output comprises sixty-plus mélodies (certainly not all of them are published, but those that are can easily be found), it is truly incomprehensible that not more musicians are interested in them. Moreover, they are easy to "marry," musically and poetically, in recital—with Ravel, for example. Durey adored Ravel. Additionally, while I was doing research on his TROIS POÈMES DE PÉTRONE (1918), I discovered something interesting: the first poem, *Boule de neige* (Snowball), which is, like the others, translated from Latin, deals with exactly the same theme as the first of the cycle DEUX ÉPIGRAMMES DE CLÉMENT MAROT, *D'Anne qui me jecta de la neige*, set to music by Ravel in 1899. I figured out that Marot had read the original Latin text and had made an adaptation in French, following the example of La Fontaine taking up Aesop's fables. What I don't know is whether Durey, by doing this, is paying homage to Ravel, or even if he was aware of this correspondence. It's both amusing and fantastic to see the extent to which everything intersects . . . Even research that seems marginal—there are not many texts by Petronius (Caius [or Titus] Petronius Niger) set to music (besides, we know now that this poem was only *attributed* to Petronius)—ends up creating intriguing relationships. I'm speaking only of Durey, but I'm pretty sure that there are countless more. Felicity Lott, for example, a great champion of French mélodie, doesn't understand why the mélodies of Maurice Delage are so rarely heard. Personally, I have never sung Delage's songs—besides, they are better suited to a high voice. Perhaps every composer is waiting for "his" singer?

Returning to the subject of rediscoveries to be made, I think that we must first look into the twentieth century. The body of unknown mélodies from the nineteenth century is enormous, but it is an established fact that the golden age of the mélodie falls between the turn of the nineteenth century and the first third of the twentieth. And if, in the more contemporary mélodies, there are certainly marvels that have been ignored, I don't think that there is a true "body of work" to discover, nor that there is a composer completely devoted to French art song who is still unknown. Jacques Leguerney, author of sixty mélodies, is not a total unknown: his work has been recorded. I'm still convinced that the most fruitful period begins in 1870 and stops at World War II. For example, Nadia Boulanger wrote a good number of beautiful songs that are unknown. It's the same with Claude Arrieu, Marcel Delannoy, Mel Bonis, Henriette Puig-Roget, Maurice Thiriet, and Florent Schmitt, to name but a few.

3

To Perform

For Which Singers?

Let us now address the question of tessitura, vocal type, and keys. The majority of French art-song composers wrote for specific singers whom they knew personally. Berlioz wrote several works for Pauline Viardot (herself a composer of mélodies, also of fairly good quality, as we will see in the second part of this book), as did Gounod, Saint-Saëns, and Fauré. Fauré dedicated his first mélodies "in duet" to Pauline's two daughters, Marianne and Claudie, as did Saint-Saëns and Massenet, the latter of whom dedicated numerous mélodies to the women who gave first performances of the heroines in his operas, Sybil Sanderson and Marie Trélat. Later on, Debussy composed for the very unusual voice of his dear Marie Vasnier, whom he accompanied at the piano. The list is long, and I'm only speaking here of dedications to women performers! There's an equally long list of men: tenors like Maurice Bagès and baritones like Jean-Baptiste Faure (who also wrote songs). But there's no general rule: Duparc's dedicatees are usually members of his family, or friends. And even with Fauré—who, at the beginning, wrote for specific singers—matters become more abstract later (except for his last vocal work, *L'HORIZON CHIMÉRIQUE*, dedicated to Charles Panzéra, then a young baritone).

Whoever the dedicatee, it was quite clear to the first great French art-song writers that, in order to get their songs published and then sung, they had to cast a wide net and publish each song in a minimum of two different keys. It was for this reason that, as regards the mélodies of Gounod, for example, the publisher systematically published each song in two keys: one for high voice, the other for middle voice, and sometimes even a third version in low voice. As the tessitura and especially the key were not, at that time, thought to impact on the function of the text and the atmosphere, composers didn't see any inconvenience in writing songs in multiple keys. With Debussy and his successors, this method became more problematic, for in their mélodies, the piano part was not interchangeable but participated directly in the musical interpretation of the poetic text and its coloration; additionally, these piano parts were often very difficult to transpose, especially in the lower registers, and, consequently, there were issues with the position of the pianist's hands on the keyboard and, more generally, the clarity of the harmonic discourse.

The relative indifference of composers to the idea of transposition, knowing the symbolic importance that the choice of key takes on, may surprise some. But when the mélodie came into being, the symbolic aspect of the key didn't have the

Le Chant Intime. François Le Roux and Romain Raynaldy, Oxford University Press. © Oxford University Press 2021.
DOI: 10.1093/oso/9780190884178.003.0004

same strength as it did during the era of Mozart and Masonry, for example. It's rather a question of color. In Debussy, there are many sharp keys, either major or minor. Fauré prefers the flat keys. But I don't think that publishing songs in several keys bothered the composers, as long as the works remained singable. For example, in Fauré, there is rarely a distance of more than a minor third between two editions of the same work, and the tessituras are rarely extreme. One must always keep in mind that, above all else, the musicians wanted the text to be presented clearly, which, practically speaking, excluded ranges that were too extended. Only great experimenters like Charles Koechlin dared to ask a soprano to sing above B♭5 in the great cycles for women. The Romantic—or, rather, "classic"—voice of the nineteenth-century song repertoire was generally the mezzo-soprano or the medium-range tenor.

Generally speaking, we cannot say that there existed an "optimum" tessitura for French song. On the other hand, we know, by virtue of having explored them, what tessitura or what voice type is preferred by such-and-such a composer. Debussy, for example, began by writing for high soprano (up to C♯6), the tessitura of Marie Vasnier. But in the second part of his life, he turned toward light mezzos and *zwischenfach* sopranos, voice types that corresponded to that of "his" interpreter of the period: Jane Bathori (1877–1970), a remarkable musician (singer and pianist) who was a favorite of Ravel as well. The "modern" music of these two great composers already requires complete singer-musicians, who are able to read quickly and almost instantly understand the style of the works that they must perform. In a certain way, there has been an evolution of the mélodie written for a specific performer—which, by its name, assures continuity to the work—to the "lab" mélodie or experimentation, which would eventually find a singer to sing it. Poulenc is the exception that proves the rule: at first for his original performers, like soprano Suzanne Peignot, then for Bernac after 1936, Poulenc writes only according to who is performing his work. Moreover, for Bernac, he would not rest until he'd fully discuss interpretation and vocal appropriateness with him. Olivier Messiaen, on the other hand, writes somehow *in abstracto*, mostly for soprano—indeed, for dramatic soprano in the HARAWI songs, for which seasoned artists are strongly recommended! Henri Dutilleux wrote for Charles Panzéra, yet his writing doesn't seem to have been guided in a specific manner by this choice of artist. Finally, it's like the choice of an instrument: at the beginning, a composer writes according to existing technical knowledge, then moves on to more abstract experimentation, and finally ends up enlarging the technique and the repertoire of the instrument. The problem for vocal music is that a composer can introduce technical progress only to the detriment of the original quality; we see that quite clearly, at the opera, in the transition from Baroque style to Classical style (from Lully to Gluck), or from Rossinian bel canto to Verdi: each time, there is a gain in one direction but equally a loss. It means that singers who have extended repertoires must be "multi-technical," which isn't always possible; even if the evolution seems less drastic for the intimacy of voice with piano, it still exists: from the classical songs of Gounod, we get to the "recto tono/uniform tone" (or almost spoken style) of Debussy.

Man or Woman?

More than the tessitura or the key, it's the "gender neutrality" of the performer that could raise questions: in general, the poetic text of a mélodie is written by a male poet, and therefore the poetic expression is "masculine." There are, of course, women poets like Marceline Desbordes-Valmore or Anna de Noailles, for example, whose work has been set to music; nevertheless, for a very long time, the "voice" of the poet has not implied any choice of sex of the performer. To be more precise, for a female singer to sing about a man's love for a woman is no problem at all. Therein lies a basic piece of societal information: crossover sexuality, which goes only in one direction; it would never occur to a man to sing Debussy's TROIS CHANSONS DE BILITIS (even if I myself have done it several times . . .)! Moreover, it is, I think, this acceptance of female crossover sexuality that has allowed the success of "lesbian" texts at the turn of the century and right up to World War II. Fauré wrote the cycle MIRAGES, on poems of baroness de Brimont, who, although married, was a lesbian—though it's not too blatant when one reads the poems. On the other hand, we don't know any overtly male homosexual poem set to music. These sexual questions are interesting, and we will come back to the topic. But the relationship between composer and performer must also be explored from this angle. For example, I find it interesting to see that Debussy asked his lover, Madame Marie Vasnier, whom he accompanied on the piano, to sing texts that include what he himself wanted to say to her, in a thinly veiled declaration (think of the ARIETTES OUBLIÉES).[1] It's very troubling; there is a terrible distortion! Additionally, he chose the poems—in my opinion, they both chose them together—that are rather erotic, like C'est l'extase langoureuse. The preceding generation was more prudent. It is amusing to see how Verlaine was set to music by Saint-Saëns in 1912 (that is, twenty-five years after Debussy!): when he, too, sets C'est l'extase—to which he gives the title Le vent dans la plaine (The wind in the plain), he stops at "roulis sourd des cailloux" (the dull rolls of pebbles), and basta! No more "âme qui se lamente" (lamenting soul)! He writes a refrain with "C'est l'extase" and, at the end, his work becomes, certainly, a very pretty song, but one that has nothing to do with the ecstatic and the languorous! He who pays scrupulous attention to the poem allows himself a highly symptomatic mutilation here.

---

[1] The composition of the "Vasnier" song cycle, first published in 1888 by Veuve Girod under the title ARIETTES, was still intended for her; the later and revised edition, by Durand in 1903, has the following dedication: "À Miss Mary Garden, inoubliable Mélisande, cette musique (déjà un peu vieille) en affectueux et reconnaissant hommage" (To Miss Mary Garden, unforgettable Mélisande, this music [already a little old], in affectionate and grateful homage). It seems that, after the premiere of Pelléas et Mélisande in 1902, Mary Garden asked the composer about songs, and Debussy "recycled" for her the cycle, from a high-soprano version to a more central one.

I think that "musical sexuality" is still explored very little by scholars. Yet, it would be highly instructive to understand how, for example, singing in the salon could serve as a release, and how the most erotic poetry of the period was strongly appreciated. Mallarmé's poetry also has strong erotic connotations, but as his poems are more obscure, only the "initiated" can grasp this aspect. The first ones to risk it were Debussy (as early as 1883 with *Apparition*, written for Madame Vasnier) and Ravel (*Sainte* dates from 1896), who were from a generation for whom eroticism posed no problem.

Art Song or Opera?

As I stated earlier, the stance of the performer of French mélodie is the negation of that of an opera singer, who must incarnate a character. The aesthetic posture is also a bit more "neutral" than that of the lieder performer, for the expression of the lied is very rarely as distanced: the lied is often a sort of dramatic mini-scene, in which the poet only expresses himself, without a mask, and in which the music depicts intimate emotions. The difference between the lied and opera is, as Dietrich Fischer-Dieskau once said in a master class, that in opera, one should completely exteriorize the emotion, while in the lied, the exteriorization is the first step, but then one should re-interiorize and channel the emotion.

The particularity of the mélodie is that it is never a direct expression of the poet, of a voyager, or of a hero. We have previously established that the poetry that best suits the mélodie is allusive, sublimating a situation or an experience, and that the music operates as an additional vibration: it creates the indefinable resonance. Take the poem *Lamento* by Théophile Gautier as an example ("Connaissez-vous la blanche tombe"), set to music by I can't tell how many composers from successive generations. Its emotion is indirectly presented (and with a question to the audience, to begin with). Berlioz sets it superbly (to the title *Au cimetière*), in a simple strophic form (ABA'), just barely ornamented with a few variants, perfectly embracing the classic form of six sestets chosen by Gautier, where we clearly hear the throbbing obsession of a "dead" song, which, however is only suggested. It's only at the beginning of the second verse ("Oh! jamais plus, près de la tombe / Je n'irai, quand descend le soir / Au manteau noir . . .) that a first-person "I" first appears. Moreover, it's because of this "I" that Duparc, in eliminating several lines of the poem, was able to write a superbly dramatic mélodie—or rather a lied.[2] But if we study the poem in its entirety, we notice that the sentiment of the poet is not that "I feel fear when I go to meditate at the white tomb," but rather, "It's weird; there are strange and fascinating things that happen at that tomb, and I think it would not be good for my sanity to return there." Thus, it is no longer romanticism the way we generally

---

[2] French musicologist Rémy Stricker (1936–2019), author of the book *Les mélodies de Duparc* (Arles, France: Actes Sud, 1996), refers to the lieder of Duparc.

think of it, in that it is not the representation of a situation and the resonance of the accompanying emotion of the poet, nor is it the state in which he finds himself at that moment in natural surroundings. In lieder, on the other hand, it is generally this Romantic attitude that prevails. It took a long time for another attitude—such as Expressionism—to appear (though Expressionism is, ultimately, only a distortion of Romanticism that goes to the depths of a space of latent morbidity—we see this transformation clearly in Schoenberg, for example, in his *Gurrelieder*).

In France, however, the poetry used for mélodie remains more aesthetic, more experimental, less cathartic. The poet is not there (except for rare exceptions) to express his sadness. This is the reason that the poetry of Heine, who had quite an ironic distance in his works, was more fully appreciated in France (in the translation by Gérard de Nerval) than in Germany.

What are the consequences for the singer? Let's see how events unfolded during concerts during which first performances of mélodies were given. The singer was generally an amateur performing for a small audience. This status inspired more of a collective enjoyment of "initiates"—very well described by Proust—than a collective catharsis. Not that the singer had less of a voice, but because the musical writing induced it. The style of writing is also why the mélodie made its entry into actual concert halls much later than the lied. I don't think that, generally speaking, one can ascribe a solemn or "liturgical" character to a mélodie recital. One could possibly conceive of it for Schubert's *Winterreise*, which is kind of a dramatic journey without a true breaking down, but there is no equivalent in French mélodie. Besides, not even the greatest French song cycles are as lengthy: *Winterreise* is over an hour long. The rare experimentations of this type, like Guy Ropartz's QUATRE POÈMES D'APRÈS L'INTERMEZZO DE HEINRICH HEINE, which is fifteen minutes long, are pretty dense. And if the German influence is obvious (already by the choice of poems—although they are translated into French), they are rather more similar to the Brahmsian lied: the piano part is very individualized and dense, hinting at an orchestration—which Ropartz eventually did.

In mélodie, cycles are not longer than nine or ten songs[3] and do not exceed a half-hour of singing. If we are looking for a German model, it would be Schumann's *Dichterliebe*—but, again, not in the expression; or as Heine had conceived it, I think, at the beginning, in his *Intermezzo lyrique*, with irony—contrary to Schumann, for whom the poet does everything for himself.

Stylization Rather Than Emotion

The slight distance between text and affect in the performance of mélodie doesn't mean that emotion and realism are banned from poems that have been set to

---

[3] We have said earlier that Lili Boulanger's CLAIRIÈRES DANS LE CIEL is, with its thirteen songs, the longest French song cycle. Its duration is around thirty minutes.

music. There are also poems of emotion felt and poetic realism, like those of Jean Richepin, yet these remain marginal in the musical setting. Moreover, it is amusing to note that the poems chosen by composers often have musical titles already. That characteristic entitles the poet to casually appropriate the musical domain. Let's take the example of Théophile Gautier again. He didn't write a "Lamentation": he wrote a *Lamento*. In this way, poets adopt forms that create distance, through older references such as the rondel. And composers don't like following indications to the letter: when a poem is called, for example, *Chanson* (Song) or *Guitare* (Guitar), they title the mélodie otherwise by what it inspires, and sometimes that choice creates a real nightmare for the performer who wishes to find the corresponding poem in its original edition. Yet, beside the title, the line structure and the versification generally induce a corresponding musical treatment, line by line, verse by verse. It is thanks to the sophistication of the form and the asymmetrical or free line that the music emancipates itself and that the mélodie discovers its own style.

Debussy pushes stylization to the maximum. It seems to me that Debussy always tackles the poem through declamation, in a chanted fashion, as if an actor were saying it. He further interprets a work that is already stylized because of its very poetic essence. His music isn't preconceived, even before the poem has been read. Thus, we have to deal with a double perspective, which necessitates considerable work to achieve a result at the limits of song, free of all melismas. It is the return to the *recitar cantando* so dear to Monteverdi, but a typically French *recitar cantando*, with a very limited range. And even when the range is extended, as in *La chevelure*, the second of the TROIS CHANSONS DE BILITIS, it's for the purpose of obtaining a precise effect. These mélodies, composed shortly after *Pelléas et Mélisande* (1897–1898) are, for me, the most important cycle among Debussy's art-song works. Instead of emphasizing the voyeuristic, unhealthy, or libidinous aspects of Pierre Louÿs's erotic poems-in-prose, the composer breathes a sensual purity into them that antedates the original sin as well as a symbolic questioning. In fact, Debussy's cycle was not considered scandalous, while Louÿs's book was. Music can always permit things that are forbidden in literature—within limits, though . . . Just think of the reception of Bizet's *Carmen*! In any case, the dated aspect of the poet's eroticism is, thanks to Debussy, completely sublimated. The serious error would consist, for the singer, to believe it: In *La chevelure*, Bilitis recounts what a man told her about a dream he had; one cannot be more indirect!

This point takes us to the sexuality of the performer. Currently, the vocal register doesn't have as much importance as one might thing: in a society like ours, where collective pathos overrides intimate expression, the sexual component carried by the voice (a secondary sexual character, according to doctors) has almost no importance. Whether Schubert's *Winterreise* is sung today by a mezzo-soprano or a tenor, it poses no problem in the eyes of the public (I was tempted to add "unfortunately"). By the same token, a woman can sing Mahler's *Kindertotenlieder*, even though Mahler wrote them explicitly for a man's voice, for it's a father who is mourning for his children. If a woman sings them, the work's perspective completely changes: the father-child relationship is nothing like the one between a mother and her child! While French mélodie was historically much more frequently performed and given first performances by women, the masculine sexual aspect of the texts is even more influential, and, in this sense alone, it didn't pose any problems: as I said previously, we can't imagine a man singing *TROIS CHANSONS DE BILITIS* or Bizet's *Adieux de l'hôtesse arabe*. Although we find cross-gender performance such as in the *Thousand and One Nights* in the Orient, it is a typically Western attitude to accept that a woman slides into a man's role without raised eyebrows; even feminine homosexuality is admitted, as long as it doesn't strike a blow upon good taste or decency. On the other hand, for men, it is complicated, even if it wasn't always the case: the *castrati* never bothered anyone at the time—perhaps because they sang the roles of virile heroes!

The attitude of mélodie singers is thus a bit paradoxical, for if the voice is individualized and sexualized, it should be used to express sentiments that are often exterior or strange to the singer. Thus, being too specialized would be risky: if one sings only mélodie, the singing will quickly become affected, because the quest for aesthetic effect will end up prevailing over personal expressivity. We had such an example in the last recorded recitals of Pierre Bernac: he tended more and more toward subtlety of expression and sound, toward all that can contribute to disembodiment, which then substitutes for internalization. The problem, for me, is that it erases his individuality and disembodies his voice, rendering it pale. All of a sudden, despite his perfect diction, we hear nothing other than effects and technical tricks. Nothing is left but the skeletons of the mélodies—even those of Poulenc, the very source of Bernac's information. Whereas, when Bernac was in full possession of his vocal means—in the recordings made prior to 1950, for example, and even when he was using the same methods—he didn't have the same unfortunate musical results. This is the usual evolution: the more time passes, the more the singing becomes overly refined, intellectualized, and, finally, desexualized. We might say the same thing about Dietrich Fischer-Dieskau in his last recordings, in comparison to those before 1980.

It's also for this reason that the singer should be completely at ease with their voice and not fake it or tamper with it. The voice should be in perfect harmony with the self. If the singer doesn't "play fair," it creates a considerable distance between who they are and what is being sung. Suddenly, we see only the performer, or should I say "Your Highness"? What is being communicated is not "I am transmitting this song," but "I know how to perform." Whence arises as well, for the singer, the necessity of choosing melodies with texts that speak to them, to which they feel close; for those to whom they feel less close, the work should be even deeper and more controlled, by themselves and a professional partner: either the coach-accompanist or the voice teacher. The risk is extreme "sophistication," such as that which I emphasized before regarding Bernac. But it takes more to get to this extreme than to go to oversimplification—which is equally risky: it's a trap that consists of singing without knowing anything about the song! Anyway, Bernac was in an unusual situation: Poulenc intentionally wrote some vocal "effects" for him—not because he admired Bernac's voice, but because he admired the interpreter of his music, a very different concept. Poulenc didn't write the same way for more "vocal" singers. He was never so infatuated with the vocal quality as he was with the overall personality of the performer: think of Denise Duval or Suzanne Peignot. More than the instrument, it was the personality—or the person—that interested Poulenc, while it seems to me that other composers, such as Massenet, were fascinated by the voice itself. (In his book *Diary of My Songs*, Poulenc did say, however, that he wanted singers to sing his music as if it were Verdi!)[4]

I think it is always interesting to know who gave the first performance of a mélodie (when possible, thanks to some well-documented sources). Where it was sung for the first time is also very insightful. If the performer had the honor of being recorded, in this mélodie or in something else, listening to this sonic testimony will make us understand what genre of voice the composer had in mind. It is also helpful to know the name of the concert hall, its capacity, and anything else pertaining to the sonic and declamatory dimensions of the space.

Putting Together a Program

Now, let's address the putting together of a recital program. There should always be a "connecting thread" to create coherence. The first rule, purely musical and rather obvious, is to blend and match the keys. Don't ever play around, moving from half step to half step in key signatures throughout the recital. And don't blend keys that clash with one another. Another big rule: manage the contrasts. It doesn't mean that you necessarily have to confine yourself to the traditional slow-fast-slow-fast! Also, avoid singing only sad songs, or finishing with the same old trick that is the amusing "end-of-concert" piece. It would feel as if you were saying, "Enough of the headache, let's have fun now!" Additionally, be wary of the placement of works that are too violent or aggressive for the voice, rich in text and in articulations: putting forth too much at once kills the voice, and it becomes difficult to get to the end of the recital. The converse is also true: no need to hold onto long legatos; it's too tiring. The essential is to vary the palette of expressions, whether they are contemplative, vehement, mixed, or serene. Additionally, if you wish to best capture the attention and the understanding of the public, it is best to try not to exceed seventy minutes of music (whether or not there is an intermission). It's really the maximum for a recital of French *mélodie*.

The beginning of the recital must be prepared with care, for oneself as well as for the public. There are composers with whom it is difficult to begin, like Debussy,

---

[4] In *Diary of My Songs*, published in French with English translation (London: Kahn & Averill, 1985; reprinted 2006), Poulenc says many times say that he prefers singers with a nice voice and no brains to "intelligent" singers with no voice; see pages 40–41, 68–69, 78–79.

whose music requires strong concentration and demands that all members of the audience set aside recollections of everything that they did beforehand. It is true that the public is generally very "open" at the beginning of a recital, excited by its appetite for music. But Debussy requires more than that: a true intellectual and sensory availability. For this reason, putting his songs at the end of the first half or the beginning of the second half seems preferable to me. Certain long mélodies by Debussy, like those on the five great poems by Baudelaire or the PROSES LYRIQUES, require the singer to be at the best of their vocal capabilities, both physically and expressively, as is rarely the case at the beginning of a recital. Finally, it is preferable, if a singer chooses to program one or more cycles, to sing them in their entirety, as they were conceived, rather than creating one's own "playlist." The composer has always chosen the order of a cycle and the number of songs within it, and the performer should respect that choice.

Another important point: international audiences require special attention, and the performer should take into account the specificities of the country in which they are singing. Germans, for example, don't know much French mélodie. If singers choose to perform a recital that is solely devoted to French mélodie in Germany, they have to go slowly and choose a repertoire of relatively progressive difficulty to engage the audience. If the singer chooses to do a recital of half lieder and half mélodie, then even more attention has to be paid to harmonic, chronological, and poetic connections. In Great Britain, on the other hand, there's nothing to worry about, for the British are passionate about French mélodie, and have been for a long time. As for the United States, the work of Pierre Bernac continues to bear magnificent fruit, thanks to his book, *The Interpretation of French Song*.[5] Other great names of French song kept mélodie before the public: particularly, Martial Singher (1904–1991), who gave the first performance of Ravel's DON QUICHOTTE À DULCINÉE, taught at Mannes, Curtis, and the Music Academy of the West.

As for the number of composers to put on a program, I'd say that seven or eight should be the limit. Beyond that number, the recital takes on a patchwork quality, and, in the end, the public won't remember anything. Because the median length of a song is short, one risks ending up with a catalogue of miniatures. A good balance would be the presentation of three composers on each half, not necessarily following chronological order. I often end up finishing a recital with Ravel's short cycle DON QUICHOTTE À DULCINÉE, after having sung some Poulenc, which follows chronologically: even if sublime Poulenc songs are being offered, it's hard to sing them after the Don Quichotte songs, which end with the extraordinary *Chanson à boire*.

It's equally important not to program composers whose works collide and clash. Programming Messiaen after Debussy works well because there's affiliation between them, but Messiaen after Fauré is rather difficult. In the same way, Poulenc

[5] Pierre Bernac, *The Interpretation of French Song* (New York: Norton Library, 1978; London: Kahn & Averill, 2006).

and Gounod go very well together, while Poulenc and Fauré work less well. Fauré works well with Albert Roussel and *very* well with Saint-Saëns, who pairs well with Ravel. Chausson works well with Fauré, but even better with Duparc; even if their writing is very different, there is a big musical and poetic coherence between them—and they were close friends. Anyway, all of that must be discovered through experience, and everyone should find their own personality. In addition to musical coherence, you must not neglect poetic coherence, which should get obvious as the recital is being built. Yet, you'd better be careful there, too. If a performer chooses two cycles on poems by Mallarmé, it is not necessarily a good idea to put them back to back, even if that placement anchors the program, for Mallarmé's poetry is quite enigmatic. Obviously, it's possible to plan an entire program around one poet. Personally, I like to program the music of several composers around the same poem. If the songs are not too long, the audience members will respond to or remember one word, or one turn of phrase, and will suddenly find their interest piqued and make connections with the program.[6]

That doesn't mean the performer can't be original! If one is programming Duparc, for example, it's a shame to systematically choose the two Baudelaire poems—in any case, there are only two! It is more interesting to separate them and to put the two Jean Lahor poems, or the two Gautier poems in between. With a composer like Duparc, whose corpus is very small, one has to choose from a poetic point of view, because, musically, everything works! One can choose as well one single mélodie and put it in a group with which there are other affinities. For example, I like to sing the first song from Cycle I of Debussy's FÊTES GALANTES, *En sourdine*—because its "nightingale" theme, cited again in the composer's *Colloque sentimental*, is already in there—and then add the three songs of FÊTES GALANTES II, whose last is precisely this *Colloque sentimental*. This program forms a coherent group of four mélodies instead of three, allowing the performer to give the audience a little more Debussy: Apart from his PROSES LYRIQUES (around twenty minutes long) and his CINQ POÈMES DE CHARLES BAUDELAIRE (lasting almost half an hour) his other cycles are so short that none of them exceeds ten minutes! It's a shame to have so little Debussy in a recital. After all, he is a pivotal composer: we can think of the French song repertoire as being divided between "Before Debussy" and "After Debussy"! On a side note, I personally don't sing the two other mélodies of FÊTES GALANTES I (*Fantoches* and *Clair de lune*) because their tessitura is too extended for my voice. But I don't think of myself as being unfaithful to Debussy in doing so: after all, he's the one who reprises the initial motive of this mélodie in *Colloque sentimental*!

Another important aspect of the recital is the connection that the performer wants to establish with the audience. It always seems to me to be friendlier if the singer has a small talk with the audience. Personally, I do so a lot. Since, in mélodie,

---

[6] Nowadays, program booklets are given to the public, or else texts are shown as surtitles on a screen. A good translation is needed when the recital takes place in a non-French-speaking country. All these tools help the public understand the coherence of a program.

as in chanson, there is no supremacy of the performer, and even less of "hero worship" (as in the lied and its "I"), why not develop a dialogue with the audience, like in a salon? Obviously, when I sing in Poland or Japan, communication is more difficult, but it's always worth it to try to do something. This attitude will always be preferable to one of religious solemnity, which seems to affirm "listen and drink." I don't think that the lied—which, for a long time, we have been more accustomed to hearing in Western culture—requires such proximity and connection between the performer and the spectator. By connection, I mean cultural bond, and not preachiness of dubious quality. Anyway, even in a recital that mixes lieder and mélodies, simplicity of contact is always welcome.

Accompaniment

Speaking of collaboration and mutual understanding, I would now like to discuss the singer's first collaborator: the pianist. There are two types of singer-pianist relationships: the long and almost exclusive kind (Pierre Bernac and Francis Poulenc, Dietrich Fischer-Dieskau and Gerald Moore, Marilyn Horne and Martin Katz) or the short-term collaboration. Must one choose? To make a non-response, I would say that each one has advantages and drawbacks. It's good to have a special relationship with a pianist, but it would be too bad if it became exclusive, because every exclusive relationship carries the seeds of laziness and the cultivation of unwished-for habits with it. It's easy to fall into a dangerously settled work routine, while our art and our craft should remain, above all, a school for curiosity and challenge. For me, the ideal is to have special relationships with several collaborators. In this way, when we work on the same repertoire with different pianists, it allows for different approaches that keep the music fresh. Additionally, certain pianists are much more comfortable with some composers than others. The sharing of knowledge should be balanced. Otherwise, an insidious hierarchy will automatically be established, and the hierarchy makes no sense in the musical performance of chamber music: no competition, only sharing and osmosis—that is the goal to be attained. Citing some personal and pertinent examples, I can say that it doesn't bother me to make recordings with different pianists. It seemed obvious to me to make a CD of Debussy's mélodies with Noël Lee, who knew the composer down to his fingertips: he had recorded all of Debussy's works for piano and had supervised the critical edition. Plus, he was an experienced recording artist, and no time was wasted during the recording process—a great benefit to a singer, who cannot go through endless takes. On my end, I brought my experience as a recitalist and, of course, my knowledge of the roles of Pelléas and Golaud made me feel "at home" with Debussy. This way, we had plenty of time and it spared us from any superfluous discussions. To record the Ravel mélodies, I chose Pascal Rogé, with whom I had already recorded Poulenc's songs. Of course, he is, above all, one of the very finest concert soloists. I particularly appreciate the frankness and the clarity with which he imbues French repertoire. He loves the song literature and brings to it passionate and always benevolent support. Therefore, we were in sync from the very beginning.

Concerning work with a partner, there are no preestablished rules: it's different with each one. Sometimes, the work is done almost automatically. When I work with Jeff Cohen, for example, each of us understands immediately what the other wants. There is no disagreement, because we are both *listening* in the same way. In general, singers need to be sufficiently clear about what they want, to the point of giving direction, so that the pianists can understand where they should go. Singers should not be intellectually rigid, but should, in part, use their voices and their interpretations to direct the performances. When pianists don't know where they are going, it's not because they are stupid, but because singers are not precise enough with directions. And, above all, the directions should be musical, and not the result of an intellectual discourse. That goal doesn't prevent either the singer or the pianist to ask, from time to time, "Why are you doing that?" and to receive an explanation. I think that the singer must have sufficiently prepared the vocal part so as not to arrive before the pianist and make them suffer through a sight-reading session. It goes without saying that the pianist must also have worked on their part before the first meeting. The two partners must be on the same level; there should be no feeling of dependence or submission on the part of one or the other. That attitude doesn't mean that singer and pianist can't sight-read new works together. But for the real work of interpretation and performance, they must be on the same level. Bernac asserts that singer and pianist follow each other alternatively. But, for me, this is mutual interaction above all. Actually, I don't think using the word "follow" is right: if the work is done well on both sides, the interaction is continuous.

To achieve that ideal, moreover, it would be beneficial for the pianist to have the same knowledge of the poetic text as the singer. But I obviously wouldn't require the pianists with whom I work to have the same poetic and musicological library as I do. Certain pianists learn by common practice; others share the same passion with me. On the other hand, I often give them my books of poetry or rare scores so that they can see what I'm talking about. I think that it's also important to make one's repertoire passions understood through these means.

The arduous preparation of a recital, done privately at home or at the home of the accompanist, should establish the essential keys of interpretation of a work. But the recital itself must be the opportunity to offer new things to one another. Everything is important: the concert piano (a potential nightmare for the accompanist), the acoustics of the hall, the lighting, the reactions of the public. One must be a bit schizophrenic: all at once judge and jury, within and outside of oneself. If not, one repeats patterns, and the music doesn't live. For example, on two consecutive days, I sang Schubert's *Winterreise* with Graham Johnson in two different places. Well, I felt like two different people because the interaction was so lively. This experience relates back to my comment from the very beginning of this book about being the puppet and the puppetmaster.

Working on the Score

Working on a score also requires a few remarks. There are two possibilities, according to whether one is familiar with the composer or not. If the singer already knows the composer's style—because they have already sung it or know the chamber music or symphonies of that composer—then the score analysis consists of understanding how much of what has been assimilated unintentionally relates to what's written on the page. This point is also valid in the case of a well-known mélodie that one knows only vaguely, by ear. One starts with the memory to arrive at what is written.

On the other hand, when a singer approaches a composer that they know just a little or not at all, the work consists first in learning their style—the "grammar and spelling"—just as one would do with a writer. Each composer has a specific language. This language generally uses a basic terminology—notes, nuances, phrasing—but each term hides a different notion. For example, in Fauré, most of the tempo indications (*andante*, *allegretto*, etc.) mean something very precise. *Andante* means "absolutely not slow," *allegretto* means "not too fast." In Debussy, who doesn't use the traditional Italian terms (or very little, and only in his early works), the singer has to know what *triste et lent* (sad and slow) or *tristement* (sadly) means. Many indications seem completely abstract, innate. It's not easy to figure them out, but doing so comes with practice. Mastering the creative world of a composer is, above all, a question of apprenticeship. Even so, good understanding of a style doesn't make a singer forget to change their "reading grid" when they go from one composer to another. This practical apprenticeship is missing in the training of many young singers. I find that the education that one receives in music school, or even in master classes, doesn't sufficiently approach these notions of specific style. There is a lot of talk about vocal technique and ways of singing, but students are rarely given the keys to learning about style—it's left up to each individual to discover—or even, at the very least, good paths to learning how to ask questions.

Good questions, as I see it, are the following:

- What does such-and-such a tempo mean when written by a given composer?
- What did the composer write in the score?
- Why, and what does the musical writing mean in relationship to the original poem?

All these things are, of course, learned through practice. With composers who have not written many songs—or have written songs that we never hear—the performers' path is more difficult and requires more time and more work. In that case, we proceed through approximations and "family" oppositions, in taking into account what we know of other composers of the same era or the same school of thought. Fauré and Franck, for example, have nothing to do with each other. On the other hand, Chausson and Franck share many common traits, even though the poetic interpretation is subtler in Chausson and less attached to the codes of the past. Even if at the risk of kicking down an open door, the following must be stated again: everything is in the score. In studying, we realize, for example, that Fauré's tempo and dynamic markings are almost superfluous: for instance, he would write a *crescendo* over an ascending vocal line, but, if one obeys it scrupulously, the result will be excessive. It would be acceptable with an orchestra, but, with the piano, it's redundant. I think this is only about Fauré being overly careful: he wants to make sure that the singer truly gets it. Generally, one should pay more attention not to increase the sonic intensity when the vocal line ascends, or to decrease it when it descends— or not to accelerate or slow down when there is no clear indication along those lines. We know that, in French music, the German-style *rubato* doesn't exist. The *rubato* is subservient to the harmony. In order for the audience to understand that there is going to be an important change of harmony and discourse, one should, in a way, prepare it, and thus anticipate this change, at least in one's mind. It should not be left to the very moment the change happens. On the other hand, however, the singer doesn't have to sound all the bells and whistles one measure beforehand!

Some stylistic elements are unique to every composer, and it is good to know what they are. Debussy, for example, uses both eighth-note and quarter-note triplets in a very specific manner: he is seeking to use them in order to approximate the regular manner of speaking certain groups of words. So one must pay close attention when Debussy mixes rhythms in order to give them a precise value. This practice is as valuable in *Pelléas et Mélisande* as it is in the mélodies. Let's take the example of the second of the TROIS CHANSONS DE BILITIS, *La chevelure*, for the phrase "Et peu à peu, il m'a semblé" (And, little by little, it seemed to me). The syllables "peu à" are the last two eighth-notes of a triplet. If one breathes in beforehand, in the eighth-note rest between "Et" and "peu"—which one is tempted to do in sight-reading—it's a reading error: an eighth-note rest is not necessarily the equivalent of a breath. It's exactly like a comma in a written text: the comma is a suspension, not necessarily a breath. In the line from Verlaine's poem *Green*, "Voici des fruits, des fleurs, des feuilles et des branches" (Here are fruits, flowers, leaves and branches) we don't breathe at every comma—it would be as stressful as having asthma![7]

In Poulenc, the quarter-note rests and eighth-note rests often serve to mark the attack on the word that follows, especially if the word begins with a vowel. That pattern doesn't mean that one has to breathe. On the contrary, Poulenc never indicates the spot where a breath should be taken. Bernac would always say, "Naturally, you would take a breath at such and such place." "Naturally," because it's logical in the poetic phrase. For example, in *Hôtel*, when Apollinaire says, "Le soleil passe son bras par la fenêtre," Poulenc cuts between "soleil" and "passe," because he wants us to hear well the "-leil" and "pa-." A breath should absolutely not be taken there. It is true that when one sight-reads Poulenc, the writing might seem very chopped up, two measures followed by two measures. But it's a writing tick of Poulenc's, and if

---

[7] *Green* was set to music by both Debussy (1886) and Fauré (1891), among others.

one sight-reads without knowledge of his style, the poetry is ruined. In fact, Poulenc follows the line perfectly; he knows what he wants and what he doesn't want. For example, when he composed on Apollinaire's calligram *L'espionne*, on the line "Tu te déguises / À ta guise," he cuts between "déguises" and "À ta guise," in putting an eighth note and a sixteenth note for "(dé)gui-ses," followed by a sixteenth-note rest, thus conforming to what Apollinaire had "calligraphed," in detaching "À ta guise" by one line in relation to "Tu te déguises," creating two parts from one simple eight-syllable line. Paying attention to that construction means paying attention to the way the composer does things, to the elements that he uses to be perfectly comprehensible, and faithful to the poet. If Apollinaire had written a classical line and Poulenc had followed him, the singer would have had to sing the liaison between "déguises" et "À" [degizəza].

I also think that sometimes we can use our performative license to authorize ourselves certain things (as long as they're justified)—notably in "classical" writing, that which borrows from the most frequently used current parlance. For example, in *Phydilé* by Duparc, on a poem by Leconte de Lisle, I always allow the so-called mute *e* in "mille" to be lightly heard in the hemistich "germant par mille issues," by re-attacking the *i* of "issues" without a glottal stop, in order not to create an elision between "mille" and "issues," which sounds ambiguous: one could hear a word that doesn't exist, "milissues" [milisyə]. But the execution of this detail is delicate, for, ultimately, the singer shouldn't be adding a syllable to the alexandrine! In this example, the singer is not operating as a simple performer, but also making a personal interpretive choice, thinking of the audience as if the singer had never heard the work. If we think that the audience consists only of people who know the repertoire by heart, we are wrong.

As for Gounod, he wrote like Mozart: he indicated the dynamics only in the piano part, but that habit doesn't mean that the singer should not perform them in the vocal line! Additionally, he used a certain number of "italianisms," and we have to beware of turns (*gruppetti*) and appoggiaturas. Because of repeated practice, we end up doing things automatically, and we're always astonished that other singers do those things differently. Let's take the example of Gounod's famous *Sérénade*, set to a poem of Victor Hugo. In the first line "Quant tu chantes, bercée," Gounod writes two notes for the "-é-e" [e-ə] of "bercée." That creates a problem, because it adds a syllable to Hugo's hexasyllable, but it's nonetheless prettier than putting two closed *é*'s [e] back to back. It's the same thing for the third line, "Entends-tu ma pensée!" We see the difficulty of making the *é* [e] in the feminine rhymes musically mute. Finally, the real solution to this problem is to find a good tempo, so that this fillip goes unnoticed. But Gounod never indicates a metronome marking!

Tempo is a recurring problem in interpretation. In Fauré, the indicated metronome marking is always too fast. It's the same with Poulenc. The latter, I think, indicates more the line toward which it should be set to avoid the whiny side. I'm often told, "But the tempos are correct—they were calculated with Bernac!" And that's what Poulenc confirms in his *Diary of My Songs*. Except that Bernac, in *his* book, *Francis Poulenc: The Man and His Songs*,[8] confirms that the written tempos are too fast. So, there's something amiss! In fact, I think that when Poulenc worked with Bernac, he never asked any questions about tempo, whose choice seemed evident. That is to say that we shouldn't take what a composer says or writes about his music at face value! To the contrary, we have to beware of it. For his whole life, Poulenc said that he didn't like his cycle POÈMES DE RONSARD and that they weren't worth anything, simply because, one day, Auric told him that these songs weren't "real Poulenc"! Now, as far as I'm concerned, as a performer, I find that they rank among his most interesting songs; pianistically speaking, the accompaniment is very detailed, and Ronsard's poems are magnificent. These poems forced the composer to rethink his manner of writing at a turning point of his creative path, 1924, between the newly rediscovered QUATRE POÈMES DE MAX JACOB (1921) and the great flourishing of mélodies in the 1930s. (By the way, in 1934, he orchestrated POÈMES DE RONSARD.) In the same vein, many people say, "Why bother rummaging through Fauré's early songs?" But it is precisely because they are early songs that they are interesting! It's extremely important to see where a famous composer comes from—and the exploration often yields happy surprises. When we see what the young Fauré did with as long a poem as Hugo's *Tristesse d'Olympio*, in which he retains six verses of the original thirty-eight, and from these assembles a completely coherent ensemble, functioning perfectly, both musically and poetically, it must be said that, behind all that, there is a formidable culture and a good dose of chutzpah. We'll discuss this song further in the analysis in Chapter 15.

Frankly, for certain composers, I remain certain that all the music is worth it, even the disavowed or destroyed pieces. With Mozart, certainly, everything was almost perfectly rendered from the very beginning; but there is, all the same, a world of difference between the little early sonatas and the great last ones. However, no one would dare say, "Why are you playing these little sonatas?" It's like those who assert that the "real" Stravinsky stops at *Renard*. How could anyone say such a thing? It's as if someone had said of Picasso that, after his Rose and Blue Periods, there was nothing else. The same thing is true for Richard Strauss after *Der Rosenkavalier*. No matter what anyone says, Strauss remains himself to the end of his life, right up to the *Four Last Songs*. Just as Stravinsky remains himself right up through his last serial works, recognizable upon first hearing. By having a comprehensive vision of a body of work, one can better distinguish the composer's different creative paths. Certain composers, from the beginning, assimilate everything, like sponges. Others build their body of work slowly, little by little, so that, by the end of their career, they have an enormous and astonishing output. That's pretty much what happened with Poulenc: before his opera *Dialogues des Carmélites*, many thought that he was not a serious composer, even if, over a considerable period of time, he had written many

---

[8] See Pierre Bernac, *Francis Poulenc: The Man and His Songs*, 2nd edition, edited and translated by Winifred Radford (London: Kahn & Averill, 2002).

important works. It is true also that other composers—Georges Auric, for example—produced their best work right at the beginning of their careers, while, later on, a kind of weariness seemed to set in, and inspiration was overridden by workaday craft. It doesn't mean, however, that everything should be thrown out: in Auric's later film music, there are interesting things that, moreover, made him famous.

For a performer, it is certainly legitimate to have opinions and preferences. What is not all right is to have *preconceptions*. My only personal preconception is to interest myself in everything that I don't know, even if at first glance some things seem off-putting: we cannot really understand what's interesting about a work until we read through it. Because of that, we should never put up boundaries in advance. For instance, it shouldn't be decreed that Saint-Saëns songs are interesting up until 1875 and that afterwards there's nothing worth knowing. Saint-Saëns wrote mélodies right up until his death, in 1921! If we make draconian selections, even with Fauré, we miss out on many things. This point is all the more true because every "minor" work sheds light not only on a composer and their personal evolution and style, but also on the *zeitgeist*, both for the musician and for the society of their era. There are themes that can be found from one artist to another; we don't know why: it's "in the air"!

It's kind of obvious to me that to really know a song composer requires exploring their works in other genres as well. If they wrote operas, it is interesting to look into this part of their work in order to understand how the songs are written: doing so will shed light on influences and context, which are often more noticeable in a long work like an opera. In Saint-Saëns, the mélodies are rather close to his great opera arias in terms of formulas and piano accompaniment, which often serve as a basis for orchestration. In my opinion, the most interesting mélodies by Massenet are those of his important cycles, even if the majority of the poets that he chose—like Armand Silvestre—are not great authors. In his manner of "cycle-izing" his mélodies, Massenet avails himself of Schumann: he is a Romantic composer. We see that right away in his writing. The use of thematic composition is a central characteristic of the "readability" school, in which we also find Guy Ropartz and his QUATRE POÈMES D'APRÈS L'INTERMEZZO DE HEINRICH HEINE (1899).

If examining diverse kinds of works seems desirable in order to know the composer better, sometimes it is simply indispensable. Thus, if a singer who has no inclination towards Debussy's mélodies and has never studied *Pelléas et Mélisande* is asked to sing one of these works, it's not even worth trying. Obviously, the songs of any great composer are not isolated from the rest of their work. This lack of isolation is the reason that we must try to retrace the "creative path" and connect the mélodies to the rest of the composer's œuvre, especially to the chamber music—as long as it is possible: none of Gounod's chamber music, for example, is extant. We are lucky we have Saint-Saëns's chamber music, and it is magnificent—not to mention that of Fauré; with Debussy, it is beyond essential. Moreover, we can reverse the proposition as regards Debussy's piano works: chronologically, they come long after a whole series of mélodies with very pianistic accompaniments. A pianist who wants to perform Debussy should get to know his entire body of work for voice and piano.

Staying curious

I would like to end by evoking the enormous choice of works available to a young beginning singer who would like to embark on learning French mélodie. It's a rather complex problem. I don't know who is guiding voice teachers in their suggestions about French repertoire, but I suspect that they are thinking only about aspects of vocal difficulty. I don't think this selectiveness is the right move. There are interesting songs by Gounod, not only for the vocal instrument, but also for the text-music relationship. The problem is that Gounod has a reputation of being a minor musician who also uses minor poetry, a notion that is totally false: he chose poems by Hugo, Gautier, Lamartine, and Musset—not too shabby! Besides—and this point relates back to what I said earlier—I don't see why we demand more of Gounod than we do of Schubert. Be that as it may, for young singers interested in mélodie, we also have to make them love the poetry. It's the only way to get around the vocal "problem." For under the pretext of casting aside "easy" works for so-called reasons of poetic mediocrity, Fauré is suggested right off the bat—but, vocally, Fauré is very difficult! Gounod's songs were destined to singers coming from the Italian repertoire, or young women who sang very classic romances in studio class. Fauré demands more than this genre of vocal education: he experiments and works closely with the harmonies. Thus, it is very difficult to start with Fauré: the young singer is completely lost, harmonically speaking. So, then, imagine that they will be just as lost poetically speaking! For we must not forget that the majority of Fauré's best-known mélodies are written on poems by Armand Silvestre, a poet who's been totally forgotten. (Not to mention the difficulty nowadays of finding his books.)

I see too many young singers attack the pillars of the repertoire straight away. It's an error to start off directly with a great composer and to approach, without any resistance, one of their great cycles with the "greatest hits." No use arguing: the best-known mélodies of Fauré are the most difficult. Even *Après un rêve*—which is not really a French art song, since the melody has Italian roots—is very difficult to sing. It would be better to start with less-well-known works, whether the singer is starting with song or opera. Why start young singers off with a Mozart opera aria, when there are concert arias by the same composer that are not as hard—or some arias from Haydn operas that no one ever sings? In any case, to dive into French art song, one should immediately "connect" the music and the poem, even if it means starting with strophic poems and mélodies that are close to romances. It is much easier to start with Gounod's *Sérénade* (on a poem by Hugo) or *Le soir* (on a poem by Alphonse de Lamartine), both of which are magnificent songs and neither of which poses major technical problems, than to get started with Fauré's *Mandoline* or *En sourdine*, both of which require great understanding of poetry and mastery of breath control and underlying harmony in order to reach the summits of mélodie. It's a bit as if a mountain-climbing guide had started with Annapurna. It's better to remain reasonable. A mountain is beautiful no matter how high it is.

Duparc is another example of a composer who has written lesser-known songs that are easier than the "greatest hits." There is *Romance de Mignon*, for example, which I find fascinating, but very few people sing it. It's up to the voice teacher to say, "It's better that you sing this song instead of *Au pays où se fait la guerre*, whose dramatic qualities make it difficult." A young singer may go slowly into Duparc before going further. Unfortunately, the access to many songs is limited, no thanks to the meager tracking work done by publishers.[9] But the circle of aficionados of mélodie is, I believe, not very protectionist, and singers willingly give one another "useful tips."

In any case, one should not be timid in confronting the repertoire. There are two visions to consider: that of the singer and that of the voice teacher. The student and future singer should certainly not be afraid to approach vocal works in order to test them out; the voice teacher, on the other hand, should do everything possible not to frighten the student—especially by not suggesting things that could seem inaccessible or overwhelming. And the pedagogy should take into account the tastes of each one: if someone doesn't like Parnassian poems, for example, it's not worth it to sing French art song. If someone doesn't appreciate the Symbolists, one should not work on Chausson's SERRES CHAUDES or Debussy's PROSES LYRIQUES. But that shouldn't inhibit a singer from working on Debussy's FÊTES GALANTES or his ARIETTES OUBLIÉES. There's plenty of choice—except for Paul Dukas or Edgar Varèse, of which we know only a single mélodie each! And all that is left to discover awaits . . . We will now give you an overview.

---

[9] If nowadays a lot of scores are accessible online, one has to be careful about the quality of the editions presented. Critical editions, if existing, must be favoured. And they are usually not online, and cost money . . . Musical public libraries are an indispensable source.

PART II

ANALYSIS AND INTERPRETATION OF FRENCH MÉLODIES

4

Georges Auric

Le petit bois (1943)

Music by Georges Auric (1899–1983)
Poem by Jules Supervielle (1884–1960)

Presentation

Georges Auric is still well known today for his numerous film scores. One of them includes at least one song that has become immortal, thanks to its performance by Juliette Gréco: *Moulin Rouge*, from the eponymous film by John Huston. Auric was considered the most precocious composer of the Groupe des Six: when he was the young age of fourteen, his works were first performed under the auspices of the Société Nationale de Musique. He composed a large repertoire of around eighty mélodies. His biggest successes were miniatures, like the cycles ALPHABET, SEPT QUATRAINS DE RAYMOND RADIGUET (1920); TROIS INTERLUDES DE RENÉ CHALUPT (1913); and QUATRE POÈMES DE GEORGES GABORY (1927). Longer flights of lyricism seem to have frightened the composer; and yet, in the superb cycle QUATRE CHANTS DE LA FRANCE MALHEUREUSE (1943), he dared to write more lengthily—almost a quarter of an hour. In this cycle, he embraced revolt, violence—in a word, passion, incited by World War II and the Occupation, which were directly and deeply felt. He was surely inspired as well by the poets that he chose: Louis Aragon, Supervielle, Éluard, and Aragon again, whose works were published clandestinely.

The title of the cycle, written in 1943 in Antibes' Free Zone, is inspired by the collection *Poèmes de la France malheureuse* by Jules Supervielle, from which the second song of the cycle, *Le petit bois*, was taken and is presented here. I chose this mélodie and this poem because of the universality of the words, which transcend what could have been nothing but a "dated" form of expression, difficult to interpret for those who didn't live through the World War II period, despite all that still remains today in our collective memories. At 2 min 20 sec, it's the shortest song of the cycle, and yet the most moving and the most restrained in the musical sense of the term. In a medium tessitura (from $D\flat3$ to $F4$), it works well for either a male or a female performer. The whole cycle has been orchestrated, and the parts are available for rental from Éditions Salabert.

Le Chant Intime. François Le Roux and Romain Raynaldy, Oxford University Press. © Oxford University Press 2021.
DOI: 10.1093/oso/9780190884178.003.0005

Analysis

Le petit bois

J'étais un petit bois de France
Avec douze rouges furets,
Mais je n'ai jamais eu de chance
Ah! que m'est-il donc arrivé?

Je crains fort de n'être plus rien
Qu'un souvenir, une peinture
Ou le restant d'une aventure,
Un parfum, je ne sais pas bien.

Ne suis-je plus qu'en la mémoire
De quelle* folle ou bien d'enfants,
Ils vous diraient mieux mon histoire
Que je ne fais en ce moment.
     * Auric writes "De quelque"

Mais où sont-ils donc sur la terre
Pour que vous les interrogiez,
Eux* qui savent que je dis vrai
Et jamais je ne désespère.
     * Auric writes "Ceux"

Mon Dieu comme c'est* difficile
D'être un petit bois disparu
Quand† on avait tant de racines
Comment faire pour n'être plus?‡
     * Auric writes "il est"
     † Auric writes "Lorsqu'on"
     ‡ In Auric, the line ends in a period

The Little Wood

I was a little wood in France
With twelve red ferrets,
But I never had any luck.
Ah! So what happened to me?

I greatly fear I am no more
Than a memory, an image
Or the tail-end of an adventure,
Perfume, I know not what.

Am I not merely in the memory
Of some madwoman or some children?
They will tell you my story better
Than I can at present.

So where in the world are they,
That you might question them,
Those who know I tell the truth
And never despair.

My God, how difficult it is
To be a little wood that has disappeared
When one had so many roots.
What can one do to cease existing?

Musically, the whole cycle is based on chanson style, a "return to the past," which was a big trend at the time, not only in music, but also in all the arts;[1] no doubt it was a way to safeguard a little bit of French national and historical prestige, badly tarnished by the country's defeat in 1940. For this second song of the cycle, Auric invents a sort of "medieval complaint" formula, in B♭ minor, whose refrain is very simple and which should be sung *piano* (Example 4.1).

It returns every two verses (quatrains 1, 3, and 5), and the second and fourth quatrains are, in a certain way, varied couplets, marked *mezzo-forte*. The singer should sing simply, without affect or pathos, and should perform this beautiful *mélodie* like the harmonization of a popular song (as Séverac did for Yvette

---

[1] For example, *Les visiteurs du soir* (1942), an illustrious film by Marcel Carné, with dialogue by Jacques Prévert.

Example 4.1 Auric, Georges: *Le petit bois*. From *Quatre chants de la France malheureuse*, Editions Salabert, 1947 (ref. EAS. 14999), page 7, mm. 1–4.

Guilbert). It's a difficult exercise, but the tempo should be moderate: not more than 92 to the dotted quarter note. The *vif* (lively) marked at the beginning is, I think, the composer's wish for a light touch, and so the singer, for example, should try to sing the first two lines in one breath, and then the second two lines in one breath. Make the *c* in "donc" audible: "Ah, que m'est-il donc arrivé?" [akemɛtildõkarive] In the middle of the couplets, the breaks, marked in the poem by commas that are sometimes missing from the score, must be handled carefully: "Qu'un souvenir, / une peinture, / Ou le restant d'une aventure, / Un parfum, / je ne sais pas bien." For the second line, one can choose instead to sing with a discreet break: "De quelque folle / ou bien d'enfants" to avoid the unintelligible flow of [fɔlubjɛ̃]. The second couplet, introduced by two measures of piano solo, is the darkest part of the song. Classic prosody dictates that one sings [mɛzusõtildõsyrlatɛr]. In this poem, however, let us recall the rule of pronunciation for *donc*: the *c* is pronounced if it is followed by a word starting with a vowel, but is never pronounced if it is followed by a consonant.[2]

Be sure to remain *mezzo-forte* for the end of the couplet, which sounds so strong-willed and yet so powerless, with equal duration on each syllable: "Et jamais je ne désespère."

The last "refrain," slower than at the beginning (marked *lent subito*) should not be maudlin. One has the choice, for the text, of either the printed poem or the version

---

[2] For this rule, I refer, as for almost everything related to pronunciation, to the *Dictionnaire de la langue française par É. Littré*, in seven volumes (henceforth referred to in short form, as *Littré*).

This dictionary is the source to which all cultivated poets—and composers—referred up until World War II. It exists today as a mobile app.

in the published vocal score. I find stronger, for both musical and poetic reasons, the alternating succession of [k] and [s] in the printed poem: Mon dieu comme c'est difficile . . . disparu . . . Quand on . . . racines . . . Comment faire . . . And, of course, the [s] at the end of "plus" is not pronounced!

To be true to the poem, the singer must understand that the roots of the trees are almost immortal, and that total disappearance is thus inconceivable. So, it is imperative not to sound despairing, but, rather, uncomplaining, with a smile of distress; the piano concludes the song alone, in a shortened and almost unrecognizable *Marseillaise* . . . , which ends in hopeful major—timid, but hopeful, all the same.

5

Hector Berlioz

Au cimetière (1841)

Music by Hector Berlioz (1803–1869)
Poem by Théophile Gautier (1811–1872)

Presentation

I have chosen the fifth song (of six) from Berlioz's very famous cycle LES NUITS D'ÉTÉ. Four of the others have been analyzed in Pierre Bernac's book. Since then, there have been numerous musicological studies, and a remarkable critical edition has been published by Bärenreiter (2000).

Au cimetière, subtitled *Clair de lune* by Berlioz, was entitled *Lamento* by Théophile Gautier. The poet also wrote a *Lamento: La chanson du pêcheur*, also set to music by Berlioz in LES NUITS D'ÉTÉ under the title *Sur les lagunes*, and subtitled *Lamento*. In each case, Berlioz's *Au cimetière* has nothing to do with that of Fauré, written on a poem by Jean Richepin, or of Saint-Saëns, on a text by Armand Renaud.

It is interesting to note that the publication of the poems of LES NUITS D'ÉTÉ dates from 1838. Now, Berlioz started writing his mélodies in 1834–1835, thus proving that Gautier, whom Berlioz knew well, showed the composer his poems well before the publication, and that the composition followed the poetic writing very closely. The orchestrated version dates from 1856.

The cycle LES NUITS D'ÉTÉ was published for the first time in 1841 as the composer's Opus 7. It is dedicated to Louise Bertin (1805–1877), the daughter of the director of the *Journal des débats*, for which Berlioz was a collaborator. There are many other musical settings of this *Lamento*, some of which are equally precocious, sometimes in the form of romances. It is not even certain that Berlioz was the first composer to set the poem. On the other hand, he is one of the very few who sets the poem in its entirety. Fifty years later, Duparc set only verses 1, 3, and 6.

To study this mélodie, I advise using the critical edition of Peter Bloom, published by the Éditions musicales du Marais in the collection Patrimoine (1992); it is certainly a rather expensive edition, but it uses the original 1841 score (which can be downloaded from the Bibliothèque nationale de France's Gallica database). The score is very interesting in terms of the piano accompaniment. The differences are often considerable compared to the other editions, which are, in reality, reductions

Le Chant Intime. François Le Roux and Romain Raynaldy, Oxford University Press. © Oxford University Press 2021.
DOI: 10.1093/oso/9780190884178.003.0006

of the orchestra score realized by who knows whom. The most striking difference in the original piano-vocal score is the absence in the original piano-vocal score of the long introduction in the second song of the cycle, *Le spectre de la rose*, which was written expressly for the orchestra. The original key is D major, with a very high tessitura. Moreover, it's written more for a tenor than for a mezzo-soprano. A tenor of that period had a voice that was not heroic, but capable of singing very lightly, mixing resonance in the mask and head voice. For this voice, the tessitura of the original version (from E4 to G5) is particularly well written (for a tenor, the tessitura becomes from E3 to G4). For a medium or low voice, the key is B♭ major, a major third below the original key. It's far away from the original key, but it proves to be very comfortable, especially if the entire cycle is being sung.

Formally speaking, the poem is constructed in a highly regular schema: the connection of two octosyllables to a line of four feet. This four-foot line gives a powerful rhythm to the poem, which Berlioz understood perfectly, and to which he gave a special harmony, something we will presently see.

Generally speaking, the writing is very romantic. Unlike the Debussyste manner, in which the color of the vowels can call forth a precise vocal color, in Berlioz, it's the meaning of the word that determines the sound. Thus, in the second line, the word "plaintif" incites an alteration of the chord intended to fit the meaning of the word.

Here, as in many mélodies, the performer must deliver the song very simply, to better capture the nocturnal atmosphere. At the same time, the clichéd interpretation of "nocturne" that implies sadness must also be avoided. It must be remembered that, for the Romantics, the relationship with death is not necessarily somber or harmful. The cemetery is considered to be a calm place, propitious for contemplation, and not a place of terror. Moreover, the song is written in a major key, which demonstrates that Berlioz didn't want to write an excessively gloomy song. And it's not just any major key: it's D major, a joyful, sometimes glorious key. The transposition to the rich key of B♭ major doesn't change that quality, either, but adapts the mélodie to the naturally darker colors of an alto or a baritone voice.

The singer should keep the voice light and find a tone that is almost "popular." One should think of the German *volkslieder* (folk songs), which were songs that everyone knew and which people hummed without thinking about it. It was in the spirit of this idea that Berlioz worked. A German speaker himself, he knew this repertoire well and he probably wanted to avoid the banality of the romance by using the model of the German lied.

Other pitfalls to avoid: monotony and emphasis, which the length of the mélodie—more than five minutes—can sometimes encourage. To maintain interest, the singer must be alert to the poem. And, in order to do that, I think it can only be beneficial, as custom requires, to take the text, see how it moves, and recite it out loud—even more so because Berlioz set it in its entirety.

Analysis

Au cimetière

Connaissez-vous la blanche tombe
Où flotte avec un son plaintif
L'ombre d'un if?
Sur l'if, une pâle colombe,
Triste et seule, au soleil couchant,
Chante son chant;

Un air maladivement tendre,
À la fois charmant et fatal,
Qui vous fait mal,
Et qu'on voudrait toujours entendre;
Un air, comme en soupire aux cieux
L'ange amoureux.

On dirait que l'âme éveillée
Pleure sous terre à l'unisson
De la chanson,
Et du malheur d'être oubliée
Se plaint dans un roucoulement
Bien doucement.

Sur les ailes de la musique
On sent lentement revenir
Un souvenir;
Une ombre, de* forme angélique
Passe dans un rayon tremblant,
En voile blanc.
   * Berlioz writes "une"

Les belles de nuit, demi-closes,
Jettent leur parfum faible et doux
Autour de vous,
Et le fantôme aux molles poses
Murmure en vous tendant les bras:
Tu reviendras?*
   * In quotation marks in Berlioz

Oh! jamais plus, près de la tombe
Je n'irai, quand descend le soir
Au manteau noir,
Écouter la pâle colombe
Chanter sur la branche* de l'if
Son chant plaintif!
   * Berlioz writes "pointe"

In the graveyard

Do you know the white tomb
Where floats with plaintive sound
The shadow of a yew?
On the yew, a pale dove,
Sad and solitary in the setting sun,
Sings its song;

A melody of morbid sweetness,
At the same time delightful and deathly,
Which wounds you
Yet which you wish to hear forever;
A melody, such as in the heavens,
A lovesick angel sighs.

As if the awakened soul
Were weeping beneath the earth together
With the song,
And at the sorrow of being forgotten,
Murmured its complaint
Most meltingly.

On the wings of music
You sense the slow return
Of a memory.
A shadow, an angelic form,
Passes in a shimmering beam,
Veiled in white.

The Marvels of Peru, half-closed,
Shed their fragrance, faint and sweet,
About you,
And the phantom with its languid gestures
Murmurs, reaching out to you:
Will you return?

Oh! Nevermore shall I approach that tomb
When evening descends
In its black cloak,
To listen to the pale dove
From the top of the yew
Sing its plaintive song!

This mélodie is marked by a very great harmonic flexibility. It begins in D major with a measure in triple meter, like a distant memory of a waltz. Berlioz inserts a basic pattern of undulating of chords on every beat, with the dominant underneath, then hesitates between B♭ major and D minor, according to the words: "la blanche tombe" is in major and "son plaintif" is in minor. "L'ombre d'un if" is more harmonically distant: it is set in F♯ major—far from the original D major. This is an illustration of what was previously discussed: Berlioz uses harmony to accentuate the single line of four poetic feet. The new key center is short lived: after "L'ombre d'un if," the key returns to D major for one cadential measure, before changing again on "Chante son chant" to C major.

The harmonic ambiguities continue in the second verse. Berlioz vacillates, until "à toujours entendre," between A♭ major and some passing diminished chords, before modulating to C minor and finally returning to D major on "L'ange amoureux." But be careful! Following the dictates of the *Dictionnaire Littré*, the *s* of "toujours" is not connected to "entendre". So the phrase must be sung: [tuʒurɑ̃tɑ̃drə].

The third verse is marked by steady eighth notes on A in the left hand—another harmonically astonishing event, since the D, the root of the chord, disappears in measure 51 (Example 5.1).

Example 5.1 Berlioz, Hector: *Au cimetière.* From *Les nuits d'été*, Editions musicales du Marais, Collection "Patrimoine," volume XVII, 1992 (ref. E.M.M. 3520), page 28, mm. 47–51.

The steady eighth notes continue on A, leading the listener astray, since it's not clear where the music is going, harmonically speaking. This pattern is followed by a stepwise harmonic progression, with the A ostinato underneath (Example 5.2).

Berlioz continues to accentuate the four-foot line: "De la chanson" is set in G minor; this passage is followed by a chromatically ascending bass line in eighth notes. In the beginning, the beats were set to quarter notes; now they have been subdivided. A short undulation on E minor on "Bien doucement" marks the end of the harmonic voyage. The poem is at its midpoint, and another evocation begins: that of memory.

It begins with a rhythmic diminution. Having begun the song with a rhythmic pattern of three quarter notes per measure and having subsequently moved to six

Example 5.2 Berlioz, Hector: *Au cimetière*. From *Les nuits d'été*, Editions musicales du Marais, Collection "Patrimoine," volume XVII, 1992 (ref. E.M.M. 3520), page 28, mm. 52–58.

eighth notes, Berlioz now subdivides the accompaniment into twelve sixteenth notes per measure. Memory is evoked through a dance in A major and a theme, at the end of the word "souvenir" (measure 77) with the upbeat (Example 5.3).

Example 5.3 Berlioz, Hector: *Au cimetière*. From *Les nuits d'été*, Editions musicales du Marais, Collection "Patrimoine," volume XVII, 1992 (ref. E.M.M. 3520), page 30, mm. 76–79.

This evocation does not last long—the memory is fleeting—and the eighth-note undulation begins again. Berlioz employs his first poetic license with the text, by repeating "Passe dans un rayon tremblant" before "En voile blanc." Moreover, the word "tremblant" (trembling) is ornamented and followed by an interesting rhythmic figure in the piano (Example 5.4).

Example 5.4 Berlioz, Hector: *Au cimetière*. From *Les nuits d'été*, Editions musicales du Marais, Collection "Patrimoine," volume XVII, 1992 (ref. E.M.M. 3520), page 31, mm. 89–92.

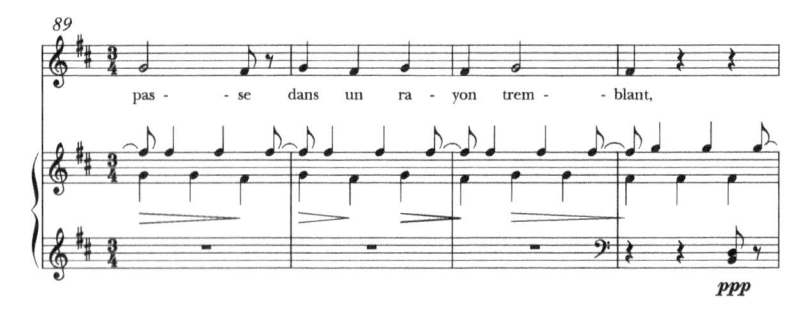

The G in the right hand, which undulates in syncopation against the left-hand F#'s on the beats, is, of course, a musical depiction of trembling, but also creates a feeling of breathlessness. This grating motion will last until just after "voile blanc." The end of the fourth verse remains suspended on a fermata and a dominant seventh chord, before beginning again on the tonic D.

The fifth verse is almost a reprise of the first phrase—the only difference being the setting of the accompanying chords in a hemiola pattern (Example 5.5).

Example 5.5 Berlioz, Hector: *Au cimetière*. From *Les nuits d'été*, Editions musicales du Marais, Collection "Patrimoine," volume XVII, 1992 (ref. E.M.M. 3520), page 31, mm. 99–105.

It is advisable to lengthen "leur" after "Jettent": it is not a question of prosody as much as an indication of typically Berliozian "unbalancing."

The last verse is related to the beginning as well, with the exception of a few details: "jamais plus" is shorter, adding to the ambiguity, and "Je n'irai, quand descend le soir" doesn't go as high as the parallel passage in the beginning. A very lovely phrase in G minor, on "Écouter la pâle colombe," follows. At the end of "Son chant plaintif" and the measures that follow, an astonishing undulation closes the song. There is no reprise of earlier material, and even the harmony is not certain— as if the sound were disappearing for lack of fighters.

In summary, the performer should always be attentive to every change in the writing—as tenuous as each one may be—and should remain clear, as much in vocal color as in the enunciation of the poem.

6

Charles Bordes

Sur un vieil air (1895)

Music by Charles Bordes (1863–1909)
Poem by Paul Verlaine (1844–1896)

Presentation

Charles Bordes is a composer of magnificent mélodies. It is certain that his position at the Schola Cantorum ultimately took its toll on his renown as a composer of mélodies, for, not having been a symphonic composer, like d'Indy, but an organist who was a great lover of poetry, he would have found himself in the camps of Debussy and Fauré. But there's nothing to do about it. His works were propagated only after his death. Bordes set to music many poems by Verlaine, but also by Jean Moréas, Francis Jammes, Camille Mauclair, Maurice Bouchor, and Jean Lahor (following the example of Saint-Saëns and Duparc, Bordes also wrote a *Chanson triste*).

The mélodie *Sur un vieil air* is quite interesting, for, instead of being turned off by all the musical allusions that Verlaine's untitled poem contains (piano, air, chant, refrain, etc), Bordes uses them superbly, to good advantage. The first line, "Le piano que baise une main frêle," is introduced by an "old air," which is none other than the very famous *Plaisir d'amour* by Johann Paul-Egide Schwarzendorf, better known by the name of Jean Martini (1741–1816) and nicknamed "Il Tedesco" (The German) by the Italians. Composed in 1784, *Plaisir d'amour* is certainly the best-known romance in the world. The words are by Jean-Pierre Claris de Florian (1755–1794), and Berlioz himself orchestrated it in 1859. Verlaine's poem speaks of memory, without indicating which air to which the titles refers, but includes, as an epigraph, this line by Petrus Borel (1809–1859): "Son joyeux, importun, d'un clavecin sonore" (Joyful sound, intrusive [sound], from a sonorous harpsichord), which seems less tearful than the eternal theme of the romance in question, but more insinuating ("importun" meaning "intrusive"). This is how Bordes treats it.

Composed in Paris in 1895 (111 years after *Plaisir d'amour*), Bordes's mélodie employs one of three keys in which the romance was published: E♭ major. *Sur un vieil air* was originally written for voice and orchestra. It was the dedicatee of the mélodie, Pierre de Bréville (1861–1949), a great friend of Bordes and his successor at the Schola Cantorum, who supervised the posthumous piano-vocal edition (Rouart-Lerolle [Salabert], 1914). The tessitura seems to indicate a mezzo-soprano

Le Chant Intime. François Le Roux and Romain Raynaldy, Oxford University Press. © Oxford University Press 2021.
DOI: 10.1093/oso/9780190884178.003.0007

voice (from E♭4 to G5), or medium tenor. The song could be transposed to D♭ major for a low voice without doing damage to either the vocal part or the accompaniment. The length of the work is approximately 3 min 20 sec.

Analysis

<table>
<tr><td>Sur un vieil air</td><td>On an Old Air</td></tr>
<tr><td>Le piano que baise une main frêle</td><td>The piano, kissed by a delicate hand,</td></tr>
<tr><td>Luit dans le soir rose et gris vaguement,</td><td>Gleams dimly in the pink grey evening,</td></tr>
<tr><td>Tandis qu'avec un très léger bruit d'aile</td><td>While, with the lightest brush of a wing</td></tr>
<tr><td>Un air bien vieux, bien faible et bien charmant</td><td>A melody, truly old, truly faint, truly charming,</td></tr>
<tr><td>Rôde discret, épeuré quasiment,</td><td>Floats quietly, as if frightened,</td></tr>
<tr><td>Par le boudoir longtemps parfumé d'Elle.</td><td>By the bedroom where long Her scent had lingered.</td></tr>
<tr><td>Qu'est-ce que c'est que ce berceau soudain</td><td>What is this sudden lullaby</td></tr>
<tr><td>Qui lentement dorlote mon pauvre être?</td><td>That slowly caresses my poor being?</td></tr>
<tr><td>Que voudrais-tu de moi, doux Chant badin?</td><td>What would you want of me, sweet playful song?</td></tr>
<tr><td>Qu'as-tu voulu, fin refrain incertain</td><td>What did you want, vague and subtle air</td></tr>
<tr><td>Qui vas tantôt mourir vers la fenêtre</td><td>That soon will die away by the window,</td></tr>
<tr><td>Ouverte un peu sur le petit jardin?</td><td>Opened a little onto the tiny garden?</td></tr>
</table>

Three *andante* measures of piano solo precede the entrance of the voice: here, the right hand plays the beginning of the theme of *Plaisir d'amour* and the left hand plays a countermelody a sixth below (Example 6.1).

Example 6.1 Bordes, Charles: *Sur un vieil air*. Editions Rouart, Lerolle, 1914 (ref. R.L.10,052 & Cie.), page 1, mm. 1–4.

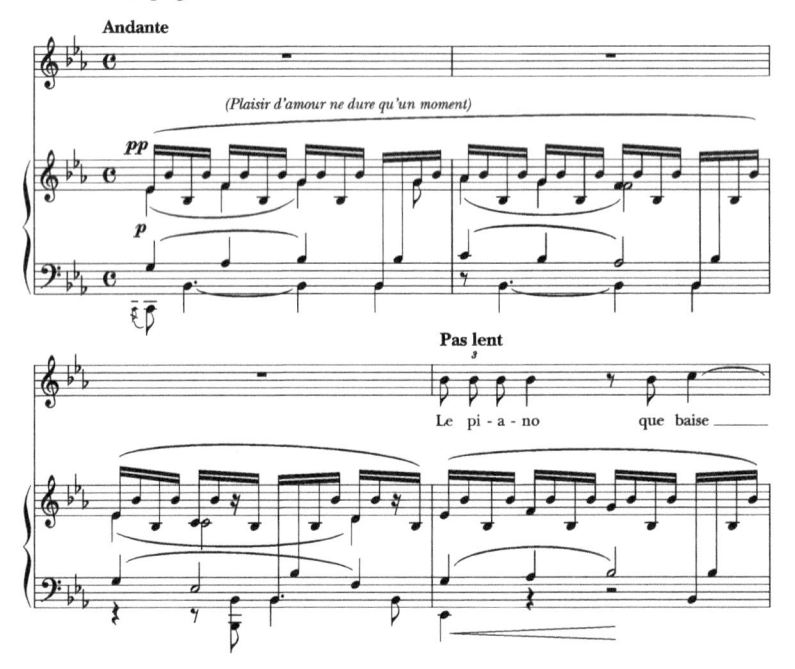

Bordes introduces the voice with the marking *pas lent* (not slowly—for the voice should not slow down the tempo of the opening). The vocal line does not so much begin with a melody—rather, it is a commentary on what has taken place in the accompaniment, thus adopting the attitude of listening demanded by the first six lines of the poem. At measure 9, the marking *cédez* (gradually slow down) (Example 6.2) allows the piano to remain "frêle" (delicate) in the sixteenth notes and to prepare the fermata (which should remain short) on the F.

Example 6.2 Bordes, Charles: *Sur un vieil air.* Editions Rouart, Lerolle, 1914 (ref. R.L.10,052 & Cie.), page 2, m. 9.

The motion then picks up again without ever really regaining the *tempo primo*, which comes at the marking *poco accel.* (measure 12, "Rôde discret" [prowling, discreet]). The *crescendo* in the accompaniment under the word "Elle" in the accompaniment applies as well to the voice, which should be bolstered with a warm vibrato, without exceeding the *mezzo-forte*. The piano continues warming the meaning and the emotion, before calming down for the return of the theme (measure 20, *tempo primo*). In the passage marked *plus mouvementé* (more active), the singer should be even more emphatic in the articulation (Bordes writes *rf—rinforzando*—for the voice) and the voice should become more sonorous, but without pathos: Verlaine writes "mon pauvre être" (my poor being), with a condescending, ironic nuance, which the performer must try to recreate; the indicated *rallentando* helps. And when the *a tempo* returns, the intensity must be maintained, for the piano remains active—as does the irony. Finally the peak of the vocal line arrives, and it would be good to attain it without taking a breath and by singing, in one go: "Qu'as-tu voulu, fin refrain incertain / Qui vas tantôt mourir"; although a *luftpause* in the score suggests a breath after "incertain", an uninterrupted ascent (i.e., without a breath) allows the performer to steadily pace the *crescendo*, which is notated in the accompaniment but which is equally applicable to the voice (Example 6.3).

Be careful: the *decrescendo* that follows should continue until "jardin," so don't become too soft too quickly. Once again, three measures of solo piano follow. Then,—and this is the only liberty that Bordes takes with Verlaine's poem—the singer takes up the next-to-last line, "Qu'as-tu voulu, fin refrain incertain?" (be sure to point out

Example 6.3 Bordes, Charles: *Sur un vieil air.* Editions Rouart, Lerolle, 1914 (ref. R.L.10,052 & Cie.), page 5, mm. 31–34.

the question mark). For the last time, the piano "exhales" the opening phrase of the romance, leading to the conclusion. The music ends less serenely than the first time, for "Chagrins d'amour durent toute la vie"—the pain of love lasts throughout life— and the romance has achieved its nostalgic effect!

7

Lili Boulanger

Reflets (1911)

Music by Lili Boulanger (1893–1918)
Poem by Maurice Maeterlinck (1862–1949)

Presentation

With Mozart, Schubert, and a few others, Lili Boulanger has the status of a genius who left us too soon: she died at age twenty-four. She was the first woman to win the Grand Prix de Rome in composition. Her sister, Nadia Boulanger (1887–1979), the great pedagogue and conductor, and a composer herself, would spend her life promoting the works of her younger sister. Today almost all of Lili Boulanger's previously unpublished music is accessible, either through recent publications or recordings; all of her achievements are now recognized. Her interest in the "New Poetry," which eschewed the Symbolist and Parnassian tendencies of the period, resulted in magnificent mélodies. In 1914, she composed the longest cycle ever written in the French song repertoire: *CLAIRIÈRES DANS LE CIEL*, on thirteen poems by Francis Jammes (1868–1939), who figured among the "New Poets" and who was also a close friend of Henri Duparc. Alas, Lili Boulanger never had the occasion to hear the cycle. In our own time, it is a "must" for tenors and sopranos. But the movement in which Francis Jammes participated was not readily adaptable to the art of the mélodie: its language, which professed to be simple and down to earth, doesn't allow for the elusion, the undefinable "moment," for which Verlaine and Mallarmé, by very different means, had previously allowed. And this great cycle—the only one that achieves the successful setting to music of this genre of poetry[1]—remains a unique case.

The other poetic route followed by Lili Boulanger was that of the Belgian symbolist writer Maurice Maeterlinck. From the start of her career, she had wanted to write an opera based on Maeterlinck's first published theatrical work, *La princesse Maleine*. Today, alas, only incomplete sketches are still extant. Like Debussy and Chausson before her, she loved the images, symbols, and sensations created by Maeterlinck's writing. She wrote two mélodies on his poetry: *Attente* (1910), and the mélodie discussed here, *Reflets* (1911). The two poems are taken from the collection

---

[1] Bordes and Milhaud, among others, also set some of Francis Jammes's poems to music.

Le Chant Intime. François Le Roux and Romain Raynaldy, Oxford University Press. © Oxford University Press 2021.
DOI: 10.1093/oso/9780190884178.003.0008

Serres chaudes, published by Léon Vanier in Paris in 1889, with illustrations by another Belgian, the designer and symbolist sculptor George Minne (1866–1941). *Reflets* was written in 1886 and published in Paris the same year in the magazine *La Pléiade*.

Analysis

Reflets	*Reflections*
Sous l'eau du songe qui s'élève,	Under the water of the surging dream
Mon âme a peur, mon âme a peur!	My soul is afraid, my soul is afraid!
Et la lune luit dans mon cœur,	And the moon gleams in my heart
Plongé dans les sources du rêve.	Plunged in the sources of the dream.
Sous l'ennui morne des roseaux,	Under the dismal boredom of the reeds
Seuls les reflets profonds des choses,	Only the deep reflection of things,
Des lys, des palmes et des roses,	The lilies, the palm trees and the roses,
Pleurent encore au fond des eaux.	Are still crying in the depths of the waters.
Les fleurs s'effeuillent une à une	The flowers shed their petals one by one
Sur le reflet du firmament,	In the reflection of the firmament
Pour descendre éternellement	To descend for eternity
Dans* l'eau du songe et dans la lune.	Under the dream's water and in the moon.
* Boulanger writes "Sous"	

The first (posthumous) publication of the score (Ricordi, Paris, 1919 [op. posth.]) contains an error in the return of the second quatrain: "Seul **le reflet** . . . Pleur**ent** encore. . . ." A singular noun cannot be followed by a plural verb. The 2000 Durand edition, which contains revisions based on the manuscripts, has corrected the error. On the other hand, the certainly intentional change that begins the last line, in which Lili Boulanger replaces "**Dans** l'eau du songe et dans la lune" with "**Sous** l'eau du songe et dans la lune" was, of course, preserved.

The mélodie is in F♯ minor, and shows a great "Fauréenne" influence by virtue of its frequent modulations and the simple arpeggios in the piano accompaniment. The meter is cut time. No metronome marking is given, but as the tempo marking is *sans lenteur* (not too slow), I suggest 69 to the quarter note. The tessitura is for a mezzo-soprano or tenor,[2] from C♯4 to G♯5. There are many expressive markings "à la Debussy," that is to say, giving more of an idea of the emotion required than technical information needed for realization. For example, at the beginning of the vocal

---

[2] The first performance was given by the tenor David Devriès (1881–1934), with the composer at the piano, on December 6, 1913, at the Salle Pleyel; on March 9, 1918, at a concert of the Société Nationale de Musique, it was Claire Croiza (mezzo soprano) who performed it, and it was she as well who gave the first performance of the orchestral version on January17, 1923, at the Salle du Conservatoire, by the Orchestre de l'Opéra, conducted by Henri Büsser.

line, we find *monotone, expressif, las* (weary); then, in measure 21, in the piano part, *douloureux* (sad). The prosody also owes much to Debussy, as shown for the verse "Et la lune luit dans mon cœur", where the length of the strong syllables (lu-, luit, dans, cœur) is varied, and finishes with a syncopated rhythm on "dans mon", bar 14 (Example 7.1).

Example 7.1 Boulanger, Lili: *Reflets*. From *Quatre mélodies*, Editions Durand & Cie, 2000 (ref. D. & F. 15284), page 2, mm. 13–16.

Through the extremely varied rhythmic values, the elocution is precise and efficient but always fluid, never overemphasizing the frequent and obvious alliterations: the [s] of "Sous l'eau du songe qui s'élève," for example, or the [r] of "morne des roseaux, / Seuls les reflets profonds."

The new tempo marking appearing at the beginning of the seventh line: *un peu mouvementé* (slightly livelier) (measure 35), followed two measures later by *animez un peu* (move forward slightly) should not sound too dramatic. The effect of the syncopated C octaves in the right hand of the piano (measure 41–44) is in itself a surprising change in relation to the regular arpeggios; to this is added the marking *retenu* (held back) (the measure at C), and the *decrescendo* for the voice and the piano. The last quatrain is superbly descriptive in the piano, illustrating, by syncopated dotted notes in the left hand, the falling leaves (measures 45–49) creating ripples in the water (measure 50); the contrast between this passage and the vocal part, marked *pp* and *lointain, effacé* (far-off), speaks for itself. It is worth noting the decision by the composer to transform the next-to-last octosyllable into a nona-syllable: "Pour des-cen-**dre** / é-ter-nel-le-ment." The decision was made, I believe, to clarify the declamation, for the [ə] of "des-cen-**dre**" is in a *decrescendo*, and the first beat on "-**cen**-dre" creates a natural stress. The four last syllables "et dans la lu-(ne)," marked *pp* and *à l'aise* (meaning with flexibility) would preferably be sung in the version that goes up to F♯5, although an *ossia* on the octave below is suggested (Example 7.2).

The mélodie is about 2 min 30 sec long. The light that it suggests, despite the malaise embedded in the poem, suggests a different perspective from that of the five SERRES CHAUDES set by Chausson (1893–1896), which doesn't include this poem. The palette of colors demanded of performers in order to do justice to this mélodie is exceptionally rich. The composer also orchestrated the song.

Example 7.2 Boulanger, Lili: *Reflets*. From *Quatre mélodies*, Editions Durand & Cie, 2000 (ref. D. & F. 15284), page 4, mm. 55–57.

Le retour (1912)

Music by Lili Boulanger (1893–1918)
Poem by Georges Delaquys (1880–1970)

Presentation

Composed in August 1912 at Gargenville,[3] this mélodie requires a completely different approach from that in *Reflets*. The poem was written by Georges Delaquys, an obscure poet and dramatist who was also a close family friend of the Boulanger sisters.[4] Delaquys wrote a collection entitled *La bonne clairière*, published in 1911, but it doesn't contain the poem in question here, the location of which has not been found. The title written on the first manuscript is *La nef légère* (The light ship) but the first edition has *Le retour* as its title.[5]

The mélodie, relatively lengthy at four minutes, is dedicated to the baritone Hector Dufranne, who, in 1902, gave the first performance of Golaud in Debussy's *Pelléas et Mélisande*. Throughout, the tone is noble—not heroic, like in a ballad, but

---

[3] Gargenville is a village situated along the banks of the Seine approximately 45 km west of Paris, where the Boulanger family spent restful periods, thus permitting the young and fragile Lili to breathe cleaner and more salutary air than that in Paris.

[4] Georges Delaquys was the son-in-law of the pianist Raoul Pugno (1852–1914), who was, until his death, the companion and mentor of Nadia Boulanger, with whom he composed a cycle of mélodies worth rediscovering: LES HEURES CLAIRES (1909), on eight poems by Émile Verhaeren. Even before her sister, Nadia Boulanger composed two mélodies on poems of Delaquys: *Chanson* (1909) and *Le beau navire* (1910), both published by Hamelle.

[5] The work was deposited at the SACEM under the title *Le retour d'Ulysse*.

firm and wide, without emphasis, like declamation; it could suit any type of warm-voiced man or woman. The tessitura is medium range, from B3 to D♯5. The key is F♯ major.

Analysis

Le retour	*The Return*
Ulysse part la voile au vent,	Ulysses is leaving, setting sail
Vers Ithaque aux ondes chéries	Towards Ithaca's beloved waves.
Avec des bercements la vague roule et plie	Rocking to and fro the waves roll and curl.
Au large de son cœur la mer aux vastes eaux	Off his heart the great sea water
Où son œil suit les blancs oiseaux	Where his eye follows the white birds
Égrène au loin des pierreries.	Ripples in the distance like precious stone.
Ulysse part la voile au vent,	Ulysses is leaving, setting sail
Vers Ithaque aux ondes chéries	Toward Ithaca's beloved waves.
Penché, œil grave et cœur battant	With a stern look and a beating heart
Sur le bec d'or de sa galère	He bends over the golden beak of his galley.
Il se rit, quand le flot est noir, de sa colère	He mocks the black anger of the waters
Car là-bas son cher fils pieux et fier attend	For ahead, his dear son pious and proud awaits him
Après les combats éclatants,	After the fierce battles,
La victoire aux bras de son père.	Victory in the arms of his father.
Il songe, œil grave et cœur battant	He dreams with a stern look and a beating heart
Sur le bec d'or de sa galère	Over the golden beak of his galley.
Ulysse part, la voile au vent	Ulysses is leaving, setting sail
Vers Ithaque aux ondes chéries	Toward Ithaca's beloved waves.

If, by virtue of its mix of different meters, the form of this poem is not easy to decipher, at least the subject is. Ulysses (Odysseus), the hero of Homer's *Odyssey*, appears, like a subject in a painting, in the pose of a ship's captain, determinedly scrutinizing the horizon with one goal in mind: Ithaca. After leaving the places where his sagacity assured the victory of the Greeks over the Trojans, and having escaped the island where the nymph Calypso kept him captive for seven years, he travels in hope of returning to his island kingdom and his beloved son (interestingly there is no mention here of his wife, Penelope).

The markings, like in the preceding mélodie, are more suggestive of atmosphere than of technical elements. The piano, after two measures of a bassline constructed on a regular and dynamic rhythm, presents the first melodic element, with, above, the marking *comme à travers la brume* (like moving through the mist). The two-against-three patterns and the juxtaposition of dissonant harmonies over various pedal points (for example, in measure 5, the right-hand C♯-major chord against the F♯-C♯ dyad in the left hand) are the principal elements in the piano part. Another thematic element appears later (for the first time in measure 19), an "orientalizing" *gruppetto*, marked *souplement* (flexibly) (Example 7.3).

Example 7.3   Boulanger, Lili: *Le retour*. From *Quatre mélodies*, Editions Durand & Cie, 2000 (ref. D. & F. 15284), page 9, mm. 18–20.

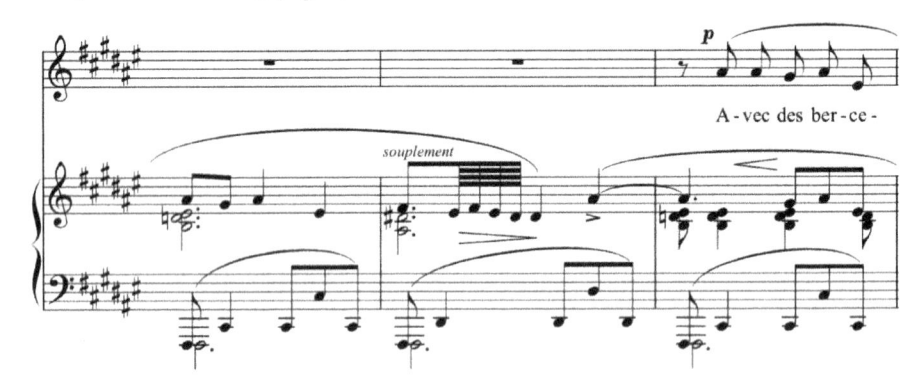

In the vocal part, the first two lines of the poem, which serve as a "refrain," will conclude the mélodie unchanged. The repetition of the middle (measures 39–40) contains several differences: the marking *en se rapprochant* (coming together) and the piano repeats the "orientalizing" element throughout (Example 7.4).

Example 7.4   Boulanger, Lili: *Le retour*. From *Quatre mélodies*, Editions Durand & Cie, 2000 (ref. D. & F. 15284), page 11, mm. 38–41.

As the singer must, above all, maintain an impeccable level of declamation, certain instructions are necessary: the syllables of the second line must not be sung in a way that runs them together [vɛritakozõdəʃeriə], because that will sound, to an uninitiated ear, like one long strange word. And no liaison should be made between the *s* of "vers" and "Ithaque"! [vɛrzitak]. So, the line must be sung this way: [vɛr/itak/ ozõdəʃeriə], which will divide the octosyllable into 3 + 5 (the silent *e* at the end of the word "Ithaque" should obviously not add a syllable to the line). As for the following alexandrines, Lili Boulanger treats them classically, with each hemistich dividing into 6 + 6 syllables:

> Avec des bercements / la vague roule et plie.
> Au large de son cœur / la mer aux vastes eaux

The silent *e* of "va-gue" and "lar-ge" should be well supported and *cantando*. However, the word "rou-**le**" should be treated differently: a pause is recommended after the silent *e*, so as not to create the word [ruleplis], which doesn't exist in French. Consequently, it would be better to sing [rul/epliə] (this last *e* should be sung, since there is a note written for it—but it should not be accentuated).

All the long phrases and rests, the roundings-off of phrase, and the *legato* are marked clearly, and demonstrate a great respect for the art of lyrical declamation. It may be useful—indeed, necessary—to write out what that approach means for the middle section:

> [Pãʃe / œj grav / ekœrbatã
> Syrlebɛkdɔrdesagalɛr
> Ilseri / kãleflo/ ɛnwar / desakɔlerə
> Karlaba / sõʃɛrfis pijøzefiɛr/ atã
> Aprɛlɛcõbazeklatã
> Laviktwar / obradesõpɛr
> Ilsõʒ / œj grav / ekœrbatã
> Syrlebɛkdɔr / desagalɛr]

In the same manner as the late vocal works of Fauré (from the period of *La chanson d'Ève* to *L'horizon chimérique*), the declamation guides the sung line. A good knowledge of the rules of classic French declamation is the key to a respectful interpretation of this magnificent *mélodie*.

8

Emmanuel Chabrier

Pastorale des cochons roses (1890)

Music by Emmanuel Chabrier (1841–1894)
Poem by Edmond Rostand (1868–1918)

Presentation

Of the four "animal" mélodies composed by Chabrier in 1889, this one, at five minutes, is the longest and also the most difficult to perform, for it is strophic (in four "couplets," groupings of four lines in an AAAB/CCCB rhyme scheme), and the humor that permeates it should not be demonstrated through effects, in order to preserve a pastoral tone (in the eighteenth-century sense). At the same time, it should be taken neither too seriously nor at face value. As humor is, by its essence, a notion with many connotations (and as the jokes presented here are a bit dated), what we consider humorous today must be presented in abstraction. The singer must try to portray a good-natured naiveté, combined with subtle social criticism, which was a hallmark of the period (especially in the operettas) and which exemplified a knowledge of poetic and theatrical styles.

The song is dedicated to the singer Lucien Fugère, famous for his staged characterizations of grotesque or noble personalities (first at the Ba-Ta-Clan Cabaret, then at the Opéra-Comique), and as the originator of the role of Fritelli in Chabrier's opera, *Le roi malgré lui* (1887). The *Pastorale* illustrates marvelously the ambition of the composer, who wanted to treat light works with as much art and seriousness as any large-scale work—a desire born of his admiration for the success of Wagner's *Die Meistersinger von Nürnberg*. Edmond Rostand only published this poem (under the title *Les cochons roses*) eleven years after the publication of the mélodie, in 1911, in a new edition by Fasquelle of his *Musardises*. The *Pastorale des cochons roses* had its first performance at the Théâtre du Vaudeville in Paris, on March 7, 1890, sung by the singer to whom it is dedicated, and with (possibly) the composer at the piano.

As regards the edition of Chabrier's mélodies, I advise the choice of Heugel-Leduc, in two volumes edited by Roger Delage, from the collection Le Pupitre-Musica Gallica (1997), whose sharpness of detail and level of excellence in the critical apparatus is far superior to the old Enoch editions. The *Pastorale des cochons*

Le Chant Intime. François Le Roux and Romain Raynaldy, Oxford University Press. © Oxford University Press 2021.
DOI: 10.1093/oso/9780190884178.003.0009

roses and the three other "animal" mélodies are in the second volume, as well as *Tes yeux bleus*, which will be discussed later on.

Analysis

Pastorale des cochons roses	*Pastorale of the Pink Pigs*

Le jour s'annonce à l'Orient,	Day is dawning in the East
De pourpre se coloriant,	With light of crimson hue;
Le doigt du matin souriant	Smiling morning's finger
Ouvre les roses;	Opens up the roses;
Et sous la garde d'un gamin	And herded by a boy,
Qui tient une gaule à la main,	A long stick in his hand,
On voit passer sur le chemin	You can see along the way
Les cochons roses.	The pink pigs pass by.
Le rose rare au ton charmant	The rare pink of charming tint,
Qu'à l'horizon, en ce moment,	That on the distant horizon,
Là-bas, au bord du firmament,	Deep in the sky
On voit s'étendre,	You cannot see spreading,
Ne réjouit pas tant les yeux,	Does not so gladden the eye,
N'est pas si frais et si joyeux	Is not so fresh and joyous
Que celui des cochons soyeux	As the silky pigs
D'un rose tendre.	With their gentle tinge of pink.
Le zéphyr, ce doux maraudeur,	The West Wind, that sweet marauder,
Porte plus d'un parfum rôdeur,	Brings more than one meandering scent,
Et, dans la matinale odeur	And in the morning fragrance
Des églantines,	Of the wild roses
Les petits cochons transportés	The blissful little pigs
Ont d'exquises vivacités	Are exquisitely pugnacious
Et d'insouciantes gaîtés	And carelessly vivacious,
Presque enfantines.	Almost childlike.
Heureux, poussant de petits cris,	Happy, emitting little cries,
Ils vont par les sentiers fleuris,	They pass along the flowery paths,
Et ce sont des jeux et des ris	Playing and laughing
Remplis de grâces.	With such grace;
Ils vont, et tous ces corps charnus	And these fleshy bodies, as they progress,
Sont si roses qu'ils semblent nus,	Are so pink as to seem nude,
Comme ceux d'amours ingénus	Like innocent putti
Aux formes grasses.	With their folds of fat.
Des points noirs, dans ce rose clair	The black specks in this pale pink,
Semblant des truffes dans leur chair	Like truffles in their flesh,
Leur donnent vaguement un air	Make them seem a little
De galantine,	Like galantine,
Et leur petit trottinement	And as they trot along,

À cette graisse, incessamment,	Their fat keeps
Communique un tremblotement	Wobbling
De gélatine.	Like gelatine.
Le long du ruisseau floflottant	Along the gurgling gutter
Ils suivent, tout en ronflotant,	They snortingly pursue
La blouse au large dos flottant	The broad cloth smock
De toile bleue;	Of fluttering blue;
Ils trottent, les petits cochons,	They trot, the little pigs,
Les gorets gras et folichons	Those fat and playful porkers,
Remuant les tire-bouchons	Waggling the flails
Que font leur queue.	Of their corkscrew tails.
Et, quand* les champs sans papillons	Then when the fields with no butterflies
Exhaleront de leurs sillons	Emit from their furrows
Les plaintes douces des grillons	The cricket's repetitive complaint,
Toujours pareilles,	Always the same
Les cochons, rentrant au bercail,	The pigs return to the sty,
Défileront sous le portail,	And pass through the door,
Agitant le double éventail	Waving the dual fan
De leurs oreilles.	Of their ears.

    * Chabrier writes "Puis quand"

	And, when yonder in the West,
Et quand, là-bas, à l'Occident,	The burning sun begins to wane,
Croulera le soleil ardent,	At the hour when evening falls
À l'heure où le soir descendant	And closes the roses,
Touche* les roses,	Peacefully at rest in the round,
Paisiblement couchés en rond,	Next to the chestnut-colored trough,
Près de l'auge peinte en† marron,	Satiated they fall asleep,
Bien repus, ils s'endormiront,	The pink pigs.
Les cochons roses.	

    * Chabrier writes "Ferme"
    † Chabrier writes "couleur"

To give an idea of how this song should be performed, think, for example, of the ballet of the hippopotamuses in Walt Disney's animated film *Fantasia* (released in 1940): the incongruity of the scene comes from the paradox between the weight of the animals, associated with ridiculous clumsiness, and the elegance of the attitudes of the star dancers. Here, the refined—and somewhat stupid—words that are employed, most often associated with poetic images, seem to have been displaced for the pigs. Certain adjectives ("floflottant," for example—a word invented by Rostand) clearly show that one doesn't have to be fooled. Nonetheless, the performer must remain imperturbably styled, and all the vocal figures used by Chabrier—mordents, ascents in thirds, etc.—should be impeccably executed. Chabrier divides this romance into four verses, each one comprising two poetic stanzas. It suffices to say that the harmonic and prosodic differences between the four verses are very subtle, and they must be memorized in order to interpret them each in their turn. This mélodie should be examined like an instrumental work, in which each detail is indispensable. The *animé* (lively) tempo should not be varied, except for the four last lines, and Chabrier notes at the end of each verse: *sans ralentir* (without slowing down) (Example 8.1), which shows the extent to which he knows the natural tendencies of performers to "close" a verse with a perfect cadence!

Example 8.1 Chabrier, Emmanuel: *Pastorale des cochons roses*. From *Mélodies en 2 volumes, second volume*, Editions Heugel, Collection "Le Pupitre-Musica Gallica" (L.P. 76), 1997 (ref. H. E. 33709), page 75, mm. 34–36.

Tes yeux bleus (1883)

Musique d'Emmanuel Chabrier (1841–1894)
Poème de Maurice Rollinat (1846–1903)

Presentation

A mélodie dating from 1883 and published only after the death of the composer, in 1913, it was orchestrated by Chabrier himself and subtitled *Romance*. Chabrier personally knew Maurice Rollinat, a poet and musician-singer at Le Chat Noir and a friend of many musicians and poets. Rollinat's volume, *Les névroses* (1883), in which this poem appears, was in Chabrier's library. Rollinat idolized Baudelaire, and the very "Wagnerian" musical setting of the poem[1] renders homage to the great poet's Wagnerism—and to Wagner himself, who had just died in February 1883. There is something of a kinship of musical writing with Duparc's very chromatic *Extase* (1887), on a poem by Jean Lahor. The original title of the poem is *Les yeux bleus*. The mélodie was published in two keys: C major, for high voice (D♭4 to A♭5) and B♭ major for medium voice (C♭4 to G♭5).

---

[1] The piano writing can easily be compared to that of *Traüme*, the last of Wagner's WESENDONCK LIEDER (1857).

Analysis

Tes yeux bleus

Tes yeux bleus comme deux bleuets
Me suivaient dans l'herbe fanée
Et près d'un lac aux joncs fluets
Où la brise désordonnée
Venait danser des menuets.
Chère Ange, tu diminuais
Les ombres de ma destinée,
Lorsque vers moi tu remuais
    Tes yeux bleus.

Mes spleens, tu les atténuais,
Et ma vie était moins damnée
À cette époque fortunée
Où dans l'âme, à frissons muets,
Tendrement tu m'insinuais
    Tes yeux bleus!

Your Blue Eyes

Your blue eyes, as two cornflowers
Followed me through the wilted grass,
And up to the lake filled with slender reeds,
Where a disorderly breeze
Came to dance some minuets.
Dear Angel, you weakened
The shadows hanging over my destiny
When you moved upon me
    Your blue eyes.

You eased my melancholy
And my life was less cursed
At that fortunate time
When, into my soul, by mute shivers,
You tenderly wormed
    Your blue eyes!

Unlike with *Pastorale des cochons roses,* the performance must be soaring, following the marking at the entrance of the voice after three measures of piano introduction: *très doux et mystérieusement* (very softly and mysteriously). Chabrier writes in one single manner the response "Tes yeux bleus," which punctuates the melody three times, in a two-against-three pattern (the meter is $\frac{3}{4}$), while the accompaniment is varied only in the left hand. Only the last iteration is extended by one measure, which reaches the height of intensity at the end of a long *crescendo,* introducing a beautiful postlude in a piano solo lasting eleven measures. The entire mélodie is made of rising and falling waves on harmonic pedals, during which the *legato* should be perfect. We can imagine an instrument such as a horn to understand the "coppery" timbre that is asked for. The *crescendos* are also "coppery," starting from *ppp* and peaking at *f.* All of this must be achieved in a soaring manner, without any overheated dramatics: it's almost an extension of a minuet filmed in progressively slowing motion. It's a good exercise in *legato* singing and heavy doses of intensity, as much for the piano as for the voice. The mélodie lasts around three minutes, and it will be (as Duparc would say) three minutes of ecstasy for the audience, if the performer does justice to Chabrier's writing.

9

Cécile Chaminade

Malgré nous (1893)

Music by Cécile Chaminade (1857–1944)
Poem by Rosemonde Gérard (1866–1953)

Presentation

The music of Cécile Chaminade, who enjoyed worldwide notoriety at the end of the nineteenth century (especially in the English-speaking world) before disappearing almost completely from concert halls, has today regained some public favor. Chaminade's music is based on magnificent melodic writing and a light spirit, never oriented toward emphasis or drama. She composed almost 150 mélodies, often set to sentimental poems, whose poets are today mostly forgotten. Many of the poets are women whom Chaminade knew personally.[1] Some of her mélodies were so well known that they are easy to find in the repertoires of renowned singers of the period, including Emma Albani and Pol Plançon. Thus, *L'anneau d'argent* (1895), on a poem of Rosemonde Gérard,[2] was as successful as, for example, Fauré's *Après un rêve*, and was even adapted (minus the words) for numerous instrumental soloists, as well as for orchestra.

I have chosen a different poem by Rosemonde Gérard. Born Louise-Rose-Étiennette Gérard, she was the wife of celebrated poet and dramatist Edmond Rostand (author of *Cyrano de Bergerac*). In 1889, Alphonse Lemerre published a collection of Gérard's poems entitled *Les pipeaux*; that volume contains two poems chosen by Chabrier for his famous humorous portraits of animals: *Villanelle des petits canards* and *Les cigales*. Chaminade set to music five poems taken from this volume. I have chosen *Malgré nous*, the third poem of the chapter. It bears no title, and the one that appears here was given by Chaminade.

Dedicated to Liza Lehmann (1862–1918, the same dates as Debussy), an English composer and singer, this is a lively mélodie (marked *gai, animé*), which lasts only

---

[1] Among the poets whose works Cécile Chaminade set to music: Marguerite Dreyfus, Rosemonde Gérard, Louise Hameau, Thérèse Maquet, Suzanne Mercey, Madame Mesureur (née Amélie de Wailly), Baroness Cécile d'Ottenfels, Louise Perny (who wrote under the pen name Pierre Reyniel), Emma di Rienzi, Countess Joseph Rochaïd (née Béatrix Piccioni), and Jenny Thénard. Other than Rosemonde Gérard, none of these poets are known today.
[2] *L'anneau d'argent* was dedicated to the famous soprano Madame Henri Conneau (née Juliette Pasqualini), who was also the dedicatee of several works by Gounod, Saint-Saëns, and Massenet.

Le Chant Intime. François Le Roux and Romain Raynaldy, Oxford University Press. © Oxford University Press 2021.
DOI: 10.1093/oso/9780190884178.003.0010

1 min 20 sec. Written in 1893, it is the third mélodie in the second volume of twenty mélodies by Chaminade that were published by Enoch et Costallat (there are four volumes). The poem, which, unusually, only has two rhyming devices (one masculine, "-eu," and one feminine, "-orte") is transformed into a ternary (ABA) composition: the first two quatrains are put together to form part A, and the third verse makes up part B. The mélodie was published in only one key, A♭ major; the tessitura (from C♯4 to F5) indicates a medium tenor or a mezzo-soprano. A transposition could nonetheless be made for a lower voice; I suggest F major.

Analysis

Malgré nous

Ce n'est pas la faute à nous deux
Si nous nous aimons de la sorte:
Un jour le dieu des amoureux
De notre cœur força la porte.

Or nous faisons de notre mieux,
Vous et moi, pour que l'intrus sorte;
Ce n'est pas la faute à nous deux
Si nous nous aimons de la sorte.

Contre un hôte si dangereux
Nul n'osa nous prêter main forte;
La raison fut sourde à nos vœux,
L'amitié même fit la morte . . .
Ce n'est pas la faute à nous deux.

Despite ourselves

It is not the fault of us both
If we love each other like this:
One day the god of lovers
Broke down the door of our hearts.

So we are doing our best,
You and I, to get the intruder to leave;
It is not the fault of us both
If we love each other like this.

Against such a dangerous guest
No one dared lend us their aid;
Reason was deaf to our pleas,
Even friendship played dead . . .
It is not the fault of us both.

The meter is in $\frac{2}{4}$, and the tempo marking is *très vite* (very fast); the metronome marking is 104 to the quarter note. The elocution is alternatively strong (for lines 1 and 3, with the "masculine" rhyme) then rapid (lines 2 and 4, with the "feminine" rhyme) (Example 9.1).

The risk for the singer is to perform the sixteenth notes *staccato* and thus make the phrase sound agitated; on the contrary, it should sound calm and fluid. As my former voice professor, Elisabeth Grümmer (1911–1986), once said, *"Long notes are long, but short notes are also long!"* In other words, don't shorten short note values—rather, use the entire length of each vowel to sing fully.

The first line, which is also the last line, should emphasize the journey that lasts from "Ce" [sə] to "deux" [dø], for this line contains a number of specific French vowels. Phonetically, the line should sound like this: [sənɛpalafotanudø].

The piano part, which consists only of arpeggios, should also maintain its fluidity and limit its dynamic range throughout from *p* to *mf*, according to the markings. Each beat seems to imitate a beating heart—but without accents! The *poco rit.* at

Example 9.1 Chaminade, Cécile: *Malgré nous.* From *Mélodies*, Editions Enoch & Costallat, 1895 (ref. E. & C. 3163), page 55, mm. 1–6.

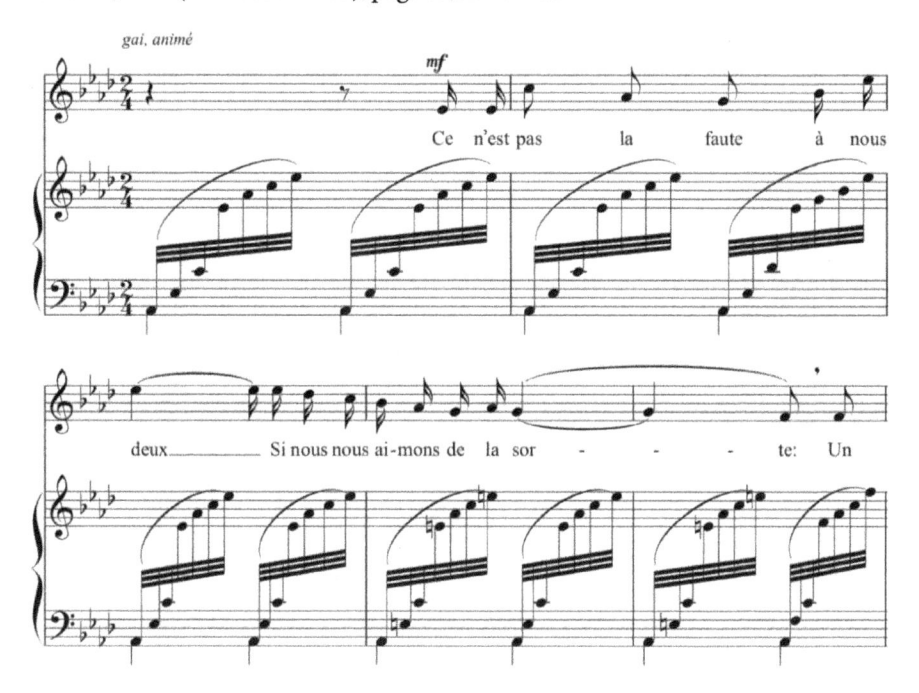

the end of the A section should not be excessive: it's a kind of musical rendering of a knowing smile. The *rit.* at the end of the middle section is associated with the *dolce* marking in the vocal line (the piano line is marked *p*). Part B is in G♯ minor. The dots on "Contre un hôte" (it should sound [kõtrœ̆not]) are instrumental: they introduce the new key, in a kind of light *rallentando*, and are not meant to indicate a bouncy vocal line. The return of the A section is a kind of intimate echo of the excuse "there's nothing we can do, if we both love each other like this."

This is a mélodie that is both romantic and light—or, as Verlaine would say, "sans rien qui pèse ou qui pose"—with nothing that weighs down or strikes a pose.

Mignonne (1894)

Music by Cécile Chaminade (1857–1944)
Poem by Pierre de Ronsard (1524–1585)

Presentation

While the majority of poems chosen by Chaminade were written by her contemporaries, she wrote some of her most beautiful mélodies on earlier poetry, including works by Victor Hugo (1802–1885), Hippolyte Lucas (1807–1878), and Alfred de Musset (1810–1857). The oldest of Chaminade's texts dates from around 1550: it is by Ronsard, the most famous of the French Renaissance poets. This *Ode à Cassandre*, already set to music during Ronsard's lifetime by Guillaume Costeley, has since been one of the favorite poems of composers: in the nineteenth century alone, it was chosen by—to name only a few—Victor Massé, Théodore Gouvy, Ernest Guiraud, the Hillemacher Brothers, and even Wagner (in 1839).

Dedicated to the singer Marie Brousse, the mélodie is published in two keys, F major and E♭ major by H. Tellier (Paris, 1894). The extended tessitura is clearly meant for a mezzo-soprano: in the version in F major, the range is from A3 to F5. The general color is fresh, young, and ardent. The length of the mélodie is approximately 3 min 30 sec.

Analysis

Mignonne

Mignonne, allons voir si la rose
Qui ce matin avait déclose
Sa robe de pourpre au soleil,
A point perdu ceste vesprée
Les plis de sa robe pourprée,
Et son teint au vostre pareil.

Las! voyez comme en peu d'espace,
Mignonne, elle a dessus la place
Las! las ses beautés laissé choir!
Ô vraiment marastre Nature,
Puis qu'une telle fleur ne dure
Que du matin jusques au soir!

Donc, si vous m'en croyez, mignonne,
Tandis que vostre âge fleuronne
En sa plus verte nouveauté,
Cueillez, cueillez vostre jeunesse:
Comme à ceste fleur la vieillesse
Fera ternir vostre beauté.

Sweetheart

Sweetheart, let us see if the rose
That this morning has disclosed
Her scarlet dress to the Sun
Has lost once more this evening,
The folds of her scarlet dress
And its complexion, so like yours.

Alas! See how in such short space,
Sweetheart, she has let
Her beauty fall all over the place!
O Nature, truly you are a cruel stepmother
For such a flower lasts only
From dawn to dusk!

So if you believe me, Sweetheart,
While time still flowers for you
In its greenest novelty,
Cull, cull your youthful bloom:
As it has faded this flower,
The doom of age will tarnish your beauty.

Chaminade's version is in no way a pastiche of early music (apart from the light mordent at the end of verses 1 and 3), even if this song is similar to a "courtly dance," a sort of minuet.

In ternary (ABA) form, following Ronsard's sestinas exactly, it is remarkable for the counterpoint between the vocal and piano parts. The meter is $\frac{3}{4}$, with a tempo of 52 to the quarter note. The piano begins alone for three measures, and then the voice enters, *dolce*. Each line should be sung in one long phrase where the prosody moves along quickly, set to numerous sixteenth notes (Example 9.2).[3]

Example 9.2 Chaminade, Cécile: *Mignonne*. Editions Heugel, nondated (ref. H. 28.371), page 2, mm. 4–7.

[3] Concerning the example, an important detail: in order not to add a syllable to the first line, the singer should not pronounce the final "-ne" of the word "Mignonne" on the second sixteenth note (B♭), but on the A, in making a short glottal stop before "Allons": [Miɲɔn/alɔ̃]. On the second page, it's completely different: the composer notes a long silent *e* for this word, which closes the line (Example 9.3). What refined prosody!

Example 9.3. Chaminade, Cécile: *Mignonne*. Editions Heugel, nondated (ref. H. 28.371), pages 4–5, mm. 28–29.

Let us address the question of pronunciation of Renaissance French: should the singer attempt a "restitution" of the early pronunciation or modernize the language? For mélodies of the nineteenth and early-twentieth centuries, I recommend using modern French, especially when a poem (like this one) is so well known (in France, this poem is routinely taught in school). The *s* should not be pronounced in words when the letter is replaced by a circumflex in modern French: [vɛpreə], and not [vɛspreə]; [vɔtrə], and not [vɔstrə] (a possessive adjective that appears four times in the poem: once in the first verse and three times in the third); [marɑtrə], and not [marɑstrə]; [sɛtə] and not [sɛstə]. On the other hand, an *s* should be sounded in "Puisqu'une" [pɥiskynə], although there is no hyphen to create an elision between "Puis" and "qu'une." Another point of pronunciation: according to the *Dictionnaire Littré*, in Chaminade's era, actors didn't sound the final *s* of "las," a word that appears three times in the second verse. It's better to sing [lɑ], with a posterior [ɑ]. The middle verse is marked *mf* for the first two lines; the voice should begin *pp* in the next line, in order to achieve a good *crescendo*—arriving at *mf*—that extends from "Las" to "choeir" (note: the *e* is not sounded; the pronunciation is [ʃwar] like in modern French). The double *crescendo* of the two following lines should be balanced, and not forced by the singer. The last line of the second verse is written for the voice as it would be for an instrument, with the sixteenth notes connected, two by two: [kə-ədy-yma-atẽ-ɛ̃ʒy-yskəzoswar]. The two last lines of the third verse include a *crescendo* for the voice, ending *f* on "**ternir**"; the *forte* dynamic should continue until "beauté," with great reverence.

This is a very pretty—and rarely performed—musical rendering of this well-known poem, which observes both the spirit and the form of the poem to perfection.

10

Ernest Chausson

La chanson bien douce (1898)

Music by Ernest Chausson (1855–1899)
Poem by Paul Verlaine (1844–1896)

Presentation

Chausson wrote three songs on poems of Verlaine. The first, *Apaisement*, op. 13, no. 1 (1885) is the well-known poem from *La bonne chanson* that begins, "La lune blanche / Luit dans les bois"; it has been set to music by many composers, most famously by Fauré and Hahn. The two mélodies from op. 34 (1898), based on poems taken from the collection *Sagesse*, are *La chanson bien douce* (no. 1) and *Le chevalier Malheur* (no. 2, which will be discussed later). The latter, while written on the first poem from Verlaine's collection, was composed seven months after *La chanson bien douce*, the sixteenth poem of the collection. This order indicates that Chausson had perhaps not intended to create a Verlaine cycle.[1] No contemporary edition of Chausson's mélodies includes both songs of op. 34. *La chanson bien douce* had its first performance on January 27, 1900 at the Salle Érard, Paris, by Jeanne Remacle, with possibly Blanche Selva at the piano, in a set that included the mélodie from op. 36, *Dans la forêt du charme et de l'enchantement*, on a poem by Jean Moréas.

La chanson bien douce is easy to find: it is included in a volume of *Vingt mélodies* by Chausson that was published by Rouart-Lerolle (Salabert) and in three American publications of Chausson's songs: *33 Songs* (Kalmus-Belwin Mills), *20 Songs* (International Music Company), and *Selected Songs* (Dover). Chausson's setting is published in only one key, C minor (the most religious and funereal key that exists) even in volumes for different voices (high and low) published by IMC; admittedly, it is written almost entirely in the medium range (from D4 to E5). A singer who finds the tessitura too high can always transpose the song down a step to B♭ minor without posing any problems.

One might say that *La chanson bien douce* is one of the most Verlainian songs in the repertoire, taking into account the work of all composers. Chausson is one of the

---

[1] The front page of the manuscript of *Le chevalier Malheur* displays, with a musical short sketch, the first verse of another Verlaine poem, the twenty-first from *Sagesse*: "Va ton chemin sans plus t'inquiéter" (Go your way without worrying too much).

Le Chant Intime. François Le Roux and Romain Raynaldy, Oxford University Press. © Oxford University Press 2021.
DOI: 10.1093/oso/9780190884178.003.0011

rare composers to have set this poem. I know of six other musical versions: by Nadia Boulanger,[2] Alphonse Diepenbrock,[3] Gabriel Grovlez,[4] Pierre Hermant,[5] Marguerite Canal,[6] and Paul Dessau[7]; there is also a chanson by Léo Ferré (1895), recorded but not published. Four of these composers set the entire poem, whereas Chausson and Grovlez leave out the fourth quatrain. For those fascinated by the musical settings of Verlaine poems, I suggest consulting a reference book: Ruth L. White's *Verlaine et les musiciens* (Paris: Minard, 1992). White, a professor of French at the University of British Columbia-Vancouver, has created an extensive documentation of musical settings of Verlaine that are housed in the major libraries of Europe and North America.

Chausson dedicated his mélodie to his daughter Étiennette. It's rather surprising that he wrote a "chanson triste" (sad song) for his daughter, but, as is often the case with Chausson, it's unwise to look for hidden meanings. His songs should be taken as they appear at first glance: as we will see, there is really no sadness in this mélodie.

While, as was mentioned previously, *La chanson bien douce* precedes *Le chevalier Malheur* in order of composition, I prefer to reverse the order when I perform op. 34 in recital, for *La chanson bien douce* begins very abruptly, without introduction, after a brief eighth-note rest. Starting a cycle this way is not only unusual, but also quite difficult. *Le chevalier Malheur* begins in a similar manner, but at least Chausson allows for two full beats before starting the vocal line.

Analysis

La chanson bien douce	*The very gentle song*
Écoutez la chanson bien douce	Listen to the very gentle song
Qui ne pleure que pour vous plaire.	That weeps but to delight you.
Elle est discrète, elle est légère:	It is discreet, it is delicate:
Un frisson d'eau sur de la mousse!	A shiver of water on moss!
La voix vous fut connue (et chère?),	The voice was known to you (and dear?),
Mais à présent elle est voilée	But is at present veiled

---

[2] Nadia Boulanger's (1887–1979) setting of *La chanson bien douce*, in E♭ major (1905), has been published by Alphonse Leduc in the third volume of her songs; the manuscript is in the Bibliothèque nationale de France.

[3] Dutch composer Alphonse Diepenbrock (1862–1921) wrote a setting of *La chanson bien douce* in E major (Halsbach and Co., 1898).

[4] The setting of *La chanson bien douce* by Gabriel Grovlez (1879–1944) is written in D minor (1909); it is part of a cycle of five mélodies, SAGESSE (Schott, 1910).

[5] Pierre Hermant (1869–1928) set *La chanson bien douce* in G major; it is the fourth mélodie of his long collection of twelve songs for voice and orchestra, entitled SAGESSE (Enoch, 1904), downloadable on Gallica, the website of the Bibliothèque nationale de France.

[6] Marguerite Canal (1890–1978) composed a cycle of six mélodies on the poems of *Sagesse* (Heugel, 1931); the last of the cycle, *Écoutez la chanson bien douce* was composed in memory of Edmond Clément, a great tenor of the Opéra-Comique. Canal's setting is in C major/A minor.

[7] The setting of *La chanson bien douce* by the German composer Paul Dessau (1894–1979) is a curiosity: written in French, for high soprano, it dates from 1939, and was recently published by Peters (2009) in the volume *Lieder aus dem Nachlass für Singstimme und Klavier*.

Comme une veuve désolée,	Like a disconsolate widow,
Pourtant comme elle est encore fière,	And yet like her still proud,
Et dans les longs plis de son voile	And in the long folds of her veil
Qui palpite aux brises d'automne,	That flutters in the autumn breeze,
Cache et montre au cœur qui s'étonne	It hides and shows the astonished heart
La vérité comme une étoile.	The truth, emblazoned like a star.
Elle dit, la voix reconnue,	It says, the voice you recognize,
Que la bonté c'est notre vie,	That kindness is our very life,
Que de la haine et de l'envie	And that of hate and envy
Rien ne reste, la mort venue.	Nothing remains, once death has come.
[Elle parle aussi de la gloire	[It also talks of the glory
D'être simple sans plus attendre,	Of being candid without delay
Et de noces d'or et du tendre	And of weddings of gold and of the tender
Bonheur d'une paix sans victoire.]*	Happiness of peace achieved without victory.]
*Quatrain omitted by Chausson	
	Welcome the voice that continues
Accueillez la voix qui persiste	Its simple bridal song.
Dans son naïf épithalame.	Come! Nothing so becomes the soul
Allez, rien n'est meilleur à l'âme	As making a soul less sorrowful!
Que de faire une âme moins triste!	
	It is transient and in travail,
Elle est en peine et de passage,	The soul that suffers without wrath,
L'âme qui souffre sans colère	And how manifest its moral is!…
Et comme sa morale est claire!…	Listen to the very wise song.
Écoutez la chanson bien sage.	

In order to sing this song well, the voice must be extremely malleable and very light; otherwise, the singer will become terribly tired. The tessitura extends only from D4 to E5, with most of the pitches falling between F4 and E♭5, that is, completely within the high-medium range. For a singer with a low voice or a rich medium-range voice, it is practically impossible to remain for so long in the center range before going up into the high range. That range is one of the principal difficulties—underestimated, in my opinion—in singing Chausson's songs, and this song in particular is particularly challenging. Consequently, a singer should not hesitate to transpose it, in order not to be dealing with a tessitura that must be managed delicately.

Another difficulty, previously alluded to, is that the singer must jump into the vocal line and establish an atmosphere with only a brief eighth-note "introduction" in the first measure; moreover, the first syllable is a closed [e]. Additionally, the only tempo marking is *sans hâte* (not fast), and the only dynamic marking is the initial *piano*. After that, nothing!

This "artistic fuzziness" is not uncommon in Chausson's mélodies: no dynamic markings; no metronome marking (also problematic in Duparc); and tempo descriptions limited to *modéré* (*moderato*), *mouvementé* (*animato*), *lent et triste* (slow and sad), and *sans lenteur* (not slow). It seems to me that with these ambiguous markings, Chausson is not indicating what he wishes, but what he *doesn't* want. At the end of the nineteenth century, whether it was Fauré, Duparc, or Chausson, composers preferred to suggest what they wanted rather than imposing their wishes in a peremptory manner. They left a lot of latitude to the performer, perhaps to find out if what they wrote could function as it was, deciding later to modify (or destroy) their work. This reticence was certainly true for Chausson who, despite a comfortable material life and a happy home life, was extremely anxious and never ceased to doubt himself.

As far as *La chanson bien douce* is concerned, the interpretative goal is more about inspiring good listening than making a vocal demonstration, as is appropriate when Verlaine is set to music.

Moreover, the song begins precisely with the imperative "Écoutez" (Listen), sung *piano* in triple meter and accompanied by steady sixteenth notes, evoking the water that runs in a calm and regular manner. The prosody of the two first lines is marvelous. The lengths of the notes are elongated on "douce" (soft), "pleure" (cry), and "plaire" (please). Chausson perfectly understood and offered musical renditions of Verlaine's assonances between "pleure" and "plaire" and made the most important word—"douce"—stand out. Without forcing or exaggerating, the singer must manage to sing one long phrase from "Écoutez" until "pour vous plaire," with a lovely *legato piano*. It's difficult, especially for a low voice, even more so when the highest note of the phrase, on "qui," should be treated like the others, simply and unforced. The harmony is at once rich and very fluid, passing from C minor to D♭ major in four measures, before landing in G♭ major; the passage is so well written that we hardly notice. The phrase "Elle est discrète, elle est légère" is set almost in a *parlando* style, while with "Un frisson d'eau sur de la mousse," we find, in mirror image, the calm of the opening, with a dotted quarter note on "eau" and "mousse," as previous (Example 10.1).

In the quatrain that follows, we see that Verlaine has placed "et chère" in parentheses, followed by a question mark. Chausson doesn't follow this notation. It is difficult for a performer to interpret, through singing, the idea of a parenthetical phrase, because the musical line is rising to D♭ on "chè-" before coming down again to a G on the silent *e*. The singer can, however, try to inject a sense of sadness or personal questioning, since the line that follows is even sadder, more interiorized. On "elle est voilée," Chausson writes an eighth-note triplet, which should be brought out, but without exaggeration. Chausson's triplets are similar to those in Debussy—who tries to reproduce spoken rhythms—but are a bit more sententious, as if the composer were trying to press more deeply into his thoughts. "Elle est voilée" set to a triplet creates a rather emphatic sense of declamation, whereas Debussy would seek only a simple *rallentando* in the emission.

Verlaine's discourse doesn't stop at the end of the second quatrain but continues until the end of the third. Chausson follows the poet and links the two musically, recreating with "Et dans les longs plis" a *parlando* rhythm. In terms of prosody, one would have difficulty doing better. Chausson changes meters (to $\frac{4}{4}$ and $\frac{2}{4}$,

Example 10.1 Chausson, Ernest: *La chanson bien douce.* From *Recueil de 20 mélodies,* Editions Rouart, Lerolle, 1910 (ref. A.R. 5847 L. & Cie.), pages 69–70, mm. 6–9.

respectively) before returning to ⅔ on "Cache" (measure 22), with a total change of harmony, in E major. The phrase ends in luminous C major, on "comme une étoile." In the two-measure preparation of this resolution in a major key on a perfect authentic cadence, the singer must be careful not to be too emphatic or too declamatory: there must be no increase in volume, contrary to what the musical phrase might suggest. It will suffice to sing the text, without adding anything. And if it feels as if some limits had been overstepped, it will be possible to come down again by several degrees in the next quatrain.

An interesting change in the accompaniment occurs next, producing a rhythmic destabilization in the right hand. It can barely be heard, because the strong beats are still given to the bassline (Example 10.2).

In this manner, Chausson illustrates the "voix reconnue," which hushes up things that cannot be clearly perceived. The singer should then make a long instrumental *legato*, while lightly separating each line—otherwise, things become redundant. Chausson creates a filigree on Verlaine's already "lacy" rhythms. It's astonishing to see so many variations in just four lines; Chausson was guided—like Debussy, I suppose—by his own sense of diction. Then, in place of the poem's fifth quatrain (omitted by Chausson), there are four measures of piano solo (measures 33–36), a unique, purely musical moment within the work: the piano sums up all that has been previously said, with the right hand still playing steady sixteenth notes, while the left hand offers a lovely countermelody, an interior but lyrical voice, like a hazy perfume. In measure 37, the music returns to the pattern from the start of the

Example 10.2 Chausson, Ernest: *La chanson bien douce.* From *Recueil de 20 mélodies,* Editions Rouart, Lerolle, 1910 (ref. A.R. 5847 L. & Cie.), pages 72 and 73, mm. 26–32.

song: sixteenth notes in both hands, like flowing water. This entire, relatively long measure seems "empty" without the voice. Why? Because the voice still persists, as Verlaine tells us: it is the sweet interior voice, the title's "chanson bien douce"— which is not the voice of the singer!

The first two lines of the next-to-last quatrain are the exact reply to the first phrase of the song. The harmony changes again with the next two phrases, where the singer should take care to make the circumflexed *â* [ɑ] on the word "âmes" darker. Chausson set the words this way on purpose to give them the same weight by giving them the same duration (a dotted quarter note for one and a quarter note tied to an eighth note for the second) to show that they are equal.

In the following quatrain, I think that it is necessary to take a little breath between "peine" and "et": the way it's written, if the two words are connected, they will sound like "Elle est en [pɛne] de passage" [ɛlɛtãpɛnedɔpasaʒ]. Be careful as well to clearly pronounce "Elle" [ɛl] and "Et" [e] clearly at the beginnings of the first and third lines, respectively. There should be no *rallentando* anywhere: none is written and even one would be superfluous, especially since the accompaniment is already sparing. Here, we arrive at what Verlaine calls a "morale claire"—a clear moral, as opposed to something serious or dark. Simplicity is the best approach. The voice now sings the highest note, the E5 ("**Et** comme sa morale est claire"), which should spring forth from the chord without any particular emphasis or marked intention: always let the meaning be insinuated, not affirmed. One final detail for the last line ("Écoutez la chanson bien sage"): Chausson didn't write a note on the last syllable of "sage." Like Duparc, who was Chausson's close friend, Chausson avoids stressing the final consonant by writing a note. I think that it is more interesting to let the [ʒə] get lost in the final chord. One can stimulate listening only by leaving the phrase open at its ending, and I think that's what Chausson, a good Verlainian, would have wanted. Besides, the final chord of the piano doesn't fall on the beat: nothing is concluded.

Le chevalier Malheur

Music by Ernest Chausson (1855–1899)
Poem by Paul Verlaine (1844–1896)

Presentation

Unlike the first of the two op. 34 mélodies, *La chanson bien douce*, the second, *Le chevalier Malheur* is hard to find, which may explain why it is sung so infrequently. It was first published by itself in a supplement of *La revue musicale* (December 1, 1925), in a special issue that paid homage to Chausson. The mélodie is included in only two American publications: a collection of *14 Songs* by Chausson (Masters Music Publications, 2003) and as a separate piece of sheet music (Eroica Music Publications, 2003).

Here, we find a dramatic side, similar to a ballade, and not unlike certain mélodies of Chausson's close friend Duparc—for example, *La vague et la cloche*, which also speaks of a strange dream. The Christian aspect of the poem could not have escaped Chausson, or the evocations of *Parsifal* in the main theme: lances, armor, blood, iron fingers, and so forth. And the musical setting, which seems to call for an orchestra, is related to that of Chausson's only opera, *Le roi Artus*. It is a shame that the libretto of this work, written by the composer himself, didn't retain the concision and the mystery of the admirable first poem of Verlaine's collection, *Sagesse*.

Analysis

Le chevalier Malheur

Bon chevalier masqué qui chevauche en silence,
Le malheur a percé mon vieux cœur de sa lance.

Le sang de mon vieux cœur n'a fait qu'un jet vermeil
Puis s'est évaporé sur les fleurs, au soleil.

L'ombre éteignit mes yeux, un cri vint à ma
                    [bouche
Et mon vieux cœur est mort dans un frisson
                    [farouche.

Alors le chevalier Malheur s'est rapproché,
Il a mis pied à terre et sa main m'a touché.

Son doigt ganté de fer entra dans ma blessure
Tandis qu'il attestait sa loi d'une voix dure.

Et voici qu'au contact glacé du doigt* de fer
Un cœur me renaissait, tout un cœur pur et fier.
   * Chausson writes "gant" (glove)

Et voici que, fervent d'une candeur divine,
Tout un cœur jeune et bon battit dans ma poitrine.

Or, je restais tremblant, ivre, incrédule un peu,
Comme un homme qui voit des visions de Dieu.

Mais le bon chevalier, remonté sur sa bête,
En s'éloignant me fit un signe de la tête

Et me cria (j'entends *encore* cette voix):
"Au moins prudence! Car c'est bon pour une fois."

The Knight Ill-Fortune

Good masked knight who rides in silence,
Ill-fortune has pierced my old heart with his lance.

The blood of my old heart made only one red spurt
And then dried out on the flowers, in the sun.

The shadow blinded my eyes, a cry came to my
                    [mouth
And my old heart died with a wild shudder.

Then the knight Ill-fortune came close,
Dismounted and touched me with his hand.

A finger of his steel gauntlet entered my wound
While he recited his law in a harsh voice.

And behold, with the icy contact of his iron finger
A heart within me was reborn, pure and proud.

And behold, ardent with divine candor,
A good young heart started beating in my breast!

Trembling I stayed, drunk, somewhat in disbelief,
Like a man who has seen visions of God.

But the good knight, back on his mount,
As he rode off nodded his head at me

And cried out to me (I *still* hear that voice):
"Prudence at least! Once should be enough."

As previously mentioned, this mélodie was not published until 1925 (Chausson had died in 1899!) in a special issue of *La revue musicale* that commemorated Chausson. It is to this publication that I will refer, as the American editions are only reproductions of this one. In C♯ minor, it requires a medium voice (the tessitura extends from C♯4 to E5) and lasts three minutes. Like the preceding song from op. 34, it begins almost dryly (only two beats in the piano before the voice enters). Chausson faithfully follows Verlaine's format of subdividing each verse into two lines. The steady arpeggiated sixteenth notes suggest a gallop (but not a hammering), like a winged Pegasus suspended in mid-air, while the left hand of the piano provides a dark and serious harmonic pedal (Example 10.3). There is no pedal indicated. The meter is $\frac{4}{4}$, and for a good flow, a metronome marking of 84 or 88 to the quarter note would seem correct to me. We see how much Chausson likes to lighten up the strong beats, in order to limit the weightiness to that which seems essential to him.

Example 10.3 Chausson, Ernest: *Le chevalier Malheur*. From the *Supplément de* La revue musicale, *numéro spécial Ernest Chausson*, December 1, 1925, page 1, mm. 1–6.

The music should remain at a *piano* dynamic for the entire first part: it's only at the phrase "un cri vint à ma bouche" that the intensity should increase, to arrive at the *forte* of "Alors le chevalier . . . ," which becomes even stronger at "Et voici qu'au contact." It's not clear to me why Chausson chose to replace the word "doigt" (finger) with "gant" (glove), and the performer is free to choose one or the other. On the arpeggio at measure 32 (Example 10.4), the singer can choose to start *a tempo* (in a

Example 10.4 Chausson, Ernest: *Le chevalier Malheur*. From the *Supplément de La revue musicale, numéro spécial Ernest Chausson*, December 1, 1925, page 5, mm. 31–32.

surprise *mp*), or to wait a bit for the arpeggio to roam about, if the pianist doesn't play it too fast. It's a harp-like figure, which is often found in the orchestrations of Chausson, and the performer is offered many interpretive choices. The following section, in *parlando* style, should remain incredulous, like the underlying harmony that hesitates. Then, at measure 47, the opening theme reoccurs, but this time in E major. With the remarkable effect and simple procedures typical of Chausson, the narration starts up again, giving an equivalent to the penultimate line, written in parentheses in the poem. The word "encore" (in italics in Verlaine's poem) should not be given too much weight in the phrase "J'entends *encore* cette voix": sung in one breath, and unaccompanied, the phrase is sung on one repeated pitch until the word "voix," sung a minor third higher, before the final *subito mf.*

It is important not to create too menacing a tone, as if the last line were being sung by a boogeyman—especially since the six measures of piano solo suggest the simple gait of a nice guy.

With the two highly contrasting mélodies of Chausson's op. 34, a singer can really put their skills in phrase and enunciation to good use, by juxtaposing a distanced tone and dramaticism—in short, all the skills required in a good recitalist, capable of quickly passing from a mini-theatrical scene to the intimacy of a confidential communication.

11

Claude Debussy

NUITS BLANCHES (1898)

I. *Nuit sans fin*
II. *Lorsqu'elle est entrée*

Poems and music by Claude Debussy (1862–1918)

Presentation

The discovery of these two mélodies was without a doubt one of the great Debussyste events of the late twentieth century. According to the announcement of the publisher Hartmann, the complete cycle of *NUITS BLANCHES* comprised five pieces, but the three others remained undiscovered. A number of the early songs that Debussy had written for Madame Vasnier, had been unearthed, scattered throughout the world in private collections or libraries, but there had been no discoveries of later works, dating from Debussy's essential creative periods.

These manuscripts were found in the library of Arthur Honegger and it was his daughter, Pascale, who located them. They are now in the Music Department of the Bibliothèque nationale de France. The *NUITS BLANCHES* had never been published—or, it would seem, even performed—during Debussy's lifetime. Happily, in 1991, this music was finally brought before the public: I gave the first public performance on the French radio station France Musique on October 18, 1991, with Noël Lee[1] on piano. Together we made the first commercial recording for Le Chant du Monde in 1999, as part of a CD of Debussy mélodies that included two other unpublished songs. Finally, the two mélodies of *NUITS BLANCHES* were published by Durand in 2001.

---

[1] Born on December 25, 1924 (hence the first name), American-born Noël Lee came to France as a student of Nadia Boulanger and settled definitively in Paris after World War II. A friend of Ned Rorem, Elliott Carter, and Henri Dutilleux, he was a composer, a great solo pianist and a magnificent and highly sought-after accompanist. His many recordings attest to his wide-ranging repertoire and prodigious musicality. In 1997, he was among the founding members and, until 2011, one of the core faculty members of the Académie Francis Poulenc (Tours), whose mission is the exploration of the rich repertoire of French mélodie and its interpretation. Noël Lee died in Paris in 2013.

Le Chant Intime. François Le Roux and Romain Raynaldy, Oxford University Press. © Oxford University Press 2021.
DOI: 10.1093/oso/9780190884178.003.0012

These mélodies seem interesting to me for two reasons: first, they date from 1898, shortly after Debussy finished composing *Pelléas et Mélisande* (1895); second, the poems were written by Debussy himself. Hartmann, Debussy's publisher at the time, presented these NUITS BLANCHES as a second volume of PROSES LYRIQUES (a cycle dating from 1892 to 1893). However, the texts of the PROSES LYRIQUES—two of which were published in the journal *Entretiens politiques et littéraires* as independent poems, without music—are purely symbolist, with few personal references. These two texts of NUITS BLANCHES, on the other hand, are stranger and much more difficult to classify. Absent any indication of what Debussy might have wanted to name them, they have both been given titles that come from their respective incipits.

The first of the two mélodies, *Nuit sans fin*, in B minor, is dated July 14, 1898 (the manuscript notes the day of the French national holiday), and the second, *Lorsqu'elle est entrée*, in D♭ major, is dated September 1898. The tempo markings, respectively, are *triste et lent* (sad and slow) and *lent et douloureux* (slow and painful); these markings relate to those often found in *Pelléas*. For those who want a deeper understanding of Debussy's work during this crucial period, these two mélodies cannot be overlooked.

Finally, it bears mentioning that, although these two songs are chronologically close to the composition of the famous TROIS CHANSONS DE BILITIS (1897–1898), on texts of Pierre Louÿs, they are extremely distant from a stylistic point of view: the sadomasochism of the narrator of the NUITS BLANCHES, very contrasting and relatively orchestral in texture, stands in stark opposition to the feminine sensuality of Bilitis, illustrated by fluid and purely pianistic music. The only point in common between the two cycles is the tempo: *lent et sans rigueur de rythme* (slow and rhythmically relaxed) for *La flûte de Pan*; *assez lent* (rather slow) for *La chevelure*; and *très lent* (very slow) for *Le tombeau des Naïades*.

Analyses

I. *Nuit sans fin*

Nuit sans fin.
Tristesse morne des heures où l'on attend!
Cœur rompu,
Fièvre du sang
Rythmant les douces syllabes de son nom.
Qu'elle vienne la trop désirée,
Qu'elle vienne la trop aimée,
Et m'entoure de son parfum de jeune fleur.
Que mes lèvres mordent le fruit de sa bouche,
Jusqu'à retenir son âme entre mes lèvres.
Ai-je donc pleuré en vain,
Ai-je donc crié en vain,

I. *Endless night*

Endless night.
Dim sadness of the hours of waiting!
Broken heart,
The fevered blood
That beats out the sweet syllables of her name.
May she come, the overmuch desired,
May she come, the too-much loved,
And enfold me in her fragrance of opening flowers.
May my lips bite into the fruit of her mouth,
Until I taste her soul upon them.
Have I wept in vain,
Have I called out in vain,

Vers tout cela qui me fuit! . . .	To all that is now gone by! . . .
Tristesse morne,	Dim sadness,
Nuit sans fin!	Endless night!

The first remarkable aspect of the poem is the interesting mirror effect between the beginning and the end, which act as bookends to the song.

Nuit sans fin lasts around two minutes; it is much shorter than the mélodies of the PROSES LYRIQUES, all of which are longer than three minutes. It's as if Debussy had concentrated to the maximum agony and waiting. Unlike the happily amorous waiting of Duparc's *Phidylé* (on a poem of Leconte de Lisle), Debussy's style of waiting is not positive but anguished, even if the middle part ("Que mes lèvres") is extremely sensual, in the high register of the voice, and *pp*, which requires great flexibility from the singer.

Given the brevity of the mélodie, I will address some general considerations of melody, rhythm, and tessitura, without doing a measure-by-measure analysis.

The dynamic markings are astonishing. Most of them are *piano* and *pianissimo*, but the *forte* is strong to the point of vehemence, since it is accompanied by double accents, which is very rare—indeed, almost unheard of—in Debussy (Example 11.1).

Example 11.1 Debussy, Claude: *Nuits blanches—I. Nuit sans fin*. Editions Durand & Cie, 2000 (ref. D. & F. 15359), page 3, m. 16.

Like in the PROSES LYRIQUES, the tessitura is extremely wide. *Nuit sans fin* is among Debussy's most demanding works for voice, since the range extends from C♯4 to F×5. One could almost say that it's a "Pelléasian" tessitura, which is not a coincidence: in many ways, *Nuit sans fin* resembles the monologue "C'est le dernier soir" (act 4, scene 4—"It's the last evening") of *Pelléas*—which is also about waiting. "Il est tard, elle ne vient pas" ("It is late, she's not coming")—all that belongs to the same universe. If one compares the two scores, it becomes apparent that the musical line of "C'est le dernier soir" (Example 11.2) is not unlike our mélodie: (Example 11.3).

Example 11.2 Debussy, Claude: *Pelléas et Mélisande*, act 4, scene 4. Voice & Piano score, Editions Durand, 2010 (Ref. D. & F. 15808), page 243, number 35, mm. 534–535.

Example 11.3 Debussy, Claude: *Nuits blanches—I. Nuit sans fin.* Editions Durand & Cie, 2000 (ref. D. & F. 15359), page 1, mm. 1–3.

The rhythmic complexity is, however, greater in *Pelléas*, because of the orchestra. But numerous relationships can be found between the two works: first, because, like here, the character Pelléas speaks for himself, in a single monologue; and, second, because there are parallels in the music itself—for example, in the use of syncopations, and the division into sections that follow the emotions closely. In a certain way, the melody is closer to dramatic expression than the discretion associated with a traditional mélodie.

It is very difficult to know what voice type should sing *Nuit sans fin*. Being perfectly Pelléasian in expression, it seems to be intended for a male voice. The range of C♯4 to F×5 also suggests that it's meant for a light baritone or a medium tenor. But we don't know if Debussy was thinking of a specific kind of performer. There are, as always in Debussy, very few interpretive markings in the vocal line. The first phrase, "Nuit sans fin. / Tristesse morne des heures où l'on attend!" (Endless night. / Dim sadness of the hours of waiting!) is extremely static, with a rather strange rocking between two chords. This is odd because the "resolution" in the third measure accompanies a "majorization" of the harmony, since we begin in B minor and end in F♯ major. Note, however, that—again, in customary Debussyste style—the major chord is ultimately "sadder" than the minor chord: it's a "resigned" resolution. Moreover, the major-minor oscillation seems to depict the poetic vacillation between resignation and hope.

In this mélodie in general and in the song's beginning in particular (and as is true for many works of Debussy as well), the performer has to prepare—and anticipate—each change of harmony. The performer must make the waiting "visible" by developing the vocal colors—that is to say, by utilizing soft and bright colors, in places where the sadness of the words is obvious, in order not to darken the mélodie excessively, in a sort of redundancy: this technique is what I call "dialecticism." It doesn't have to be a melodrama to make you cry.

The musical motion is completely static; the "action" goes nowhere. Consequently, there should be an interior sense of motion felt by the singer—and not only because the singer has to know where to breathe. The rocking back and forth should be well "corporealized," as if it were part of a mechanical lullaby.

The two major-harmony resolutions on "où l'on attend" and on the conclusive "Nuit sans fin!" reveal the ambiguity of this waiting: it is neither despairing nor trembling with desire. Thus, the arrival of the F♯ major should sound bright: the assumed resignation—or fatalism—of the harmony sounds a bit like parallel passages in Duparc's *Soupir*, in which the "Toujours" (always) is the equivalent of "sans fin" (endless). In the second system, the rocking between two chords should be thought of in half-note pulses, then one pulse per bar, despite the fact that the song is written in quadruple meter, followed by a typically Debussyste three against two (Example 11.4).

Example 11.4 Debussy, Claude: *Nuits blanches—I. Nuit sans fin*. Editions Durand & Cie, 2000 (ref. D. & F. 15359), page 1, mm. 4–5.

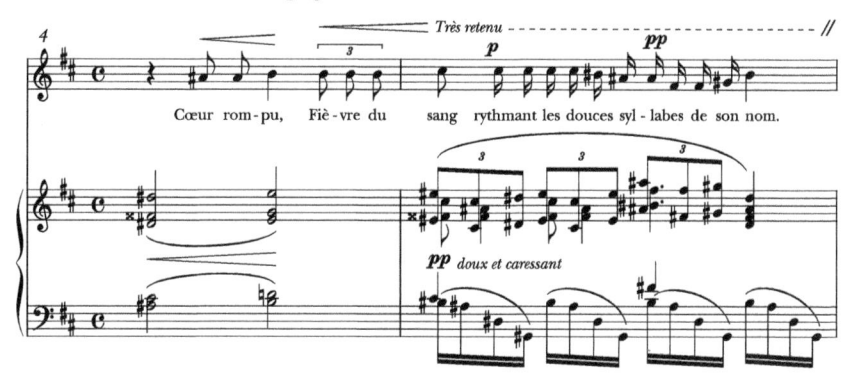

We also see the great rhythmic complexity of the accompaniment, especially in the last measure of the second system, on "sang / Rythmant les douces syllabes de son nom," featuring steady sixteenth notes in the right hand and eighth-note triplets in the right hand. The rhythmic patterns from the beginning then return, but with the repetitive figure in the right hand, on a syncopated rhythm in the left hand. This is followed by a fragmentation of the pulse into four quarter notes (measures 8 and 9), which will expand to six beats (measures 10–16), until the music halts altogether (measure 11), making way for the final return of the initial half-note motion (Example 11.5).

Example 11.5 Debussy, Claude: *Nuits blanches—I. Nuit sans fin.* Editions Durand & Cie, 2000 (ref. D. & F. 15359), page 3, mm. 14–17.

It's an astonishing procedure. To offer a way in, I would say that it's as if there were an opposition between "I, Debussy" and "She, the object of the poem."

II. *Lorsqu'elle est entrée*[2]	II. *When she came in*
Lorsqu'elle est entrée, il m'a semblé	When she came in, I felt that
Que le mensonge traînait aux pieds de sa jupe.	Falsehood was caught in the folds of her skirt.
La lueur de ses grand yeux mentait,	The glow of her eyes was but a lie,
Et dans la musique de sa voix,	And in the music of her voice,
Quelque chose d'étranger vibrait.	Something strange was vibrating.
C'étaient les doux mots que je connais si bien	I recognized the sweet words I know well,
Mais ils me faisaient mal	But they were hurting me
Et entraient en moi douloureusement.	And penetrated in me painfully.
Qui donc a usé son regard?	Who then has exhausted her glance?
Qui donc a fané la rougeur de sa bouche?	Who then has made the redness of her lips wilt?
D'où vient cette lassitude heureuse,	Where from comes her felicitous tiredness,
Qui semble avoir brisé son corps	Which seems to have broken her body
Comme une fleur trop aimée du soleil . . .	Like a flower that the sun loved too much?

---

[2] According to a recently discovered notebook of sketches, it appears that Debussy considered as a title *Pourquoi* (*Why*).

Oh! torturer une à une	Ah! to torture one by one
Les veines de son cher corps.	The veins of her beloved body.
L'anéantir et le consumer,	To destroy it and to extinguish it,
Ensevelir sa chair dans ma chair,	To drown her flesh in mine,
Avec la joie amère de l'impossible pardon.	With the bitter joy of the impossible forgiveness.
Tout à l'heure ses mains	In a moment her hands
Plus délicates que des fleurs	More delicate than flowers
Se poseront sur mes yeux	Will land on my eyes
Et tisseront le voile de l'oubli . . .	And will weave the veil of oblivion . . .
Alors mon sang rebattra.	Then my blood will beat again.
Les plaies rouges de mon cœur saigneront,	The red wounds of my heart will bleed,
Et le sang montera*	And the blood will go up and up
Noyant son mensonge	Drowning her lie
Et toute ma peine.	And all my grief.

* In the musical setting, "montera" is repeated

The extended tessitura must be pointed out right away: from D♭4 to G♯5, that is to say, an octave and a half. *Lorsqu'elle est entrée* is an extremely difficult mélodie to perform, but it is logical when one knows the work of Debussy: it brings together all the prosodic and interpretive gifts of the composer, blending *parlando* and pure singing, even including operatic momentum. The mélodie is dated September 1898.

The song opens with two measures of piano solo. The voice then enters on an E pedal and continues in an extremely limited range. The use of the single pitch E for "Lorsqu'elle est entrée, il m'a sem-" is a quasi-amplification of speech. With "la musique de sa voix," the music takes on an almost religious manner, which will, of course, be heard again in *Pelléas*. The next passage (measures 13–17) returns to Debussy's version of *Sprechstimme* (spoken/sung) up until "soleil," where a rhapsodic figuration announces the sun. From "torturer une à une" onward (measures 19–24), we return to the speech amplification from the beginning, and on it goes. This alternation is eminently Debussyste.

This mélodie also features modal writing of great complexity, with unstable harmonies that sometimes gives it an extremely modern color. The key centers are equally unstable: four modulations can occur in two measures.

This mélodie, over three minutes long, is much closer in its development to the PROSES LYRIQUES than to *Nuit sans fin*: it is closer still to act 4, scene 4 of *Pelléas*. Moreover, it is written (with the exception of measures 25–31) in a meter of ⁹⁄₈, the emblematic meter of *Pelléas*. Contrary to the static quality observed at the beginning of *Nuit sans fin*, we have here a two-measure introduction filled with movement, with a vacillation between two tritone-related keys, B♭ and E major, this latter contaminating the B♭ and turning it into B natural. When the voice enters, the key center is still uncertain. The entire mélodie vacillates unceasingly, but subtly, between major and minor. Once the chord has been established by the piano (measure 3), nothing more moves, before the "restart" in the following measure. There exists a kind of stasis that allows the voice, in an almost "operatic" fashion, to return when it wants to (Example 11.6.).

Example 11.6 Debussy, Claude: *Nuits blanches—II. Lorsqu'elle est entrée*. Editions Durand & Cie, 2000 (ref. D. & F. 15359), page 4, mm. 1–4.

Here, we find a sense of free declamation, *quasi-recitativo*. This very same thing happens in act 4, scene 4 of *Pelléas* (see the example 11.2 on page 94). The writing is different—a double bar in *Pelléas*, a fermata at the end of the second measure, then a rest of one beat in the mélodie—but the result is the same: the singer can take a bit of time before starting up once more.

Next, the rhythm from the piano part at the beginning reappears, inverted. All these vacillations and hesitations—this time, between an A natural and an A flat—represent, I think, the idea of a lie. One must be careful to make a distinction between the major and minor thirds, especially since, in Debussy, the minor thirds are often luminous and the major thirds sad (admittedly, it is unwise to generalize). There is a major third on "mensonge traînait," another on "pieds de sa jupe," and a third on "La lueur de ses grands yeux," which is transformed into a minor third on "mentait." It goes without saying that what's worthwhile for the thirds is true for every interval: take care with them; explore their subtleties.

A typically Debussyste element appears in measures 9–10: an eighth-note triplet, on "C'étaient les doux mots que je connais si bien, / Mais ils me faisaient mal." The phrase embodies the same principle as that used in measure 2: a note that is stretched out—without a fermata, this time—and leaves open every dramatic and interpretive possibility. Vocally, the line ends on "douloureusement," followed by a measure of rest in the vocal part. The piano, which resolved with the voice, retains the sound with a tie over the barline, then drops an octave. Because of the tie, all sense of meter is completely lost, until the quarter notes of the bassline, beginning on B♭ (measure 12), recapitulate the rhythmic figure from the beginning of the song. And yet, once again, it will be the voice that determines the rhythm flow.

Three "questions" follow, two with question marks and one followed by an ellipsis, without any augmentation, since Debussy—even if he marks a *crescendo*—obliges the voice to redescend in each new measure, up until the long *crescendo* on "trop aimée du soleil" (measure 16).

The ascending *fioratura* in the piano's left hand precedes a passage of rhythmic fragmentation via languorous syncopations. And a rhythmic figure that had already appeared in *Nuit sans fin* appears little by little, suggesting a cyclic treatment of *NUITS BLANCHES*'s thematic material. Thus, we find the rhythmic motive of *Nuit sans fin*, measure 14, in *Lorsqu'elle est entrée*, measure 18 (Example 11.7).

Example 11.7 Debussy, Claude: *Nuits blanches—II. Lorsqu'elle est entrée.* Editions Durand & Cie, 2000 (ref. D. & F. 15359), double example: (a) page 7, m.18, compared to (b) first measure of the last example of *Nuit sans fin* (page 3, m. 14).

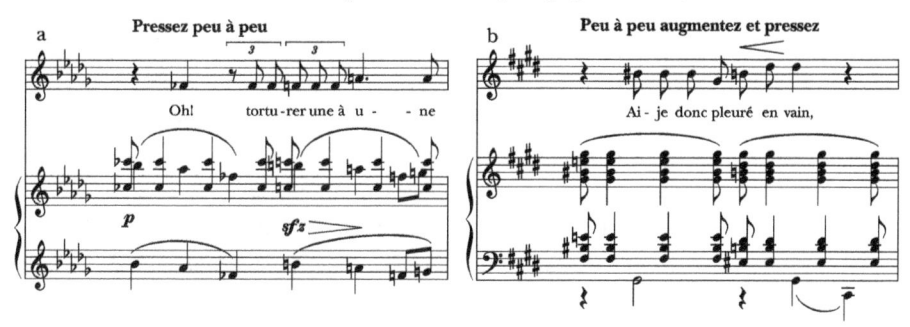

The parallel is uniquely rhythmic, in the right hand of the piano, since the left hand retains the musical theme of the beginning, while the voice remains completely independent.

At that point, the color is at its most passionate, with two *sforzatos* illustrating "L'anéantir et le consumer." Care must be taken with the accents in this passage: on "le consumer," the accent in the piano is on "le," while, in the voice, it falls on "con-." In the same vein, on "Avec la joie amère," pay attention to the two accented *a*'s: "**A**vec la joie am**è**re." In this way, the singer is forced to reattack "amère" in order not to create an elision with "joie," which is phonetically close.

In the highly agitated passage on "l'impossible pardon," the voice ascends to a very high point, coming to a close on the G♭, and the piano attains its maximum intensity. Then, all of a sudden, the picture changes completely. The flats disappear and the meter changes from 𝄔 to 𝄴, while a *diminuendo* begins a long descent beginning on G♯ (measures 25–27), leading to a magnificently simply theme, swirling around a syncopated rhythm, in a sort of orientalist dance (Example 11.8).

Example 11.8 Debussy, Claude: *Nuits blanches—II. Lorsqu'elle est entrée*. Editions Durand & Cie, 2000 (ref. D. & F. 15359), page 8, mm. 24–27.

This duality is reinforced by the voice, at once calm and voluble. These elements are all gathered into three measures (measures 28–30), finally arriving at the initial E♭ on "oubli." This phrase appears like a voluptuous parenthesis, re-establishing, in the interlacing of the voice and the piano's left hand, the woven-like image evoked in the poem.

This alternation of violent and voluptuous passages marvelously illustrates the story of betrayal in love, the falseness that both gnaws away at and fascinates the lover. The music seems to allow its listeners to understand the duality of feelings that assail us when we are facing a beloved who has betrayed us, or who is in the process of betraying us.

The piano returns again, suddenly (measure 31), with the intensity of the preceding page, with syncopations in the right hand set against the initial theme (C♭-E♭-F-C♭-E♭-G♭) in the left hand (Example 11.9).

Example 11.9 Debussy, Claude: *Nuits blanches—II. Lorsqu'elle est entrée*. Editions Durand & Cie, 2000 (ref. D. & F. 15359), page 8, m. 31.

This figure is followed by the poetically strange phrase: "Alors mon sang rebattra. (. . .) Et le sang montera, montera." Preferably, the second *r* of "rebattra" will be rolled, while the singer listens attentively so that the pianist can set the top of the arpeggio with G♯ (the original manuscript is not very clear). The ascending syllables on "montera, montera" should become progressively more attached. At the top of the phrase, "noyant son mensonge," I think that the singer should take advantage of the marked accents to broaden and relax the tempo, providing that the music returns to *tempo primo* for the last two measures: the mélodie finishes in a brutal fashion, without reprise, and no *rallentandos* should be used to sugarcoat its starkness. Such an ending seems to prove that this mélodie was not the last of the cycle and that another (at least one more) more conclusive piece should have followed.

Apparition (1884)

Music by Claude Debussy (1862–1918)
Poem by Stéphane Mallarmé (1842–1898)

Presentation

Apparition, which is dated February 8, 1884 in Debussy's manuscript, seals the poetic meeting of the composer with Mallarmé. The poem had just been published in the journal *Lutèce* in November 1883. It was only later—after the first face-to-face meeting of Debussy and Mallarmé, apparently in 1890—that the former became a fixture in Mallarmé's "Tuesdays," an elite circle in which Debussy was the only composer. But already, in this mélodie dedicated to Madame Vasnier, the refinement of the images—the lyrical outpouring of the Symbolist text—allowed Debussy to go very far into musical experimentation. The song was published only long after the death of the composer, in May 1926, in a supplement of *La revue musicale* devoted to Debussy's early period that included three other mélodies: *Pantomime*, *Clair de lune* (first version) and *Pierrot*.

Analysis

Apparition	*Appearance*
La lune s'attristait. Des séraphins en pleurs	The moon grew sad. Weeping seraphim,
Rêvant, l'archet aux doigts, dans le calme des fleurs	Dreaming, bows in hand, in the calm of hazy
Vaporeuses, tiraient de mourantes violes	Flowers, drew from dying viols
De blancs sanglots glissant sur l'azur des corolles.	White sobs that glided over the corolla's blue.
—C'était le jour béni de ton premier baiser.	—It was the blessed day of your first kiss.
Ma songerie aimant à me martyriser	My dreaming, glad to torment me,

S'enivrait savamment du parfum de tristesse	Grew skilfully drunk on the perfumed sadness
Que même sans regret et sans déboire laisse	That—without regret or bitter aftertaste—
La cueillaison d'un Rêve au cœur qui l'a cueilli.	The harvest of a Dream leaves in the reaper's heart.
J'errai donc, l'œil rivé sur le pavé vieilli,	And so I wandered, my eyes fixed on the old paving stones,
Quand avec du soleil aux cheveux, dans la rue	When with sun-flecked hair, in the street
Et dans le soir, tu m'es en riant apparue*	And in the evening, you appeared laughing before me
Et j'ai cru voir la fée au chapeau de clarté	And I thought I glimpsed the fairy with her cap of light
Qui jadis sur mes beaux sommeils d'enfant gâté	Who long ago crossed my lovely spoilt child's slumbers,
Passait, laissant toujours de ses mains mal fermées	Always allowing from her half-closed hands
Neiger de blancs bouquets d'étoiles parfumées.	White bouquets of scented flowers to snow.

   * In the musical setting, "apparue" is repeated

There was, between Mallarmé and Debussy, an immediate comprehension, and the musical setting helps to illuminate the aspect of precious obscurity desired by the poet. It must not be forgotten that the *Prélude à l'après-midi d'un faune* of the composer (1894), based on Mallarmé's *Églogue*, was for this latter a revelation, inspiring the poet to write, on the copy of *L'après-midi d'un faune* that he gave to the composer, this compliment:

Sylvain d'haleine première	Sylvan creature of the first breath,
Si ta flûte a réussi	If your flute has succeeded,
Ouïs toute la lumière	Listen to all the light
Qu'y soufflera Debussy.	That Debussy will blow through it.

The dedication enlightens us as to the type of voice for which Debussy composed this mélodie: Madame Marie Vasnier, his first muse, was an amateur soprano with a light and agile voice (a fact known thanks to a few journalistic critics) for whom he wrote thirty-odd mélodies, through the *ARIETTES OUBLIÉES*. Her stratospheric vocal range explains the high tessitura of many of Debussy's "mélodies de jeunesse" (early songs), and *Apparition* is a typical example. The range is from D4 (on "l'archet aux doigts") to C6 (on the second "apparue"). Of course, special attention must be paid—as always—to articulation of the words in the high register, but the melodic writing is so accomplished that there shouldn't be much difficulty in pulling it off.

Debussy follows the poem in a rather simple manner, by musically isolating each part of the phrase to make it intelligible. The mélodie begins, in E major, with an exhibition of "pianistic arrows" in the right hand, followed by an ecstatic vocal line that moves very little. (One note: the B, on "La lune s'attristait" is set in duplets, creating a typically Debussyste gesture of two against three in the context of the $\frac{9}{8}$ meter.) This figure is followed by grand operatic lyricism in the style of Massenet ("C'était le jour béni de ton premier baiser," in G♭ major). Note that the meter changes to $\frac{3}{4}$ on "Ma songerie": this is not marked in the voice part. The music returns to stasis with "J'errai donc" (C major) for four measures; then the progression that begins on "Quand avec du soleil aux cheveux" is marked with *animez peu à peu* (moving forward step by step), followed by a *crescendo, toujours plus animé* (moving forward even more), which explodes with the grand lyricism of "tu m'es en riant apparue" (B♭ major), "apparue" being repeated twice (which is not in the poem), with a vocal ascent up to C6. The tempo can be broadened in order to allow the voice to blossom at the highest point. The *diminuendo* must not begin too soon (it's marked only for "d'enfant gâté"), in order for the expressive surprise of "passait," on the *pianissimo* high A, to be really surprising.

Finally, calm descends, and *en allant toujours se perdant* (going on fading progressively), the song ends by returning to G flat major, *pianissimo*; with the reiteration of the last hemistich, Debussy gives the singer one more magnificent *pianissimo* B♭♭ on "parfumé-é-es." Here, the golden, taunting Mallarmé is well served by an incredible lyrical effusion, in the piano and in the voice. This song is a "must" for a high soprano who loves mélodie.

TROIS POÈMES DE STÉPHANE MALLARMÉ (1913)

I. *Soupir*
II. *Placet futile*
III. *Éventail*

Music by Claude Debussy (1862–1918)
Poems by Stéphane Mallarmé (1842–1898)

Presentation

Claude Debussy's last cycle dates from 1913. The first public performance, by soprano Ninon Vallin,[3] with the composer at the piano, took place on March 21, 1914, in Paris's Salle Gaveau. The cycle is dedicated *"to the memory of Stéphane Mallarmé."* Like many of Debussy's late cycles, it consists of three mélodies. The three poems chosen are more obscure than *Apparition* (especially the last one, *Éventail*), but Debussy illuminates them with a limpid musical setting, treating them as refined sketches of an astonishingly modern language. It always astounds

---

[3] Ninon Vallin (1886–1961) joined the Opéra-Comique in 1911 and became one of its stars. She sang all the lyric soprano roles: Micaëla in Bizet's *Carmen*, the title roles of Charpentier's *Louise*, Massenet's *Manon*, Mélisande, and the Countess in Mozart's *Le nozze di Figaro*. In addition to giving the first performance of Debussy's TROIS POÈMES DE STÉPHANE MALLARMÉ, with the composer at the piano, she also gave the first performances, in 1917, of three works by Manuel de Falla, including his SIETE CANCIONES POPULARES ESPAÑOLAS. Fluent in Spanish, she became, starting in 1916, the symbol of French singing in South America, where she sang at Buenos Aires' Teatro Colón. In 1917 she was engaged at La Scala. Her truly international career brought her to the former USSR, Australia, and New Zealand. In partnership with star tenors Georges Thill and Enrico Caruso in recordings for Columbia, she recorded many of her soprano roles (including a famous Marguerite in Gounod's *Faust*), but also Charlotte (a mezzo role) in Massenet's *Werther*. She remained active through the 1940s. In 1953, she founded the Music Conservatory of Montevideo (Uruguay), where she taught for many years. She was also professor of singing at the Conservatoire de Lyon from 1957 to 1961, the year of her death. Even to our modern ears, her voice remains an exemplar of extraordinarily natural singing.

me that this cycle is programmed less frequently than the TROIS BALLADES DE FRANÇOIS VILLON or LE PROMENOIR DES DEUX AMANTS. Reading the score makes it easier to understand both the poems themselves and Debussy's incredible sensitivity to this highly affected language, which is often caricaturized.[4]

Analyses

I. *Soupir*

Mon âme vers ton front où rêve, ô calme sœur,
Un automne jonché de tâches de rousseur,
Et vers le ciel errant de ton œil angélique
Monte, comme dans un jardin mélancolique,
Fidèle, un blanc jet d'eau soupire vers l'Azur!
—Vers l'Azur attendri d'Octobre pâle et pur
Qui mire aux grands bassins sa langueur infinie:
Et laisse, sur l'eau morte où la fauve agonie
Des feuilles erre au vent et creuse un froid sillon,
Se traîner le soleil jaune d'un long rayon.

I. *Sigh*

My soul rises toward your brow where, calm sister,
An autumn strewn with russet spots is dreaming,
And toward the restless sky of your angelic eye
As in some melancholy garden,
A white fountain faithfully sighs toward the Azure!
—Toward the tender Azure of pale and pure October
That mirrors its infinite languor in the vast pools:
And, on the stagnant water where the tawny agony
Of leaves wanders in the wind and digs a cold furrow,
Lets the yellow sun draw itself out in one long ray.

Soupir (A♭ major, $\frac{3}{4}$) is a portrait of a woman's face worthy of a Japanese brush. The piano executes the first brushstroke with an ascending parallel phrase in the two hands, which ends on A♭1, whence is heard the same phrase in rhythmic diminution; taken together, the two seem to move in rapid concentric circles. The voice enters in measure 6, singing alone—nakedly—for two measures before being joined by the piano, playing broken half-note chords on "sœur, / Un automne" (measures 9–10). The first line must be sung in a near-whisper in order to attain the desired mystery in this intriguing a cappella setting. The singer must sustain the initial intention until the belated appearance of the verb "Monte", so that the public can understand that it is the soul ("Mon âme") that is rising ("Monte"); if the music is too chopped by marked breathing silences or changes in nuances, then one loses the meaning of this typical building of a sentence by Mallarmé. The same holds true for the third line, similarly declaimed "in the nude," which leads to "jardin mélancolique" (measure 14), where the fountain is illustrated in the piano by the triplets on E covering two octaves, cascading down to a third bass-clef E at the end of the phrase (measure 18). The vocal phrase "Vers l'Azur attendri" reaches F5 (not everyone can sing in Madame Vasnier's range!) and then redescends ("Et laisse"). The frequent two-against-three patterns created between the vocal line and the left hand of the piano, which should never exceed a dynamic of *mezzo-forte*, depict the leaves dancing in the wind. Finally,

---

[4] Perhaps the most notable caricature of Mallarmé's poetic style is found in *Le gendarme incompris*, a short comic theater piece with a text by Jean Cocteau and Raymond Radiguet, set to music in 1920 by Poulenc. In this work, *Placet futile* (in a version that is only slightly different from the one chosen by Debussy for the second song) has been placed in the mouth of a police commissioner!

the "soleil jaune" (yellow sun) spreads out across an eighth-note/quarter-note pattern in triplets, ending with a fade-out in the voice on a long E♭5 ("long rayon") accompanied by a reprise of the piano's initial motive (*ppp*); here, the voice should follow the piano's dynamic markings. Some advice for preparing the sustained E♭ of the last two measures: with a two-syllable grouping in mind [rɛj-jõ], place the A♭ on [rɛj], and [-jõ] on the E♭. The doubling of the [j] will allow for perfect understanding of the word and a bright nasal coloration, like a ray of golden sunshine!

II. *Placet futile*	II. *Futile supplication*
Princesse! à jalouser le destin d'une Hébé	Princess! In envying the fate of a Hebe
Qui poind sur cette tasse au baiser de vos lèvres,	Who appears on this cup at the kiss of your lips,
J'use mes feux mais n'ai rang discret que d'abbé	I expend my ardor but have only the modest rank
Et ne figurerai même nu sur le Sèvres.	[of an abbot
	And shall not figure even naked on the Sèvres.
Comme je ne suis pas ton bichon embarbé,	Since I am not your bearded lapdog,
Ni la pastille, ni du rouge, ni Jeux* mièvres	Nor patch, nor rouge, nor affected Games,
Et que sur moi je sais ton regard clos tombé,	And know you look on me with indifferent eyes,
Blonde dont les coiffeurs divins sont des orfèvres!	Blonde, whose divine coiffeurs are goldsmiths!
*Debussy writes "jeux" without a capital	
Nommez-nous . . . toi de qui tant de ris framboisés	Appoint me . . . you whose many laughs like raspberries
Se joignent en troupeau* d'agneaux apprivoisés	Are gathered in a flock of docile lambs
Chez tous broutant les vœux et bêlant aux délires,	Grazing through all vows and bleating at all frenzies,
*Debussy writes "troupeaux" in the plural form	
	Appoint me . . . so that Love winged with a fan
Nommez-nous . . . pour qu'Amour ailé d'un éventail	May paint me there, fingering a flute and lulling this fold,
M'y peigne flûte aux doigts endormant ce bercail,	Princess, appoint me shepherd of your smiles.
Princesse, nommez-nous berger de vos sourires.	

Placet futile (B♭ major, $\frac{3}{4}$) is a pastiche in the manner of the eighteenth century, filled with precious speeches filled with references intended to arouse a smile. Mallarmé himself, in a letter to Henri Cazalis (the poet Jean Lahor) May 24, 1862, defined it as a *"Louis XV sonnet."* Debussy utilized a slow minuet figure to craft this pastiche. The tone is intentionally obsequious (the voice "bows" on the word "Princesse"), and the discreet eroticism is evoked through vocal ornaments, such as the grace notes on "Et ne figurerai même **nu** sur le Sèvres" (measures 9–10). The woman reveals herself to be a little put out (the rapid flutterings of her fan, represented by descending sixteenth-note triplets in the right hand, from "Sèvres" to "pastille" in measures 10–13),—then flattered (more fan fluttering under "coiffeurs divins sont des orfèvres!" in measures 17–18). The pedant gets a bit worked up ("Chez tous broutant . . . aux délires," which rises to G♭5) and ends up evoking Arcadia ("pour qu'Amour ailé . . . ce bercail)—at which point the fan becomes, through the grace of a trill, a flute. The singer should control the *crescendo* so that the *forte* arrives only on "bêlant aux délires." The contrast between the *staccato* notes of "peigne flûte aux doigts" and the triplets of "doigts endormant ce bercail" evokes a snake charmer, and the singer must really make the sound on the triplets "drowsy." Hold the E♭ of "bercail" until after the end of the piano part.

The return of the opening theme leads to the conclusion via an affected-sounding alexandrine, "Princesse, nommez-nous berger de vos sourires," where the *i* of "sourire" should become as bright and smiling as possible. The fan closes on the held E in the voice. Two low G's punctuate in the piano—by acquiescing to the request? Or by recusal?—the mute response in G major. The singer must, through precise diction and adherence to the dynamics, maintain a distanced reserve in order for the pastiche not to become a caricature; throughout, they should imagine witty and highly stylized conversation from the court of Louis XV.

III. *Éventail*

Ô* rêveuse, pour que je plonge
Au pur délice sans chemin,
Sache, par un subtil mensonge,
Garder mon aile dans ta main.
    *Debussy writes "O"

Une fraîcheur de crépuscule
Te vient à chaque battement
Dont le coup prisonnier recule
L'horizon délicatement.

Vertige! voici que frissonne
L'espace comme un grand baiser
Qui, fou de naître pour personne,
Ne peut jaillir ni s'apaiser.

Sens-tu le paradis farouche
Ainsi qu'un rire enseveli
Se couler du coin de ta bouche
Au fond de l'unanime pli!

Le sceptre des rivages roses
Stagnants sur les soirs d'or, ce l'est,
Ce blanc vol fermé que tu poses
Contre le feu d'un bracelet.

III. *Fan*

O dreamer, that I may plunge
Into pure pathless delight,
Contrive, by a subtle deception,
To hold my wing in your hand.

A twilight freshness
Reaches you at each flutter,
Whose captive stroke distances
The horizon delicately.

Vertigo! See how space
Shivers like an immense kiss
Which, mad at being born for no one,
Can neither burst forth nor abate.

Can you feel the wild paradise
Just like buried laughter
Flow from the corner of your mouth
Deep into the unanimous fold!

The scepter of rose-colored shores
Stagnating over golden-evenings—such is
This white furled flight that you set
Against a bracelet's fire.

The original title of the poem is *Autre éventail de Mademoiselle Mallarmé* ("Another fan for Miss Mallarmé"—Mallarmé wrote this poem for his beloved daughter Geneviève, and there are more!) but Debussy changed it to *Éventail* (*Fan*) for his mélodie. In ⅜, with an indeterminate key center, it is connected through its title to the preceding song. But, here, the fan is a bird that is constantly escaping; "on the wing," as the poem says, it opens and closes in rapid succession—which explains the unstable and very brief rhythms gestures. For the two performers, the precision work (like that of goldsmiths, as the abbot of *Placet futile* would say), which should be polished to perfection, should also sound like a game. A very short piano introduction is followed by a *rubato* passage, where the voice and the fan (represented by dry "flips" in the piano's right hand) alternate, intersecting for the first time only on "Sache" (measure 8); this is also the first place where an actual key, G♯ major, is perceived—and then quickly refuted. The following phrase ("Une fraîcheur," measures 14–24) seems to bring a brief "calm before the storm": it features a "limping" accompaniment of quarter notes in the right hand and offbeat eighth notes in the left hand (the pattern is varied slightly on "Dont le coup prisonnier"). Suddenly, on "Vertige!" (measures 25–26) the chase resumes, punctuated by increasingly more complicated flips of the fan (measures 27–35), which ease up only after "s'apaiser" with the return to the "limping" rhythm of the "coup prisonnier," where the lady hides her face behind the fan. "Sens-tu" should be an ample and lyrical pulling back that includes a light portamento on the descending minor seventh. Set to triplets, "Au fond de l'unanime pli!" (measures 44–45) should remain quite enigmatic. The "pli" (fold) at the end of the phrase should sound almost like a question, as if the narrator were daring to lift the fold with an exploratory finger. The transformation of the fan into a scepter, after a last toss of the fan (under "rivages roses") converts the pursuit into bedazzled adoration ("contre le feu d'un bracelet"), with a D♯ extending and adorning the E-minor harmony. Also, a typical Mallarmean poetical ambiguity is used here: "ce l'est" (This is it) sounding [səlɛ] is totally homophonic to "ce lait" (this milk) for a French ear. It is, of course, linked to the white colour of the "blanc vol fermé" (white furled flight), thus making the interpretation very visual, as well as musical. Besides, like in all Symbolist poetry, all the images that come to mind can be used in the interpretation!

12

Henri Duparc

Sérénade (1869)

Music by Henri Duparc (1848–1933)
Poem by Gabriel Marc (1840–1901)

Presentation

A contemporary of Duparc, the poet Gabriel Marc, most of whose works are largely unknown, has been pretty much forgotten by posterity. This poem comes from the collection *Soleils d'octobre* (1869). As the date of composition of the mélodie is also 1869, we might wonder if Duparc knew Gabriel Marc personally, and if Marc might have placed the poem in Duparc's hands. Originally, Duparc's *Sérénade* was the second mélodie in a volume entitled CINQ MÉLODIES, op. 2, published by Flaxland in 1869. This edition, very rare today—the composer did not wish the volume to be republished as it was originally—, also consisted of I. *Soupir* (on a poem by Sully Prudhomme, pseudonym of René-François-Armand Prudhomme), III. *Romance de Mignon* (Victor Wilder, after Goethe), IV. *Chanson triste* (Jean Lahor, pseudonym of Henri Cazalis), and V. *Le galop* (Sully Prudhomme). Ultimately, Duparc kept, in later editions of his songs and after reworking them, only *Soupir* and *Chanson triste*.

I use an American edition of Duparc's songs, *Complete Songs for Voice and Piano* (Dover, 2009), which includes all the mélodies published by the composer, and thus has the advantage of being truly complete. In addition to *L'invitation au voyage* and *La vie antérieure*, another poem by Baudelaire, *Recueillement* (incipit: "Sois sage, ô ma Douleur, et tiens-toi plus tranquille"), was in the works, but no trace of it has ever been found. Duparc's archives were burned after his death in a house fire, and all song sketches and completed works have completely disappeared.

As practical as it is, the Dover edition nonetheless has one fault: all the songs are presented in only one key, that of the first edition. Singers who need a transposition may use the 2005 Peters edition by Roger Nichols of the seventeen songs; it exists in one volume for medium-low voice, along with the volume in the original keys. Or they can avail themselves of the French edition Salabert (formerly Rouart-Lerolle), *Treize mélodies,* which is, unfortunately, incomplete, but does offer a choice of high voice and medium voice (the thirteen songs are also sold separately). The transpositions for this edition have been approved by the composer.

Le Chant Intime. François Le Roux and Romain Raynaldy, Oxford University Press. © Oxford University Press 2021.
DOI: 10.1093/oso/9780190884178.003.0013

I have tried to convince a French publisher to publish a complete edition of Duparc's seventeen songs, but it is difficult, because they are widely dispersed.[1] It's really a shame. Moreover, because it is incomplete, the Salabert edition only provides grist for the mill for those who think that Duparc's early songs hold no interest, since the composer himself didn't want to republish them. Duparc's judgment was questionable, given his chronic depressive state and severe lack of confidence in himself. The history of music has often shown that if composers could be trusted to decide what was and was not worthwhile in their output, many interesting works would never have seen the light of day.

As we return to *Sérénade*, if a transposition is desired (as the Peters edition keeps the original key in the volume for medium-low voice), I would advise choosing a key close to the original G major: for example, E major for low voices or A major for high voices. On the other hand, avoid the key of D major, which is too solemn; avoid F major as well: besides being a flat key, it would give this mélodie a rather sententious feeling.

For those interested in Duparc, I highly recommend Remy Stricker's monograph, *Les mélodies de Duparc* (Arles: Actes Sud, 1996), the only really interesting modern study of the composer. The author uses the word lieder to define Duparc's mélodies; while this is a highly pertinent analysis, it must nonetheless be pointed out that *Sérénade* is one of Duparc's rare mélodies that is *not* in lied form. It is close to the romance or early serenades: very simple, with an unchanging piano accompaniment whose arpeggios evoke the guitar. The singer must never lose sight of this simplicity while singing, and must trust Duparc, who was always very precise in his writing. The poem, while rather forgettable, has within it a lightness and freshness that the performer should try to put across.

If several mélodies by Duparc are to be sung in recital, this *Sérénade* will lighten the song group—not a small thing.

Analysis

Sérénade	*Serenade*
Si j'étais, ô mon amoureuse,	If, my beloved, I were
La brise au souffle parfumé,	The scented breeze,
Pour frôler ta bouche rieuse,	I would come, timid and rapt,
Je viendrais craintif et charmé,	To brush your laughing lips.
Si j'étais l'abeille qui vole,	If I were a bee in flight,
Ou le papillon séducteur,	Or a beguiling butterfly,

---

[1] Among the complications associated with Duparc's mélodies: the Flaxland scores were edited by two heirs who, in addition to not republishing op. 2, are the owners of two mélodies "disavowed" by the composer. Another mélodie (the duet *La fuite*, on a poem by Théophile Gautier) belongs to a private owner; another (*Le galop*), to Durand Editions; and Salabert has the thirteen others.

Tu ne me verrais point*, frivole,
Te quitter pour une autre fleur.
    *Duparc writes "pas"

Si j'étais la rose charmante
Que ta main place sur ton cœur,
Si près de toi toute tremblante
Je me fanerais de bonheur.

Mais en vain je cherche à te plaire,
J'ai beau gémir et soupirer,
Je suis homme, et que puis-je faire?
T'aimer … te le dire … et pleurer!

You would not see me skittishly
Leave you for another flower.

If I were the charming rose
Your hand placed on your heart,
I would, quivering so close to you,
Wither with happiness.

But I seek in vain to please you,
In vain I moan and sigh.
I am a man, and what can I do?
Love you … Confess my love … And cry!

In this *Sérénade*, as in the *Sérénade florentine* and many mélodies by Duparc, it is important to try to "globalize" the classic quatrain—that is to say, to create for each quatrain a sense of continuity from the beginning of the first line to the end of the fourth. Here, Duparc's compositional scheme is clear from the first quatrain: the first two lines are written in absolutely parallel fashion; the third serves as the high point, and the fourth as the conclusion. This design is why the performer must not take the rests in the vocal line too literally: these should be regarded as written-out "breaths" (later on, we will see the same ambiguity in Poulenc's writing). In these specific cases, real silences accompanied by breaths may make some phrases sound ridiculous; on the other hand, with a discreet pause, the singer can go to the high point, then to the accent, and the result is much better (Example 12.1.).

Duparc has written a *decrescendo* on the two measures of "Pour frôler ta bouche rieuse," which leads to a slight accent on the E of "bouche." At the end of the first quatrain, relax the tempo a bit in order to lead into the fermata on the final eighth note. Be especially careful of the half steps and chromatic alterations, like on "rieuse" (D♯ and D natural) or "craintif" (C natural). We can already see the refinement in Duparc's chromaticism—which comes from the Greek word for "color"—and this must not be forgotten when singing.

Duparc then writes *très doux* (very soft) to accompany the change of key: having been in G major, the music moves to E major (Example 12.2).

In singing the B, baritones and mezzo-sopranos might find it challenging to find the right timbre. Be careful not to seek too rich a sound, especially since the text is speaking of bees and butterflies, two insects traditionally symbolizing lightness. These are not bumblebees!

The two first lines are thus identical, musically speaking. Bring out the E5, tied over the barline (measures 15–16), on "Tu ne me verrais pas" (Example 12.3).

Here, Duparc writes *Suivez la voix* (follow the voice), which suggests that, during Duparc's lifetime, singers had trouble performing this passage. For us, there is no reason to imagine difficulties. Remain strictly *a tempo*, while making a light *diminuendo*. Between "Tu ne me verrais pas" and "frivole," which is relatively high, I advise going from *forte* to *mezzo-forte* in order to make a lovely *piano* color

Example 12.1 Duparc, Henri: *Sérénade*. From *Complete Songs for Voice and Piano*, Dover Publications, 1995 (ref. ISBN 0-486-28466-2), page 76, mm. 1–11.

Example 12.2 Duparc, Henri: *Sérénade*. From *Complete Songs for Voice and Piano*, Dover Publications, 1995 (ref. ISBN 0-486-28466-2), page 76, mm. 12–15.

Example 12.3 Duparc, Henri: *Sérénade.* From *Complete Songs for Voice and Piano*, Dover Publications, 1995 (ref. ISBN 0-486-28466-2), pages 76–77, mm. 15–16.

on "Te quitter pour une autre fleur." Be attentive to the light *portamento* on "une autre," indicated by the slur, which should be performed very delicately. Above all, don't make too much of it: Duparc only writes it only to avoid an accent on the *n* of "une."

The second quatrain finishes with four measures given over entirely to the piano. Pianists tend to want to avoid these interludes, especially in romances, because the accompaniment doesn't seem very interesting; often, pianists will rush through it, as if they were in a hurry to get back to the vocal part. Let's not go there. The first two measures of the interlude (measures 20–21) are identical, and they should be played identically, with no thought of differentiating them, for this method is a kind of illustration of the "brise" (breeze), the "abeille" (bee), and the "papillon" (butterfly), written in a guitar-like manner (a serenade was usually sung with a guitar accompaniment, played by the singer, under the window of the beloved). And the butterfly won't be happy to have to go faster or more slowly just to impress the spectator.

For the third quatrain, Duparc returns to the original key of G major. Here again, the first two lines are musically identical—but everything changes with the sudden *forte* outpouring on "Si près de toi," set on brief stepwise tonicizations of F (measure 28) and E♭ (measure 29), respectively. It is important to perform this surprise effect without seeking to minimize it—but also not forgetting the *diminuendo* written on "toute tremblante." Duparc treats the third and fourth lines more or less like hemistiches: "Si près de toi / toute tremblante / Je me fanerais / de bonheur." Note the F♯ on "Je," the *fortissimo* high point of the tessitura, after which the intensity is lessened almost immediately via a *diminuendo*, to reach a dynamic of *piano* on "bonheur," in the harmonically remote key of F♯ major (measure 32) (Example 12.4). Nothing is as calm and simple as it might have seemed at the beginning!

The fourth quatrain (*un poco agitato*) features an astonishing progression of mediant relationships (F♯ minor–A minor–C major–E major, measures 3–38) before returning to the tonic G major (approached by the mediant E major) in measure 39. Take care to respect the *poco* in *poco agitato*. The opening "Mais en vain" should not be too rushed—otherwise, it will become too explosive, and I don't think that's what Duparc would have wished for. If the basic tempo is around 60 to the dotted

Example 12.4 Duparc, Henri: *Sérénade*. From *Complete Songs for Voice and Piano*, Dover Publications, 1995 (ref. ISBN 0-486-28466-2), pages 77–78, mm. 28–33.

quarter note, I would advise a maximum tempo of 72. In measures 35–36, take care with the pronunciation of the two [ʒɛ] sounds—"J'ai" and "gé-(mir)," a poetic device that Gabriel Marc obviously wanted.

I think that the very interesting quasi-recitative of the ending on "Je suis homme, et que puis-je faire" can be performed completely out of tempo, while still counting the six eighth notes. The written dynamic is *pianissimo*, so the singer should almost murmur the line, with a nice liaison between "suis" and "homme" [ʒɛsɥizɔmə]. The motion becomes *ritenuto* and finally *lento*. Be careful to bring out the upbeat of "pleurer," skillfully written by Duparc in order to avoid a heavy accent on the first syllable of "pleurer": don't make the sound cry! On the second beat of this measure, the piano resumes *a tempo* (Example 12.5).

Example 12.5 Duparc, Henri: *Sérénade*. From *Complete Songs for Voice and Piano*, Dover Publications, 1995 (ref. ISBN 0-486-28466-2), page 78, mm. 42–45.

Romance de Mignon (1869)

Music by Henri Duparc (1848–1933)
Poem by Johann Wolfgang von Goethe (1749–1832), translated into French by
   Victor Wilder (1835–1892)

Presentation

This 1869 version of Mignon's famous song "Kennst Du das Land" is a true art song, or better still, a lied in two strophes. There are numerous translations of this song into French: one by Louis Gallet that Gounod set to music (1871), and, of course, Jules Barbier and Michel Carré's version for Ambroise Thomas's opera *Mignon* (1866). I will not speak here of the many lieder by Beethoven, Schubert, Schumann, Liszt, Wolf, and so forth. Victor Wilder is known especially as the author of French versions of Wagner's operas. As Duparc was a fervent Wagnerian, the relationship between the two men seems logical.[2]

Analysis

Romance de Mignon

Le connais-tu, ce radieux pays
Où brille dans les branches l'or des fruits?
Un doux zéphir embaume l'air
Et le laurier s'unit au myrte vert.
Le connais-tu, le connais-tu? Là-bas,*
Mon bien-aimé, courons porter nos pas!
   * Repeated twice by Duparc

Le connais-tu, ce merveilleux séjour
Où tout me parle encor de notre amour?
Où chaque objet me dit avec douleur:
Qui t'a ravi ta joie et ton bonheur?
Le connais-tu, le connais-tu? Là-bas,*
Mon bien-aimé, courons porter nos pas!
   * Repeated twice by Duparc

Mignon's romance

Do you know it, that radiant land,
Where golden fruit gleams among branches?
A gentle breeze scents the air,
Laurel and green myrtle intertwine.
Do you know it? Do you know it? There,
My beloved, let us make our way!

Do you know it, that wondrous abode,
Where everything still speaks of our love,
And every object asks me with sorrow:
Who has stolen your delight and joy?
Do you know it? Do you know it? There,
My beloved, let us make our way!

Goethe's poem has three verses, the last speaking of mountains—in fact, of Mignon's native Italy. Here, as in the later *L'invitation au voyage*, Duparc retains only the

---

[2] Victor Wilder was the translator in French for a lot of German lieder, and of Wagner's opera librettos, apart from *Rienzi, The Flying Dutchman, Tannhaüser,* and *Lohengrin* (translated already earlier by Charles Nuitter); his translation of *Die Walkyrie* was used by the Paris Opera until the years 1930.

verses that determine neither a place nor a particular person, giving a "universal" resonance to his musical setting. He uses the last line as a sort of refrain, or rather an antiphon quivering with hope and desire. I can only strongly advise following the written dynamics scrupulously, because Duparc thinks of everything, as we will see.

The original keys—E major for the "couplet" and G major for the "refrain"—allow a soprano (or a high mezzo)[3] to remain bright and to avoid overly "dramatizing," for the tessitura always stays in the high-medium register (from A4 to G5), and permits a crisp articulation and a constant search for colors. Four measures of piano solo introduce the theme to the whole song, like a call from a distant horn (Example 12.6).

Example 12.6 Duparc, Henri: *Romance de Mignon*. From *Complete Songs for Voice and Piano*, Dover Publications, 1995 (ref. ISBN 0-486-28466-2), page 71, mm. 1–5.

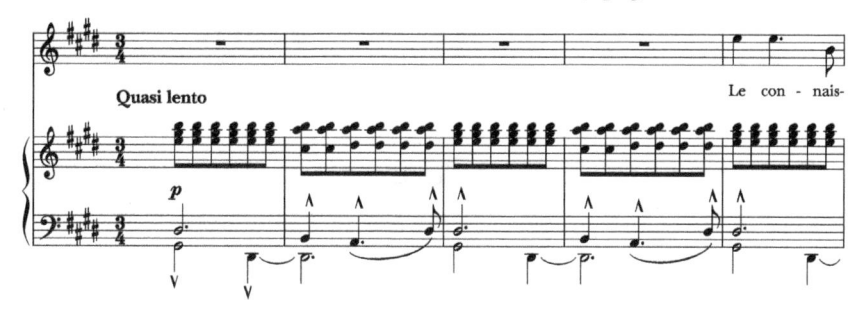

Duparc uses the simplest means in the vocal line, subdividing the first two lines into two hemistiches and using only two notes, E and B. The dynamic is *piano*, which should become softer for the question "l'or des fruits?" and increase again in volume with the fourth line. Then, the two instances of "Le connais-tu?" should be almost murmured (the dynamic in the accompaniment is *pp*). The *forte* dynamic of the refrain is prepared by two measures of *crescendo molto* in the piano, and the singer can accentuate the upbeat of "Là-bas" by expanding the tempo a bit, like a conductor, but, of course, without exaggerating. Immediately afterwards (measure 27), the original tempo should resume and the two-measure passage that follows should be sung *forte*, coming down again on "Mon bien-aimé" (measure 29), all the while retaining the feeling of trembling. The *forte* dynamic returns again on the second iteration of "Là-bas / Mon bien-aimé" (measures 33–34), but the singer should reserve some strength so that the third and final "Mon bien-aimé," marked *ff* (measures 38–39), can be even more impassioned. The two iterations of "Là-bas" at the end should be as intimate and dreamy as possible, much like the ending of *L'invitation au voyage*: "Là, tout n'est qu'ordre et beauté / Luxe, calme et volupté." The second "Là-bas," marked *pp*, (measures 41–42) should in fact be written *ppp*, just as

---

[3] The volume for medium-low voice in the 2005 Peters edition by Roger Nichols gives the transposition a minor third lower: D♭ major for the "couplet," and E major for the "refrain." This transposition will be convenient for an alto (tessitura from F♯4 to E5).

it is at the end of the second verse (perhaps this was a printing error). The second verse is constructed similarly, with even more perceptible sadness in the fourth line, "Qui t'a ravi ta joie et ton bonheur?" The line is marked *più forte* and reinforced by accents over every note (measure 63) (Example 12.7).

Example 12.7 Duparc, Henri: *Romance de Mignon*. From *Complete Songs for Voice and Piano*, Dover Publications, 1995 (ref. ISBN 0-486-28466-2), page 74, mm. 59–66.

Only the coda in the piano part provides a kind of dreamy calming, emphasized by a brief *rallentando* (Example 12.8). No romanticizing *rubato* need be added.

Example 12.8 Duparc, Henri: *Romance de Mignon*. From *Complete Songs for Voice and Piano*, Dover Publications, 1995 (ref. ISBN 0-486-28466-2), page 75, mm. 93–100.

Le galop (1869)

Music by Henri Duparc (1848–1933)
Poem by Sully Prudhomme (1839–1907)

Presentation

After a mélodie written specifically for a woman, here is a mélodie for a man's voice. The original edition was published in the key of F major for the voice, and it's only in the recent edition by Durand that the song has been published in the key of G major. The manuscript of this 1869 mélodie was given by the composer to the famous baritone Charles Panzéra[4]; Panzéra subsequently gave the manuscript to Durand in preparation for its Duparc volume, not published until 1948. The song is also available today, published separately. But using the complete Dover edition facilitates the work![5]

Analysis

Le galop	*The gallop*
Agite, bon cheval, ta crinière fuyante;	Flourish, good horse, your flying mane,
Que l'air autour de nous se remplisse de voix!	That the air about us be filled with voices!
Que j'entende craquer sous ta corne bruyante	That beneath your clattering hooves I hear
Le gravier des ruisseaux et les débris des bois!	The gravel of streams and the wood's broken boughs!
Aux vapeurs de tes flancs mêle ta chaude haleine,	Mingle your hot breath with the steam of your flanks,
Aux éclairs de tes pieds, ton écume et ton sang!	Your foam and your blood with the sparks from your hooves!
Cours, comme on voit un aigle en effleurant la plaine	Run, like an eagle we see skimming the plain,
Fouetter l'herbe d'un vol sonore et frémissant!	Lashing the grass with its quivering loud wings!
"Allons, les jeunes gens, à la nage! à la nage!"*	"Come, young men, swim your horses across!"
Crie à ses cavaliers le vieux chef de tribu;	Cries the old tribal chief to his horsemen;

---

[4] Swiss baritone Charles Panzéra (1896–1976) made his debut at the Opéra-Comique in 1918, but he quickly abandoned the theater to devote his career to concerts and recitals. In 1921, he gave the first performance of Gabriel Fauré's song cycle L'HORIZON CHIMÉRIQUE, op. 118, of which he was the dedicatee. Between 1920 and 1940 he gave many first performances of contemporary works, including Arthur Honegger's *Le roi David* and *La danse des morts*. Considered to be one of the finest singers of the French répertoire of his time, he specially distinguished himself as Mephisto in Berlioz's *La damnation de Faust*, which he sang more than 150 times in concert. While he lacked spectacular vocal means, Panzéra was a master of refined expression, superb musicality, and exemplary diction. He was a professor of voice at the Paris Conservatoire, and inspired Henri Dutilleux to write songs for him. He was the author of several books, all included in the bibliography at the conclusion of this study.

[5] The Peters volume for high voice keeps the original key.

Et les fils du désert respirent le pillage,

Et les chevaux sont fous du grand air qu'ils ont bu!

    * Duparc writes, "Allons! Les jeunes gens,"
      and repeats the line twice

Nage ainsi dans l'espace, ô mon cheval rapide,

Abreuve-moi d'air pur, baigne-moi dans le vent;*

L'étrier bat ton ventre, et j'ai lâché la bride,

Mon corps te touche à peine, il vole en te suivant.

    * Duparc puts a period instead of a semicolon

Brise tout, le buisson, la barrière ou la branche;

Torrents, fossés, talus, franchis tout d'un seul bond;

Cours,* je rêve et sur toi, les yeux clos, je me penche …

Emporte, emporte-moi dans l'inconnu profond!

    * Repeated in Duparc

And the sons of the desert are eager for plunder,

And the horses are crazed with the air they have drunk!

Swim thus in space, O my swift mount,

Quench my thirst with pure air, bathe me in wind;

The stirrup strikes your belly, I've slackened the rein,

My body scarcely touches you, it flies in your wake.

Break down everything, bush, gate, or branch;

Cross torrent, ditch, embankment with a single bound;

Race on, I dream, bending over you with closed eyes …

Transport me, transport me to the deep unknown!

This poem, later set to music by Théodore Dubois (1837–1924) and Georges Enesco (1881–1955), is at once an example of intoxication of the senses, a tribute to speed, to the call of the wild (before the arrival of race cars), and to parachute jumping! Here, Duparc follows the example of numerous musical "jumps into the abyss," like Schubert's *Erlkönig*, or, in opera, the final race ("Hop! Hop!") of Mephistopheles and Faust in Berlioz's *La damnation de Faust*. The duet *La fuite* by Duparc is also a sketch of breathless racing, but it's about escaping pursuers, while here, one races eagerly toward nothingness! The key is G minor, at once dark and majestic. The main theme in the piano is a descending chromatic scale (Example 12.9).

Example 12.9 Duparc, Henri: *Le galop.* From *Complete Songs for Voice and Piano*, Dover Publications, 1995 (ref. ISBN 0-486-28466-2), page 43, mm. 1–3.

Another prevalent motive is the "galloping" dotted-eighth/sixteenth-note figure that appears in the accompaniment of the third verse, describing the horses as "fous du grand air qu'ils ont bu!" (Example 12.10).

Example 12.10

But the vocal part remains quite lyric, and adheres most of the time to a division of each line into two hemistiches ("Agite bon cheval / ta crinière fuyante"). The only real problem that faces the singer is not going beyond their own means and finding with their collaborator the correct balance between the piano and the voice. Curiously, this mélodie, unlike *La vague et la cloche* or *Le manoir de Rosemonde*, which are similar in mood, was not, it seems, conceived to be orchestrated. But the piano sound is written in a grand, orchestral manner, and the tessitura is demanding (from G2 to F4), so the singer must really be careful! The tempo should not be too slow, but very judiciously Duparc indicates *Allegro non troppo ma con fuoco* (Not too fast, but with fire). What counts most is the ecstasy, as if the subject were intoxicated by the speed, by the words. Carefully work out the expenditures of air in the *crescendo*, in a dynamic range that goes from *mezzo-forte* to *forte*, and make a beautiful line, in contrast with the *legato crescendo-decrescendo* on the second line ("Que l'air autour de nous") (Example 12.11).

Example 12.11 Duparc, Henri: *Le galop*. From *Complete Songs for Voice and Piano*, Dover Publications, 1995 (ref. ISBN 0-486-28466-2), page 43, mm. 4–10.

The first written *forte* is found in the first line of the second quatrain ("Aux vapeurs de tes flancs"), and it's *ff* in the following line. So, measure out this gradation, and deliver it with declamatory emphasis rather than with extreme loudness. In measure 31, just before "Cours, comme on voit un aigle," the pianist should come down to *mezzo-forte* (it's not written, but it supports the *mf* in the vocal line). The attack on the following line ("Allons! Les jeunes gens"), repeated twice by Duparc, should be as biting as possible. Make sure to cut the "-lons!" [-lõ] with the piano, in order to start the phrase "Les jeunes gens" almost on the breath. Duparc's clear dynamics—*energico*, then, further on, *passionato*—should always be rendered with imagination. Make a good contrast between the *legato* phrases ("Nage ainsi) and the strident phrases ("Brise tout"). In measure 79, the "Lisztian" chromatic scale in the left hand can be delivered more effectively by scaling back the volume from the preceding *fff* (perhaps coming down even to *pp*) and playing the passage just slightly under the tempo, on the condition that the music returns to a strict *a tempo* in measure 80 (Example 12.12).

Example 12.12 Duparc, Henri: *Le galop.* From *Complete Songs for Voice and Piano*, Dover Publications, 1995 (ref. ISBN 0-486-28466-2), page 48, mm. 77–80.

Finally, for the last two lines, where Duparc reiterates "Cours" the extraordinary effect of the *stringendo* followed by the *diminuendo-crescendo* up until the *forte* should act as a respite from the hallucinatory dream before the final leap. And, of course, the "galloping" tempo returns (this marking is missing, but it's obvious) on the first beat of bar 95 "**toi**, les yeux clos," and should be maintained up until *en élargissant* (broadening), which prepares the sinking of the final G2. If the performer is afraid that the low G won't sound, it could be sung up an octave, but only if the suicidal effect is retained: this last note should not sound triumphant. Moreover, the piano should sound, as it nears the end, as if the earth had opened and swallowed up the instrument; by the last measure, almost nothing should be heard.

Le galop is a fascinating mélodie, for the singer, the pianist, and the audience, and improves with further acquaintanceship. It contrasts well with *Élégie* or *Soupir*, by the same composer.

13

Louis Durey

TROIS POÈMES DE PÉTRONE (1918)

    I. *La boule de neige*
   II. *La métempsycose*
 III. *La grenade*

Music by Louis Durey (1888–1979)
Poems attributed to Caius (or Titus) Petronius Niger, aka. Arbiter (ca. A.D. 27–ca. A.D. 66), called Petronius, translated by Charles Héguin de Guerle (1793–1881)

Presentation

Here, two names appear together in odd juxtaposition: Petronius, the famous and scandalous author of the *Satyricon*, and Louis Durey, the forgotten and the most discreet member of the Groupe des Six. The other unwritten but implicit name—cited by Durey in his still-unpublished *Catalogue commenté de mes œuvres* (Annotated catalogue of my works), and evoked as a sort of patron saint—is Erik Satie, whose *Socrate* had strongly impressed the young composer. There are few Latin poems used in French mélodie. But here Durey achieves a master stroke (and he would do it again with his four *ÉPIGRAMMES DE THÉOCRITE*, also dating from 1918), and illustrates in an exemplary manner the principles of the founding manifesto of the Groupe des Six, formulated by Jean Cocteau in *Le coq et l'arlequin* (*Cock and Harlequin)*: simplicity of means, clarity of diction, freshness of expression, concision. This cycle only lasts seven minutes. But it is indeed a cycle, and a complete one: two fast movements around a slow movement, and a unique musical motive that can be found, in varied form, in all three. A little history: Ravel and Durey knew each other. Ravel even considered Durey to be the most promising of the composers of Les Six. As such, Ravel presented Durey to Jacques Durand, who agreed to publish this very Petronius cycle (Durey's first engraved work), and the *ÉPIGRAMMES DE THÉOCRITE*, in 1919. It's one of the reasons that, of all of Durey's vocal output, I decided to choose this cycle, because it can still be found in music stores that sell used scores. It's difficult to find, but it's possible!

Le Chant Intime. François Le Roux and Romain Raynaldy, Oxford University Press. © Oxford University Press 2021.
DOI: 10.1093/oso/9780190884178.003.0014

Analyses

I. *La boule de neige*

Je ne croyais pas que la neige renfermât du feu. Mais l'autre jour Julie me jeta de la neige, et cette neige était de feu. Qu'y a-t'il de plus froid que la neige ? Et pourtant, Julie, la neige lancée par tes mains embrasa mon cœur. Où trouver à présent un refuge pour m'abriter des pièges de l'amour, si même cette eau glacée recèle sa flamme ? Julie, tu peux éteindre cependant l'ardeur qui me consume, non pas avec la neige, non pas avec la glace, mais en brûlant d'un feu pareil au mien.

I. *The Ball of Snow*

I didn't think that snow contained fire. But the other day Julie threw snow at me, and this snow was made of fire. What could be colder that snow? However, Julie, the snow thrown by your hands set fire my heart. Where can I henceforth find a refuge to protect me from the traps of love, if even this frozen water conceals its flame? However, Julie, you can extinguish this fire, not with snow, not with ice, but by burning with a similar flame.

I include the Latin poem, as it is found in Riese's *Anthologia Latina*, in its entirety—for, returning to what I said in the first part of this book, it is useful to remind readers of the relationships of this mélodie with the epigram of Marot, set to music by Ravel, *D'Anne qui me jecta de la neige*, which refers to it as well; we will speak of this again later.

> Me niue candenti petiit modo Iulia. Rebar
> Igne carere niuem: nix tamen ignis erat.
> Quid niue frigidius? nostrum tamen urere pectus
> Nix potuit manibus, Iulia, missa tuis.
> Quis locus insidiis, dabitur mihi tutus Amoris,
> Frigire concreta si latet ignis aqua?
> Iulia, sola potes nostras extinguere flammas,
> Non niue, non glacie, sed potes igne pari.

Did Durey know Ravel's mélodie (Demets, 1900)? Surely he did. Did he make the connection with Petronius's poem? Without a doubt. So, we could be dealing with a discreet and flattering homage to Durey's friendship with Ravel. As the poem is attributed only to Petronius (and we have since learned that it is, in essence "Petrarchian," and thus a fake Renaissance poem), one has, thus, successive "stories within stories" and cover-ups. There's no doubt that a direct homage to Ravel would have aroused a reaction from Cocteau, who at the time considered him a relic from the Impressionist past, a follower of Debussy. It was also apparently because Cocteau had reprinted in the journal *Le coq* Satie's famous remark—"*Ravel refuses the Legion of Honor but all his music accepts it*"—that Durey distanced himself from Les Six. I own a signed copy of the TROIS POÈMES DE PÉTRONE, and Durey formulated the undated dedication this way: "*To Maurice Ravel, this modest homage of my gratitude and my admiration.*"

The key chosen by Durey is B♭ minor. The tessitura is for a medium tenor (from E♭3 to G♭4). Contrary to the archaic form of Ravel's work on the poem of Marot (described in chapter 28, on pages 226–229), Durey adopts a form of a sort of childish dance—marked *enjoué* (playful) from the opening ⅔—for four measures of piano introduction (*mf*). Then the simple melody is heard in one uninterrupted phrase, while the piano becomes more discreet, almost dreamy (Example 13.1).

Example 13.1 Durey, Louis: *Trois poèmes de Pétrone—I. La boule de neige.* Editions Durand & Cie., 1919 (ref. D. & F. 9673), page 1, mm. 1–10.

It begins again, alone, but this time in piano, the rhythm of the opening, for five measures. Then the melody takes up again, uninterrupted, the next phrase, with only a brief pause (not a breath!) between "me jeta de la neige" and "cette neige était de feu." The musical construction alternates in this way between playful movement, for the lively addresses to Julie, and the calmer tone of thoughts about the "feu glacé." Only the phrase "Où trouver à présent . . . recèle sa flamme?" benefits from special treatment: marked *attristé (sans ralentir)* (saddened, but without slowing down), the voice doesn't have to sound sad—it's banter that plays at sadness, so there's no need for irrelevant sentimentality. Besides, the music returns quickly to the "playful" tempo to conclude.

II. *La métempsycose*

Tandis que je cueillis un suave baiser sur les lèvres de mon ami et que j'aspirais sur sa bouche entr'ouverte le frais parfum de son haleine, mon âme, enivrée, se précipita sur mes lèvres, et s'insinuant entre les siennes, s'efforça de m'échapper. Ah ! Si la tendre union de nos lèvres eût duré un instant de plus, mon âme, enflammée d'amour, passait dans la sienne et m'abandonnait. Ainsi, ô merveille ! mort par moi-même, j'aurais continué à vivre dans le sein de mon ami.

II. *Metempsychosis, or Transmigration of the Souls*

While snatching a sweet kiss from the lips of my beloved and inhaling from his half-open mouth the cool perfume of his breath, my intoxicated soul came to my lips, and, sneaking through his lips, tried to escape from me. Ah! if the soft union of our lips had lasted one more instant, my soul, inflamed by love, would have joined his and abandoned me. And thus, oh marvel ! having died by myself, I would have continued to live in the bosom of my lover.

Marked *modéré* (moderato), this mélodie is in F♯ minor (⁴⁄₈). The tessitura is a little more extended than in the preceding song (from C♯3 to F♯4). Like the first song, the singing should be free of sentimentality, but marked by a delight of discovery, through the senses, of a sort of suspension of time (I won't say eternity, for that would be too pompous for the object in question). The singing must be *legato*, but light, and the phrase lengths should be respected. The breaths should be discreet (for example, for the first phrase, the simplest is to make a brief pause after "je cueillais," which avoids a rather difficult liaison, and gives the momentum to go up until "mon ami"). All the markings must be done lightly, e.g., the *En pressant un peu* (measure 27). And the *forte* at measure 41 is relative, given the accompaniment: it is an exteriorized exclamation of love rather than a valiant *forte*.

III. *La grenade*

Lesbie, lumière de mon âme, m'a envoyé une grenade; Maintenant, je fais peu de cas des autres fruits ! Je dédaigne le coing au blanc duvet, et la châtaigne hérissée de dards; je ne veux ni des noix ni des prunes luisantes. De tels présents sont assez bons pour le grossier Corydon. Lesbie m'a envoyé aussi des gâteaux que ses dents ont légèrement mordus; le miel de ses lèvres en a augmenté la douceur. Je ne sais ce qui est meilleur à respirer, du doux parfum du miel ou de son haleine, plus embaumée que le thym de Cécropie.

III. *The Pomegranate*

Lesbia, light of my soul, sent me a pomegranate; Henceforth, I have no consideration for other fruits! I reject in disdain the quince covered by white down and the chestnut, prickly with stingers; I don't want either nuts or gleaming plums. Such presents would be good enough for rusty Corydon. Lesbia also sent me sweetmeats gently bitten by her teeth; the honey of her lips has thus increased their sweetness. I don't know which is better to breathe, the soft perfume of honey, or her breath, more fragrant than Cecropian thyme.

The last song of this short cycle is full of frank sensuality without ulterior motives; perhaps the allusions of the text sound a bit daring for our era, but the music remains both innocent and knowing, exempt from Christian sentiments of sin: we are in a Roman pantheist country. Moreover, the opening marking, *gracieux* (graceful), sums up the sought-after attitude. In C♯ minor, bright-sounding (the tessitura is exactly the same as in the preceding song), the tempo (𝄴) suggests the swaying rhythm of a nursery rhyme. The first pages must be sung with momentum, which stops (the comma noted at the bottom of the page) all of a sudden, to change the discourse or rather to soften it a bit, up until the following stopping point—this time indicated by a fermata on the barline.

The lower tessitura used to allude to "grossier Corydon" denotes the speaker's contempt, which should be applied only in a fleeting manner; for, after the piano measure marked *p (mais clair)* (*piano*, but bright), the open gaiety returns and remains until the end, with just a softer nuance for the last phrase. Cécropie (Cecropia) is the ancient name of Athens (from the name of King Cecrops, founder of the city), and, more generally, of the Attic region around this city; it gives an idea of the odor of thyme—and the performer must try to bring the scent to the audience!

14

Henri Dutilleux

San Francisco Night (1963)

Music by Henri Dutilleux (1916–2013)
Poem by Paul Gilson (1904–1963)

Presentation

Henri Dutilleux is certainly a unique composer: his music derives from no "school," and his body of work, consisting of few opuses, is a rare jewel. In this respect, he belongs to a glorious musical lineage that stretches from Rameau to Berlioz to Debussy. The titles of his works seem to continue the tradition of Debussy's titles: *Tout un monde lointain* (A whole far away world), *Ainsi la nuit* (So the night) . . . and so forth. He composed at least one music-theatrical work: his cantata for the Prix de Rome (which he won in 1938), entitled *L'anneau du roi* (The king's ring), dedicated to his teacher Henri Büsser, and sung in December 1938 by sopranos Germaine Hoerner and Irène Joachim and baritone Charles Panzéra, under the direction of Philippe Gaubert. Very critical of his early works, he refused to allow them to be performed, and often apologized for not having written more for the voice—although late in his career, he wrote two large works for voice and orchestra: CORRESPONDANCES (2003) and LE TEMPS L'HORLOGE (2009). It goes without saying that his very short list of mélodies doesn't make him a composer much sought after by recitalists: to date, only twelve mélodies have been published.[1] They all date from before 1965. The collection of QUATRE MÉLODIES, composed in 1942 and published by Durand in 1943, were dedicated to Charles Panzéra. These were followed, in 1943, by a musical setting of a sonnet by Jean Cassou, entitled *La geôle* (published by Durand in 1946), then by DEUX SONNETS DE JEAN CASSOU, composed in 1954 and published in 1956, also by Durand. These seven mélodies have been orchestrated.

Dutilleux's last known mélodie, *San Francisco Night*, was composed in 1963. It was a commission from Alice Esty, a wealthy American amateur singer, who

---

[1] After *Chanson de la déportée*, published by Alphonse Leduc in 2010, three more songs were released in 2016 by the same publisher, with an introduction that I wrote. These have been reconstructed according to manuscripts, dated 1941, that had been in the possession of Charles Panzéra and that were subsequently placed in the Bibliothèque nationale de France. This is music worth discovering!

Le Chant Intime. François Le Roux and Romain Raynaldy, Oxford University Press. © Oxford University Press 2021.
DOI: 10.1093/oso/9780190884178.003.0015

was the dedicatee of Poulenc's song cycle LE TRAVAIL DU PEINTRE (1957). After Poulenc's death in January 1963, Esty, wanting to pay homage to the composer, organized a concert comprised of Poulenc's songs and works composed specially for the occasion. In addition to Henri Dutilleux, she contacted (among others) Darius Milhaud, Vittorio Rieti, Manuel Rosenthal, Henri Sauguet, and Germaine Tailleferre. And thus, *San Francisco Night* was given its first performance on January 13, 1964, in Carnegie Recital Hall in New York, as part of an "Homage to Francis Poulenc," performed by Alice Esty and pianist David Stimer. Dutilleux's song remained unpublished until 2002, and it was only after the first public performance in France—at the Théâtre des Champs-Élysées, on March 26, 1999, by American soprano Dawn Upshaw and pianist Jérôme Ducros—that it was published by Alphonse Leduc.

Dutilleux knew poet Paul Gilson (not to be mistaken with the Belgian composer (1865–1942) who bears the same name!) through his work on French national radio as a jazz specialist. He was deeply affected by his sudden death that also occurred in 1963. With this mélodie, Dutilleux realized a double homage: to Poulenc and to Gilson.

Analysis

San Francisco Night

Je crois qu'il n'a jamais fait plus noir que ce soir,*
où la sirène pleure au bord du monde en ruines,
mais la merveille vaut le prix du désespoir.
Aussi profil perdu d'amour je te dessine

en aveugle, et j'attends nocturne de l'enfance
que l'enchanteur ranime un oiseau mort de froid
sans avoir révélé le secret de la chance.
Amour, amour, toujours dans mon rêve à l'étroit.

   * All the punctuation has been added by Dutilleux

San Francisco Night

I think no evening was so dark before:
the world is wrecked, the siren's tears are
                                    [flowing
And yet the wonder's worth its price, despair.
Lost profile, love, it's you I'm blindly drawing.

Childhood nocturne: I hope the enchanter may
bring back to life a bird that died of cold:
nor is luck's secret his to give away.
Love love forever in my dream's tight hold.
(*Translation by Timothy Adès*)

The collection of twenty-seven poems by Paul Gilson, entitled *Au rendez-vous des solitaires*[2] (Seghers, 1947), is a magnificent volume about exile: not necessarily true exile, but amorous exile. In an interview, the poet explained, "*Always in exile, the poet lives like the immigrants.*"[3] The titles of the majority of poems in this collection are in English (*Remembrance, Vacuum Cleaner, Absent Minded*, etc.), but they

---

[2] The English translation of this title could be *At the meeting of lonely people*.
[3] Interview with Paul Gilson, in the collection of monographs *Poètes d'aujourd'hui*, number 70 (1959, reprinted in 1976 by Seghers), devoted to Paul Gilson. It was perhaps here that Henri Dutilleux read and chose the poem *San Francisco Night*, which was reproduced in the volume.

contain wonderful alexandrines that make up the poetic rhythm. Gilson, a great jazz lover, invented a sort of French "blues," blending the influences of American and French cultures in order to open uncharted paths to the mind and the ear. He was a friend of many musicians; his work has often been set to music, and *San Francisco Night* has been set by at least one other composer, Jean-Michel Damase (1928–2013), in his 1952 collection of six songs (this one is the fifth) on poems by Paul Gilson, entitled NO EXIT (Salabert, 1954). It would be interesting to listen to these two musical versions of the same poem performed together in recital (hint, hint . . .).

In Dutilleux's mélodie, the publisher has marked measure numbers, to which I will refer. Henri Dutilleux adds punctuation to the printed poetic text: commas at the ends of the first and second lines; a period at the end of the third line of the first quatrain; a comma after "en aveugle" at the beginning of the second quatrain; a period at the end of the next-to-last and last lines; and a comma after each "amour" in the last line. These details are useful to the singer in understanding how the composer "interprets" the poem: in a slow rhythm (*Calme*, 54 to the quarter note), the song becomes a nocturne, a Debussyste blues, with a languorous length of around 4 min 30 sec. The tessitura (C♯4 to F♯5) is in the middle of the vocal range; it is probably best suited to a woman's voice or a tenor (although I myself have sung it in recital). The voice should remain light. The general dynamic of the mélodie is a dreamy *p*, with a few expressive breaths (measures 14, 35, 36, 42, 43). The only *mp* appears on the repetition in the last line of "Amour, amour"; here, the voice becomes a little fuller in order to conclude in the low register without disappearing completely. The accompaniment is rich and rhythmically complex. There are some written-out build-ups in measures 12 and 18, where the dynamics expand from *pp* to *f*. The accompaniment should give the impression of a written-out improvisation that uses the entire palette of the post-Ravelian piano.

As is often the case in modern vocal repertoire, the performer should control the vibrato, allowing the register to sound homogenous in the long phrases, such as the first three lines. Then, the phrases seem easier. The breaths and catch breaths add rhythm to the discourse: between "Aussi" and "profil perdu," the same between "et j'attends" and "nocturne de l'enfance," and before "que l'enchanteur," where the punctuation previously pointed out and the division of the lines into hemistiches ("Sans avoir révélé / le secret de la chance") come into play. But the "gliding" aspect remains in force: this technique is not about declamation. The choice of making liaisons between words—or not—seems to me to be clearly indicated, by the presence—or lack—of slurs written above the staff. In measure 22, for example, the silent *e* of "dessine" is "assimilated"; so, it is performed [ʒətədɛsinãnavœgl]; in measure 30, there is a single *r* to enunciate after the *tenuto* on "eu" in the word "enchanteur" (and there is a possible catch breath to be taken after "ranime"): [kəlãʃãtəranim'œ̃n wazomɔrdəfrwa].

One could not be more precise than Henri Dutilleux, both technically and expressively, to bring together as closely as possible poetic development, the evocation of being cut off physically because of the absence of the beloved, and the nocturnal flight of the song of a human nightingale, dreaming of joining the absent lover. In some ways, Dutilleux is close to the Ravel of the *TROIS POÈMES DE MALLARMÉ*, but he achieves his means through simple and evocative vocalism that is very "blue," both serious and passionate. A magnificent mélodie.

15

Gabriel Fauré

L'absent (1871)

Music by Gabriel Fauré (1845–1924)
Poem by Victor Hugo (1802–1885)

Presentation

L'absent is an interesting mélodie for a number of reasons: it's an early work by Fauré—it dates from 1871, when the composer was twenty-six years old—and the poem is one of the very rare excerpts from Victor Hugo's *Châtiments* (1853) ever to have been set to music; moreover, it is exceptionally short, in a collection of very long texts. It's also one of the rare dramatic poems that the young Fauré set to music during this period.

It is the eleventh of Fauré's *Vingt mélodies, volume I*, assembled by the publisher Choudens in 1879 and reprinted today by Hamelle (Leduc). Fauré designated the song as op. 5, no. 3. There exist three early mélodies by Fauré on poems of Victor Hugo, which remained unpublished until recently; two of these will be discussed below. *Puisque j'ai mis ma lèvre* (December 1862) and *L'aurore* (1870) are both from the volume *Les chants du crépuscule* (1836). The dramatic and very beautiful *Tristesse d'Olympio* (undated, probably from 1865), from the collection *Les rayons et les ombres* (1840), is based on an extremely long poem (more than thirty verses), from which Fauré, in an astonishing feat of paring down, retained only six verses! (See the following analysis.) *L'aurore* was published for the first time in Fritz Noske's book *La mélodie française de Berlioz à Duparc* (Presses Universitaires de France, 1958) and reprinted in the English-language version, *French Song from Berlioz to Duparc* (Dover, 1988).

L'absent is dedicated to Romain Bussine (1830–1899), a poet, singer, and professor of voice at the Paris Conservatoire. He is the author of the French text of Fauré's famous mélodie *Après un rêve*, op. 7, no. 1, and numerous retranscriptions of Italian songs.

L'absent is published in two keys. The original, for medium voice, is in A minor. It is transposed for soprano to C minor, which gives it a very dramatic tension. The wide tessitura—B3 to E5 in the original key (an octave and a half)—is rare in Fauré. At more than four minutes (if the tempo is adhered to), it is also a relatively long

Le Chant Intime. François Le Roux and Romain Raynaldy, Oxford University Press. © Oxford University Press 2021.
DOI: 10.1093/oso/9780190884178.003.0016

mélodie. Here, as he usually is, Fauré is highly respectful of the text—a practice to be expected all the more with someone as eminent as Victor Hugo—and he sets the music line by line, verse by verse. This mélodie may be an early one, but it is already very "Fauréen": the accompaniment features well-balanced, unlyrical minimalism, over which soars a vocal line that is very instrumental and extremely lyrical—a bit like the great mélodies of the second volume and the beginning of the third. Additionally, the trajectory of the dynamics is already typical of the composer: from *piano* to *mezzo-forte*, disrupted only by the grand conclusion of the third quatrain, which reaches a dynamic of *forte*.

Hugo's untitled poem, constructed as a series of questions and answers, includes a format that denotes dialogue, a visual aspect that disappears in the score. I don't know if this format was in the original edition or on Fauré's manuscript, but it's important to keep this wonderful dialogic construction in mind: in the first two quatrains, the question takes up three lines and the response only one, while in the two last quatrains, the questions and the responses are organized in hemistiches. Thus, there is an augmentation of poetic rhythm and a mounting anxiety, perfectly understood by Fauré, who amplifies the accompaniment in the third quatrain, before returning, for the last, to a pared-down piano part similar to the beginning.

Analysis

L'absent

—Sentiers où l'herbe se balance,
Vallons, coteaux, bois chevelus,
Pourquoi ce deuil et ce silence?
—Celui qui venait ne vient plus.

—Pourquoi personne à ta fenêtre?
Et pourquoi ton jardin sans fleurs?
Ô maison!* où donc est ton maître?
—Je ne sais pas, il est ailleurs.
　　*Fauré writes a comma instead of an exclamation point

—Chien, veille au logis!—Pour quoi faire?
La maison est vide à présent.
—Enfant, qui pleures-tu?—Mon père.
—Femme, qui pleures-tu?—L'absent.

—Où s'en* est-il allé?—Dans l'ombre.
—Flots qui gémissez sur l'écueil,
D'où venez-vous?—Du bagne sombre.
—Et qu'apportez-vous?—Un cercueil.
　　* Fauré writes "Où donc"

The absent one

Paths of swaying grass,
Valleys, hillsides, leafy woods,
Why this mourning and this silence?
—He who came here comes no more.

—Why is no one at your window,
And why is your garden without flowers,
O house! where is your master?
—I do not know, he is elsewhere.

Dog, guard the home.—For what reason?
The house is empty now.
—Child, who is it you mourn?—My father.
—Woman, who is it you mourn?—The absent one.

—Where has he gone?—Into the shadow.
—Waves that moan against the reefs,
From where do you come?—The dark convict
　　　　　　　　　　　　　　[prison.
—And what do you carry?—A coffin.

The big pitfall to avoid in *L'absent* is making a mélodie that is already naturally dark even darker. The song is in A minor, a relatively somber key (not to mention C minor, the key used in the version for high voice). As Louis Jouvet used to say, "Ne pas mettre la flamme sur la flamme"—don't add fuel to the fire. I would even say, to the contrary, that, if the score is read carefully enough, there are certain luminous passages that will shine through.

The first question ("—Sentiers où l'herbe [. . .] et ce silence?") is in A minor and the response is in E major. For once, the performer can simply use the major key to brighten the mood, in particular at the moment of descent to the B3 at "ne vient plus," which can be lightened up to the maximum, almost with a smile, rather than weeping buckets of tears.

The second quatrain begins with a series of poignant questions. Fauré depicts the questions through a harmonic vacillation between D minor and F major and a chain of descending second-inversion parallel harmonies in the accompaniment, rendered all the more poignant by a series of suspensions in the interior right-hand line. Harmonically, the song is already great Fauré, creating subtle harmonic changes that sound clear and easy: this is his trademark.

We see that the dynamic marking for the first quatrain is *piano* but that the marking at the beginning of the second is *dolce*. It's a typical Fauré marking, this way of refining the color by varying it very little—for it is a question of nuance and not of intensity. It is possible to mark a *crescendo* before the *decrescendo* of "où donc est ton maître?": it is found in the earliest edition, and it appears to have been left out by accident in the recent edition.

At the end of the quatrain, pay attention to the pronunciation of "il est ailleurs" [ilɛtajœr] (he is elsewhere), which, to a French ear could easily become, because of too strong a liaison between "est" and "ailleurs," "il est tailleur" (he is a tailor). Therefore, although the liaison is obligatory, the [t] should be pronounced very lightly. Fauré wrote what was needed rhythmically, so that there would be no confusion, in giving a long note value to "est" (Example 15.1). But it would be going too far to make a space between the [t] of the liaison and "ailleurs."

Example 15.1 Fauré, Gabriel: *L'absent*. From *Mélodies et duos, volume I—Premières mélodies*, Editions J. Hamelle, 2010 (ref. HA 9 729), pages 74–75, mm. 28–30.

In my opinion, the *tempo* could also be slightly slowed down before attacking the *un poco più mosso* at the third quatrain, making it easier to hear. The passage is further marked by repetitive triplet figures, set against duple subdivisions in the vocal line. Pay attention to the dynamic marking of *mezzo-forte*—it should not be sung *forte*, which is tempting to do.

"Chien" is sung in the high part of the tessitura—C5 in the medium-voice version, E5 for the high voice—but the *crescendo* should not begin too soon: it should come later, especially since on "Pour quoi faire?" the dynamic returns immediately to *piano*. The anxiety, carried by the triplets in the accompaniment, increases from question to question. Don't do too much, however, with the response of the child, "Mon père": remember that it is a child who is singing. On the other hand, when the woman weeps for "L'absent," the performer should imagine a heart-rending cry. It bears mentioning that Fauré himself wrote all the exclamation points that end the responses; in that respect, he reveals himself to be more expressively dramatic than the poet. Nonetheless, I suggest, instead of arriving on an enormous *forte*, holding back a bit, in order to make a *crescendo* on the high E5 (G5 in the high-voice version) (Example 15.2).

Example 15.2 Fauré, Gabriel: *L'absent*. From *Mélodies et duos, volume I—Premières mélodies*, Editions J. Hamelle, 2010 (ref. HA 9 729), page 76, mm. 43–47.

For, just afterwards, Fauré writes a *crescendo* in the piano part that will end in a *fortissimo*, a rare dynamic marking in his songs.

With the fourth quatrain, the music returns to *piano*. There again, I advise the performer not to go too fast, for a big *crescendo* to *mezzo-forte* must be undertaken on "Flots qui gémissez sur l'écueil." In some editions, there is a wrong note written on the "-sez" of "gémissez." The accompaniment should follow suit, and thus, the passage should read as given in Example 15.3.

To the extent possible, try to brighten "bagne sombre" and "un cercueil" and, especially, be careful in placing the "-ueil" of "cercueil," which runs into the *diminuendo* at the end of the measure. The singer can put the syllable either on the last eighth note of the last triplet of the measure or even on the following chord.

Finally, in this quatrain, a tiny modification of Hugo's original text should be noted: Fauré has substituted "Où donc est-il allé," for the poet's original "Où s'en est-il allé?" If—as is most likely—Hugo chose the "s'en" because he had already written,

Example 15.3 Fauré, Gabriel: *L'absent*. From *Mélodies et duos, volume I—Premières mélodies*, Editions J. Hamelle, 2010 (ref. HA 9 729), page 77, mm. 56–60.

in the second quatrain, "Ô maison! où *donc* est ton maître?" I don't understand why Fauré decided on this change. Perhaps it was a fault of the editor. In any case, as the rhythms are the same and the change in sonority negligible, the singer may, if desired, restore the original text.

Puisque j'ai mis ma lèvre (1862)

Music by Gabriel Fauré (1845–1924)
Poem by Victor Hugo (1802–1885)

Presentation

This mélodie remained unpublished for a long time. It was published recently, first by the French musicologist and Fauré specialist Jean-Michel Nectoux in a volume of Fauré's *Mélodies et duos, volume I—Premières mélodies, 1861–1875* (J. Hamelle, 2010); and then in the critical edition by Roy Howat and Emily Kilpatrick, *Complete Songs, Volume I: 1861–1882* (London: Peters, 2015), in two keys, C major (in the "high voice" volume) and B♭ major (in the "medium voice" volume).[1] It is very interesting: first, because it's one of the very first works by Fauré (he was not yet twenty years old); second, because the untitled poem, from *Les chants du crépuscule* (1835), was set to music by other great composers—Saint-Saëns (1860), César Franck (1880), and Reynaldo Hahn (ca. 1900), among others—but never by such a young man. One finds in Fauré's version incomparable enthusiasm and freshness. It's a romance with a simple structure (AA'BA'), constructed on the alternation between C major (parts AA') and A minor (part B, including the third and fourth quatrains), with a shortened

---

[1] I was able to consult the manuscript, which belongs to my friend Thierry Bodin, who serves as an expert consultant for music for the Paris auction houses. The manuscript, one of two in existence, is dated September 30, 1863 (see the notes in the 2010 Alphonse Leduc edition, page 175). The mélodie is in C major. It was reproduced in its entirety in the first edition, in French, of this book (Fayard, 2004), pages 176–179.

conclusion, based on A', which is a simple solution for a poem of five verses. It's very classic, but it also shows great faithfulness to the poem. Finally, it has a high tessitura, perfect for a real *tenore di grazia* (E4 to A5), which is rare in mélodie.

Analysis

Puisque j'ai mis ma lèvre

Puisque j'ai mis ma lèvre à ta coupe encor pleine;
Puisque j'ai dans tes mains posé mon front pâli;
Puisque j'ai respiré parfois la douce haleine
De ton âme, parfum dans l'ombre enseveli;

Puisqu'il me fut donné de t'entendre me dire
Les mots où se répand le cœur mystérieux;
Puisque j'ai vu pleurer, puisque j'ai vu sourire
Ta bouche sur ma bouche et tes yeux sur mes yeux;

Puisque j'ai vu briller sur ma tête ravie
Un rayon de ton astre hélas! voilé toujours;
Puisque j'ai vu tomber dans l'onde de ma vie
Une feuille de rose arrachée à tes jours;

Je puis maintenant dire aux rapides années:
—Passez! passez toujours! je n'ai plus à vieillir!
Allez-vous-en avec vos fleurs toutes fanées;
J'ai dans l'âme une fleur que nul ne peut cueillir!

Votre aile en le heurtant ne fera rien répandre
Du vase où je m'abreuve et que j'ai bien rempli.
Mon âme a plus de feu que vous n'avez de cendre!
Mon cœur a plus d'amour que vous n'avez d'oubli!

Since I have placed my lip

Since I have put my lip upon your still
[brimming cup;
Since I have rested my pale brow in your hands;
Since I at times have inhaled the sweet breath
Of your soul, a fragrance buried in the
[shadow;

Since I have been blessed to hear you say
The words wherein love's mystery is abundant;
Since I have seen you cry, since I have seen you
[smile
With your mouth upon mine and your eyes in my
[eyes;

Since I have seen, on my delighted head, shine
A ray of your star, alas so often veiled;
Since I have seen, in the flow of my life, fall
One rose-leaf snatched from your days;

I may now tell the swift years:
"—Pass by! Pass forever! I will not age!
Take all your withered flowers and go;
Within my soul there is a flower none can steal!

Your wings brushing the jar I've filled to the brim
Will spill nothing from it.
My soul has more flame than you have ashes!
My heart has more love than you have
[forgetfulness!"

I make reference to the version in C major, for a tenor (or soprano); if neither of the two published keys is suitable for a medium voice, the performer can transpose the mélodie into A major, which will preserve the freshness of the writing. A lower key would change the atmosphere. After seven measures of piano solo, the singer performs a long phrase that incorporates the first two lines, then another, which, similarly, corresponds to the two lines that follow. Note Fauré's tiny coquetry: he adds a syllable to the first line by writing a distinct note for the "-vre" of "lèvre," as well as for the end of the eighth line, with the "-che" of the second "bouche" (Example 15.4). The treatment of the silent *e* is an eternal problem for French composers!

Example 15.4 Fauré, Gabriel: *Puisque j'ai mis ma lèvre*. From *Mélodies et duos, volume I—Premières mélodies*, Editions J. Hamelle, 2010 (ref. HA 9 729), page 20, mm. 36–38.

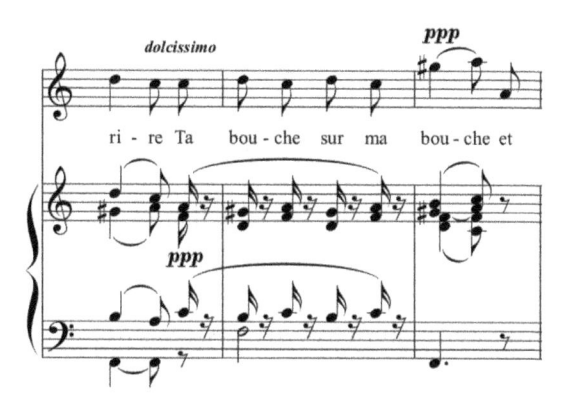

The dynamic is *piano* for the voice and the accompaniment, and, the higher the tessitura goes, the more important it becomes to sing softly (in the phrase that ascends to A, on "Puis**que** j'ai respiré," Fauré writes *pp*!), thus indicating that the voice should be extremely flexible. The accompaniment suggests a sort of guitar and is similar to a later mélodie, on another poem by Victor Hugo, *Rêve d'amour*. The part in minor doesn't include any indications of increased intensity, and the words and the minor key largely suffice to change the emotional temperature. Only an *animato* emphasizes the ecstasy in the fourth quatrain of "Je puis maintenant dire." The passage concludes on a *rallentando* ("fleur que nul ne peut cueillir!"), which leads to the *a tempo* in the last verse, where the ascent on *pp* to the A5—which includes a diphthong on "amou-our"—is accompanied by an expressive *rallentando* that, this time, continues until the last note in the piano part (Example 15.5).

Example 15.5 Fauré, Gabriel: *Puisque j'ai mis ma lèvre*. From *Mélodies et duos, volume I—Premières mélodies*, Editions J. Hamelle, 2010 (ref. HA 9 729), page 23, mm. 88–92.

Tristesse d'Olympio (ca. 1865)

Music by Gabriel Fauré (1845–1924)
Poem by Victor Hugo (1802–1885)

Presentation

Like the preceding mélodie, this one remained unpublished for a long time. It is now published in the Hamelle and Peters editions previously cited. It dates from around 1865.

I have already spoken lengthily about this work by Fauré—a prime example, to my way of thinking, of Fauré's first explorations of poetry. He makes a drastic reduction of the original text: of the thirty-eight sestinas of this poem, from the collection *Les rayons et les ombres* (1837), he sets only six (numbers 1, 8, 9, 10, 31 and 32) to music. These sestinas are divided into two distinct musical parts: the two first sestinas, set in a ternary rhythm marked *grave* (slow and serious), are treated like a sort of slow march; they are similar in character to a German lied like Schubert's *Der Wanderer*, which depicts wandering. The second part (in cut time) is tormented in nature: it seems to owe much more to Gounod's romantic songs (see, for example, the 1868 mélodie *Le départ*—written three years after this one—on a poem by Émile Augier). The manuscript copy, housed in the Music Department of the Bibliothèque nationale de France, is not written in Fauré's hand. It bears the dedication "*À mon ami Adam Laussel.*" Laussel (1845–1893), affectionately nicknamed "Gaston," was a close friend of Fauré and a colleague in Louis Dietsch's composition class at the École Niedermeyer. Perhaps Laussel wrote this copy.

Analysis

Tristesse d'Olympio

The sadness of Olympio

Les champs n'étaient point noirs, les cieux n'étaient [pas mornes;	The fields were not black, the sky not bleak; No: daylight shone in boundless azure
Non, le jour rayonnait dans un azur sans bornes Sur la terre étendu,	Over the earth,
L'air était plein d'encens et les prés de verdures	The air was filled with incense, and the meadows [were green
Quand il revit ces lieux où par tant de blessures Son cœur s'est répandu!	When he saw those places again where through [so many wounds His heart poured forth!
....	....
Hélas! se rappelant ses douces aventures,	Alas! Remembering his sweet adventures,
Regardant, sans entrer, par-dessus les clôtures, Ainsi qu'un paria,	Gazing over the fences from afar, Like an outcast,
Il erra tout le jour. Vers* l'heure où la nuit tombe,	

Il se sentit le cœur triste comme une tombe,
   Alors il s'écria:
   * Fauré writes "À l'heure"

—O* douleur! j'ai voulu, moi† dont l'âme est
                              [troublée,
Savoir si l'urne encor conservait la liqueur,
Et voir ce qu'avait fait cette heureuse vallée
De tout ce que j'avais laissé là de mon cœur!‡
   * Fauré writes "Ô"
   † Fauré adds a coma after "moi"
   ‡ Sung twice in Fauré

"Que peu de temps suffit pour changer toutes
                              [choses!
Nature au front serein, comme vous oubliez!
Et comme vous brisez dans vos métamorphoses
Les fils mystérieux où nos cœurs sont liés!
. . . .

"Eh bien! oubliez-nous, maison, jardin, ombrages!
Herbe, use notre seuil! ronce, cache* nos pas!
Chantez, oiseaux! ruisseaux, coulez! croissez,
                              [feuillages!
Ceux que vous oubliez ne vous oublieront pas.†
   *Fauré writes the plural "ronces" and "cachez"
   † Sung twice in Fauré

"Car vous êtes pour nous l'ombre de l'amour même!
Vous êtes l'oasis qu'on rencontre en chemin!
Vous êtes, ô vallon, la retraite suprême
Où nous avons pleuré nous tenant par la main!
. . . .["]

He wandered the whole day. Around nightfall
His heart felt heavy as a stone,
   Then he cried out:

"O pain! I wanted, with my troubled soul,
To know whether the urn still held the liquor,
And to see what this happy vale had made
With whatever was left behind of my heart!

"How little it takes for everything to change!
Nature of the unspoilt brow, how you forget!
And how you and your metamorphoses will
                              [sever
The mysterious threads whereby our hearts are
                              [bound!
. . . .

"Lo! Let house, garden and shade forget us!
Let the grass wear our doorstep! Bramble, hide
                              [our footsteps!
Let the birds sing! Let the brooks run! Let the
                              [boughs grow!
By those they forget, they will not be forgotten.

"For us you are the shadow of very love!
You are the oasis one meets on the way!
You are, o vale, the dearest shelter
Where we cried and held hands!
. . . .["]

This highly romantic poem, which speaks of memory and forgetting, is rendered relatively dark by the key chosen by Fauré: E minor.[2] Written in a central tessitura (D4 to E5), it suits all voice types, and it doesn't have to be artificially darkened. The accompaniment in the descriptive first part is very simple and sometimes doubles the vocal line (e.g., measure 7) (Example 15.6).

It is only at the moment when the heart "s'est répandu" that a fluid accompaniment appears, dividing the measure in two (Example 15.7).

In this narrative section, for which the manuscript contains no dynamic markings indicating the level of intensity (I would recommend a dynamic of *mezzo-piano*), the flow of the vocal line is very calm, and the enunciation and assonances ("**Sur** la

[2] The "high voice" volume of the Peters Edition (2015) offers a transposition up a step, in F♯ major.

Example 15.6 Fauré, Gabriel: *Tristesse d'Olympio.* From *Mélodies et duos, volume I—Premières mélodies*, Editions J. Hamelle, 2010 (ref. HA 9 729), page 24, mm. 1–7.

Example 15.7 Fauré, Gabriel: *Tristesse d'Olympio.* From *Mélodies et duos, volume I—Premières mélodies*, Editions J. Hamelle, 2010 (ref. HA 9 729), page 25, mm. 17–20.

terre étendu," ". . . paria, Il erra . . . il s'écria," etc.) should be carefully attended to. It's when the poet addresses himself to Nature that it becomes more difficult to find a good balance between diction and melodic phrasing. To do so, the tempo marking *Allegro non troppo* is essential. A tempo of 88 or 92 to the half note seems right to me, for the phrasing—very instrumental—should really encompass two verses at a time. For intensity, the dynamic can be raised to *mezzo-forte*, but no more. It's through beautiful phrasing, shaped by well-understood enunciation and calm, measured breathing—which will avoid choppiness and/or panting in the impassioned text—that the performer will render justice to this little-known work. It is imperative not to insert *rubatos* or *rallentandos*—especially at the ending, which should conclude abruptly, as if the farewell to the happy past were definitive.

Cygne sur l'eau (1919)

Music by Gabriel Fauré (1845–1924)
Poem by Baroness Antoine de Brimont (1880–1943)

Presentation

We previously discussed three early mélodies by Fauré; here, we introduce Fauré in his late maturity. The cycle MIRAGES, op. 113, which consists of four songs, dates from 1919. The whole cycle deserves to be sung: it is fascinating, but rarely performed. Let us hope that our discussion of one of the poems will inspire the reader to look into the other three.

The Baroness Antoine de Brimont (following the custom of the period of identifying a woman by her husband's name) was born Renée de la Bonninière de Beaumont. She came from an impressive lineage: she was the great-niece of Lamartine, and was related to the famous Boniface "Boni" de Castellane, and therefore has ties to the Proustian circle. Proust knew her personally, as attested to by their correspondence. She was a highly erudite woman who, among her other accomplishments, translated Rabindranath Tagore into French.

Her collection of poems *Mirages* also dates from 1919. Fauré set the cycle to music the same year as its publication, by Émile-Paul Frères. Hard copies of the book are extremely difficult to find, as the volume was published in only a limited edition of five hundred numbered copies, with beautiful illustrations by Georges Barbier, one of the great artist-engravers of the period. It has been made available online through the Universities of Toronto and Ottawa, Canada (https://archive.org/details/miragespomes00brim).

The title of the mélodie is the same as that of the poem, *Cygne sur l'eau*, but Fauré set to music only five of its nine verses, numbers 1, 3, 4, 5 and 6. Here are the four quatrains not set by Fauré:

Il glisse … et lentement se déroule, s'allonge,	He glides … and slowly his collar unfolds, [lengthens,
son col, tel un serpent vaguement balancé,	like a snake vaguely cradled,
et son aile luisante est la conque où le songe	and his glossy wing is the conch where the [dream
repose avec l'oubli, la paix et le passé.	lies with oblivion, peace, and the past.
. . . .	. . . .
"En cette heure où les voix se taisent une à une,	
où le silence tisse un fabuleux réseau,	

demeurez, chaste amant fidèle de la lune,	"At this hour when voices stop one after the [other,
oui, demeurez captif des reflets et des eaux;	where silence weaves a fabulous net,
	stay, chaste and trustful lover of the moon,
votre sillage meurt en gouttes de lumière,	yes, stay captive of reflections and waters;
parmi les nénuphars et les presles tremblants...	
Que votre nostalgie ait une grâce fière,	your aftermath dies in drops of light,
Et votre solitude un grand air nonchalant!"	among water lilies and trembling [horsetails...
	May your longing look gracefully proud,
Et sur l'onde sans fond du rêve, du mirage,	and your loneliness a nonchalant air!"
de l'écho, du brouillard, de l'ombre, de la nuit,	
ma pensée est un cygne harmonieux et sage	And on the fathomless waters of dreams and [delusion,
qui glisse lentement aux rivages d'ennui.	of echo, of mist, of shadow, of night,
	my mind is a gentle, harmonious swan
	gliding slowly along the shores of ennui.

I think that Fauré found the swan too "personalized," too anthropomorphic, in these last quatrains, and that he preferred to leave them out, even if it meant losing, as a result, the cyclic style of the poem, whose first and last two lines are absolutely identical.

This poem is the first in the Baroness de Brimont's collections, with the exception of a sort of introduction, also in the form of a poem, entitled *Méditation au miroir*—Meditation to a mirror—where the narrator explains that they are going to speak in the subsequent pages of a person through natural imagery. This introduction has a post-Romantic feeling about it, where Nature only echoes what is being lived through at any given moment, but sends back the image (the mirage?) of someone—or of a feeling—that has disappeared.

The song cycle MIRAGES (eponymous with the Baroness de Brimont's collection) is relatively short, at around twelve minutes in length. It comprises four mélodies. The first three—*Cygne sur l'eau, Reflets dans l'eau*, and *Jardin nocturne*—are taken from the first part of the collection, *De l'eau et des paysages*, and the fourth, *Danseuses*, comes from the second part, *Des songes et des paroles. Cygne sur l'eau* lasts around three minutes, depending on the *tempo* chosen by the performers. Fauré writes *Andantino*, with a metronome marking of 66 to the quarter note. Let me here interject a word about Fauré's metronome markings: most of his mélodies—and especially those in Volume II— are performed too slowly, even though Fauré wanted to avoid performances that were too languid. The printed metronome mark should be used as a kind of correction to instinct. I always advise singers and pianists to begin with a spontaneous first reading, to see what comes naturally. Then, do a strictly metronomic reading, to see what Fauré's tempo marking *does not* allow. The tempo marking is never perfectly exact, but it is fundamental—contrary to what many say—in order to have an inkling of what each line presents and what must be avoided.

The published key is F major: there is no other version. The tessitura is extremely narrow, extending only from C4 to E♭5.

Analysis

Cygne sur l'eau	*Swan on the Water*

Ma pensée est un cygne harmonieux et sage
qui glisse lentement aux rivages d'ennui
sur les ondes sans fond du rêve, du mirage,
de l'écho, du brouillard, de l'ombre, de la nuit.

My mind is a gentle, harmonious swan
gliding slowly along the shores of ennui
on the fathomless waters of dreams and delusion,
of echo, of mist, of shadow, of night.

·   ·

Il glisse, roi hautain fendant un libre espace,
poursuit un reflet vain, précieux et changeant,
et les roseaux nombreux s'inclinent lorsqu'il passe*,
sombre et muet, au seuil d'une lune d'argent;
   * Fauré writes "quand il passe"

He glides, a haughty monarch cleaving a path,
pursuing a vain reflection, precious and fleeting,
and the countless reeds bow as he passes,
dark and silent, before a silver moon;

et des blancs nénuphars chaque corolle ronde
tour à tour a fleuri de désir ou* d'espoir . . .
Mais plus avant toujours, sur la brume et sur l'onde,
vers l'inconnu fuyant glisse le cygne noir.
   * Fauré writes "et"

and each round corolla of the white water-lilies
has blossomed by turn with desire or hope . . .
But ever forward on the mists and the waves,
the black swan glides toward the receding
                    [unknown.

Or j'ai dit: "Renoncez, beau cygne chimérique,
à ce voyage lent vers de troubles destins;
nul miracle chinois, nulle étrange Amérique
ne vous accueilleront en des havres certains;

And I said: "Renounce, beautiful chimera of a
                    [swan,
this slow voyage to troubled destinies;
no Chinese miracle, no exotic America
will welcome you in safe havens;

les golfes embaumés, les îles immortelles
ont pour vous, cygne* noir, des récifs périlleux;
demeurez sur les lacs où se mirent, fidèles,
ces nuages, ces fleurs, ces astres et ces yeux."†
   * Fauré writes "Cygne" with a capital
   † End quotation marks are added by Fauré

The scented gulfs, the immortal isles
await you, black swan, with their perilous reefs;
remain on the lakes, which faithfully reflect
these clouds, these flowers, these stars, and these
                    [eyes.

·   ·

Fauré began to lose his hearing in 1898; by 1905, when he assumed directorship of the Paris Conservatoire, his deafness had advanced considerably. These physical and psychological hardships didn't diminish his capacities as a composer, since he could hear internally what he wrote, but this sensory constraint certainly had an impact on his style, which, after 1908, featured extreme economy of means and pared-down textures. Running parallel with the evolution of this new style was Fauré's desire to modernize the curriculum for singers at the Conservatoire. Among the reforms instituted by the composer were the requirements to study song repertoire and vocal declamation. Fauré's curricular preoccupations were consistent with the aesthetic values that permeate the style of his late vocal works, a style that requires an ascetic sobriety. Like all of the cycle MIRAGES from which it derives, *Cygne sur l'eau* perfectly reflects this late-period style.[3] It requires the singer to maintain an exemplary level of declamation; the supporting piano part should be concise, but firmly in the background.

Unlike what we saw in *L'absent*, in *Cygne sur l'eau* there is no true setting the poem to music line by line. (It also bears noting that, unlike in the classical poetic tradition, not every line begins with a capital letter.) This is a much more discursive composition. First, Fauré includes the first verse in its entirety, which creates some problems for the singer, since, between "Ma pensée" and "de la nuit," there are no rests and there is no rest! The parts of the text are separated only by commas, and, for once, we should consider these as punctuations for the vocal line as well—otherwise, it would be necessary to put breaks in the accompaniment to accommodate the singer's need to breathe. For example, there are no rests in the voice part in the first line of the poem, but, in the piano part, which doubles the voice, there is a slur that stops on the F (measure 4, beat 2). The singer could thus breathe after the slurred G-F of "sa-ge" (measure 4) and, similarly, after "d'ennui" (measure 7) (Example 15.8).

In any case, it's important not to reconstruct the line too much, since doing so is clearly not what Fauré would have wanted. Creating a sense of musical fluidity relates to the movement of the swan on the water, movement that is guessed at but not seen. In essence, the ideal would be not to breathe (!), but since breathing is necessary, it is necessary to be very careful not to rhythmicize the short note values or make them even shorter.

In terms of dynamics, Fauré gives no markings for the voice at the beginning but writes a *piano* in the accompaniment. So there's no need to give too much voice, especially since the *crescendo* that precedes the *decrescendo* in the second line happens almost by itself: the voice goes higher in the tessitura, then comes back down. I find it much more interesting to work with a medium amount of voice, which will facilitate the representation of the mirror effect and the seemly motionless gliding of the swan on the water.

---

[3] Katherine Bergeron, in her remarkable book, *Voice Lessons: French Mélodie in the Belle Époque* (New York: Oxford University Press, 2010), writes at length about Fauré's late style; she devotes an entire chapter (pages 320–327) to *Cygne sur l'eau*.

Example 15.8 Fauré, Gabriel: *Cygne sur l'eau.* From *Mirages,* Editions Durand & Cie, 1919 (ref. D. & F. 9809[1]), page 1, mm. 1–7.

The second verse offers a change of texture in the accompaniment, which, for the next twenty-two measures (measure 13–35) will feature *tremolando* sixteenth notes. The sixteenth notes should neither be rhythmicized nor rushed. This section can serve as a baseline to determine the *tempo* for the entire mélodie.

With "Il glisse, roi hautain," a separation must be made between "roi" and "hautain," with a well-detached "hau-." A breath can be taken at every available opportunity, but the full note values must nonetheless be maintained, like on "précieux" (measure 18) (Example 15.9).

I would further suggest making maximum use of liaisons, such as "précieux et changeant" [presijøzeʃãʒã], to emphasize the *legato* and the effect of gliding. One of the problems often encountered in Fauré is that if a breath is taken during a *crescendo* (something that the writing seems to invite), it chops up the progression, and so the singer has to start again more loudly. This difficulty appears in the phrase "Et les roseaux nombreux s'inclinent quand il passe, sombre et muet, au seuil d'une lune d'argent." I think that it would be better to breath after "passe" rather than somewhere between "sombre" and "argent." Moreover, there is a comma after "passe," and connecting "passe" and "sombre" is difficult, taking the alliteration into account. I just want to point out that in the original poem, the text is "lorsqu'il passe" and not "quand il passe." The reason for the change is a mystery: was Fauré trying to facilitate the vocal line? Impossible to know . . .

The third quatrain, which evokes the blossoming of "hope and desire," is set to a rising octatonic scale (C-D♭-D♯/E♭-E♮-F♯-G-A-B♭) that begins in the piano and is

Example 15.9 Fauré, Gabriel: *Cygne sur l'eau*. From *Mirages,* Editions Durand & Cie, 1919 (ref. D. & F. 9809[1]), page 2, mm.15–18.

joined at "et des blancs" by the vocal line. The last line reaches the summit of the tessitura, with the E♭5 on "vers l'inconnu" (Example 15.10).

Example 15.10 Fauré, Gabriel: *Cygne sur l'eau*. From *Mirages,* Editions Durand & Cie, 1919 (ref. D. & F. 9809[1]), page 3, mm. 30–32.

This E♭ is not sung *forte*, but *mezzo-forte*, even though it is preceded by a *crescendo*. I would advise breathing after "fuyant," to make it clear it is the unknown that is fleeing, not the swan! Finally, be careful not to further darken the "cygne noir": the text alone suffices to make the point.

After "cygne noir," the fourth verse begins with the word "Or" (translated here as "And"), which suggests that the poet is lost in her own thoughts, talking to herself. It is important to give the impression of singing to oneself, but it must be done without overemphasis. It should sound like a personal reflection.

The *staccatos* within the slurs that appear next in the accompaniment should not "contaminate" the voice with a pointillistic sound. On the contrary, I advise the pianist to connect everything well, so that the image of the swan will always be present. The only interesting breaths are to be found in the third verse, where two hemistiches begin with "nul," accompanied by an interesting change of rhythm (Example 15.11).

Example 15.11. Fauré, Gabriel: *Cygne sur l'eau*. From *Mirages*, Editions Durand & Cie, 1919 (ref. D. & F. 9809[1]), page 4, mm. 41–43.

To bring them out, the singer can either re-accentuate or cut the phrase before each hemistich. On the other hand, absolutely no cut should be made after "Amérique," as there is an immediate connection with the next line, both in terms of syntax and meaning.

With the fifth verse, a new, calmer undulating pattern gradually takes over the right hand of the accompaniment. On "les golfes embaumés, les îles immortelles," the piano parallels the rhythmic patterns in the voice (Example 15.12).

Example 15.12 Fauré, Gabriel: *Cygne sur l'eau*. From *Mirages*, Editions Durand & Cie, 1919 (ref. D. & F. 9809[1]), page 4, mm. 46–47.

A short *luftpause*—but not a breath—can be inserted between the two hemistiches. It bears mention that the beginning of the verse is modeled musically—but not rhythmically—on the first phrase of the mélodie. I find it interesting to use the same procedure: breathe as little as possible while making all the liaisons—for example, between "îles" and "immortelles," and between "immortelles" and "ont" (this is an audacious enjambment! Only an option . . .). The phrase is easy to sing: it's just a question of the amount of vocal expenditure. It's somewhat equivalent to *parlar cantando*[4]—imitating speech through song—that is often found in Debussy, but with less harmonic support. Fauré's accompaniments are even more pared down, but the singer and pianist have to find just the right vocal/instrumental balance and timbre in order to obtain a slightly more intensified declamation. The singer has to be careful, however, not to end up with an overblown declamation.

For the last two lines, I suggest taking a breath in the following places: "Demeurez sur les lacs" (breath) "où se mirent" (a very discreet *luftpause*), "fidèles" (an optional breath), and "Ces nuages, ces fleurs, ces astres [breath] et ces yeux"; the singer can try to insert a *luftpause* before each of the "ces," but the most important thing is not to get too soft too soon. On "fidèles," the singer has arrived at a dynamic of *mezzo-forte*, the only relatively important dynamic marking for the voice in the entire score, and this *mezzo-forte* should be maintained: no *diminuendo* should take place until after "ces astres."

Here, too, if possible, the performers should continue to function as "mirrors," to render homage to the "pensée calme" (calm thought). The white swan[5] is a symbol of purity and enigma; it is a bird that doesn't fly but advances, by gliding silently on the water (according to tradition, it sings only when it's getting ready to die). In Fauré's setting of the Baroness de Brimont's poem, there is no underlying irony, as there is in the mélodie *Le cygne* in the HISTOIRES NATURELLES by Jules Renard and Maurice Ravel. The singer must remain serious in order to best serve the poet's beautiful lines.

---

[4] Between 1300 and 1600, the Italian poetic treatises referred to *parlar cantando*, literally "speaking through singing," or *stile recitativo rappresentativo*, a specific practice of sung declamation, which flourished in opera—a new genre—at the beginning of the sixteenth century during the period of the Florentine Camerata. The practice of adapting singing to the inflections of ordinary speech is especially associated with Claudio Monteverdi.

[5] The black swan is rare; according to tradition, it has either hidden its whiteness or was condemned to lose it.

16

Charles Gounod

Ô ma belle rebelle (1850)

Music by Charles Gounod (1818–1893)
Poem by Jean-Antoine de Baïf (1532–1589)

Brandus published this mélodie, dated March 20, 1850 on the manuscript, in 1855. It is the second of a collection of six mélodies, subsequently included in the first volume of *Twenty Songs* by Gounod, published by Brandus in 1867 (three more volumes would follow). Today, this mélodie can be found in many editions, even in Japanese publications. It is interesting first of all because it is written on a sixteenth-century poem, by Jean Antoine de Baïf. In his choices of poetry Gounod was highly eclectic; as such, he was the precursor of many composers of mélodies. He set to music the poems of his contemporaries (Émile Augier, Jules Barbier), as well as those of earlier poets: in addition to Baïf, he also set the works of Jean Passerat and Ronsard, all three of whom date from the sixteenth century. Obviously, Gounod liked to poke around everywhere—as Ravel would do—to multiply his sources of inspiration.

The original key, for high voice, is G minor. For medium voice, F minor was the key chosen: it's a very pretty key—a little bit unexpected, as four flats is less "medieval" than G minor; it's more discreet and more modern.

This is a strophic song, which thus invites (as I already said with regard to Berlioz) a relationship with a lied of, let us say, Mendelssohn: it is inspired by popular song, and, while it should be sung simply, its colors should be varied in accordance with the verse and the sentiments therein.

As is always the case with mélodies based on early texts, the performers also have to think about the dances that might have inspired the music—and not necessarily dances from Baïf's time. Moreover, in Gounod's case, the connection between music and dance is clearly identifiable: it could be marches, or sarabandes, or pavanes—often slow dances. Each accent, each upbeat must be considered: each of these little details signals the preparation of a dance step or a bow. Obviously, today, anyone who had studied early or Baroque music would automatically think of these matters.

Ô ma belle rebelle is three minutes long, a typical length for this kind of song.

Le Chant Intime. François Le Roux and Romain Raynaldy, Oxford University Press. © Oxford University Press 2021.
DOI: 10.1093/oso/9780190884178.003.0017

Analysis

Ô ma belle rebelle	*O my rebellious belle*

Ô ma belle rebelle,	O my rebellious belle,
Las! que tu m'es cruelle,	Alas! How cruel you are,
Ou quand d'un doux souris	When with a sweet smile
Larron de mes esprits,	You steal my soul,
Ou quand d'une parole	Or with a soft
Mignardètement molle,	Seductive word,
Ou quand d'un regard d'yeux	Or with a proud
Fièrement gracieux,	And winning glance,
Ou quand d'un petit geste	Or with a little gesture,
Tout divin tout céleste	So heavenly and divine,
En amoureuse ardeur	Into ardent rapture
Tu plonges tout mon cœur	You plunge my heart.
(bis)	(repeat)

Ô ma belle rebelle,	O my rebellious belle,
Las! que tu m'es cruelle,	Alas! How cruel you are,
Quand la cuisante ardeur	When the burning desire
Qui me brûle le cœur	That consumes my heart
Fait que je te demande	Compels me to beg you
À sa brûlure grande	A single kiss
Un rafraîchissement	To quench
D'un baiser seulement.	Its conflagration.
Ô ma belle rebelle!	O my rebellious belle,
Las! que tu m'es cruelle,	Alas! How cruel you are,
Quand d'un petit baiser	When with a little kiss
Tu ne veux m'apaiser	You will not soothe me.
(bis)	(repeat)

Me puissé-je un jour, dure!	May I one day, O callous one!
Venger de ton injure,	Return the harm you caused me,
Mon petit maître Amour	May my little master, Cupid,
Te puisse outrer un jour	Pierce your heart one day,
Et pour moi langoureuse	And make you
Il te fasse amoureuse,	Pine for me,
Comme il m'a langoureux	As he made me pine
Pour toi fait amoureux.	With love for you.
Alors par ma vengeance	By my revenge
Tu auras connaissance,	You then shall know
Quel mal fait du baiser	The harm you cause
Un amant refuser	In refusing a lover a kiss.
(bis)	(repeat)

Ô ma belle rebelle consists of three strophes—one might almost say three couplets—all treated in identical fashion, with no variation. The guiding principle is to phrase the music as if it were being played on an instrument such as a violin, viola, or viola da gamba. The performers have to find the right way to articulate accordingly—without, however, getting stuck in the redundancy of the rhythm, which is almost always the same throughout. This mélodie makes me think of a succession of three increasingly large loops, each one interlocking with the others, like the variations of amorous seduction.

The first couplet describes the "cruelty" of a woman, whose manner of comporting herself has plunged the heart of the narrator into "amoureuse ardeur." The second couplet sees the narrator begging for "the refreshment of a kiss" to soothe his pain, while the third couplet speaks of blackmail and the menace of vengeance—all of which is recounted in a light manner.

As for the accompaniment, the piano should not sound as it were imitating another instrument like a spinet or a harpsichord. Even the relationship to the lute is not pertinent, for the left hand plays a countermelody, a rhythmic variation of the first phrase of the voice.

Right from the start we can see Gounod's remarkable work as a prosodist, who gives to the line *Ô ma belle rebelle* a rhythm modeled on the spoken phrase. If we dutifully follow the musical line, we see that there are no rests—and thus, no time to breathe—between the first line and "Fièrement gracieux." So we have to return to the text, and in particular the scansions created by the "Ou" 's, which result, poetically speaking, in the pushing of the meaning of the phrase to the end of the verse. And Gounod, to better emphasize the importance of the two last lines of each verse, repeats them—a very classical procedure.

A small point, but an important one: the "Las!" of the second line should be pronounced [lɑ] and not [lɑs], so that the connection with "que" will not sound like an awful-sounding, non-existent word: "lasque" [lɑskə].

Vocally speaking, there are no real difficulties. The mélodie is beautifully written for the voice, as is always the case with Gounod. Be careful of the inverted mordent at the end of each verse, on "tout" (verse 1), "m'apaiser" (verse 2), and "refuser" (verse 3), the kind of Italianate details of which Gounod is so fond (Example 16.1). Also of importance: there is a delicate change in rhythm between the repeated lines. In a certain way, Gounod has displaced the durations by equalizing them, like on "am**ou**re**u**se ardeur, / Tu plonges **tout** mon cœur" (Example 16.2).

It's apparently these lines that inspired him to make the changes: he uses long and relatively deeply placed vowels in order to allow the voice to be placed for a longer time. Therefore, the singer must, at all costs, avoid making accents or attacks, so that these light pauses don't create sighs or swoons. Certain singers often remark that "cruelle" is one of the most difficult words to pronounce when the *r*'s are not rolled, because the [k] sound creates a glottal attack. To manage it, the singer must avoid glottalizing the *r* and sing it as discreetly as if lightly rolling the consonant.

Example 16.1 Gounod, Charles: *Ô ma belle rebelle*. From *Vingt mélodies*, Editions Choudens, 1874 (ref.: A.C. 1803). Triple example: page 27, mm. 33–35; page 29, mm. 65–67; page 31, mm. 102–105.

Example 16.2 Gounod, Charles: *Ô ma belle rebelle*. From *Vingt mélodies*, Editions Choudens, 1874 (ref.: A.C. 1803), page 27, mm. 31–33.

Another rule that I must repeat over and over: be very attentive to the upbeats. Thus, [omabɛlørebɛlø] is forbidden. Of course "-le" and "re-" have the same rhythmic value (two eighth notes), but they don't have the same weight: "re-" falls on the upbeat of "rebelle," while "-le" is only the flexional ending of "belle," that is, a silent *e*, which should always sound like a schwa [ə].

In the same vein, pay close attention when there are very different vowels in the same spot in each of the three verses—like, for example, each third syllable of the fifth lines: "Ou quand d'**une** parole," "Fais que **je** te demande," "Et pour **moi** langoureuse." With a sound going from [y] to [e], two round sounds, it's important not to explode onto [wa], a sound that is certainly open, but upon which Gounod has placed no accent.

Generally speaking, in the third verse, rich in open vowels, be careful not to push the voice too much and to listen carefully in order to maintain vocal control. This mélodie is an excellent exercise in creating "homogenous" phrasing.

Ma belle amie est morte (Lamento) (1872)

Music by Charles Gounod (1818–1893)
Poem by Théophile Gautier (1811–1872)

Presentation

Gounod had already set this poem to music in 1841, under the title *Lamento, la chanson du pêcheur*, which was only published, posthumously, in 1895, by Choudens. The version about which we are speaking here dates from 1872, the year of Gautier's death; it was published by Henry Lemoine in 1877. Curiously, the first known mélodie by Gounod, written in 1839, is also based on Théophile Gautier's poetry: it is titled *Où voulez-vous aller?* and, like this *Lamento*, is one of the poems set to music by Berlioz in LES NUITS D'ÉTÉ. As far as I know, apart from these three mélodies, all chronologically distant from one another, Gounod set only one other poem by Gautier: *Premier sourire du printemps*, written sometime between 1852 and 1858 and entitled *Primavera* by Gounod. *Où voulez-vous aller?* is a lovely, cheerful romance; *Primavera* is more complex. The *Lamento* that we will explore is neither a romance nor joyful. By virtue of its later date of composition, as well as its style and the reduction of the poetic text, it is more closely related, in affect and in spirit, to Fauré—or to Duparc, who wrote another *Lamento* (incipit: "Connaissez-vous la blanche tombe")—than to Berlioz.

Analysis

Ma belle amie est morte	*My dearest love is dead*
Ma belle amie est morte:	My dearest love is dead;
Je pleurerai toujours;	I shall weep for evermore;
Sous la tombe elle emporte	To the tomb she takes with her
Mon âme et mes amours.*†	My soul and all my love.
Ah! comme elle était belle	Ah! how beautiful she was
Et comme je l'aimais!	And how I loved her!
Je n'aimerai jamais	I shall never love a woman
Une femme autant qu'elle.	As I loved her.
Que mon sort est amer! (bis)	How bitter is my fate! (repeat twice)
Ah! sans amour s'en aller sur la mer!	Alas! To set sail loveless across the sea!
Sans amour, s'en aller sur la mer!	To set sail loveless across the sea!
Ma belle amie est morte:	My dearest love is dead;
Je pleurerai toujours. (ter)	I shall weep for evermore. (repeat three times)

* Gounod writes an exclamation point
† Gounod repeats the third and fourth verses twice

This first remark is essential: in its first version (1841), Gounod set the entire text to music in strophic form (in three absolutely identical strophes). But in the version discussed here, composed in March 1872 in London, Gounod sets only about half of Gautier's poem: he retains the first four lines of the first verse, completely eliminates the second ("La blanche créature") and then retains only the last six lines of the third. In this manner, he has created something of a new poem, but has erased the element of "refrain," consisting of the last two lines ("Que mon sort est amer! / Ah! sans amour s'en aller sur la mer!") of *La chanson du pêcheur*, the subtitle of Gautier's poem. He sets music to these lines only once, in the center of the mélodie. Moreover, he repeats one time at the end of the first part the last two lines of the first "quatrain," and, to end the mélodie, he uses the first two lines of the poem, by reiterating twice "Je pleurerai toujours," which is thus heard three times.

Here is the complete poem by Gautier:

Ma belle amie est morte	*My dearest love is dead*
Ma belle amie est morte:	My dearest love is dead;
Je pleurerai toujours;	I shall weep for evermore;
Sous la tombe elle emporte	To the tomb she takes with her
Mon âme et mes amours.	My soul and all my love.
Dans le ciel, sans m'attendre,	Without waiting for me
Elle s'en retourna;	She has returned to Heaven;
L'ange qui l'emmena	The angel who took her away
Ne voulut pas me prendre.	Did not wish to take me.
Que mon sort est amer!	How bitter is my fate!
Ah! sans amour, s'en aller sur la mer!	Alas! To set sail loveless across the sea!

La blanche créature	The pure white being
Est couchée au cercueil.	Lies in her coffin.
Comme dans la nature	How everything in nature
Tout me paraît en deuil!	Seems to mourn!
La colombe oubliée	The forsaken dove
Pleure et songe à l'absent;	Weeps, dreaming of its absent mate;
Mon âme pleure et sent	My soul weeps and feels
Qu'elle est dépareillée.	Itself adrift.
Que mon sort est amer!	How bitter is my fate!
Ah! sans amour, s'en aller sur la mer!	Alas! To set sail loveless across the sea!
Sur moi la nuit immense	The immense night above me
S'étend comme un linceul;	Is spread like a shroud;
Je chante ma romance	I sing my song,
Que le ciel entend seul.	Which heaven alone can hear.
Ah! comme elle était belle	Ah! how beautiful she was
Et comme je l'aimais!	And how I loved her!
Je n'aimerai jamais	I shall never love a woman
Une femme autant qu'elle.	As I loved her.
Que mon sort est amer!	How bitter is my fate!
Ah! sans amour, s'en aller sur la mer!	Alas! To set sail loveless across the sea!

Following Mozart's practice, Gounod writes dynamic marks only for the accompaniment—but the singer should obey them as well. Written in a central tessitura, this mélodie—in E minor for the high voice and D minor for the medium/low voice—is rather similar to Fauré's famous *Les berceaux*, because of its atmosphere, its rocking barcarolle rhythm,[1] and its putative "popular" style. It is relatively lengthy, lasting longer than three minutes.

After five measures of piano solo, where the main theme is played in the right hand, the voice enters *piano*, but, beginning in the second line, begins a *crescendo* that rises to *forte* on "tombe." The [õ] vowel must be very dark in order to give the high point of the *crescendo* a truly funereal character (measure 10). The *decrescendo* that follows (measures 12–17) should not be too pronounced, since the voice goes into the low register. The two lines that follow are more tender memories than lamentations; they should be sung in a bright, warm color. Be aware of the prosody in "Je n'aimerai jamais / Une femme **aut**ant qu'elle," which unbalances the line with the addition of a foot, but allows the singer to lightly emphasize the attack on "**aut**ant." This is followed by a long *crescendo*, whose high point will occur on the *piano subito* marked in the piano part, but which should be followed by the voice as well, beginning on the second "s'en al**ler** sur la mer" (measure 29) (Example 16.3).

---

[1] The word "barcarolle" comes from the Italian *barcarola* (or *barcaruola*), which literally means "a barque that rolls." The musical rhythm creates a good sonic depiction of the boat's movement.

Example 16.3 Gounod, Charles: *Ma belle amie est morte*. Editions. H. Lemoine, 1877 (ref.: HL 7348), page 4, mm. 27–30.

After this passage, a long conclusion begins, featuring a descent by degrees. The performers should listen to—and make audible to the audience—the dissonance created by the vocal line, which "rubs" against the pedal points in the left hand of the piano on "**Ma** belle amie est mor**te**"; this lovely tension should be brought out, but without exaggeration. Don't get too soft too soon, so that the low D's of the last "Je pleurerai toujours" can be sonorous; and don't darken the sound too much, because the two [u]'s are already sung far back in the throat. Finally, one last remark: with the piano, make a *crescendo*, without exaggerating, on the last "tou**jours**," in order to keep the line moving right up until the resolution to the tonic in the lowest register of the piano (an E octave in the high version, a D octave in the medium/low version), two measures before the end.

17

Reynaldo Hahn

En sourdine (1893)

Music by Reynaldo Hahn (1874–1947)
Poem by Paul Verlaine (1844–1896)

Presentation

This mélodie, in A major, is published by Heugel. It's the fourth song (of seven) in the collection CHANSONS GRISES, on poems by Verlaine. It was published—like all the mélodies in the cycle—in only one key. Any transpositions that might be found are not by Reynaldo Hahn. I have nothing against transposed versions of single mélodies, but, when we are speaking of a cycle, as we are here, I advise the performer to respect the original keys and their order.

The seven mélodies of CHANSONS GRISES were composed in 1893, during Verlaine's lifetime. At that time Reynaldo Hahn was nineteen years old. He knew the poet, and went to visit him at the Broussais Hospital, where Verlaine, suffering from chronic drug addiction and alcoholism, was a "guest" during the last years of his life. The two exchanged several letters related to the setting of poems to music. I own one of Hahn's letters, not dated but probably written in 1893, in which the composer—who, at the time, was also setting *Fêtes galantes* (his version of the poem called *Mandoline*)—asked Verlaine, "*Should the song be called Fêtes galantes or La fête galante? Isn't [the latter] more symbolic?*" On the letter, one can see that Hahn had first written "*symboliste*," before opting for "*symbolic*." He writes as well about "*two other mélodies*" that he wanted to bring to Verlaine "*in person*"—but, alas, we don't know to which songs Hahn was referring.

The poems in CHANSONS GRISES come from different collections; in order, *Poèmes saturniens* for *Chanson d'automne*; *La bonne chanson* for *Tous deux*; the *Paysages belges* from *Romances sans paroles* for *L'allée est sans fin*; *Fêtes galantes* for *En sourdine*; *La bonne chanson* again for *Paysage triste*, and, once again, *La bonne chanson* for the mélodie of the same name, the last of the cycle. Eminently "Verlainian," this cycle is quite successful, musically speaking. Simple and strong, it almost evokes the chanson—which would not have displeased Verlaine, who was always glad to have his poetry set to music (which is not surprising, if one reads his poem *Art poétique*), even if it was by the *chansonniers* of the club Le Chat Noir.

Le Chant Intime. François Le Roux and Romain Raynaldy, Oxford University Press. © Oxford University Press 2021.
DOI: 10.1093/oso/9780190884178.003.0018

En sourdine is a magnificent mélodie. It is rather short, lasting 2 min 30 sec, and I often use it as an encore in recital. It should be performed very simply, without additional effects. With a minimum of means, Hahn has truly written a "muted" mélodie. It is completely faithful to the title and to the kind of harmony that the poem suggests. Fauré and Debussy[1] demonstrated similar fidelity to the spirit of the poem, but through completely different means. This song demonstrates, once again, that Verlaine is an inexhaustible source of inspiration.

Analysis

En sourdine	*Muted*
Calmes dans le demi-jour	Calm in the twilight
Que les branches hautes font,	Cast by lofty boughs,
Pénétrons bien notre amour	Let us steep our love
De ce silence profond.	In this deep quiet.
Fondons nos âmes, nos cœurs	Let us mingle our souls, our hearts,
Et nos sens extasiés,	And our enraptured senses
Parmi les vagues langueurs	With the hazy languor
Des pins et des arbousiers.	Of arbutus and pine.
Ferme tes yeux à demi,	Half-close your eyes,
Croise tes bras sur ton sein,	Fold your arms across your breast,
Et de ton cœur endormi	And from your heart now lulled to rest
Chasse à jamais tout dessein.	Banish forever all intent.
Laissons-nous persuader	Let us both succumb
Au souffle berceur et doux	To the gentle and lulling breeze
Qui vient à tes pieds rider	That comes to ruffle at your feet
Les ondes de gazon roux.	The waves of russet grass.
Et quand, solennel, le soir	And when, solemnly, evening
Des chênes noirs tombera,	Falls from the black oaks,
Voix de notre désespoir,	That voice of our despair,
Le rossignol chantera.	The nightingale shall sing.

The tempo is *Andantino très modéré*—but there's no metronome marking. Hahn is rather stingy with his interpretive markings. The tempo marking is the only "lead," but it suffices to give us an idea of what he wants: a long *legato* in the vocal line, sung with a minimum of vocal efforts, in a *piano* dynamic that continues through the first verse, until "ce silence profond." Despite the fact that the range of this first

---

[1] Fauré's setting of Verlaine's *En sourdine* is the second of the CINQ MÉLODIES DE VENISE, written in 1891. Debussy's setting is the first of three songs in the cycle FÊTES GALANTES I, also dating from 1891.

phrase is relatively wide—from C♯4 to B4—the singer should remain *piano* and *legato*, without bringing out anything in particular.

I must point out that the short *luftpausen*, indicated with commas, are not necessarily breath marks. The one that follows "Calmes," for example, is only there to caution the singer not to sing [mø] at the end of the word. In the same spirit, in Hahn's mélodies, the frequent *tenuto* markings mean only that the singer should lean into the note, just long enough to place it.

The piano accompaniment must be extremely regular up until "arbousiers," at the end of the second verse (measures 16–17). The only motion comes from the chromatic triplets in the left hand, and the bell-like octave leaps in the right hand (Example 17.1).

Example 17.1   Hahn, Reynaldo: *En sourdine*. From *Chansons grises*, Editions Heugel, 1893 (ref. 8240 H. et Cie. 7784 [4]), page 11, mm. 13–15.

The beginning of the second verse is even more subdued, notwithstanding the ascending line from E4 to E5 on "sens extasiés". The natural tendency would be to "let loose" a bit on the high E5, but Hahn forbids it: the verse begins *pianissimo* on "Fondons," and the marking is reiterated on "Parmi"—thus, six full measures are sung *pianissimo*. Never forget that Hahn was a good pianist *and* a good singer (a tenor) himself, and thus he anticipated all the "temptations" of the performers.

The *tenuto* marking on the C natural of "Et **nos** sens" is only there to remind the singer to make audible the chromatic alteration. It's just a style of writing, and certainly not an invitation to make too much of the *n*, as I often hear it performed. It's enough just to take a little time and to place the C natural carefully. In that passage, Hahn marks *suivez* (*colla voce*, follow the voice) in the piano part, which will allow for a slight *rubato*. On the other hand, the *tenuto* on the *a* of "extasiés" seems to indicate that Hahn wanted the [a] to be as elongated as possible.

Unlike in Debussy, the triplet on "vagues langueurs" is not for Hahn a reproduction of speech: it is simply a regular triplet, a sort of effacement of the word's rhythm. Care should be taken as well to make a good liaison between "Des pins et des arbousiers" so that it sounds like [depɛ̃zedɛ]; a stopping after "pins" will create an accent on "et," something that Hahn would not have wanted, and all the more true with the leap down the minor seventh that occurs in that passage.

The piano then begins the second theme, which the voice takes up on "Ferme tes yeux à demi." Hahn writes no slurs in the vocal part, which is accompanied only by a block chord in the accompaniment—but that doesn't mean, however, that the line should be connected. This chord is just, for Hahn, a way of inviting the performer to sing in a more supported manner. And here's something curious: two notes for one vowel! The setting of "Ferme tes yeux à demi-i" is no doubt a tender way of accompanying, with a tender gesture, the amorous request. An ascending scalar gesture in the left hand of the accompaniment leads to "Croise tes bras sur ton sein," which lightly varies the pattern; here, we find the preceding effect: "Croise tes bras sur ton sein-ein" (Example 17.2).

Example 17.2 Hahn, Reynaldo: *En sourdine.* From *Chansons grises*, Editions Heugel, 1893 (ref. 8240 H.et Cie. 7784 [4]), page 11, mm. 19–22.

The *tenuto* marking on "tes" is the same as the one that we saw earlier on "et nos sens": it's only meant to indicate the return to C♯, so there's no need to lean into the *t*. There should be a little *rubato* on "endormi" and an accent on "jamais" to emphasize the upbeat.

The sudden change to a meter of $\frac{3}{4}$ is the only rhythmic "disruption" in the score (Example 17.3).

Example 17.3 Hahn, Reynaldo: *En sourdine.* From *Chansons grises*, Editions Heugel, 1893 (ref. 8240 H.et Cie. 7784 [4]), pages 11–12, mm. 24–27.

Morever, it's a brief disruption, because the meter returns immediately to $\frac{4}{4}$. Combined with Hahn's rhythmic choice on the syllables "-mais tout des-" (from "jamais tout dessein"), this metric change marks a shortening of the flow—Hahn indicates *sans retenir* (*senza rallentando*)—in order to keep the phrase from "falling asleep." Meanwhile, underneath "dessein," the accompaniment echoes the theme from "Ferme tes yeux à demi," but without providing any particular relief, since the triplet vocal line that follows is marked *Également*. The voice doesn't take up the theme again, but does appropriate the short ascending scalar gesture previously encountered in the piano part.

The fourth verse contains a few unexpected twists: a shake-up of the *tempo* on the last beat of measure 29, incited by an "antagonistic" cross-rhythm between the voice and the piano on "Qui vient à tes pieds rider," leads to an implied pulling back of motion (Example 17.4).

Example 17.4 Hahn, Reynaldo: *En sourdine*. From *Chansons grises*, Editions Heugel, 1893 (ref. 8240 H.et Cie. 7784 [4]), page 12, mm. 29–31.

The next section, marked *Animez un peu* (*poco animato*), which also includes a brief sidestep into the mediant key of C major on "Les ondes de gazon roux," acts as a sort of "correction" that brings back the *tempo primo* and the sense of forward motion. All of this is done in two measures (30–31).

A brief piano interlude (measures 32–33) reestablishes the original key of A major. At the same time, the rhythm in the vocal line changes from that at the beginning of the mélodie, becoming appreciably more stretched out. Thus, the initial "Et" of the fifth verse enters on the fourth beat, while, in the first verse, "Calmes" entered on the third beat. Hahn again accentuates the effect of slowing down—as if he had neither wanted to divulge nor anticipate what was going to happen—by clearly separating "Et quand, solennel," and "le soir," to which he attributes longer note values. Be aware that the commas mark punctuations of the text and not breaths. Be sure as well not to make inopportune accents: the line is always *legato*.

At "Des chênes noirs tombera," Hahn marks *très doux* (very soft) and not *pianissimo*. There's no point in putting an accent on the F natural of "**désespoir**," since a *crescendo* is in progress. The *crescendo* arrives at its peak at "-poir" of "désespoir," but, as the line is written in the middle range, I suggest continuing the *crescendo* up until "rossignol," so that the *diminuendo* that follows is even clearer (Example 17.5). To facilitate the passage, I advise breathing after "désespoir" in order to connect the last two lines.

Example 17.5 Hahn, Reynaldo: *En sourdine*. From *Chansons grises*, Editions Heugel, 1893 (ref. 8240 H.et Cie. 7784 [4]), page 13, mm. 39–42.

An alternative would be to breathe between "rossignol" and "chantera," but it will take a certain skill to make the *l* of "rossignol" audible without accenting "chantera," which is very difficult. The high point of the tessitura—the F♯ of "chant**er**a-a" (once again, two notes for one vowel!)—should be sung very softly and delicately; on this F♯-E slur, be careful not to slow down, for the vocal line is continued in the piano, and it's the solo piano that ends the melody. These two notes are no doubt a very pared-down illustration of the song of the nightingale, which is emitted like a moan. This song brings to mind the famous story: the nightingale, once a bird with beautifully colored plumage, lost his colors when he understood that he would never be the lover of the stabbed dove—but he acquired his beautiful voice . . .

Au pays musulman (1906)

Music by Reynaldo Hahn (1874–1947)
Poem by Henri de Régnier (1864–1936)

Presentation

First published separately by Heugel, this mélodie is now available in the third volume published by Alphonse Leduc in 2016. This collection has brought together seventeen mélodies (including four in English), and *Au pays musulman* is the fourth of the collection. It deserves special treatment, because it is somewhat exceptional in Hahn's vocal output, in part because of its length (almost 7 min 30 sec!), in part because of its subject matter: the narrator dreams of changing his life—or meeting his death—in an Orient at once close and quite different from that in all the mélodies (by Delibes, Félicien David, and Saint-Saëns, among others) inspired by this theme of escaping industrial society. But the most significant aspect of this mélodie is its extraordinary musical treatment, by virtue of its economy of means and its refined details. Reynaldo Hahn composed this mélodie in 1906, in Constantinople, on the Golden Horn—in direct contact with the ambience! Its text is taken from a poem in Henri de Régnier's volume, *La sandale ailée* (Le Mercure de France, 1906), entitled *Le souhait* (The wish).

Analysis

Au pays musulman

In the Muslim country

Peut-être si j'avais choisi mon temps où vivre,
Eussé-je, grave et doux, vieilli sous le turban,
Et ma vie eût passé ses jours calmes à suivre
L'ombre du cyprès noir et du minaret blanc.

Maybe, had I elected my time to live,
Would I have aged severe and tender wearing a
[turban,
And my life would have spent its calm days
[following
The shade of black cypresses and of white
[minarets.

Dans la fraîche mosquée où mille fleurs
[sont peintes
Sur la faïence lisse autour du nom d'Allah,
J'aurais, les yeux levés vers les lampes éteintes,
Attendu qu'Azraël, à mon tour, m'appelât;

Inside the cool mosque, where thousands of
[flowers are painted
On the smooth tile walls around the name of
[Allah,
With eyes staring up at the extinguished lamps,
I would have waited for Azrael to call for my
[turn.

À la fontaine pure où coule une onde claire,
J'aurais lavé mes pied, mon visage et mes mains
Et prosterné mon corps au tapis de prière,
Chaque fois qu'au ciel bleu chantent les muezzins;

In the pure fountain where fresh water flows,
I would have washed my feet, my face and my
[hands
And bowed down my body on to the prayer rug
Every time the muezzins sing to the blue sky;

Et, sur la Corne d'Or par la nuit étoilée,
Mon caïque eût fendu le flot pareil aux cieux;
Et ma femme pour tous jalousement voilée,
N'eût montré qu'à moi seul les astres de ses yeux.

And, on the Golden Horn by a starry night,
My caique[2] would have split up the heaven like
[stream;
And my wife, to all others' glances jealously
[veiled,
Would have but to me showed the stars of her
[eyes.

Ainsi j'aurais vécu dans la demeure close,
Mêlant à la senteur en feu du tabac fin
Le parfum du santal et l'odeur de la rose,
Sous quelque vieux Sultan au nom sonore et saint.

Et dans le cimetière où se pressent les tombes,
Harmonieusement et du haut des cyprès,
La voix des rossignols et la voix des colombes

---

[2] A caique is a small fishing boat used in the Middle Eastern countries.

Auraient bercé*, là-bas, mon sommeil sans regrets.
  * Hahn writes "Enchanteraient"

Mais, qu'importe sa* vie à qui peut par son rêve
Disposer de l'espace et disposer du temps!†
Qu'importe, puisque j'ai, d'une illusion brève,
Satisfait pour jamais mon désir d'un instant,‡
  * Hahn writes "la vie"
  † Hahn writes "?"
  ‡ Hahn writes "!"

Et qu'à travers Stamboul et dans la verte Brousse,
J'ai ressenti l'attrait du pays musulman
Où s'allonge, le soir, sur la terre âpre et douce,
L'ombre du cyprès noir et du minaret blanc!

Thus would have I lived into my closed house,
Mixing the scent of fine burning tobacco
With the fragrance of sandalwood and the
                              [perfume of roses,
Under the rule of a Sultan whose name would be
                              [old and revered.

And in the graveyard where many tombs are
                              [gathered,
Harmoniously, from the height of cypresses,
Voices of nightingales and voices of doves
Would have enchanted, there, my slumber void
                              [of regrets.

But what life matters to the one who can through
                              [dream
Dispose of space as well as of time!
What matters, if I can, in a brief illusion,
Satisfy forever my instant desire,

And if, throughout Istanbul and in the green
                              [Bursa,
I have felt the attraction of the Muslim country,
Where, at evening time, on the rough and soft
                              [ground,
Stretches the shade of black cypresses and of
                              [white minarets!

Curiously, either Reynaldo Hahn or the editor added to the poetic text a number of commas that didn't exist in the literary edition. They are used in the song as scansions of word groups. Perhaps Hahn had seen a manuscript by the poet with the additions, given that he and Régnier were from the same "circle." But they were certainly not intended to break up the flow!

The very first marking above the first measure, *Profondément calme et contemplatif*, describes the general mood. The meter is an expansive $\frac{4}{2}$, and the piano part features a rocking dotted-half-note/quarter-note *ostinato* (with a *tenuto/staccato* marking on the quarter note) that will not change for two-and-a-half pages (Example 17.6).

The vocal line is very simple, close to the *parlar cantando* so dear to Monteverdi,[3] and allows the imagination to color the images that Régnier's poetic lines inspire. The tessitura—from C4 to G5—matches that of Hahn's tenor voice (which he never forced), but a mezzo-soprano will do just fine as well in this tessitura. (The text is obviously "masculine," but even more ostensibly

---

[3] See footnote 4 page 148 in Chapter 15, on Fauré.

Example 17.6 Hahn, Reynaldo: *Au pays musulman*. From *Mélodies—Troisième volume*, Editions Alphonse Leduc, 2016 (ref. AL 30 682), page 16, mm. 1–3.

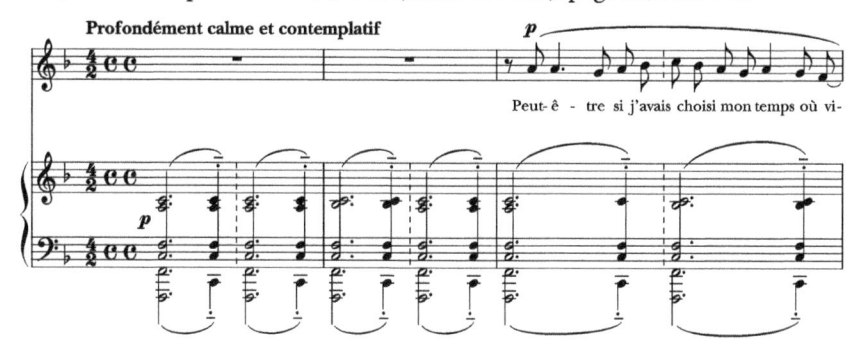

"virile" texts are often sung by women.) The key, F major, maintains its classically oratory color (like in Mozart's Masonic symbolism), but a baritone could make a transposition to E♭ major without any problem. The dynamics and performance indications on the page all suggest a contemplative atmosphere: *p*, *pp*, *simplement*, *comme un rêve* (like a dream). The entire first page—which corresponds to the first quatrain—is a magnificent exercise in creating homogeneity within a limited range (from F4 to C5) in the high middle register. The rhythm of the prosody should not be rushed, and, on this subject, the quintuplet of "et du minaret" should be imperturbably regular. The second quatrain features sophisticated prosody, with an alteration of duplets and triplets, and even an accented ornament on "où mille fleurs sont **pein**tes," as if the mosque had transformed the narrator into a muezzin.[4] These effects do not, however, imply dramatization or anguish: serenity is always present. The third quatrain ("A la fontaine") allows Hahn to use a figure that ascends by degrees—a musical rendering of purification and prostration, in which the voice rises with the soul: "J'aurais lavé mes **pieds** (E5) . . . Et prosterné mon **corps** (F5) . . . Chaque fois qu'au ciel bleu chan-**an**-tent" (G5, prepared by an accented lower neighbor). This ascent, a kind of seeking death—or heaven—leads to the quatrain that speaks of the "ultimate voyage" (in a caique), which Hahn illustrates through arpeggiated chords evoking bells or harps, before the image of the veiled woman brings back to earth (to put it euphemistically) the dreamer; it leads to the return of the initial rhythm and a pacified tessitura.

The fifth quatrain is all about smells, and filled with harmonic changes, on the regular bass F-C-F-C and, in the vocal line, small alterations of "foreign" notes (Example 17.7).

---

[4] In certain Muslim, Hebraic, and Sikh traditions, Azraël is the angel of death, the intercessor of souls. The name comes from Biblical Hebrew, and means "Helper of God." Azraël's name appears in the work of many artists, painters, and musicians.

Example 17.7 Hahn, Reynaldo: Au pays musulman. From *Mélodies—Troisième volume*, Editions Alphonse Leduc, 2016 (ref. AL 30 682), page 21, mm. 25–28.

The sixth quatrain restores to the initial calm. And then, in the seventh quatrain, the mood changes: the dynamic becomes *mezzo-forte* and the music more intense (the meter changes, too, to common time). It is imperative not to overly dramatize this passage. Be attentive to the rhythmic patterns of "et disposer du temps," which should not be bumpy, but should remain simple. The only stopping point on the dominant seventh, "mon désir d'un in**stant**," should be well supported and sung without *diminuendo* (it is a sustained whole note—and Hahn puts an exclamation point at the end, to keep the singer from going to sleep). Finally, the last quatrain, which marvelously sums up all the preceding enunciation, compels us, alas, to leave this dream by stretching out the words, accompanied by a more classic eighth-quarter-note/eighth-quarter-note pattern, to end on a contemplative *piano*. If the attention of the singer remains constant, the waking dream will be shared by all, the performers and the audience, for a moment that is truly "suspended in time"!

18

Philippe Hersant

Paroles peintes (1995)

Music by Philippe Hersant (b. 1948)
Poem by Paul Éluard (1895–1952)

Presentation

Born in Rome in 1948, Philippe Hersant won a First Prize in Composition in the class of André Jolivet at the Paris Conservatoire. He subsequently received grants to study at the Casa de Velázquez in Madrid and the Villa Medici in Rome. He is the winner of many prestigious prizes: the Prix Nadia Boulanger (1970), the Prix Enesco (1982), and the SACEM prize for the best new contemporary work (1986), for his String Quartet no. 1. He is the author of two operas as well as numerous mélodies and lieder. He received the "Composer of the Year" award in 2005, 2010, and 2016 from Victoires de la Musique Classique, the French classical-music equivalent of the Grammys.

This mélodie, an homage to the poet Paul Éluard, was commissioned in 1995 by the Festival de Saint-Denis. It is special to me, in part because it was written for my voice and because I gave its first performance—on June 13, 1995, with the pianist Noël Lee—and also because it is composed on a wonderful poem by Éluard, taken from the volume *Cours naturel* (1937). For me, it is something of an extension of Poulenc's majestic cycle, LE TRAVAIL DU PEINTRE (1957), also on poems of Éluard.

There is a second version of this work, for baritone, flute, cello, and piano, modeled on the instrumentation of the CHANSONS MADÉCASSES by Ravel. I had suggested this "orchestration" to Philippe Hersant just after the first performance of the version for voice and piano, because the relationship of the writing between the two works struck me, and also, more practically speaking, I wanted to have a coherent programmatic complement to the CHANSONS MADÉCASSES when I performed them in recital. Hersant confided to me that he himself had originally imagined these *Paroles peintes* for voice, cello, and piano. Adding a flute was no problem for him. I premiered this second version one year after the first version, on September 16, 1996, in Saint-Nazaire, as part of the "Consonances" chamber music festival, with flutist Emmanuel Pahud, cellist Gary Hoffman, and pianist Pascal Devoyon. The atmosphere of this music is very close to the second of the three CHANSONS

Le Chant Intime. François Le Roux and Romain Raynaldy, Oxford University Press. © Oxford University Press 2021. DOI: 10.1093/oso/9780190884178.003.0019

MADÉCASSES, *Méfiez-vous des blancs* (Beware of the White people), by virtue of the vague tension and the incantatory, shaman-like character that pervades it.

These *Paroles peintes* can be considered to be "mature work." Philippe Hersant, who loves the human voice, had previously written a good number of songs, including a lied that I also premiered, *Was es gilt?* (What is at stake?), on a German poem by Goethe, and a pretty duet for mezzo-soprano and baritone on a verse from Théophile Gautier's *Lamento*. It's amazing how poetry and piano-vocal writing still interests contemporary composers!

Unfortunately, *Paroles peintes* is not published commercially, even though it is written on paper from Durand Editions. It is accessible only through a photocopy of the manuscript. But, on the plus side, Philippe Hersant's handwriting is perfectly legible.

This is a long mélodie, lasting eleven minutes. Hersant has conceived it in little subsections: to the composer's thinking, if the *words* were *painted*, they could be presented in different ways. Thus, he follows the subdivisions of the poetic line that parallel its appearance on the printed page, but he elongates the phrases in order to allow the singer to maintain a high degree of lyricism.

The expression is often emphatic, and it requires a rather sturdy singer, even if, intonation-wise, this is not a difficult song. The challenge is to find a way to create an atmosphere exclusively based on the text, in the manner of an incantation, since the poem is based on eleven repetitions of the word "Pour" (For). And the key to understanding is given at the end: "Donner / Mon / Bien / Donner / Mon / Droit" (Give / My / Goods / Give / My / Right).

It's an atmospheric mélodie, very pianistic and very striking for the audience, even in its chamber-music version. That quality is why it always works well in recital, as occurs rather rarely with a contemporary song.

Analysis

Paroles peintes	*Painted words*
Pour tout comprendre	In order to understand all
Même	Even
L'arbre au regard de proue	The tree that looks like a prow
L'arbre adoré des lézards et des lianes	The tree adored by lizards and lianas
Même le feu même l'aveugle	Even the fire even the blind
Pour réunir aile et rosée	In order to gather wing and dew
Cœur et nuage jour et nuit	Heart and cloud day and night
Fenêtre et pays de partout	Window and all countries
Pour abolir	In order to abolish
La grimace du zéro	The grimace of nought
Qui demain roulera sur l'or	That soon will be high on the hog

Pour trancher	In order to cut short
Les petites manières	The little manners
Des géants nourris d'eux-mêmes	Of giants fueled on themselves
Pour voir tous les yeux réfléchis	In order to see all eyes reflected
Par tous les yeux	By all eyes
Pour voir tous les yeux aussi beaux	In order to see all eyes as beautiful
Que ce qu'ils voient	As what they see
Mer absorbante	Absorbing sea
Pour que l'on rie légèrement	In order to laugh lightly
D'avoir eu chaud d'avoir eu froid	Of having been hot having been cold
D'avoir eu faim d'avoir eu soif	Having been hungry having been thirsty
Pour que parler	So that to speak
Soit aussi généreux	Be as generous
Qu'embrasser	As to embrace
Pour mêler baigneuse et rivière	In order to mix swimmer and stream
Cristal et danseuse d'orage	Crystal and dancer of storm
Aurore et la saison des seins	Dawn and the season of breasts
Désirs et sagesse d'enfance	Desires and wisdom of childhood
Pour donner à la femme	In order to give the woman
Méditative et seule	Meditative and lonely
La forme des caresses	The form of the caresses
Qu'elle a rêvées	She has dreamed of
Pour que les déserts soient dans l'ombre	So that deserts be in the shade
Au lieu d'être dans	Instead of in
Mon	My
Ombre	Shadow
Donner	Give
Mon	My
Bien	Goods
Donner	Give
Mon	My
Droit	Right

The tessitura sits rather high, and the song begins directly on a series of high F's (F5). Philippe Hersant's idea was that, right from the start, the music should bring out the rather strong incantatory quality of the poem. Starting out in this tessitura while declaiming an impassioned line is very difficult, and the challenge for the singer will be not to get worn out all at once!

The first musical figure—a big pianistic commotion in D minor—has this same incantatory character; its clangorousness evokes Oriental percussion instruments. A second figure appears rather quickly in the piano (Example 18.1), while the voice reaches the height of the tessitura on a G♭5.

Example 18.1 Hersant, Philippe: *Paroles peintes*. Editions Durand & Cie, 1995 (no ref.), page 1, mm. 1–2.

We were in D minor, and now we are in D flat major. The music oscillates between the two key centers, with the F acting as a pivot (Example 18.2).

Example 18.2 Hersant, Philippe: *Paroles peintes*. Editions Durand & Cie, 1995 (no ref.), page 1, mm. 10–12.

Then a third figure bursts forward in the piano, which ascends from B♭2 to arrive on "même l'aveugle" (Example 18.3), before a kind of strange stasis sets in (quarter note = 92) in the piano's left hand, which leads to a Debussyste—or Messiaenesque—mixture (Example 18.4).

The incantation reappears with a phrase comprised of low notes and long note values, like the E♭4 on "Pour réunir, pour réunir" (the repetition is by the composer), before a clear diminution on "Pour abolir / La grimace du zéro / Qui demain roulera sur l'or / Pour trancher / Les petites manières / Des géants nourris d'eux-mêmes." New accents appear, still based on incantation, but the mood changes on the *piano* of "Par tous les yeux," with wide intervals, such as B3–C♯5 (Example 18.5).

Example 18.3 Hersant, Philippe: *Paroles peintes*. Editions Durand & Cie, 1995 (no ref.), page 2, mm. 22–26.

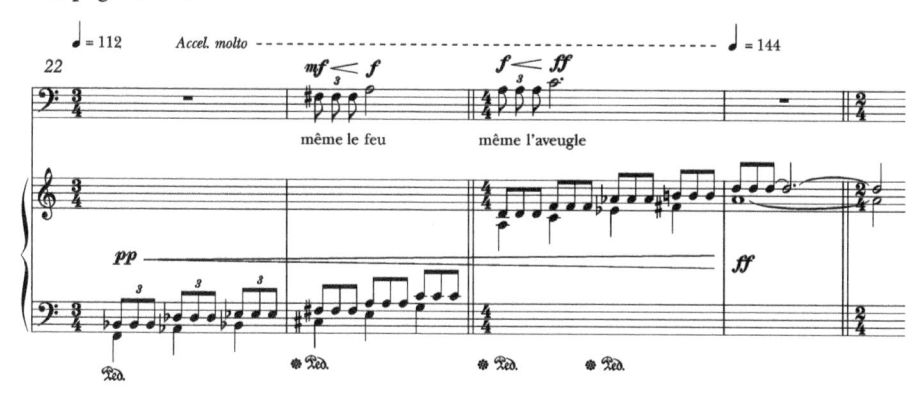

Example 18.4 Hersant, Philippe: *Paroles peintes*. Editions Durand & Cie, 1995 (no ref.), page 3, mm. 27–34.

The section beginning with "Pour que l'on rie légèrement" features the appearance of a trill, like a laughing figure, in the piano. We then return to *fortissimo* intensity, after the accents in measure 145. "Pour que parler / Soit aussi généreux / Qu'en embrasser" is repeated once (which is not the case in the poem), with a rhythmic augmentation at the end of the line, at the repetition.

The phrase "Pour mêler" reproduces exactly the rhythmic oscillation that occurred at the beginning, on "Pour réunir," with an effect that is both dancelike and slippery. "Pour donner à la femme / Méditative et seule / La forme des caresses /

Example 18.5 Hersant, Philippe: *Paroles peintes*. Editions Durand & Cie, 1995 (no ref.), page 8, mm. 87–93.

Qu'elle a rêvées" illustrates one of the principal themes of Éluard's poetry: the woman, seen in the man's gaze, who finally realizes the dream of the man through her own willfulness. With "Pour que les déserts soient dans l'ombre / Au lieu d'être dans / Mon / Ombre" (the composer repeats the last part) (Example 18.6), we see here how the poet subdivides the line into four elements: the first consisting of five syllables, with a "masculine" ending, the three others consisting of three syllables, with a "feminine" ending.[1] The result is a very "Madécassian" augmentation, not so much in the rhythmic organization as in the very steep ascents.

The agitated conclusion presents a little rhythmic change between the two "Donner," and features the return of almost all the themes, recited with extraordinary vehemence, as if creating the striking of gongs in echo. The piano prolongs this echo in repeating the same large chord held by the pedal, until it fades away. In order to produce the desired effect, a concert grand piano is needed—otherwise, the sustained sound will be too short, and that would be too bad! Additionally, if the singer and the pianist have a good rapport, and if the acoustics in the hall allow it, the best idea is to open the piano to full stick, like in a piano recital.

---

[1] In French, we speak of a "masculine ending" if the syllable in question is accentuated and a "feminine ending" if the last syllable is silent, usually ending on a silent *e* [ə]. This difference in sound results in different phrasings: the first goes right to the end, the second releases the tension after the last "accented" syllable, that is to say, the next-to-last syllable. In the same way, the French speak of masculine rhymes and feminine rhymes for the same procedure, the last "silent" syllable of a feminine rhyme not counting as a true syllable.

Example 18.6 Hersant, Philippe: *Paroles peintes.* Editions Durand & Cie, 1995 (no ref.), page 18, mm. 216–222.

19

Augusta Holmès

***Rondel* (1872)**

Music by Augusta Holmès (1847–1903)
Poem attributed to François Villon (ca. 1431–after 1463)

Presentation

As famous during her lifetime as George Sand, Augusta Holmès is an example of a marginalized nineteenth-century woman artist. If it was difficult for a woman writer to become known and enjoy success, it was practically impossible for a woman composer. Remember: in the Western musical world of the period, a woman could certainly be a performer, but, for bourgeois society, performing on-stage was considered shocking, close to prostitution. This state of affairs is what gave rise to the private salon, where a woman was permitted to perform for a circle of friends and specially invited guests. Marriage meant the abandonment of dreams of a career.

Augusta Holmès followed her own path. Of Irish origins (she added the grave accent to the *e* of her family name so that it would sound more French), she was celebrated for her beauty and her talent. The list of her admirers and her suitors was long—even Saint-Saëns, who affectionately referred to her as "l'outrancière" (the excessive woman), asked for her hand in marriage! Although she never married, she maintained a fifteen-year liaison with poet Catulle Mendès. They had five children together—having them never caused Holmès to give up her independence nor her compositional career. The opposite of mild-mannered, she mostly wrote many large-scale works. Holmès briefly wrote under the masculine pseudonym Hermann Zenta, but not for long. Of her five symphonic poems, two— *Irlande* and *Pologne*—were written to promote national liberty; both enjoyed great success. Her best-known choral work was the *Ode triomphale* (1889), which commemorated the centenary of the French Revolution; it was written on a scale that would have made Berlioz green with envy: 1200 choristers and an orchestra of 500 musicians. Another choral work, *Hymne pour la paix*, was performed in Florence in 1890 and her opera *La montagne noire* was performed at the Paris Opera

Le chant intime. François Le Roux and Romain Raynaldy, Oxford University Press. © Oxford University Press 2021.
DOI: 10.1093/oso/9780190884178.003.0020

in 1895.[1]. In his book *Harmonie et mélodie* (Paris: Calmann Lévy, 1885), Saint-Saëns devoted a chapter to one of her monumental works, the opera *Les argonautes*, demonstrating that he considered her to be an exceptional case—indeed, *sui generis*.

Holmès wrote more than one hundred mélodies, most of them settings of her own poems. Her father had been a poet, and the fact of living with Catulle Mendès, whose works were often used by composers, encouraged her to write her own texts. It is difficult to determine if the words came before the music, or the opposite. In addition to Mendès, she personally knew poets Stéphan Bordèse, Auguste Brizeux, Emmanuel des Essarts, Jean Lahor, and Louis de Lyvron, among others; she set some of their work to music—but, curiously, never used any of Mendès's poems. She also wrote musical settings of older poets, including Hugo, Musset, and even Khwaja Shams-ud-Din Muhammad Hafez-e Shirazi, aka Hafiz, a fourteenth-century Persian poet.

One of Holmès's mélodies, *Trois anges sont venus ce soir* (Three angels have come tonight), dated 1884, for which she wrote the words, became so famous that it is still sung today during Christmas; great singers like Ninon Vallin and Mado Robin[2] have recorded it. The subtitle "Chanson populaire," written on the score, was, for once, not usurped: popular French singers (like Tino Rossi,[3] for example) and amateur choirs have performed it. Like many songs integrated into the collective memory, no one knows—or knows anymore—that Augusta Holmès wrote it.

Holmès was also a contralto who captivated her audiences not by the beauty of her voice but by the emotion that it aroused and by her ability to sing exceptionally low notes.

Composed in 1872, *Rondel* is dedicated to Holmès's close friend Geneviève Breton, granddaughter of the publisher Louis Hachette.[4]

---

[1] *La montagne noire* ran for only thirteen performances; its short stage life was attributed to a cabal. It is really unclear, as she had been supported also by such prominent people like Victorin Joncières and Octave Mirbeau. She was taxed as "Wagnerite," which was like a curse for conservative circles.

[2] Born in 1918, Mado Robin began studying voice at age thirteen with Mario Podesta. In 1937, she won the First Prize for sopranos at the Paris Opera. She became world famous for her excursions in the stratospheric vocal range because of her ability to sing a high D (D6), the highest note ever sung, earning her the nickname "The French Stratospheric Coloratura." An American newspaper quipped that she had "broken the sound barrier." In 1952 she recorded the title role in Delibes's *Lakmé* for Decca. She died of cancer in 1960. Immensely popular in France, she made numerous recordings of mélodies and traditional songs.

[3] Constantin Rossi, known as Tino Rossi (1907–1983), was a tenor "of charm" and a screen actor. During his lifetime, he sold more records than did any other French artist.

[4] Geneviève Breton was the fiancée of the painter Henri Regnault (1843–1871), killed during the Franco-Prussian War in 1870. In 1866, Regnault had asked Augusta Holmès, who was then twenty years old, to pose for his painting *Thétis apportant à Achille les armes forgées par Vulcain* (Thetis bringing to Achilles the arms forged by Vulcan), which won him the Grand Prix de Rome. Augusta Holmès is depicted as a sculptural goddess with red hair and bare breasts, bringing to her son Achilles, who is leaning over the body of Patrocles, a golden casket and a round shield.

Analysis

Rondel

Les biens dont vous estes la dame
Ont mon cueur si très fort espris,
Qu'il feust mort, s'il n'eust entrepris
De vous aymer plus que nul ame.

Quant à moy, point je ne l'en blasme,
Pour ce qu'ilz ont de tous le pris
Les biens dont vous estes la dame.

De ce qu'il fault que je vous ayme,
Je scay trop bien que j'ay mespris;
Mais qui en doit ester repris?
Non pas moi. Qui donc? Sur mon ame,
Les biens dont vous estes la dame.

Rondel

The goods of which you are the owner
Have so well taken my heart
That it would have died, if it would not have
[decided
To love you more than any other.

As for me, I do not blame it,
For they surpass all others,
The goods of which you are the owner.

To have to love you,
I know that I have been wrongly forced to:
But who should be blamed for this?
Not I. Who then? Upon my soul,
The goods of which you are the owner.

On the cover of the score (which can be seen on *Gallica*, the database of the Bibliothèque nationale de France), the poem appears in scripted characters for the title and the name of the poet, as if on parchment, to underline the medieval source of the composer's inspiration. The poem can be found on page 133 of *Œuvres complètes de François Villon* (Alphonse Lemerre, 1876). It is the first poem of the last section, which assembles all the works attributed to the fifteenth-century poet (attributions that are still considered questionable today). It is a *rondel*: a poem in which a line reappears unchanged but in a different position in each strophe. In the mélodie, it's the first line of the first verse, the third of the second, and the last of the third. The spelling is early French, but my opinion is that the pronunciation should be modernized so that the audience can understand the meaning of the words. In Holmès's era, no one would have thought of "restoring" the pronunciation of early French, as scholars of our time are now looking for. Nonetheless, since the meaning of the poem remains ambiguous, I propose here a non-poetic explanatory version:

Vos biens (charmes, ou appâts), Madame,
Ont tant conquis mon cœur
Qu'il serait mort, s'il n'avait pas voulu (décidé)
De vous aimer plus qu'aucune autre âme.

Il n'en est pas à blâmer,
Puisque qu'ils (vos biens) surpassent
Tous les autres.

Je sais bien que j'ai eu tort
De penser que je devais vous aimer

Your goods [charms, or lures], Madame
Have so conquered my heart
That it would be dead, if it hadn't decided
To love you more than any other living soul.

It [my heart] is not to blame,
Since they [your goods] surpass
All others.

I know well that I am wrong
To think that I should love you

(ou: Je sais que vous méprisez*	(or I know that you disdain*
mon amour pour vous)	my love for you)

* The form "mespris" can come from the verb "méprendre" (be mistaken) or "mépriser" (be disdainful of), whence the ambiguity of the meaning.

	But who is to blame?
Mais qui est à blâmer?	Not me. Who, then? Upon my soul,
Pas moi. Qui alors? Sur mon âme,	Your goods have conquered my heart.
Vos biens ont conquis mon cœur.	

As I said earlier, I think that the pronunciation should be updated:

estes = êtes [ɛtə]

espris = épris [epri]

mespris = mépris [mepri]

cueur = cœur [kœːr]

feust = fût [fy]

n'eust = n'eût [ny]

fault = faut [fo]

Other words are written differently today, but shouldn't cause difficulties:

ilz = ils. A liaison should be made with "ont": [ilzõ]

pris = prix [pri], without pronouncing *s* or *x*

ayme = aime [ɛm]

scay = sais, pronounced with a closed *e* [se]

j'ay = j'ai, also pronounced with a closed *e* [ʒe]

ame = âme [ɑm], pronounced with a posterior [ɑ]

blasme = blâme [blɑm], also pronounced with a posterior [ɑ], since it rhymes with "âme"

It is important to make good contrast between the closed *é* [e] and the open *è* and *ê* [ɛ].

François Villon, known for his courtship of many women, here celebrates the beauty of one woman and the love that she inspired. This adulation is rendered musically by a sort of elegant dance in Renaissance style, in common time and marked *andantino*. I suggest a tempo of 100 to the quarter note. The mélodie exists in two keys: D minor for baritone or mezzo-soprano and E minor for tenor or soprano. Whatever key is chosen, the tessitura remains in the central range: D4 to E5 in D minor, E4 to F♯ 5 in E minor. The piano begins alone with an introduction of four measures. The first three lines of the first and last verse are identical, musically speaking. No dynamics are written in the score, but, as there is a *p* in the piano part, it should apply to the two performers. On the third system, the written phrasing seems to indicate that the singer should take a good breath after "mespris," at the end of the second verse, in order to sing "Qu'il feust mort, s'il n'eust entrepris / De vous aymer plus que nul ame" in one breath, since the comma after "mort" is missing from the score (Example 19.1).

Example 19.1 Holmès, Augusta: *Rondel*. Editions Alphonse Leduc, undated (ref. A.L. 4371), page 1, mm. 8–11.

The following verse, marked with a double bar—which implies a possible stopping point—contains numerous markings: the vocal line starts *dolce* (first line), which rises to *f* via a long *crescendo*, emphasizing the superiority of the "charms" described in the second line, and finally ends on a *decrescendo* that falls to *p*, for the third line. The first line of the third verse also contains a *crescendo*, but this one rises only to *mf*, in such a way that the last line (marked *f* and *rallentando*) becomes the true high point. And the little ornament on the last word, "dame," acts as a sort of final bow, allowing the song to end in major.

In sum, this lovely *Rondel* offers a romantic approach to the universe by a composer whose mélodies deserve to be rediscovered.

20

Arthur Honegger

TROIS POÈMES DE PAUL FORT (1916)

I. *Le chasseur perdu en forêt*
II. *Cloche du soir*
III. *Chanson de fol*

Music by Arthur Honegger (1892–1955)
Poems by Paul Fort (1872–1960)

Presentation

Arthur Honegger composed a great deal of vocal music, including more than fifty mélodies. Associated with many brilliant performers—especially Claire Croiza[1]—he wrote beautifully for the voice. And yet his mélodies, written on poetic texts of the highest quality, are rarely heard today. I have chosen an early cycle, whose great strength and lovely balance belies the relative youth of its composer. Chronologically, it is the second cycle published, after QUATRE POÈMES (1914–1916). Strongly influenced by Bach, Fauré, and Debussy, Honegger was an important figure in twentieth-century French music. He wrote his mélodies during two periods, 1915–1924 and 1939–1955 (the year of his death). This cycle dates entirely from 1916. The first mélodie was orchestrated in the late 1920s and received its Paris premiere in this version on January 25, 1930, with mezzo-soprano Lina Falk (1889–1943) and the Pasdeloup Orchestra, conducted by Albert van Raalte. Each of the three mélodies is dedicated to a different female singer[2] and thus indicates that the cycle was conceived for female voice. Nonetheless, a baritone could sing the cycle without a problem, as the tessitura is perfectly adapted to a medium male voice

---

[1] Claire Croiza (1882–1946), born Claire Connolly, was the daughter of an American colonel. In 1906, she gave her first performance at the Théâtre de la Monnaie in Brussels, where she would subsequently perform often, and made her debut at the Paris Opera in 1908. Although well known as an opera singer, she became recognized as a singer of French mélodie, of which she became one of the great interpreters. She gave first performances of works by André Caplet, Roussel, Milhaud, and Honegger, with whom she lived (without marrying) and with whom she had a son. In 1922 she became a professor of voice at the École normale de Musique, and in 1934 she joined the faculty of the Paris Conservatoire. Her students included Gérard Souzay. During World War II she collaborated with the Nazis, which destroyed her reputation. She died in 1946.

[2] One of the dedicatees, Rose Armandie, to whom *Cloche du soir* was dedicated, was also one of the composer's favorite singers.

Le chant intime. François Le Roux and Romain Raynaldy, Oxford University Press. © Oxford University Press 2021.
DOI: 10.1093/oso/9780190884178.003.0021

(the last mélodie is higher, but doesn't go above F♯5). The entire cycle is around seven minutes long. The first publisher was Demets (1922), then Salabert. The TROIS POÈMES DE PAUL FORT cycle can easily be found at the beginning of the collection of forty-eight mélodies published by Salabert in 1995, the anniversary of the composer's death.

The poems of Paul Fort constitute a mixture of post-symbolism and a return to the tradition of myths, stories, and songs of popular origin; the poet uses a more simple and direct language than his predecessors. In a way, his output can be considered "neo-classical," or perhaps "neo-medieval," an aesthetic that matches Honegger's musical culture perfectly. Most of Fort's enormous poetic output, dating from 1897 to 1958, has been gathered together into a giant collection, consisting of more than forty books, under the global title *Ballades françaises*. Paul Fort's works have been set to music by many composers, from Ernest Chausson (who in 1898 wrote a *Ballade française*, which is still unpublished) to Georges Brassens[3] (who set *Le petit cheval* and *Si le bon dieu l'avait voulu*). The three poems chosen by Honegger come from *Complaintes et dits* (in Volume XV, published in 1913), whose subtitle is "Chansons pour me consoler d'être heureux" (Songs to console me to be happy).

Analyses

I. *Le chasseur perdu en forêt*

Quand le son du cor s'endort, gai chasseur, ne tarde!—Déjà les sentiers regardent, avec l'œil creux de la Mort, passer l'avalanche des hauts chevaux sous les branches.

Cavalier, quel beau squelette enfourche ta bête? Adieu, chasse! Adieu galops!—Alors s'éveille indistincte, puis s'enfle la plainte de l'étang rouge aux oiseaux.

I. *The hunter lost in the forest*

When the sound of the horn sleeps, merry hunter, don't tarry!—Already, the paths watch, with the hollow eye of Death, the avalanche of tall horses passing beneath the branches.

Horseman, what handsome skeleton mounts your beast? Farewell, hunt! farewell gallops!—Then, indistinct, the lament of the red pond of the birds wakes and rises.

This mélodie falls neatly into the line of numerous French musical evocations of the hunt, of macabre dances, and of horn calls, including—to name but two— Ange Flégier's *Le cor*[4] and Debussy's *Le son du cor s'afflige vers les bois*, on a poem

---

[3] Georges Brassens (1921–1981) was the most famous of the singer-songwriters of ballads and protest songs of the second half of the twentieth century in France. He accompanied himself on the guitar. He wrote almost 200 songs, about thirty of which are set to texts by well-known writers (Villon, Victor Hugo, Francis Jammes, Paul Fort); the most famous ones, however, are based on his own texts, including *Les sabots d'Hélène* (1954) and *Les copains d'abord* (1965).

[4] In France, Flégier's song *Le cor* is so well known that its composer has been forgotten. The poem, by Alfred de Vigny, is the famous *Poème pittoresque*, which begins with the words "J'aime le son du cor. . . ."

of Verlaine. But Honegger's setting also contains Teutonic tropes such as those found in Weber's *Der Freischütz* or Brahms's *"Edward" Ballade* for piano, op. 10. However, the text suggests a lightly ironic distance, with this sound that "sleeps" and a "merry hunter" who is late returning home. The horn theme (in rapid triplets) alternating with the dotted-eighth/sixteenth "galloping" rhythm also seems ironic, slightly diabolical, passing from *f* to *mf* then to *pp*, before the voice *freely* produces its warning of prudence. Don't take such a fast *tempo* that the difference between the triplets and the dotted rhythms will disappear; conversely, too slow a tempo will weigh down a distanced stance. And the voice, especially, should not sound too menacing; it should, rather, "insinuate," separating from the sharply articulated piano part to get louder, by way of a progressive *crescendo*, almost reaching *forte* on "sous les branches." The following phrase is the only really diabolical one, in the mocking sense of the term. The two "adieu"'s, both marked *piano*, can be well contrasted through their rhythmic differences (Example 20.1).

Example 20.1 Honegger, Arthur: *Trois poèmes de Paul Fort—I. Le chasseur perdu en forêt*. From *Mélodies et chansons*, Editions Salabert, 1995 (ref. E.M.S. 4752), pages 6–7, mm. 22–26.

Finally, after three measures in which the piano's right hand plays a quasi-Wagnerian theme, the voice, in a beautifully lyrical passage (expansive tempo, an ample *crescendo*), sings of the enigma of the red birds who inhabit a red swamp (the symbolism is half-Arthurian, half-Goethean), followed, in conclusion, by the piano calling out in eleven successive E's.

II. *Cloche du soir*	II. *Evening Bell*
Ah! ce soir-là, vraiment, tout était si paisible que le Champ du Repos était sur le chemin,	Ah! Truly that night, everything was so peaceful that the Field of Rest was along the wayside,
et l'angélus du soir d'une cloche invisible, croisait deux beaux sons clairs sur le front des humains.	and the evening Angelus from an invisible bell, crossed two beautiful bright sounds on the brow of humans.

La lumière de l'ombre, et ce halo de lune, les sons de l'angélus et leur mystique appel

versaient des charités dans l'âme. O crépuscule! —Un petit cimetière ouvre une heure éternelle.

L'angélus va mourir. Que dis-je? il est encore. C'est lui qui tremble aux bords de ce nuage d'or.

C'est lui qui tremble aussi dans le signe de croix que font ces deux rayons d'argent croisant leurs voies.

Ah! ce soir-là mourut de l'éternel bonheur que le Champ du Repos offre sur le chemin,

et l'angélus mourant vint planter sur mon cœur sa blanche croix mystique et signa mon destin.

The light of the shadow, and the halo of the moon, the sounds of the Angelus and their mystic call

brought mercifulness into my soul. O dusk!— A small cemetery brings about an hour of eternity.

The Angelus will die. What do I say? it still is. It is that which trembles on the edge of this golden cloud.

It is that too which trembles in the sign of the cross that these two silver rays form by crossing their paths.

Ah! That evening died of the eternal happiness that the Field of Rest offers up along the wayside,

and the dying Angelus came to plant in my heart its white mystical cross, and sealed my fate.

At more than three minutes, this is the longest of the three mélodies, and also that which evokes the great composer of oratorios—first, by virtue of the choice of the poem, radiant with religious serenity, and second, by the musical phrasing, which has the dignity of a prayer. The choice of the key of D major adds to the sense of luminosity. Because of the allusion to bells, we hear the influence of Debussy. But we also hear the similarity to Déodat de Séverac, especially in his mélodies *Un rêve* and *L'éveil de Pâques*, which illustrate the Angelus bell in their respective accompaniments through a well-known figure (Example 20.2), and then a counter-melody in triplets (Example 20.3).

Example 20.2 Honegger, Arthur: *Trois poèmes de Paul Fort—II. Cloche du soir.* From *Mélodies et chansons*, Editions Salabert, 1995 (ref. E.M.S. 4752), page 8, mm. 1–3.

Example 20.3 Honegger, Arthur: *Trois poèmes de Paul Fort—II. Cloche du soir.* From *Mélodies et chansons*, Editions Salabert, 1995 (ref. E.M.S. 4752), pages 8–9, mm. 12–14.

In every part of the tessitura (from B3 to F5), the voice should exhibit a faultless homogeneity. The full, abundant vocal line follows a strict versification in alexandrines; only "O crépuscule" (measure 18) marks a sort of contemplative halt to the highly active, pervasively chromatic lines that had preceded it: in the two subsequent measures, the vocal line peacefully descends until "une heure éternelle" (measures 20–21) and the accompaniment is reduced to one harmony per measure. The initial lyricism and unsullied diatonicism is resumed in the last four verses, but the lengths of the sung phrases are then extended into two lines each—ideally speaking, for if the singer needs to breathe, the phrasing can still be adhered to by going line by line. The ending of the song is typical of the composer: after eight measures of angelic pentatonic *arpeggios* (measures 34–41), Honegger inserts, in the penultimate measure, a cadential passage, set chorale-style on gritty chromatic harmonies—which then resolves, guilelessly, in pentatonic radiance (Example 20.4) worthy of Ravel's song *Sainte* (which will be discussed further on).

Example 20.4 Honegger, Arthur: *Trois Poèmes de Paul Fort—II. Cloche du soir.* From *Mélodies et chansons*, Editions Salabert, 1995 (ref. E.M.S. 4752), page 10, mm. 43–44.

III. *Chanson de fol*

Les sorciers et les fées dansent sur le coteau.
Leurs pas brûlants font des 8* noirs sous les
méteils. Ils dansent de la nuit venue au jour
nouveau pour honorer le saint qui nourrit les
abeilles.

    * Honegger writes "huit," in letters

Et sept nuits et sept jours ils font la ronde
encor, jusqu'au huitième soir où, géantes
cigales, les fées jouent de la flûte et les sorciers
du cor, pour honorer le dieu qui nourrit les étoiles.

III. *Song of the madman*

The sorcerers and fairies dance on the hillside.
Their blazing footsteps trace black figure 8's
under the mixed grains. They dance from dusk
till dawn to honor the saint who feeds the bees.

And for seven nights and seven days they
continue to dance around until on the eighth
night, like giant cigales, the fairies play the flute
and the sorcerers play the horn, to honor the god
who feeds the stars.

This lively piece in some ways recalls Ravel's a cappella choral work *Ronde* and Debussy's *Noël des enfants qui n'ont plus de maison*. Less than a minute long, it illustrates a pantheism that unites the satanic paganism of the first mélodie of the cycle with the Christian meditation of the second. The "huit noirs" (black eights) stand in opposition to the "sept jours et sept nuits" (seven days and seven nights): according to some traditions, eight is a "satanic" number, while seven is eminently Christian. In the Christian faith, the "saint who feeds the bees" is St. Ambrosius, patron saint of beekeepers; on the other hand, the reference to the "saint who feeds the stars" is an enigma. A similar ambiguity is inherent in the words chosen by the poet: "méteil" is a mixture of wheat and rye grains that have been sown together (separating the wheat from the chaff is difficult!).

The accompaniment features a delicious mash-up of pandiatonicism, pentatonic and whole-tone scales, and a bit of bitonality; and the two concluding *arpeggios*—which, taken together, create a Ravelian extended chord (B^{13})—do nothing to resolve the delightful ambiguity. The singer should always think of an elfin dance, but should always maintain the duple meter ($\frac{2}{4}$), without falling into a one-pulse-per-measure motion; this metric clarity is especially important in the piano solo, which functions almost as an additional "verse" inserted between the two sung quatrains.

The performer should carefully articulate the words: for example, the *t* in "huit noirs" (black figure eights) should be clearly pronounced so that the word doesn't sound like [ɥi] which, to a French ear, could suggest the word "huis" (front door). A male performer should sing very lightly; it might be helpful to remember the title: the mild "madness" of the narrator should be that of an imp, not of a lunatic. The dynamic marking at the beginning is *piano*, and this does not change. There are no swells in the vocal lines, despite the pitfalls of the tessitura. The final F♯, held for six-and-a-half beats, can be sung in head voice by a baritone, if that will help maintain the necessary light tone. The ideal would be a flexible, medium-weight voice that can blend with the sixteenth notes in the accompaniment.

In sum, the cycle *TROIS POÈMES DE PAUL FORT*, through its contrasts, can show the full expressive range of a singer and can fit perfectly into a Debussyste or Ravelian repertoire, while possessing the added attraction of being rarely heard!

21

Vincent d'Indy

L'Amour et le crâne (1884)

Music by Vincent d'Indy (1851–1931)
Poem by Charles Baudelaire (1821–1867)

Presentation

As famous during his lifetime as Debussy, and his greatest opponent (although he recognized the great qualities of *Pelléas et Mélisande* in a critical piece that appeared in the monthly magazine *Occident*), Vincent d'Indy has not yet emerged from a kind of long purgatory. While his symphonies are slowly being rediscovered, his song repertoire, consisting of twenty-odd titles, is completely unknown.

I have chosen a mélodie that, in many ways, approaches the greatness of the songs by Duparc, who was a very close friend of Vincent d'Indy (moreover, the first piano-vocal version of *La vague et la cloche* is by d'Indy!). The choice of a very biting poem by Baudelaire is also revelatory in terms of the poet's importance to the composers of Duparc's generation. It would be interesting to create a "cycle" of this unique Baudelaire setting by d'Indy and the two famous songs on Baudelaire texts, *L'invitation au voyage* and *La vie antérieure* by Duparc.

The poem, published in 1855, is subtitled "Vieux cul-de-lampe." The term, which derives from medieval architecture, refers to a curved or bracketed surface that projects out from a wall and supports a weight; it is similar in form to the base of a church lamp. Baudelaire's poem was inspired by an engraving by Hendrick Goltzius (1556–1616) on a vanitas theme, in which Death and Time are the masters of the world; it is similar to the medieval visions very much in vogue at the end of the nineteenth century.

D'Indy's musical setting of the poem dates from 1884, falling between the musical settings of Baudelaire by Duparc (1870–1884) and Debussy (1887–1889). The song is also similar to Saint-Saëns's famous *Danse macabre*, on a poem by Jean Lahor (1873). *L'Amour et le crâne* was published on December 15, 1885, in an *Album* of musical works offered by the daily newspaper *Le Gaulois* to its subscribers. The first official publication of the song dates from roughly 1892, by Loret et Freytag.

Written for tenor voice (the tessitura extends from F4 to G5—that is, barely more than an octave), the mélodie is in C minor. A baritone could transpose it to B♭ minor with no problem. Its length is approximately 2 min 30 sec.

Le chant intime. François Le Roux and Romain Raynaldy, Oxford University Press. © Oxford University Press 2021.
DOI: 10.1093/oso/9780190884178.003.0022

Analysis

L'Amour et le crâne	*Love and the skull*
L'Amour est assis sur le crâne	Eros is seated on the skull
De l'Humanité	Of Humanity
Et sur ce trône le profane	And on this throne the profane one
Au rire effronté,	Insolently laughing,
Souffle gaiement des bulles rondes	Gaily blows round bubbles
Qui montent dans l'air,	That rise in the air
Comme pour rejoindre les mondes	As if to join the worlds
Au fond de l'éther.	Hidden in the ether.
Le globe lumineux et frêle	The luminous, frail globe
Prend un grand essor,	Leaps ahead,
Crève et crache son âme grêle	Explodes and spits out its spindly soul
Comme un songe d'or.	Like a golden dream.
J'entends le crâne à chaque bulle	With each bubble, I hear the skull
Prier et gémir:	Pray and moan:
—"Ce jeu féroce et ridicule,	"This fierce and ridiculous game,
Quand doit-il finir?	When will it end?
Car ce que ta bouche cruelle	"For what your cruel mouth
Éparpille en l'air,	Scatters in the air,
Monstre assassin, c'est ma cervelle,	Monster murderer, it is my brain,
Mon sang et ma chair!"	My blood and my flesh!"

At the opening, the $\frac{6}{8}$ meter is skewed by an *ostinato* hemiola in the piano line, creating a kind of "hiccup" effect; the meter is righted only by the entry of the vocal line, which stabilizes the compound duple meter (Example 21.1).

Example 21.1 D'Indy, Vincent: *L'Amour et le crâne*. From the journal *Album du Gaulois*, 1885 (no ref.) page 158, mm. 1–3.

In addition to the *animé* (lively) indication, the vocal line is also marked *bien accentué* (well accented). This instruction doesn't mean that the singer should not connect the phrases, for, in his musical setting, d'Indy groups two lines at a time: "L'Amour est assis sur le crâne / De l'Humanité." It is important to avoid the same pitfalls that arise in Duparc's *Le galop*: the voice risks being drowned out by the rich texture in the accompaniment, so it is imperative to maintain the balance between the piano and the voice. The third quatrain is the exception: the voice is marked *doux* (soft) and the piano is marked *pp très lié* (very connected); these markings are reinforced by a change of meter (⁹₈), a slower *tempo* and a murmuring accompaniment in triplet eighth notes. The marking of *rit.* at the end of the verse, on "songe d'or," allows for a beautiful dreamy color in the three-measure piano solo that follows. The fourth quatrain (*Animé, 1° tempo*) returns to the obsessive driving rhythm from the beginning, which may be a reflection of the "headache" of the narrator-singer. However, in the middle of the verse, the music shifts to triple meter and the passage is marked *un peu plus lent* (*poco più lento*), with the further indications *déclamé* (declaimed) in the vocal line and *très soutenu* (*molto sostenuto*) in the piano accompaniment; here, the singer should create a *legato* line that allows the words "Quand doit-il finir?" (When will it end?) to be heard as a declaimed question (Example 21.2).

Example 21.2 D'Indy, Vincent: *L'Amour et le crâne*. From the journal *Album du Gaulois*, 1885 (no ref.), page 160, mm. 36–42.

This passage is followed by a kind of *colla parte*, emphasized by a throbbing syncopated pedal point in the left hand of the piano, ending in a cross-rhythm between voice and piano (marked *énergiquement*) on "Monstre assassin," which thrusts the music into the final return to *Animé, 1° tempo*. The climactic setting of "et ma" on a ringing high G should be well accented but not held too long, so that there is enough air left for the final word "chair!" as it endures more than three beats. The concluding piano solo features the opening *ostinato* hemiola, which progressively dissipates in a *diminuendo molto* and disappears only on the last note, like a bad dream.

22

Marie Jaëll

Larmes (ca. 1893)

Music by Marie Jaëll-Trautmann (1846–1925)
Poem by Jean Richepin (1849–1926)

Presentation

A great pianist and pedagogue, Marie Trautmann, born in Strasbourg in 1846, started out as a piano prodigy. She won her first prize in piano at the Paris Conservatoire in 1862—the same year that she began her studies! In 1866, she married another piano virtuoso, the Austrian Alfred Jaëll (1832–1882). She gave many concerts and toured throughout Europe, both as a soloist and in four-hand performances with her husband. Her 1868 encounter with Liszt changed her life and her art: she became his protégée, as she did with Saint-Saëns. But the Franco-Prussian War of 1870 halted a promising international star career: a true Alsatian, she opted for French citizenship. Her husband had been on the verge of succeeding celebrated pianist Ignaz Moscheles as a professor of piano at the Leipzig Conservatory, but, in solidarity with his wife, gave up the opportunity and chose French nationality.

Thoroughly bilingual, Marie Jaëll composed lieder on German texts, but, after the war, stopped speaking the language almost completely. Her career became essentially French, and, in many ways, Parisian. She became a member of the Société Nationale de Musique, which had been founded to promote new French music, and under whose auspices she was featured as both composer and pianist. She also wrote numerous books and articles on piano technique, works for which she is best known today.

On the other hand, her mélodies and lieder are very rarely programmed. She wrote two major cycles on French texts: *LES ORIENTALES*, on seven poems of Victor Hugo, and *LA MER*, on six poems of Jean Richepin; both cycles were published by Paul Dupont in 1893. These works can be downloaded from Bibliothèque nationale de France's *Gallica* database. Three other mélodies, including one based on a poem by Baudelaire, *Les hiboux,* have been published by the Université de Strasbourg.

Although it's not always advisable to choose one single mélodie from a longer cycle, I have chosen the last of the cycle *LA MER*, which has not yet been recorded.

Le chant intime. François Le Roux and Romain Raynaldy, Oxford University Press. © Oxford University Press 2021.
DOI: 10.1093/oso/9780190884178.003.0023

The collection of eponymous poems by Jean Richepin, published by Maurice Dreyfous in 1886, was very popular at the end of the nineteenth century, especially with composers: in the case of *Larmes*, Fauré set it in 1888, César Cui in 1890, and Ange Flégier in 1892. It is the seventeenth of the thirty poems in the last section of the collection, *Étant de quart*.[1]

Analysis

Larmes	*Tears*
Pleurons nos chagrins, chacun le nôtre.	Let us mourn our sorrows, each his own.
Une larme tombe, puis une autre.	One tear falls, another follows.
Toi, que pleures-tu? Ton doux pays,	You, what do you mourn? You sweet native land,
Tes parents lointains, ta fiancée.	Your distant family, your betrothed.
Moi, mon existence dépensée	And I—my existence, wasted
En vœux trahis.	On vows betrayed.
Pleurons nos chagrins, chacun le nôtre.	Let us mourn our sorrows, each his own.
Une larme tombe, puis une autre.	One tear falls, another follows.
Semons dans la mer ces pâles fleurs.	Let us bestrew the sea with these pale flowers.
À notre sanglot qui se lamente	To our sobbing lament
Elle répondra par la tourmente	It will reply with the storm
Des flots hurleurs.	Of howling waves.
Pleurons nos chagrins, chacun le nôtre.	Let us mourn our sorrows, each his own.
Une larme tombe, puis une autre.	One tear falls, another follows.
Le flux de la mer en est grossi	The flow of the sea is enlarged with them,
Et d'une salure plus épaisse,	And its saltiness thickened,
Depuis si longtemps que notre espèce	So long has our species
Y pleure ainsi.	Been weeping.
Pleurons nos chagrins, chacun le nôtre.	Let us mourn our sorrows, each his own.
Une larme tombe, puis une autre.	One tear falls, another follows.
Peut-être toi-même, ô triste mer,	Perhaps you yourself, O dismal sea
Mer au goût de larme âcre et salée,	Which tastes of acrid and salty tears,
Es-tu de la terre inconsolée	Are the inconsolable earth's
Le pleur amer.	Bitter weeping.

The key chosen by Jaëll, who set the entire poem, is C♯ minor (the key chosen by Cui as well). The evocative blue-green cover image used for all six songs of the LA MER cycle (published individually) illustrates an enormous wave breaking on the cliffs. The image foreshadows the storminess of Jaëll's musical setting of *Larmes*. Marked *Allegretto* (a metronome marking of quarter note = 72 seems appropriate to me), the

---

[1] Fauré and Flégier omitted the third verse, perhaps because of the many "non-poetic" words ("flux," "grossi," "salure," "espèce"), or because of the oblique rhyming of "épaisse" and "espèce."

mélodie lasts about 3 min 30 sec. It opens with a harmonically turbulent three-and-a-half-measure piano introduction with no discernable key center. Here, we find the two principal piano motives: a sixteenth-note anacrusis preceding each strong beat in the left hand, and a fluid group of sixteenth notes in the right hand, whose surging ascending-descending patterns resemble the waves of the cover image. No tonal stability is established until measure 5, with the strong arrival on C♯ in the vocal line and the supporting C♯ minor harmony—albeit in first inversion—in the accompaniment. The similarities to Chopin in the piano introduction are confirmed by an unmistakable quotation from that composer's "Revolutionary" *Étude*, op. 10, no. 12, in the vocal line ("chacun le nôtre"), measures 5–6 (Example 22.1).

Example 22.1 Jaëll, Marie: *Larmes*. From *La mer, poésies de Jean Richepin*, Editions Paul Dupont, 1893 (no ref.), page 2, mm. 3–6.

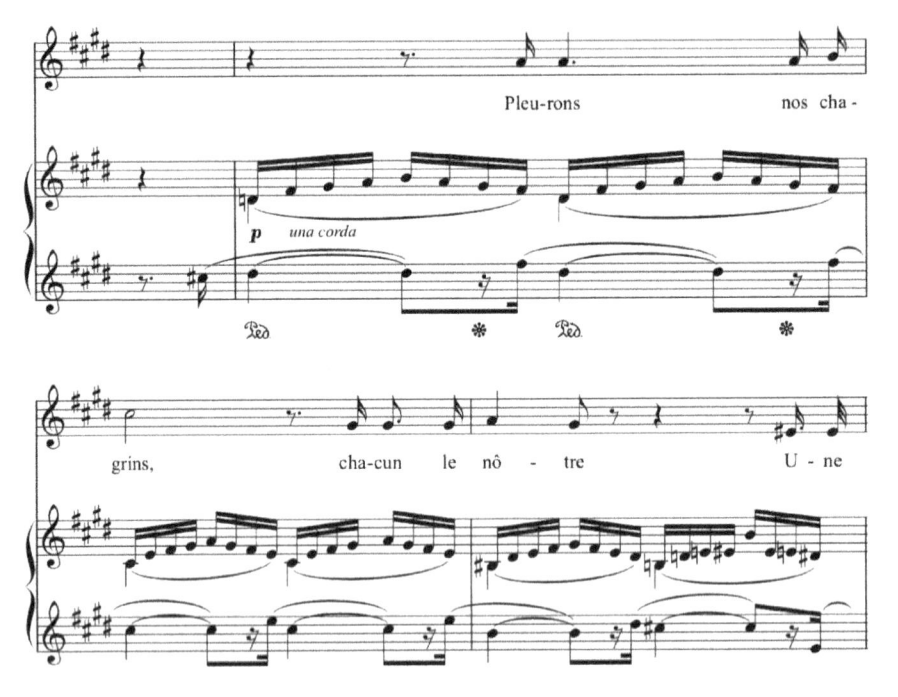

The first two lines of the poem will serve as a "refrain" throughout, and will appear four times, musically unchanged, in the vocal line. The piano part is quite varied: while the sixteenth-note "waves" motive and the dotted rhythm in the accompaniment dominate, the intercalated episodes in eighth notes—especially the searching ascending right-hand scales in verses 1 and 3, and the "walking bass" in verse 2—are particularly fascinating. The anacrusic first motive, previously mentioned, becomes increasingly virtuosic in the left hand with each new iteration; by the fourth "refrain," the leaps from the anacrusis to the downbeat can span almost three octaves!

The vocal line is medium range, from B♯3 to E5, which is mezzo-soprano or baritone range. The singer should accentuate the sixteenth-note upbeats, but should keep the line *legato*. The declamation should not be "darkened," but must be clear and intelligible throughout in order to maintain the dual bitterness and tenderness of the poem. Since the key centers fluctuate in parallel with the different aspects of the poem, nothing beyond what is written in the poem must be added to "enhance" the expressivity. The mélodie is certainly "romantic," but is not teary-eyed—the title notwithstanding—nor does it express pity for the plight of mankind. (Nor should the performers resort to any sudden violent effects at the end of Fauré's setting of the same poem.) The balance between the piano and the voice should be meticulously worked out so that the clarity of the text is not compromised. The vocal texture must always remain bright and colorful, even in the *forte* passages. This is a magnificent "water" text, which juxtaposes the vastness of the sea with the poignancy of a single tear. It is moving, certainly—but only if the performers maintain control of their own emotions!

All six songs are worth discovering. LA MER is a true Romantic cycle, lasting around twenty-five minutes in total. And, for pianists, there are plenty of beautifully crafted "Lisztian" passages. Curiosity seekers, take notice!

23

Thierry Lancino

L'Amour par terre (2000)

Music by Thierry Lancino (b. 1954)
Poem by Paul Verlaine (1844–1896)

Presentation

Thierry Lancino has an astonishing ability to change styles, especially when it comes to mélodie. It is interesting to see, even today, how a composer is capable of changing their grammar and writing, depending on the poetry being set[1] .

In addition to *L'Amour par terre*, I gave the first performance of another work by Lancino, *L'ESPRIT ET L'EAU*, a long cycle for baritone and string quartet set to one of Paul Claudel's *Cinq grandes odes*. It's a lengthy and fascinating work, in five movements, about forty minutes long.

We publish here the score of *L'Amour par terre*, with the composer's permission, since it has never been done commercially (Example 23.1). The mélodie was written in late 2000, and I gave its first performance, with Jeff Cohen on piano, in a program called "Autour de Verlaine" produced by the Bibliothèque nationale de France.

L'Amour par terre is the twentieth poem of twenty-two in the collection *Fêtes galantes* (1869), by Paul Verlaine. The title makes reference to the paintings of Antoine Watteau (1684–1721), which often depict country gatherings organized by aristocrats whose amusements included music and *masques*, theatrical performances that were improvised recreations of the Italian *commedia dell'arte*. The "Amour" of the poem's title refers to a statue of Cupid, god of Love. Lancino's choice of this poem is interesting: it is a bit more nostalgic and melancholier than many poems of *Fêtes galantes*, although it does embody the sense of irony that characterizes the entire collection. It has been set to music by only a few composers, all pre–World War II.[2]

---

[1] According to an article written by Sabine Ejdelman in *Le Courrier* français in April 1997, mentioned on his website (https://www.lancino.org/aboutE/longbio.htm), "Lancino's dual personality, classical and experimental, makes his music accessible, although he leaves no room for concession nor academic formulas. Discreet, curious and showing a singular culture, he is immersed in musical art away from dominant trends." He loves to compose for the voice, and has had commissions for many songs, including one for the 6th International Nadia and Lili Boulanger recital competition in Paris (2011). His *Requiem*, commissioned by the Koussevitzky Music Foundation, has been unanimously acclaimed.

[2] Prior to Lancino, Verlaine's *L'Amour par terre* was set to music by three composers who today are largely forgotten: Marguerite Béclard d'Harcourt (1907), Fernand Ochsé (1908), and Raoul Laparra (1927).

Le chant intime. François Le Roux and Romain Raynaldy, Oxford University Press. © Oxford University Press 2021.
DOI: 10.1093/oso/9780190884178.003.0024

Lancino's mélodie is around four minutes long and extremely Verlainian in the way that the composer makes room for air and breathing between the words, thus prolonging them. The wind that is a subject of the poem is perceived by the composer more as an interior breath than as a "pretty wind." Being far removed from the old illustrations or mandolin music, in the genre of a painting by Watteau, does not prevent this mélodie from being greatly enjoyed by the audience—to the contrary.

The tessitura is rather demanding, since it goes from A♭3 to G♯5—two octaves, which is rare for a mélodie. It is written in the key of F major, and is intended for a baritone.

Analysis

L'Amour par terre

Le vent de l'autre nuit a jeté bas l'Amour
Qui, dans le coin le plus mystérieux du parc,
Souriait en bandant malignement son arc,
Et dont l'aspect nous fit tant songer tout un jour!

Le vent de l'autre nuit l'a jeté bas! Le marbre
Au souffle du matin tournoie, épars. C'est triste
De voir le piédestal, où le nom de l'artiste
Se lit péniblement parmi l'ombre d'un arbre,

Oh! c'est triste de voir debout le piédestal
Tout seul! Et des pensers mélancoliques vont
Et viennent dans mon rêve où le chagrin profond
Évoque un avenir solitaire et fatal.

Oh! c'est triste!—Et toi-même, est-ce pas? es touchée
D'un si dolent tableau, bien que ton œil frivole
S'amuse au papillon de pourpre et d'or qui vole
Au-dessus des débris dont l'allée est jonchée.

Love on the ground

The other night's wind blew down the statue of love
That, in the most mysterious corner of the park,
Smiled while slyly bending its arc,
The sight of which made us dream all day!

The other night's wind blew it down! The marble
Whirled in the morning breeze, and scattered. It's sad
To see the pedestal, where the name of the artist
Could barely be read in the shadow of a tree,

Oh! it's sad to see the empty pedestal standing
All alone! And melancholy thoughts go
And come in my dreams, where deep sorrow
Evokes a lonely and fatal future.

Oh, it's sad!—And you yourself are touched, aren't
[you,
By such a sad scene—although your frivolous eye
Is entertained by the purple and gold butterfly that
[flutters
Above the debris strewn across the path.

The song needs to be sung from the point of view of a "narrator," like in Debussy's *Colloque sentimental*—that is to say, "objectively," a bit in the style of a voice-over done by a broadcast reporter in a news story. The nuances and intervals communicate ambiguity and mystery. The initial key is not clearly defined, although it seems to tend toward A minor. The voice begins a cappella for two measures, in a sort of stripped-down presentation. The wide intervals in the vocal line (particularly the many major and minor sevenths) require precise intonation that will need special practice, as is always the case when the style of a contemporary composer is unfamiliar.

The first phrase, which coincides with the first line (measures 1–3), presents a musical theme that will be encountered again later on. The piano then intervenes in a punctuating fashion; it will function as a "punctuator" throughout the narrative of the mélodie. Sometimes it acts as a commentator, emphasizing the statements of amorous failure—but then disappears each time that its presence is not required. In fact, the writing of the accompaniment is rarely discursive.

In the second phrase (measures 5–7), after the piano has insisted on a C (measures 3–5), the voice starts again on a B, before landing on a C♯ in a pattern similar to that in the first phrase. The piano offers a new "punctuation," including a fleeting minor third (C♯-E), which allows the singer, this time, to calmly find the C♯.

The third phrase (measures 9–10) is short and close to simple declamation, but in a high register. At the beginning of the fourth phrase, there is—as previously—a leap between the concluding and repeating note (D) of the piano and that of the attack (E) in the voice. The phrase presents a kind of oscillation, like an ironic musical commentary on the text of the poem, and closes the first verse. This is a contemporary take on adhering to the quatrains!

The second verse marks the musical arrival of the wind, with triplets in the piano, which sound like a statement of failure. This big gesture finishes with a rather piteous *rallentando*, while the voice, which suddenly experiences a good deal of movement, attacks a *crescendo* that will lead it to the high point of the tessitura, G♯. The verse continues with several rhythmic oscillations in the piano, before starting again, as if to comment on the word "tournoie."

For Lancino, the key to this agitation is clearly "le nom de l'artiste": the composer seems to be asking, "What is the artist doing in this scene?" If the artist's name can be read only as "péniblement" (literally, "painfully"; in context, "barely"), is it because the narrator is asking if it was he, or the wind, that made the statue topple over—or, literally, caused Love to fall (to fail)? "Le vent de l'autre nuit l'a jeté bas" follows an ascending line—when, naively, with the idea of "jeter bas" (throw down, or bring down), we would have expected a descending line. The end of the quatrain, "l'ombre d'un arbre", is very serious; it is also one of the rare instances where the composer writes a unison, on a low A, with the piano.

The third verse begins again with a sense of stasis, up until "tout seul," before a new "spinning" gesture begins—more calmly this time, with a *diminuendo* on "solitaire et fatal," which Lancino marks *pianissimo*. I advise using a *falsetto* for the high G of "fa-tal," but without "coming to an end": it's only a way of giving an impression of disillusionment and fatalism to this *piano* passage.

The feeling of stasis is found again in the fourth verse, again in triplets. After "Oh! c'est triste," there's nothing left but the pedal in the piano part. Then suddenly appears "Et toi-même, est-ce pas!" punctuated by the piano. *Marcato* intervals, which should be handled carefully, emphasize "D'un si dolent tableau" (measures 45–46); then the voice alone recreates a kind of swirl around itself from "bien que ton œil frivole" to "qui vole." Finally, in the last line, the composer substitutes a regular punctuation that "rubs against" the voice, as if to say that what we are seeing is not necessarily reality. The mélodie ends with an incomplete chord that is missing its root—the C. Perhaps this omission indicates a final agreement to reconcile with oneself—or to agree not to understand everything!

Example 23.1 Lancino, Thierry: *L'Amour par terre.* First published in *Le chant intime* by F. Le Roux and R. Raynaldy, Editions Fayard, Paris, 2004 (ref. 35-2272-9), pages 239–242.

L'AMOUR PAR TERRE

Pour François et Jeff

Thierry LANCINO
poème de Paul VERLAINE

où le nom de l'artis - te Se lit pé - ni - blement par - mi l'ombre d'un ar -

- - bre, Oh ! c'est tris - te de voir debout le piédestal Tout

seul ! Et des pensers mé - lan - co - li - ques vont Et viennent dans mon

rê - - ve où le chagrin pro - fond É - vo - - que un a - ve - nir so - litaire et fa -

Domaine de la Prée, 17 décembre 2000

24

Jules Massenet

Le poète et le fantôme (1891)

Music by Jules Massenet (1842–1912)
Poem by an unknown author

Presentation

This mélodie dates from 1891, the period during which Massenet enjoyed his greatest fame, thanks to his operas (*Esclarmonde* was first performed in Paris in 1889, and *Werther* would be given its first performances in Vienna in 1892). It was published by Heugel, in Volume III of his mélodies, and—as is the case for every volume—exists in versions for medium voice (in E♭ major) and high voice (in G major). Massenet was a prolific writer of mélodies: in addition to the eight volumes published by Heugel, he also wrote several cycles and separate mélodies not included in the collections.

One of the interesting aspects of this mélodie is that it is constructed as a dialogue between a poet and a ghost . . . but is not written for two voices (or, at least, is not formally specified as such). Massenet indicated, for The Ghost, and, in parentheses, *Comme une voix lointaine et surnaturelle* (Like a far-off and supernatural voice). It is for this reason that I recorded two versions of the mélodie, both for the REM label: the first, on the CD *Mélodies en duo* that I made with soprano Colette Alliot-Lugaz and pianist Jeff Cohen, where Colette personifies the "supernatural voice" of The Ghost; the second version, on my own, is included on a CD devoted to mélodies of Massenet, with Noël Lee on piano. Both versions work; nonetheless, at the end of the day, I think this mélodie is more interesting when sung by one voice, for the performer is obliged to vary the colors and create a sort of Schumanesque dialogue between "the ego and the id"—or between "the ego and the superego." This is not a contradiction in Massenet's works—quite the opposite, as we will see.

Moreover, in order to leave open many possibilities of interpretation, Massenet wrote many *ossia*, with the choice of octave left up to the artist. This device allows the singer to work on matters of color and—particularly if the mélodie is being sung by only one voice—to test different solutions. For example, in E♭ major—the key that I use—the tessitura of the poet is right in the middle range. The answers by The Ghost are clearly in a low tessitura, but an *ossia* can bring them into the middle

Le chant intime. François Le Roux and Romain Raynaldy, Oxford University Press. © Oxford University Press 2021.
DOI: 10.1093/oso/9780190884178.003.0025

range. It's really up to the singer to make these choices—and remember that the song exists as well in a high version, in G major.

Another interesting aspect of this mélodie is the fact that the author of the poem is unknown. Let's hope that, one day, the enigmatic identity is revealed. The poet could have been from Massenet's circle, or could have been one of his patrons. I doubt that Massenet himself wrote the poem, because none of his mélodies are set to his own texts. Unlike Saint-Saëns, Debussy, Ravel, or Gounod, who occasionally wrote poetry, Massenet never tried to be a "total" creative artist. This mélodie demonstrates the point to which Massenet, often very Romantic in his operas, is never so in his mélodies, contrary to what is generally thought. Granted, the subjects of the mélodies are Romantic, but not the compositional means employed. So performers should be prudent: the balance between intimacy and exteriorization is very difficult to find, and it is for this reason that these mélodies are often poorly sung. A professor can say to the student that "it's too much" or "it's not enough," that "the vocal contrasts are not sufficient," but never more than that. Approaching Massenet's mélodies in an operatic fashion completely distorts the style. And the opposite approach—"pure mélodie"—creates the risk of making the mélodie sound like faux Fauré. There's no comparison: Massenet's music requires a true musical characterization, as is the case with Schumann, whose music often presents the same problems of balance. To understand Massenet's songs, think of lieder—not the big, brawny lieder of Brahms or Wagner, but the concise Schumann lieder.

Apart from these general observations, there are really no other ways to penetrate this repertoire—either poetic or vocal. The music of Massenet is much more enigmatic than that of Saint-Saëns, Duparc, or Fauré, not least because of the lack of interpretive markings. One would think that an opera composer would at least include explicit dynamic markings, but there are none. The result is an enormous latitude as far as performance practice is concerned. In a certain way, Massenet is more closely allied with the first writers of mélodie, like Gounod, than Saint-Saëns or Fauré, who are much more generous with markings.

Analysis

Le poète et le fantôme		*The Poet and the Ghost*	
Le poète:	Qui donc es-tu, forme légère	The Poet:	Who are you, airy form
	Que devant moi je vois toujours?		That I constantly see before me?
Le fantôme:	Je n'appartiens plus à la terre.	The Ghost:	I no longer belong to this world.
	Je suis l'ombre de tes amours.		I am the shadow of your loves.
Le poète:	Ils sont bien morts les anciens charmes.	The Poet:	The old charms are all dead.
	Et je ris du temps où j'aimais.		And I laugh at the time when I loved

Le fantôme:	Je suis le spectre de tes larmes, Rappelle-toi quand tu pleurais.	The Ghost:	I am the specter of your tears, Remember when you cried.

Le poète:	Oui, j'ai souffert de durs martyres: L'oubli seul a séché mes yeux.	The Poet:	Yes, I suffered difficult agonies: Only forgetting has dried my eyes.
Le fantôme:	Je suis l'âme de tes sourires: Rappelle-toi les jours heureux.	The Ghost:	I am the soul of your smiles: Remember the happy days.

Le poète:	J'ai dû rêver toutes ces choses, Ce vain songe s'en est allé…	The Poet:	I must have dreamed all those things This futile dream has slipped away…
Le fantôme:	Oseras-tu nier les roses Parce qu'avril s'est envolé?	The Ghost:	Do you dare deny the roses Just because April has flown?

Le poète:	Fantôme ailé de ma maîtresse, Reprends ton vol et laisse-moi!	The Poet:	Winged apparition of my mistress, Take flight again and leave me!
Le fantôme:	Je suis l'âme de ta jeunesse, Rappelle-toi, rappelle-toi…	The Ghost:	I am the spirit of your youth, Remember, remember…

Le poète:	Ainsi, jadis, en ma demeure, L'amour descendit du ciel bleu!	The Poet:	Thus it was, long ago, in my abode, Love descended from the blue sky!
Le fantôme:	Si vite qu'en ait passé l'heure, Tu fus aimé, rends grâce à Dieu!	The Ghost:	As quickly as the hour passed, You were loved; give thanks to God!

Le poète:	Oh! ma jeunesse, êtes-vous morte… Où sont les jours où l'on s'aimait?	The Poet:	Oh! my youth, are you dead?… Where are the days when we loved?
Le fantôme:	Je suis celui qui les rapporte, Reviens vers moi: Dieu le permet.	The Ghost:	I am the one who brought them, Return to me: God will permit it.

Le poète:	O, fantôme qui me réclame, D'où donc peux-tu me revenir?	The Poet:	Oh, ghost who calls for me, From whence do you come to me?
Le fantôme:	J'ai ma demeure dans ton âme. Ami, je suis le souvenir…	The Ghost:	I dwell in your soul. Friend, I am the memory…

In light of what I said previously, I don't want to do a detailed analysis of the mélodie; instead, I prefer to discuss its themes.

At the risk of repeating myself, I will remind the reader that the most important thing is to remain as simple as possible so as not to slip into irrelevant expressionism. The structure of the poem is not complicated, since it's a series of quatrains. Its meaning, after the initial ambiguity caused by the question-answer form, becomes clear: The Poet is in dialogue with himself, as he looks back on his past. The theme of memory is dear to Massenet, who in 1868 wrote a beautiful cycle titled POÈME DU SOUVENIR, on poems of Armand Silvestre. There's no point in getting involved with problems of psychological interpretation: keep things simple, and don't get into vocal outbursts that might sometimes be incited by the part of The Poet. On the other hand, adhering to the lengths of the notes is crucial: be very clear about the ends of lines that end with question marks, so that the audience will immediately understand what is being affirmed and what is being questioned.

As in many of Massenet's mélodies, solutions to problems must be found vocally, without—as I said earlier—falling into the "operatic trap," especially if the voice is not particularly large.[1] On this subject, the rendering of the "faraway voice" of the ghost is a delicate matter; I think that it is above all a question of timbre. As we know that the ghost is, in reality, only a "personification" of the poet's memory, his can only be an interior voice. That said, the performer must not under-sing: the audience should hear everything distinctly. The accompaniment helps: as the piano is in *diminuendo* before the ghost enters *ppp*, the singer can almost murmur or whisper. To characterize the contrast between the two voices, I recommend that each time that the performer is The Poet they should resume the same vocal timbre and simply follow the dynamics written on the page (*piano*, *mezzo-forte*, etc.).

The musical construction that Massenet uses for the poem is equally very simple, since it is strophic. At each quatrain, the poem returns to a kind of refrain, with an accompaniment composed of descending-ascending arpeggios in the right hand and ascending-descending arpeggios in the left hand. This beautiful mixture of "liquid" colors could be the musical illustration of a mirror in which The Poet views himself and discovered an image different than his own. To this cyclic construction, however, Massenet brings a number of variations, instance of which can be found in the accompaniment—for example, at the end of the second quatrain, where the piano restates the initial phrase (a) (Example 24.1a) a whole step higher (b) (Example 24.1b).

With a slight *animato*, the poet reaches the height of his tessitura, on a *forte* F. The Ghost had already sung *forte*, but his line reached only a D.

The real dynamic of *forte* doesn't arrive until the last page, at the *rallentando*, with the heart-rending words of The Poet (Example 24.2).

This passage also contains a *rallentando* in the middle of an *animato*—typical of Massenet. But beware: the *rallentando* should be calculated only in relationship to the *animato*: it should not be emphatic. Meanwhile, the piano gets its only *forte* of the score, which quickly diminishes, to return to *piano*, then *pp*.

To sum up: remain serious and make a good contrast between the two characters—or the two faces of the characters, without artificial sadness or exaggeration. This mélodie allows for well-thought-out and detailed variations of vocal expressivity, and attentive listening—both internal and external—will provide the performer will ample opportunities for their refinement.

---

[1] Massenet wrote an orchestral version of this mélodie (in E♭), in November 1891.

Example 24.1 Massenet, Jules: *Le poète et le fantôme.* From *Mélodies—Troisième volume*, Editions Heugel, 1891 (ref. H. et Cie. 7041), double example: (a) page 63, mm. 1–2; (b), page 64, mm. 15–16.

Example 24.2 Massenet, Jules: *Le poète et le fantôme.* From *Mélodies—Troisième volume*, Editions Heugel, 1891 (ref. H. et Cie. 7041), page 68, mm. 49–52.

25

Olivier Messiaen

TROIS MÉLODIES (1930)

I. *Pourquoi?*
II. *Le sourire*
III. *La fiancée perdue*

Music by Olivier Messiaen (1908–1992)
Poems I and III by Olivier Messiaen; poem II by Cécile Sauvage, mother of
the composer (1883–1927)

Presentation

This 1930 cycle is the first published vocal work by Olivier Messiaen (he had written
DEUX BALLADES DE VILLON at the age of twelve; these have remained unpublished).
It is six minutes long, making it the shortest vocal work by Messiaen. Touched by the
death of his mother, Cécile Sauvage, two years earlier, the composer pays tribute to her
here by asking the question in the first song that always comes to mind upon the death
of a dear one: why? Messiaen's response, in the third song, is a work that, informed by
his religious faith, finds an answer in hope of a glorious life in the hereafter. As for the
second song, he employs a poem written in 1913 by his mother, a well-known poet,
whose works had just been published by Mercure de France. The poem used for the
second song is from the unfinished volume *Primevère*. It speaks of human love, but the
text could also refer to sacred love. Thus, the cycle constitutes a true Christian triptych,
and even in this early work the future Messiaen is manifested in broad daylight. The
first performance was given by soprano Louise Matha, accompanied by the composer,
at Paris's Salle Chopin on February 14, 1931, as part of the 523rd concert of the Société
Nationale de Musique.

It is not particularly vocally difficult: it is written in middle range (from C4 to F♯5).

Analyses

I. *Pourquoi?*

I. *Why?*

Pourquoi les oiseaux de l'air,
Pourquoi les reflets de l'eau,

Why are there birds in the air?
Why are there reflections in the water?

Le chant intime. François Le Roux and Romain Raynaldy, Oxford University Press. © Oxford University Press 2021.
DOI: 10.1093/oso/9780190884178.003.0026

Pourquoi les nuages du ciel,	Why are there clouds in the sky?
Pourquoi?	Why?
Pourquoi les feuilles de l'Automne,	Why are there [falling] leaves in Autumn?
Pourquoi les roses de l'Été,	Why are there roses in Summer?
Pourquoi les chansons du Printemps,	Why are there songs in the Spring?
Pourquoi?	Why?
Pourquoi n'ont-ils pour moi de charmes,	Why don't these things appeal to me?
Pourquoi?	Why?
Pourquoi, Ah! Pourquoi?*	Why, oh, why?

* Messiaen repeats the last "Pourquoi?" three times

Simply written, this mélodie is a modal song of very moderate output. Interpretively, the singer must to explain the narrator's perplexity and find a way to make the question marks clear. This is not always an easy task, for the vocal line sometimes descends to a C♯4, which acts as a close to the phrase (Example 25.1).

Example 25.1 Messiaen, Olivier: *Trois mélodies pour chant et piano—I. Pourquoi?* Editions Durand & Cie, 1930 (ref. D. & F. 11943), pages 1–2, mm. 1–8.

The singer must not amplify the sound, but must remain *ppp*, almost under the breath, as is indicated in the accompaniment (Example 25.2). The piano part has more to do than the voice, especially where it introduces the three "Pourquoi"'s (Why?) at the ending (measures 20–22) with thick chords, followed by runs in thirty-second notes.

Example 25.2 Messiaen, Olivier: *Trois mélodies pour chant et piano—I. Pourquoi?* Editions Durand & Cie, 1930 (ref. D. & F. 11943), page 2, mm. 9–15.

By all means, do not slow down at the end, and don't "jazz up" the last chord; the same goes for the last note in the vocal line, for this is a question with no response!

II. *Le sourire*	II. *The Smile*
Certain mot murmuré	A certain word whispered
Par vous est un baiser	By you is a kiss,
Intime et prolongé	Intimate and lingering,
Comme un baiser sur l'âme.	Like a kiss on the soul.
Ma bouche veut sourire	My mouth wishes to smile
Et mon sourire tremble.	And my smile trembles.

For this short love poem, Messiaen acts like a fervent Debussyste: the silence surrounding the murmur is created by rarefied music, where the right hand of the pianist plays a flute tune, and the left hand bangs out chords, while the voice, reduced to only a few notes (E–G-G♯-A-B♭-B♮-C-C♯), declaims in an understated manner, only to disappear in a breath, like a discreet Mélisande. The song requires a good *legato* and great intensity in order to properly weight the words without breaking up the phrases, all within the dynamics of *pp* and *ppp*. This little song is a masterwork of concision and tenderness.

III. *La fiancée perdue*

C'est la douce fiancée
C'est l'ange de la bonté,
C'est le vent sur les fleurs.
C'est un après-midi ensoleillé,
C'est un sourire pur comme un cœur d'enfant,
C'est un grand lys blanc comme une aile,
 très haut dans une coupe d'or!
O Jésus, bénissez-la!
Elle!
Donnez-lui votre Grâce puissante!
Qu'elle ignore la souffrance, les larmes!
Donnez-lui le repos, Jésus!

III. *The lost fiancée*

She is the gentle fiancée,
She is the angel of kindness,
She is the wind on the flowers.
She is a sun-drenched afternoon,
She is a smile as pure as a child's heart,
She is a tall lily, as white as a wing
 towering in a golden vase!
Oh Jesus, bless her!
Her!
Bestow on her your powerful Grace!
May she never know pain or tears!
Bestow peace of mind on her, Jesus!

This is the longest *mélodie* of the cycle at 2 min 30 sec. It is jubilant and exudes a radiant faith that would convert a heathen! For those put off by the overtly Christian character of the words, I would recommend coming up with a personal story in which a loved one is entrusted to a benevolent divinity—or simply to Love, with a capital L. The first part, which is marked *forte* and *vif* (*vivace*), and whose range extends from E4 to A5, should express joyful energy; this passage is followed by a fervent and restrained prayer, which should glide like an eagle on a current of triplets in the piano. Vocally, the performer must take care with the diction, which could suffer from choppy rhythm because of the short phrases in the beginning, and then from a colorless *piano* dynamic in the second part. Everything is a question of sonic quantity and balance. Thus, the *vivace* tempo must not be too bouncy, and the *modéré* (*moderato*) (Example 25.3) in the second section should be thought

Example 25.3 Messiaen, Olivier: *Trois mélodies pour chant et piano—III. La fiancée perdue*. Editions Durand & Cie, 1930 (ref. D. & F. 11943), page 9, mm. 55–58.

of in two-measure phrases, the internal pulse of which should be the half note, despite the meter signature of $\frac{4}{4}$.

And, above all, the rest must be adhered to before the final, childlike "Jésus" at the end. (Hint: counting the beats helps!)

In short, here is a simple cycle that pays dividends: it will allow a soprano to follow a Debussy group in a recital—let us say, for example, the *TROIS CHANSONS DE BILITIS*—with music written in a more modern style, but which is still very accessible.

26

Darius Milhaud

L'innocence (1913)

Music by Darius Milhaud (1892–1974)
Poem by Lucile de Chateaubriand (1764–1804)

Presentation

Darius Milhaud's vocal output is considerable: he wrote more than 250 mélodies; only between 1910 and 1915, he composed sixty-nine mélodies for voice and piano (some of which have remained unpublished). And yet, this part of his work remains unknown and rarely sung. The quality of the poems that he chose is not the problem: with famous names like Ronsard, Verlaine, Rimbaud, Claudel, Jammes, Gide, Supervielle, and Cocteau, among others, the guarantee of quality is almost implicit. In my opinion, the relative lack of interest by singers in Milhaud's abundant vocal output stems from two factors. First, no particular poet seems to have fundamentally impacted on the general style of the composer; in other words, it seems to me that, for Milhaud, poetry was only one medium among many others that shaped his musical inspiration. For some, that independence could seem to be a source of strength, even an indication of unshakable self-confidence. But it is also what makes this repertoire more or less interchangeable with that of another composer, as if it were not essential.

The second factor is that the voice is not an instrument that seemed to "stimulate" the composer. Nonetheless, there are many lovely, compositionally successful songs, like the four CHANTS DE MISÈRE on poems by Camille Paliard (1946), or the mélodies written on the poems of Léo Latil, a close friend of the composer who died young, during World War I. There are also the eight POÈMES JUIFS (1916), for which the composer made his own translations of the original Hebrew texts. And then there are short cycles by Milhaud that give to the voice an unexpected lyricism. Thus, from the TROIS POÈMES EN PROSE DE LUCILE DE CHATEAUBRIAND (published by Salabert in a volume of twenty-eight mélodies in 1991), I have selected the last, because of its freshness and immediacy. The text of *L'innocence* was taken from a new edition of the *Œuvres poétiques* (Messein, 1912) written by this sister so dear to Chateaubriand; Milhaud set it to music in 1913. This is a prose poem, but for Milhaud, who was twenty-one at the time, the challenge of setting a musical rhythm to the poem seems to have been as easy as child's play for him. It is, at heart, a kind of

Le chant intime. François Le Roux and Romain Raynaldy, Oxford University Press. © Oxford University Press 2021.
DOI: 10.1093/oso/9780190884178.003.0027

pagan prayer, inspired both by the eighteenth-century cult of nature and the idealization of classical Antiquity.

The range extends from C♯4 to G♯5, making the song perfect for either a soprano or a light tenor.

Analysis

L'innocence

> *Fille du ciel, aimable innocence, si j'osais de quelques-uns de tes traits essayer une faible peinture, je dirais que tu tiens lieu de vertu à l'enfance, de sagesse au printemps de la vie, de beauté à la vieillesse et de bonheur à l'infortune; qu'étrangère à nos erreurs, tu ne verses que des larmes pures, et que ton sourire n'a rien que de céleste.*
>
> *Belle innocence! mais quoi! les dangers t'environnent, l'envie t'adresse tous ses traits: trembleras-tu, modeste innocence? chercheras-tu à te dérober aux périls que te menacent?*
>
> *Non, je te vois debout, endormie, la tête appuyée sur un autel.*

Innocence

> Daughter of Heaven, lovely Innocence, if I dared try to make a poor attempt to paint some of your features, I would say that you embody childhood virtue, wisdom in the springtime of life, beauty in old age, and happiness in bad times; that, being unaware of our mistakes, your tears are always pure, and your smile always celestial.
>
> Beautiful Innocence! But alas, dangers surround you, envy is aiming at you with all its arrows: will you shiver, modest Innocence? Will you try to escape from the dangers menacing you?
>
> No, I see you, standing, sleeping, your head leaning on an altar.

As is always the case with Milhaud, there is a real sense of a tonal center, even when the work (including this one) doesn't have a key signature; here, the tonal center is E major. The major influences are both Debussy and the Fauré of *La chanson d'Ève*.

The right hand of the piano part contains a single cell that lasts for nineteen measures. The left hand plays a bright countermelody, like a long lyrical phrase for viola (Milhaud's favorite instrument)—or, in any case, a stringed instrument. On this "carpet," the performer sings and declaims at the same time, simply and with moderate flow. The punctuation of the poetic text must be strictly adhered to, and this task requires both meticulous attention and flexibility. After a reverential greeting ("Fille du ciel, aimable innocence"), the phrases become lengthy: four measures (measures 8–11, from "si j'osais" to "faible peinture") then nine measures (measures 12–19, from "je dirais" to "l'infortune"). The section concludes (measure 20) in the key of C♯ minor. The voice is set more theatrically in the second verse, in a quasi-recitative, accompanied by punctuating chords featuring an E-B "drone" in the left hand. A sense of rhythmic acceleration is created in the vocal line through progressively smaller subdivisions of the beat: from duple eighth notes to triplets (on "les dangers t'environnent") and then to sixteenth notes ("l'envie t'adresse tous ses traits"), bolstered by a dramatic *crescendo*, which arrives at its peak on "trembleras-tu."

The setting of the second question ("chercheras-tu à te dérober aux périls qui te menacent?") is where the influence of Debussy is most keenly felt: for seven measures (measures 44–50), the whole-tone-infused chords descend along a scalar bass line (B-A-G-F♯-E) in quasi-parallel harmony. The second question itself is posed rather coquettishly, with a dynamic of *piano* on the initial G♯ of "**cher**cheras-tu." The placid setting of "menacent" belies the "menace" of the word: supported by an extended G^9 harmony, the A in the vocal line on "me**nacent**"—the top note of the chord—is sung *piano* and is prolonged through a *rallentando*. The slide downward in the next measure, to a parallel F♯ dominant seventh chord, sounds surprisingly jarring because of the juxtaposition of the high E on "Non" (again, the high note of the chord) with the A♯'s (at the distance of a tritone) in the right hand of the piano. "Non," sustained by a fermata, should be sung *mezzo-piano* and with full vibrato. The concluding section, *Plus lent* (slower), returns to the E-centered music of the opening; the cell in the right hand of the piano is repeated for nine measures before the accompaniment cadences on E major in the last measure. The vocal line, still in a dynamic of *mezzo-piano*, should never slow down, as the two-against-three rhythm on "sur un autel" has already created a de facto *rallentando*.

27

Francis Poulenc

Poète et ténor (1921)

Music by Francis Poulenc (1899–1963)
Poem by Max Jacob (1876–1944)

Presentation

I have chosen this mélodie for several reasons: it is not included in Pierre Bernac's book on the interpretation of Poulenc's mélodies (see the Bibliography); it is written on a poem by Max Jacob; as the title indicates, it is written for tenor, which is rare; and it dates from a period that represents something of a lull in Poulenc's song output.

Bernac doesn't talk about *Poète et ténor* in his book for the simple reason that it was discovered only in 1993, with three other mélodies (*Est-il un coin plus solitaire*, *C'est pour aller au bal,* and *Dans le buisson de mimosas*), brought together under the title QUATRE POÈMES DE MAX JACOB. The original version of this cycle (according to what we know) is for tenor and wind quintet (trumpet, flute, oboe, B♭ clarinet, and bassoon). It seems that, after the first performance of the cycle, on January 7, 1922, at the Salle des Agriculteurs in Paris, Poulenc was disgusted by what he had written and threw away the score. He had, however, left a full score with Darius Milhaud, the dedicatee of the mélodies and the conductor of this first performance. It was Madeleine Milhaud (1902–2008), the composer's wife, who around 1990 found the score while going through some papers. The cycle has since been published by Salabert, both in its original version and in a piano-vocal reduction. I made the first commercial recording of the voice-and-winds version with the principal wind players of the Orchestre national de France, under the baton of Charles Dutoit. The reduction is unfortunately not written in Poulenc's hand: he had apparently prepared one, but, to date, it has not been discovered. This is too bad, for the composer's manipulation of instrumental timbres is very interesting, and the published reduction gives no idea of how Poulenc might have translated the wind colors in pianistic terms. No doubt he would have found a solution, because he surely composed this work, as always, at the piano and then developed the instrumental parts later: this was his procedure for *Le bal masqué*, his great 1932 cantata on poems by Max Jacob. Consequently, I advise pianists who want to play *Poète et ténor* to work out their own version by looking at both published scores (which are sold together).

Le chant intime. François Le Roux and Romain Raynaldy, Oxford University Press. © Oxford University Press 2021.
DOI: 10.1093/oso/9780190884178.003.0028

With the inclusion of this cycle, there are fifteen mélodies by Poulenc on texts of Max Jacob, thus modifying considerably the balance among the poets set by Poulenc. It is clear that Max Jacob was one of the "favorites," along with Paul Éluard (thirty-four mélodies), Guillaume Apollinaire (thirty-eight mélodies), and Louise de Vilmorin (thirteen mélodies).

Finally, the rediscovery of the QUATRE POÈMES DE MAX JACOB confirms that, in his early years, Poulenc seemed to prefer to write for voice and instrumental ensemble rather than for voice and piano. LE BESTIAIRE (we rather tend to forget about this original version), the COCARDES (on three poems of Cocteau), and *Rapsodie nègre* are all written for small ensembles, and it would not be until 1924 and the five POÈMES DE RONSARD that Poulenc started writing songs for voice accompanied by solo piano.[1]

Other voice-and-piano mélodies by Poulenc have been discovered during the last several decades: *La colombe*, *Le serpent*, and *La puce*, which are part of the original twelve mélodies of LE BESTIAIRE (Poulenc kept only six) on poems of Apollinaire; *Pierrot*, on a poem by Théodore de Banville, which we will explore later, and *Viens!* on a poem by Victor Hugo, composed by the young Poulenc (fourteen years old at the time), maybe his first song.

The QUATRE POÈMES DE MAX JACOB were written in August and September 1921, a period during which Poulenc's composition of mélodies was meager, especially compared to the prolific 1930s: between 1918 and 1926, he wrote only LE BESTIAIRE and COCARDES (1918–1919), POÈMES DE RONSARD (1924), and CHANSONS GAILLARDES (1925–1926).

The poem of *Poète et ténor* (entitled *Passé et présent* by Max Jacob) is taken (like the poems of *Le bal masqué*) from the collection *Laboratoire Central* (1921). The other texts of the cycle were published in *Les pénitents en maillot rose* (1925), therefore after the first performance of the musical work. I think that, in *Poète et ténor*, Poulenc liked this mixture—habitual in the work of Max Jacob—of the morbid (indeed, the macabre) and the humorous: the strangeness of a sentence like "Je divulgue les secrets des algues" (I divulge the secrets of seaweed)—an association of ideas and sounds similar to that in Apollinaire's work—must have appealed tremendously to Poulenc. The poem also embodies the underlying melancholy common to both the poet and the composer.

The musical writing in *Poète et ténor* is more Milhaud-like than any other work by Poulenc. Whether this was a conscious choice or not, I don't know. But, in any case, it seems that the instrumental ensemble is typical of Milhaud's chamber music, and the rather contrapuntal writing is written in grand classical style, even if it is similar to the first styles of Schoenberg and Stravinsky—and that likeness in itself is interesting. No doubt the dedication to Milhaud has multiple meanings!

---

[1] In 1934, Poulenc wrote a version of the POÈMES DE RONSARD for voice and large orchestra.

Vocally, this mélodie doesn't present any real difficulties, at least for a central tenor: the range goes from D4 to G♯5. The cycle, about six minutes long, consists of two fast songs alternating with two slow songs. *Poète et ténor* (the third of the four) lasts approximately two minutes.

Analysis

Poète et ténor	*Poet and tenor*

Poète et ténor	Poet and tenor
L'oriflamme au nord	Banner of the North
Je chante la mort.	I sing of death.
Poète et tambour	Poet and drummer
Natif de Colliour[2]	Native of Collioure
Je chante l'amour.	I sing of love.
Poète et marin	Poet and sailor
Versez-moi du vin	Pour me some wine
Versez! Versez! Je divulgue	Pour! Pour! I divulge
Le secret* des algues.	The secret of seaweed.
*Poulenc writes "les secrets"	
	Poet and Christian
Poète et chrétien	Christ is my good
Le Christ est mon bien	I say no more.
Je ne dis plus rien.	

As was previously discussed, there are always problems of metronome markings in Poulenc's works. For *Poète et ténor*, he writes quarter note = 60–65. Personally, I have chosen quarter note = 66, so that the song, despite its tempo marking of *Lent* (*Lento*), does not become too static and the motion goes forward.

First off, there are several little omissions and errors in the 1995 edition of the song. In the first measures, for example, there are no "courtesy" accidentals that indicate chromatic alterations, as have become customary in more recent editions. Thus, in measure 2, be careful to play D♯ and E♮ (see the oboe part in the full score, where the fault is identical); do the same with the entrance of the voice in measure 6: a D♭ has to be added to "**Poète**" (Example 27.1). In the following measure and in measure 10 (on "nord"), the D is natural on "**ténor**." Another little mistake: in the same measure, the hyphen is misplaced; it should be written between the *o* and the *è* and not between the *è* and the *t*: the correct pronunciation for these two syllables is [pɔ-ɛt]. The [ɛ] comes on the E♭ and the [t] is connected to the "et" [pɔɛtetenɔr].

---

[2] Colliour(e) (in Catalan, Cotlliure) is a little French town on the Mediterranean sea.

Example 27.1 Poulenc, Francis: *Poète et ténor*. From *Quatre poèmes de Max Jacob pour voix moyenne et quintette à vents*, Voice & Piano score, Editions Salabert, 1993 (ref. E.A.S. 19155t), page 10, mm. 6–7.

The dynamics are almost always written in the high part of the tessitura; the winds of the accompaniment require the vocal color to be relatively strong. Measure 6 should be attacked *mezzo-forte*, a dynamic that remains up until the *forte* of measure 15 ("Natif de Colliour"), which Max Jacob had excised to create the rhyme, before returning to *mezzo-forte* in the next measure. The dynamic will not change, except at measure 34 ("Le Christ est mon bien"), where the *forte* marking returns.

The keys change frequently, and in surprising ways, which is rare in Poulenc. For example, at the beginning the music is in D♭ minor—or in C♯ minor—before it changes to E major (measure 16). But, in the meantime, each instrument develops its own counterpoint. Alas, this handover of timbres vanishes completely from the piano part. It's because of that disappearance that this mélodie is more difficult to sing with just the piano than with the instrumental ensemble. Another thing worth mentioning: Poulenc wrote *Poète et ténor* line by line—something that is highly unusual for him. It's even more curious that the poem is very short: three of the four verses are tercets, and the fourth is a quatrain. Max Jacob rarely wrote so tersely.

The first phrase is entirely exposed in the oboe, and it will be repeated identically by the voice. This imitation, as well, is something extremely rare in Poulenc, at least during his early period. In *Le dromadaire* from LE BESTIAIRE, for example, there is also an instrumental introduction, but it doesn't reveal most of the vocal line, as it does here.

The vocal line is so regular and minimal that it almost seems like a cantus firmus—or like a trumpet in a Bach choral orchestrated by Hindemith or Stravinsky. This approach is surprising in a composer whose declamation is often so sensitive. Here, the declamation is rather neutral, without affect. Is this the reason that the composer disowned these pages?

From this lean writing we can extract, at measure 27, a sudden unison between the clarinet and the bassoon, which enunciate the theme, while the flute and the oboe oscillate between two half steps in a rather strange manner, as if Poulenc were hesitating between two keys. The religious affirmation of the fourth verse is perhaps the first in the output of the composer, whose "conversion" would not take place until 1936, at Rocamadour. To emphasize "Poète et chrétien / Le Christ est mon bien / Je ne dis plus rien," Poulenc begins the phrase on an E♮—up an augmented second from the D♭ at the beginning of the work (Example 27.2).

Example 27.2 Poulenc, Francis: *Poète et ténor.* From *Quatre poèmes de Max Jacob pour voix moyenne et quintette à vents*, Voice & Piano score, Editions Salabert, 1993 (ref. E.A.S. 19155t), page 12, mm. 29–31.

The very original conclusion follows the text to the letter, since everything stops with "Je ne dis plus rien." So there is no coda—only one final chord, and no fermata!

Pierrot (1933)

Music by Francis Poulenc (1899–1963)
Poem by Théodore de Banville (1823–1891)

Presentation

Published by Salabert, this *Pierrot* is another recent discovery. Written on May 18, 1933, it was dedicated to one of Poulenc's patrons, Vicomtesse Marie-Laure de Noailles (1902–1970), for whom this song may have been intended as a little gift. *Pierrot* lay dormant in Salabert's stockroom for over fifty years—it had been slipped between the pages of another score. The song must not have been of great interest for Poulenc, who seems to have forgotten about it, but the fact that the manuscript was found in the possession of his publisher proves that the composer—who must have been the one who left it there—was nonetheless hoping for something to come out of it. I sang what seems to have been the first public performance in March 1996, with Noël Lee at the piano, at the Salabert stand in Paris's Musicora Fair. The ambient noise of the large crowd at Musicora fit in quite well with the "fairground" atmosphere of the mélodie!

The composer's choice of a poem by Théodore de Banville constitutes an oddity in his vocal output, since, before this rediscovery, Poulenc had never been known to set the work of any nineteenth-century poets to music[3]. There are several hypotheses

---

[3] Another song by Poulenc on a nineteenth-century poem has been recently discovered: *Viens!*, on a poem by Victor Hugo, already set to music by many great composers, such as Saint-Saëns and Caplet. Poulenc's song was composed as a wedding present to his elder sister Jeanne. The unpublished manuscript, dated June 2, 1913 (Poulenc was fourteen years old!) is housed at the Bibliothèque nationale de France (MS-23584).

that can be proffered to explain why he made an exception. The first is that Poulenc chose this text as a result of his customary perusals of poetic literature—an entirely plausible possibility. The second is that he was influenced by Debussy, who had already set this poem to music in 1882: this mélodie had been published with three other early songs by Debussy (also written in 1882) in *La revue musicale* (May 1926). Finally, a third hypothesis is that Poulenc had modeled his song after one by Auric, who had also set Banville's poetry to music in his TROIS CAPRICES (1928)—which had been inspired by the same issue of *La revue musicale*!

It is amusing that, in Poulenc's *Pierrot*, we can hear a vague Debussyste color, by virtue of the song's dancing rhythm and its faux roguish tone. Nonetheless, there is a big difference: the author of *Pelléas* used the popular motive from the folksong *Au clair de la lune* as a motto, whereas Poulenc composed an original tune for the piano accompaniment in the style of a trumpet "reveille," whose rapid tempo and rat-a-tat rhythms set to repeated notes evoke the hustle and bustle of the fair.

Analysis

Pierrot

Pierrot

Le bon Pierrot que la foule contemple	Good old Pierrot, watched by the crowd
Ayant fini les noces d'Arlequin	Having done with Harlequin's wedding
Suit en songeant le boulevard du Temple.	Drifts dreamingly along the Boulevard du Temple.
Une fillette au souple casaquin	A girl in a flowing blouse
En vain l'agace de son œil coquin.	Vainly leads him on with her teasing eyes.
Et cependant, mystérieuse et lisse,	And meanwhile, mysterious and sleek,
Faisant de lui sa plus chère délice,	Cherishing him above all else,
La blanche lune aux cornes de taureau,	The white moon with horns like a bull,
Jette un regard de son œil en coulisse	Ogles her friend
À son ami Jean-Gaspard Deburau*.[4]	Jean-Gaspard Deburau.

* In Poulenc's manuscript, "Deburau" is wrongly spelled "Debureau" and the edition retained that mistake

Without going into great analytical detail about this mélodie, which is barely fifty seconds long, I would just like to point out that we are in A minor, that the range extends from C4 to D♯5 and that the song is in duple meter, which requires great precision in the articulation. As is always the case in Poulenc, the rests are not necessarily places to breathe, but merely breaks in the text. Poulenc trusts the singer to figure out where to breathe!

---

[4] Jean-Gaspard Deburau (often erroneously spelled Debureau), born Jan Kašpar Dvorák (1796–1846), was a famous Bohemian-French mime. He is the inventor of the character Pierrot, dressed and made up all in white, with sleeves that covered his hands. In the celebrated film by Marcel Carné, *Les enfants du paradis* (1945), he is named Baptiste, and is played by Jean-Louis Barrault.

In the seventh line, "Faisant de lui sa plus chère délice," a rhythm different from the other lines appears for the first time. On "Jette un regard," a rhythm of three rapid sixteenth notes—also found in *Le bal masqué*—is introduced. Between "taureau" and "Jette," I advise the singer to cut off dryly and to connect immediately with the next phrase.

The song ends without slowing down, voice and piano together, with a low A in the accompaniment and a low C in the voice.

To quote the composer, this mélodie should be sung seriously, so that the humor rings true, without exaggeration. This short, humorous mélodie is always welcome in recital, especially if the performer wants to find repertoire off the beaten track. It also works well as an encore. Finally, if a soprano sings Debussy's *Pierrot* in the first part, she can include Poulenc's *Pierrot* in the second, by transposing it up a major third, to E major.

28

RAVEL

Les grands vents venus d'outre-mer (1907)

Music by Maurice Ravel (1875–1937)
Poem by Henri de Régnier (1864–1936)

Presentation

Here is a mélodie that is rarely heard, no doubt because it was published separately. It's too bad, because it has great expressive strength, and, by virtue of its enigmatic character, opens up a dream world to the listener.

This mélodie dates from 1907, despite the fact that the Durand edition indicates 1906. Ravel was then at the height of his creative powers. The first performance took place on June 10, 1907, with soprano Hélène Luquiens and the composer at the piano. *Les grands vents venus d'outre-mer* is dedicated to the publisher Jacques Durand (1865–1928), who was also a poet and composer.

For the text, Ravel chose a relatively early poem by Henri de Régnier, from the collection *Tel qu'en songe*, published in 1892. The poem has no title, and was not often set to music. It is interesting to note that, unlike many composers, Ravel didn't have any favorite poets. His poetic research was wide ranging, only excited by novelty, as if each time he had wanted to rub up against a new poetic object, to find a new problem to resolve.

In fact, the forty-odd mélodies that he wrote represent a real mix: ex-Parnassians and former Symbolists like Mallarmé; New Symbolists like Henri de Régnier; newcomers like Tristan Klingsor (*SHÉHÉRAZADE*), Léon-Paul Fargue (*Rêves*), and Jules Renard (*HISTOIRES NATURELLES*); and much older poets like Évariste Parny (*CHANSONS MADÉCASSES*), Clément Marot (*DEUX ÉPIGRAMMES DE CLÉMENT MAROT*)—and Ronsard (*Ronsard à son âme*).

Régnier's poem is very short, and the text is rather intriguing, a bit like the style of Edgar Allan Poe. The mélodie is as enigmatic as the poem—that's what makes it interesting!—and necessitates great vocal expressivity, the opposite of his future *HISTOIRES NATURELLES*. In a certain way, the Régnier setting is rather close in style to *SHÉHÉRAZADE*. Moreover, certain effects seem to be of Oriental inspiration especially the music of the second verse.

Le chant intime. François Le Roux and Romain Raynaldy, Oxford University Press. © Oxford University Press 2021.
DOI: 10.1093/oso/9780190884178.003.0029

In this very detailed and dark mélodie, we also find the somewhat macabre character with which Ravel sets some of his early mélodies, including *Un grand sommeil noir* (on a poem by Verlaine), published long after his death.

The mélodie is published in two keys: the original is in E♭ minor (tessitura from C4 to F♯5); the transposition in F major is for high voice (tessitura from D♯4 to G♯5); it runs between 2 min 15 sec and 2 min 30 sec in length. I imagine that it was the publisher who asked for the transposition. But, as is always the case with Ravel and Debussy, the transposition somewhat changes the spirit of the mélodie, and is a little less easy for the piano. Nonetheless, the two versions were published during the composer's lifetime, and the transposed key is readily available in both a Durand edition of *Collected Songs* and a Dover edition.

Analysis

Les grands vents venus d'outre-mer	*The great ultramarine winds*

Les grands vents venus d'outre-mer
Passent par la Ville, l'hiver,
Comme des étrangers amers.

The great ultramarine winds
Pass through the City, in winter,
Like bitter strangers.

Ils se concertent graves et pâles,
Sur les places, et leurs sandales
Ensablent le marbre des dalles.

Solemn and pale, they scheme together
In the squares, and their sandals
Strew with sand the marble flagstones.

Comme de crosses à leurs mains fortes
Ils heurtent l'auvent et la porte
Derrière qui l'horloge est morte;

As though holding crooks in their strong hands
They ram the porch-roof and the door
Behind which the clock has died;

Et les adolescents amers
S'en vont avec eux vers la Mer!*
    * Ravel writes "mer" and ends with a period

And the bitter adolescents
Make off with them toward the Sea!

The formal divisions of the mélodie closely follow the spacing of the verses of the poem (three tercets, followed by two concluding lines). From the first two measures in 𝄴, where the piano plays alone, Ravel adopts a rather convulsive writing, with the marking *modéré très agité* (*moderato molto agitato*) for the first three beats, immediately followed by a *ralenti* (*rallentando*) (Example 28.1).

As a consequence, there is no definitive sense of pulse. The second measure repeats this pattern, and the voice enters suddenly (marked *très agité* and *mezzo-forte*). Be careful not to sing with too dark a sound; on the contrary, the sound should be quite bright, in order not to be drowned out by the piano. Ravel alternates between major and minor keys, thus prolonging the instability. In measure 5, in the left hand of the piano, an arpeggiated figure illustrates a menacing wind, which

Example 28.1 Ravel, Maurice: *Les grands vents venus d'outre-mer.* Editions Durand & Fils, 1907 (ref. D. & F. 7248), page 1, mm. 1–2.

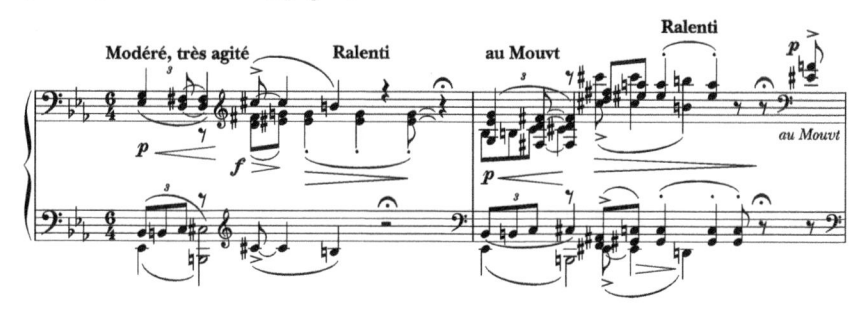

ends, after "étrangers amers," with two measures of oscillating tritones, played by left hand alone in a low range. The second verse begins in a very slow tempo. The calm returns; the vocal line enunciates the form in triplet figures. Should the final *s* of "sandales" function as an elision to "Ensablent le marbre des dalles," even though this creates an enjambment? I think so, for Ravel's musical phrase seems to indicate two spans of one-and-a-half lines, which will be repeated more clearly with the slur "et leurs sandales / Ensablent le marbre des dalles." In measures 12 and 13, the triplets should be regarded as a kind of rocking in place; the figure reminds me of the motion of some leaders of religious services and ceremonies, who turn round and round as they pray.

The third verse incites new violence. Prior to this verse, the tempo was *très lent* (*molto lento*) and *calme*; now Ravel marks *animez progressivement* (move forward step by step). The return of the voice is *forte* and *agité* (agitated). I suggest breathing after "auvent," because, next, there is a one-measure *crescendo* leading to "et la porte," ending *fortissimo* on the high F♯/G♯. The singer should remain *forte* on "Derrière qui l'horloge est morte" until the low C♯/D♯ of "morte." I think that it will be necessary to breathe before "et la porte"—otherwise, it will be difficult to stay *forte* in the long phrase that follows.

The conclusion that follows establishes a sense of calm after the storm. After "l'horloge est morte," a two-measure piano solo, with both hands in bass clef, features a written-out slowing down to accompany the marking *retenez* (hold back): the rhythmic values in the left hand progressively augment, from triplet eighth notes, to duple eighth notes, to quarter notes, while the right hand offers a few syncopated sighs and a last spasm. The vocal coda that follows (*à volonté—colla voce*) is set recitativo-style, with one low sustained bass chord in the accompaniment—the same procedure that Ravel uses in the last of the three CHANSONS MADÉCASSES. The tempo should be moderate, prolonging the mystery. The piano postlude, marked *lent—très lointain* (*slow, very far away*), ends with a series of rolled C naturals in the high register, marked *pppp*. And thus ends a song that could aptly borrow the title of a mélodie by Saint-Saëns: *Désir de l'Orient.*

In sum, let us say that a mélodie like this one requires of performers a deep commitment as well as great subtlety in order to allow the enigmatic mystery of the poem to full reveal itself.

Sainte (1896)

Music by Maurice Ravel (1875–1937)
Poem by Stéphane Mallarmé (1842–1898)

Presentation

Like Debussy, Ravel set four poems by Mallarmé to music, and this poem, written in 1865, was the first one chosen, well before the three that comprise the 1913 TROIS POÈMES DE STÉPHANE MALLARMÉ (for string quartet, two flutes, two clarinets, and piano). In its earliest version, the poem was entitled *Sainte Cécile jouant sur l'aile d'un chérubin* (Saint Cecile playing on the wing of a cherub). Need readers be reminded that Sainte Cécile is the patron saint of musicians? The mélodie *Sainte* dates from 1896, when Ravel was twenty-one years old. It is dedicated to Mallarmé's daughter, Geneviève. A short time earlier, Ravel had composed the mélodie *Un grand sommeil noir*, based on a poem by Verlaine from his collection *Sagesse*. In many ways, the writing of *Sainte* is similar: it contains the same pared-down style of piano accompaniment (described here by the composer as *liturgiquement*—liturgically). But while the extended tessitura (two octaves) of the Verlaine setting required a dark, rich voice, *Sainte* requires the voice of a monk, or of a child chorister, almost devoid of color. Written in the key of A minor, the tessitura extends from D4 to G5.[1] The mélodie is just two minutes long.

Analysis

Sainte	*Saint*
À la fenêtre recélant	At the window that harbors
Le santal vieux qui se dédore	The old sandalwood of flaking gilt
De sa* viole étincelant	Of the viol that sparkled
Jadis avec† flûte ou mandore,	Once on the flute or mandola,

   * Ravel writes "la"
   † Ravel writes "selon"

---

[1] The original version of *Sainte* was in G minor. The manuscript, however, indicates that the mélodie was written in F minor, and so, in this case, the tessitura would be even lower, from C4 to F5.

Est la Sainte pâle, étalant	Stands the pale Saint, displaying
Le livre vieux qui se déplie	The ancient unfolding book
Du Magnificat ruisselant	Of the Magnificat that glistened
Jadis selon vêpre ou complie:	Once to Vespers and Compline:
À ce vitrage d'ostensoir	At this monstrance-glass
Que frôle une harpe par l'Ange	Brushed by a harp the Angel
Formée avec son vol du soir	Forms in his evening flight
Pour la délicate phalange	For the delicate finger-
Du doigt, que, sans le vieux santal	Tip that, lacking the old, sandalwood
Ni le vieux livre, elle balance	And the ancient book, she poises
Sur le plumage instrumental,	On the instrumental plumage,
Musicienne du silence.	Musician of silence.

This exceedingly subtle poem is not so easy to grasp, and I find it interesting to reproduce here, alongside the poem itself, a sort of paraphrase in prose, written by René-Albert Gutmann (1885–1981) in his interesting—albeit biased—book, *Introduction à la lecture des poètes français* (published by Flammarion in 1946), which devotes an entire chapter to the poetry of Mallarmé:

Contre la fenêtre près de laquelle est appuyé le vieux bois de santal dédoré de la viole (celle de la Sainte), viole qui jadis étincelait (dans un trio) avec la flûte et la mandore (*sorte de luth à quatre cordes, dit aussi mandole au XVIe siècle*), la Sainte se tient, pâle, tenant un vieux livre ouvert à la page où le Magnificat ruisselle (la lumière jouant sur les enluminures), comme jadis aux offices de Vêpres et de Complies, contre ce vitrage brillant comme un ostensoir; elle frôle une harpe, (qui n'est en réalité que) le vol du soir (l'aile caressée par le soleil couchant) d'un ange; et cette harpe est formée pour la phalange délicate de ce doigt que, sans rien toucher, ni le vieux bois de santal, ni le vieux livre, la Sainte fait courir sur ce plumage devenu instrument; elle est ainsi musicienne du silence.

Against the window, alongside which is pushed the old sandalwood of the viol (that of the Saint), a viol that once sparkled (in a trio) with the flute and the mandora (a sort of four-stringed lute, also called a mandola in the sixteenth century), the Saint stands, pale, holding an old book open to the page where the Magnificat glistened (the light playing against the illuminations), as it did once during the Vespers and Compline, against this window as brilliant as a monstrance-glass; she brushes a harp (which, in reality, is) the evening flight (the wing caressed by the setting sun) of an angel; and this harp is formed for this delicate fingertip, which, without touching anything, neither the old sandalwood, nor the old book, the Saint makes it run on this plumage that has become an instrument; thus, she is a musician of silence.

Ravel phrases by quatrain, and, as always, notates what he wants very precisely: the accompaniment should remain *p sans aucune nuance jusqu'à la fin* (without any dynamic change to the end). This instruction requires the pianist to do good preliminary work, for when, at measure 16, the music goes into the high register and changes from block chords to arpeggiations, the sound will be more intense than the "liturgical" chords of the beginning.

For the singer (required by the composer to sing *p* and *très calme*—very calmly), the slurs indicate the phrasing very clearly, and Ravel takes the trouble to indicate whether or not he wants the *e*'s to be silent or not. For example, "dé**dore**" is written with slurred staccatos, while the "-re" of "man**dore**" is not placed on a separate note. That placement does not mean, however, that the sound should disappear! I advise placing the final schwa [ə] discreetly on the last beat of the tied C, which is the third beat of measure 7 (Example 28.2).

Example 28.2 Ravel, Maurice: *Sainte*. Editions Durand & Fils, 1907 (ref. D. & F. 7248), page 2, mm. 6–7.

The *crescendo-decrescendo* in measure 12 should be executed without exaggeration, as there is already an ascent of an octave in the tessitura (from G4 to G5). It is not necessary to make the double [s] for "Jadis selon": it should be sung [ʒadisəlõ]. The longest continuous phrase marked by Ravel is "À ce vitrage" (measure 16) to "Du doigt" (measure 22), but, if necessary, a breath can be taken après "vol du soir" (measure 19), providing that the F♯ that follows on "**Pour** la délicate" doesn't sound either bumpy or more intense. The apostrophe after "vieux santal" (measures 23–24) is well placed and necessary, because the next phrase should be sung in one long breath, from "Ni le vieux livre" to "balance"—a real challenge! Finally, in the last line, the only note marked *pp* should parallel the dynamic marking from the very beginning, and should be sung without expression or slowing down. The [s] of the last word "silence" should be delayed as long as possible, until the very end of the breath, as if the voice were disappearing like an echo into the arches of the church.

DEUX ÉPIGRAMMES DE CLÉMENT MAROT (1896 and 1899)

I. *D'Anne, qui me jecta de la neige*
II. *D'Anne jouant de l'espinette*

Music by Maurice Ravel (1875–1937)
Poems by Clément Marot (1496–1544)

Presentation

This is a complete cycle, although it contains only two songs and lasts only four minutes. Compared to that of Charles d'Orléans or Ronsard, Clément Marot's poetry has rarely been set to music[2]. To my knowledge, there is only one long cycle on his poems: Georges Enesco's SEPT CHANSONS (1908). Moreover, all the other musical settings date from the twentieth century. Ravel composed first what is now the second epigram: *D'Anne jouant de l'espinette*, in December 1896 (at the same time as *Sainte*); it was given its first performance in the salon of Marguerite de Saint-Marceaux in April 1898; then, three years later, the first epigram, which is a variation after a Petrarchian poem in Latin, attributed to Petronius, and set to music by Louis Durey (see chapter 13 pages 123–124). Marot transformed Petronius's Julia into Anne (no doubt Anne d'Alençon)[3]. The order with which we are familiar today was devised by the dedicatee, tenor Lucien Hardy-Thé, who gave the first performance with Ravel at the piano, on January 27, 1900, at Paris's Salle Érard, for the 280th concert of the Société Nationale de Musique. We will discuss both songs together, for the interpretation of the two utilizes the same methods. For writing the sixteenth-century French, we will use the spelling employed in the volumes of the period, reproduced in the two-volume edition of the complete works of Marot published by Classiques Garnier (1993).

Analyses

I. *D'Anne, qui luy*jecta de la Neige*

Anne (par jeu) me jecta de la Neige,
Que je cuidoys froide certainement:
Mais c'estoit feu: l'experience en ay je,
Car embrasé je fuz soubdainement.
Puis que le feu loge secrettement
Dedans la Neige, où trouveray je place
Pour n'ardre point? Anne, ta seulle grâce
estaindre peult le feu que je sens bien
Non point par eau, par neige, ne par glace
Mais par sentir un feu pareil au mien.
   * Ravel writes "me"

I. *On Anne, who threw snow at me*

Anne in a play threw snow at me,
Which I certainly thought cold:
But what I felt from it was fire,
For suddenly I was all aflame.
Since fire dwells secretly
In the snow, where shall I find a place
Where I'll not burn? Anne, your favor alone
Can quench the flame I so keenly feel,
Not water nor snow nor ice,
But by feeling a fire which matches mine.

[2] Like the other two poets mentioned, his poetry had been set to music by composers of his time (i.e., Clément Janequin [1455?–1558], Claudin de Sermisy [1490?–1562]), in a form of mixed-voice madrigals.

[3] Anne d'Alençon (1492–1562) was a French noblewoman, the niece of Marguerite de Navarre (1492–1549), sister of King of France Francis I. She was Clément Marot's patron and a platonic object of his affection. In a gesture of respect, he dedicated to her the love poems from the *Second livre d'épigrammes*.

II. *D'Anne**

Lors que je voy en ordre la Brunette
Jeune, en bon poinct, de la ligne des Dieux,
Et que sa voix, ses doigtz, & l'Espinette
Meinent ung bruyt† doulx, & melodieux,
J'ay du Plaisir & d'oreilles, & d'yeulx
Plus que les sainctz en leur gloire immortelle:
Et aultant qu'eulx, je deviens glorieux,
Des que je pense estre ung peu aymé d'elle.
  *Ravel's title: "D'Anne jouant de l'espinette"
  †Ravel writes "bruyct"

II. *On Anne playing the spinet*

When I see my neat and dark-haired lady,
Young, comely, of divine lineage,
And when her voice, her fingers and the spinet
Make a sweet melodious sound,
My ears and my eyes know greater pleasure
Than the saints in their immortal glory:
And I become as glorious as they,
The moment I feel she loves me a little.

The first problem to resolve, as with any musical work based on early French: what pronunciation? I opt for a measured modernization: for example, keep "jecta" [ʒɛkta], instead of the modern "jeta" [ʒəta], because it can be easily understood, but sing the "oy" as "ai": for example, "cuidais" [kɥide] instead of "cuidoys," which, in early French, would be pronounced [kɥidwe]. The rule is to help the audience understand most of the words, even if certain words—like the verb "cuider" ("croire"—believe—in modern French)—will be lost for some listeners; the same things for the verb "ardre,"—burn—in modern French "brûler." So, all the words that existed before our time, even if they are written differently, can be sung with the early pronunciation—which means that the singer has to learn what those words sound like. And the earlier the language, the more difficult it is to make the text comprehensible: in that context, Villon is certainly more problematic for the audience than Marot! For what concerns us, the general meaning of the two poems is clear, in any case, and even "en bon poinct"—from which the modern "embonpoint" derives—can be figured out: Anne is, as we would say today, well padded!

A curious use of prosody in Ravel: on the fourth decasyllable of the second poem, he puts two notes for "bruyct." Be careful: don't read an *e* in place of the mute *c* added in the score—in other words, don't sing [brɥijɛ] instead of [brɥi-i]—that will transform ten syllables into eleven!

The first song is in G♯ minor, and the second is in C♯ minor. The tessitura is centrally placed (from C♯4 to G♯5), but it requires soft dynamics. Given that the first performer was a tenor, the singer should be a tenor or a light baritone. But any singer can try it, on the condition that the songs not be transposed; in the case of this cycle, transposition would completely distort its very special sonority.

The first mélodie should sound as clear as rock crystal—or better, ice, in the magical piano part (for which the pedal should be well worked out) as well as in the vocal part, which sounds—like in *Sainte*—a bit colorless (in fact, on the last page, Ravel writes *très doux, presque en fausset*—very soft, almost in falsetto) (Example 28.3).

Example 28.3 Ravel, Maurice: *Deux épigrammes de Clément Marot—I. D'Anne qui me jecta de la neige*. Editions E. Demets, 1900 (ref. E. 570 D.), page 4, mm. 12–13.

The second mélodie is more of a piano piece with poetic commentary: the posture of the singer is completely disassociated from the accompaniment, since the subject listens to a sort of imitation of an early keyboard instrument (and Ravel writes in the accompaniment "*piano ou clavecin*"—piano or harpsichord, the latter of which sounds very good). The singer provides amorous commentary with classical equipoise—until, for a brief moment, in the next-to-last line, he becomes enflamed with passion and ascends to a G♯ on "glori-**eux**," while the piano (almost) imperturbably continues its solo. Altogether, the early-music mannerisms are presented discreetly. It is the task of the performers to delicately chisel the phrases and remain diaphanous and *pp*, both in the *très lent* (very slow) movement of the first song (think of the eighth note as a pulse) and in the *très léger et d'un rythme précis* (very light and rhytmically precise) motion of the second (quarter note = 80). This cycle incorporates everything Ravelian: the ethereal, dreamy magic of *Daphnis et Chloé* for *D'Anne, qui me jecta de la neige*, and the perfect, precise, music-box precision of *L'heure espagnole* for *D'Anne jouant de l'espinette*.

29

Albert Roussel

La menace (1908)

Music by Albert Roussel (1869–1937)
Poem by Henri de Régnier (1864–1936)

Presentation

La menace is Albert Roussel's op. 9. It was written in 1908 for voice and orchestra, on a poem by Henri de Régnier, who was the last great Symbolist poet of the generation of Pierre Louÿs. Roussel subsequently made a reduction for piano and voice. Dedicated to Madame Gustave Samazeuilh, it can be found in a Salabert collection of Roussel's *Douze mélodies*. Régnier's poem is taken from his collection *La sandale ailée* (1906). The mélodie, like the poem, is long, and lasts around 7 min 30 sec. The very strong text is addressed to his wife Marie de Régnier[1] and predicts, in an extremely vehement tone, what will happen to her in the future, whence the title.

Roussel is the composer who most frequently set to music the poetry of Régnier: he made nine settings of Régnier's poems. Debussy said that Régnier wrote the purest French language of his time. It's probably true, and it's also for that reason that the poetry is difficult to set to music. Writing strictly on alexandrines—even if they appear in only one of every two lines in *La menace*—Régnier breathes a regular and extremely precise rhythmicization into his magnificent language, which fits perfectly with Roussel's music. A great manipulator of rhythm, Roussel always knows how to valorize, with the orchestra in particular (it's a little less obvious with the piano) the radiance of the language. His orchestral writing is both close to that of Ravel and also very different, in the sense that, instead of working in a stripped-down manner, he prefers to carve within the thickness of the timbre, without ever becoming overly heavy. His orchestrations are always luminous—and sometimes not easy for the voice to get over! With regard to this challenge: the conductor needs to pay attention, for with two flutes, two oboes, two A clarinets, an English horn, two bassoons, four F horns, two C trumpets, three trombones, timpani and cymbals, harp and strings,

---

[1] Marie de Régnier (1875–1963) was the daughter of poet José-Maria de Heredia (1842–1905). She was a French novelist and poet who wrote under the pen name Gérard d'Houville. Although married to Henri de Régnier, she had many love affairs, including a long-term relationship with her brother-in-law Pierre Louÿs.

Le chant intime. François Le Roux and Romain Raynaldy, Oxford University Press. © Oxford University Press 2021.
DOI: 10.1093/oso/9780190884178.003.0030

we're talking about a large orchestra. In the interplay between strings and winds, we can also see the premises of Richard Strauss's FOUR LAST SONGS.

Discussion here includes both the orchestral and the piano-vocal versions, which will allow this song to be sung in a traditional recital, with the hope that all singers who study it will have the good fortune to sing it with full orchestra!

La menace is a fascinating mélodie, much more impressionistic than any mélodie of Debussy, since the subjectivity is intrinsic to the text, before being carried along by the music. It's a long mélodie, but, curiously, it works very well in recital. It's also a difficult mélodie, for the singer must find, as is often the case when singing with orchestra, a good balance between the diction and a good *legato*. The range, which extends from C4 to F♯5, is not exceptional, but it is rather wide.

Analysis

La menace	*The threat*
Vous aimerez un jour peut-être ce visage 　Qui vous plaît aujourd'hui Par le trouble le mal, l'angoisse et le ravage 　Que vous faites en lui.	Perhaps one day you will like this face 　That pleases you today For the trouble, the harm, the anguish, and the havoc 　You make in it.
Car vous aurez alors pour l'œuvre de vos charmes 　Un douloureux regret Et ce temps vous verra maudire avec des larmes 　Ce que vous aurez fait.	For then you would have as the work of your charms 　Painful regret And this time will see you tearfully curse 　What you have done.
À ces yeux détournés, à cette bouche lasse, 　Vous chercherez en vain Que l'amer souvenir disparaisse et s'efface 　De votre long dédain,	From these eyes turned aside, from this tired mouth, 　You will in vain try to make The bitter memory disappear and fade away 　Of your long disdain.
À moins que par orgueil, luttant contre vous-même 　Vous vous disiez tout bas: Que m'importe qu'il souffre et qu'il pleure et qu'il 　　　　　　　　　　　　　　[m'aime 　Puisque je n'aime pas?	Unless through pride, struggling against yourself 　You say under your breath: What if he suffers and if he weeps and if he loves me Since I do not love him?
Et, pour de cette image importune et morose 　Éloigner votre esprit Vous cueillerez l'odeur de la plus rouge rose 　Que juin gonfle et mûrit.	And, from this importunate and gloomy image 　To distance your mind, You will gather the fragrance of the reddest rose 　That June swells and matures.
Vous penserez à vous et à votre jeunesse 　Et à votre beauté. À la langueur, à la couleur, à la tendresse 　De ce beau ciel d'été.	You will think of yourself and your youth 　And of your beauty. Of the languor, of the colour, of the tenderness 　Of this beautiful summer sky.

À des pays lointains, à des villes lointaines,	Of distant countries, of distant cities
Au-delà de la mer.	Beyond the sea,
À des palais, à des jardins, à des fontaines,	Of palaces, of gardens, of fountains
Qui s'élèvent dans l'air.	That rise into the air.
Vous fermerez en vain sur ces beaux paysages	In vain to these beautiful landscapes will you close
Vos yeux, et malgré vous	Your eyes, and despite yourself
Vos yeux se rouvriront pour revoir ce visage	Your eyes will open again to see this face,
Qui vous sera plus doux,	That will be gentler to you,
Plus doux que le printemps et plus doux que	Gentler than spring and gentler than autumn,
[l'automne,	Than the earth and the sky,
Que la terre et le ciel,	Gentler than this ardent moon, crescent and yellow,
Plus doux que cette lune ardente, courbe et jaune,	The color of amber and honey.
Couleur d'ambre et de miel.	

The work is in the key of B minor, but the composer takes a good long time to establish a sense of key center. The declamatory twelve-measure introduction establishes a tonal center of E, played in unison in the orchestral version by the horns and trombones and set over a B pedal. In the piano-vocal version, the pianist must strive to replicate the clarion brass color.

The incremental harmony gives way to a chord consisting of F♯-G-A♯-B♯-C, completely ignoring the E and maintaining the tonal ambiguity, while, in three measures, the E will be hammered out on the first beats. (Example 29.1),

Example 29.1 Roussel, Albert: *La menace*. From *Douze mélodies*, Editions Salabert, 1910 and 1921 (ref. R.L. 11 273 & Cie), page 63, mm. 1–3.

The "threat" of the title is already there, in purely musical terms, and the singer must absorb it aurally, for the vocal part—which finally enters in measure 12—will never be subjected to such vehemence in the rest of the song. It's interesting to see how an introduction can gear up a singer, by exteriorizing what should be held back, in order to remain within the limits of "politeness," which may seem affected, but is certainly real in the poem.

The phrases in the first four measures are sharply demarcated, with only the E's held through the measure, like so many flashes of violence expressed then restrained, which Roussel translates into changes of meter (² ₄, ³ ₄, etc.), emphasized in the orchestral part—but not in the piano part—by double bars in the fifth, sixth, and seventh measures.

Finally, with the marking *moins lent* (less slow) (two measures before rehearsal number 1), we feel that we are moving toward something, which in this case is the entrance of the voice, marked *sombre et très soutenu* (dark and very steady). In the passage that follows, the *très modéré* (very moderate) means *less slow*: the music must be contained to be let go. The first line of the poem, "Vous aimerez un jour peut-être ce visage," is set to a highly chiseled rhythm of diverse note values (Example 29.2).

Example 29.2 Roussel, Albert: *La menace*. From *Douze mélodies*, Editions Salabert, 1910 and 1921 (ref. R.L. 11 273 & Cie), page 63, mm. 12–13.

It's with "peut-être" that the discourse truly begins, where the narrator gets going. It's a "peut-être" (perhaps) that is comparable to "n'est-ce pas" (isn't it so?) in Verlaine. It can also be taken literally: "If at least it could be like that." The following lines are quicker, with the marking *en animant* (livelier). At the end of the quatrain, marked *retenez* (hold back), we see Debussyste triplets (although the orchestration is far from that of the composer of *Pelléas*) as well as a dominant prolongation around a yearning F♯ harmony (measures 18–20)—but with still no resolution to B minor.

This first quatrain is no more than one long single phrase, and it needs to be performed accordingly, by remaining concentrated on the sound and diction so as not to be swallowed up by the orchestra. The tessitura of this quatrain (C4 to E5) is already quite demanding. The voice should be homogenous and prepared for a color that will allow the surprising Neapolitan second (C4) on "mal" (measure 16, four measures before rehearsal number 2, first beat) to cut through the orchestral texture.

The orchestra continues, at rehearsal 2, with a magnificent lyrical theme, evoking not rage or menace, but love. This phrase will blend rhythmically with the voice, at the beginning of the second quatrain, on "Car vous aurez alors," using a procedure that Roussel utilizes all the way through the mélodie and of which one must be wary: a strong rhythmic opposition between the vocal line and the orchestral (or piano) accompaniment.

There is not more to say about this second quatrain, except to signal that, far from considering the passage after "Ce que vous aurez fait" to be a conclusion (measure 30, one measure before rehearsal 3), Roussel sets up a particularly daring change of key, going abruptly from B minor to G minor. The lines of the third quatrain will be much more rhythmically demarcated: its hemistiches are set in a meter of $\frac{5}{4}$

and are punctuated by powerful chords between "détournés" and "à cette bouche" (measure 33) then between "lasse" and "Vous chercherez" (measure 35). These chords resemble those at the beginning, with the same instruments, plus trumpets and timpani. In a certain way, it's the mixture of two opposing affects: love and hate, vehemence and restraint; it's the desire to strike out or do someone harm, but finally staying the aggressing hand. With "votre long dédain" set to an unusual F♭ major chord (measure 40), Roussel chooses once more to modulate at the end of the quatrain. It's worth noting that, in the entire eleven-measure passage, there is not even one tonic G in the bassline.

The fourth quatrain, which marks the end of the first part, is less sectional. Accompanied by soft undulations in the piano part (Example 29.3), the vocal texture resembles a kind of panting—supple and devoid of anger—that seeks to calm the motion.

Example 29.3 Roussel, Albert: *La menace.* From *Douze mélodies*, Editions Salabert, 1910 and 1921 (ref. R.L. 11 273 & Cie), page 66, mm. 41–43.

At rehearsal 5 (measures 48–49, *animez un peu*), the intervals in the vocal line ("Que m'importe qu'il souffre et qu'il pleure et qu'il m'aime)" progressively expand as they ascend. The move toward resolution on B♭ in measures 50–51 ("Puisque je n'aime pas") sounds almost cadential . . . but, once again, Roussel begins the next quatrain with a change of key signature (two sharps), a change of tempo (*très modéré*) and a change of meter (to ¾). The rhapsodic orchestral theme beginning in measure 52 (*modéré*), accompanied by swirling sixteenth and thirty-second notes (Example 29.4),

Example 29.4 Roussel, Albert: *La menace.* From *Douze mélodies*, Editions Salabert, 1910 and 1921 (ref. R.L. 11 273 & Cie), page 66, m. 52.

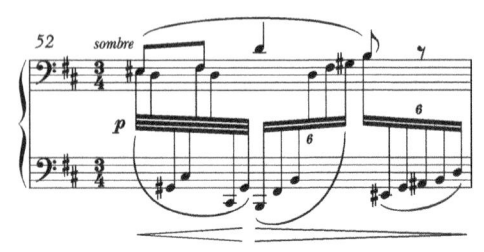

is a natural outgrowth of the expanding intervals in the vocal lines in the previous section; it will recur several times.

The fifth quatrain marks the return of the "love" theme of rehearsal 2 (measure 62, fourth measure after rehearsal number 6), transposed here to G♯ minor. At measure 64 (¹²⁄₈, *lent*), the undulating music features a prolonged F♯ dominant seventh harmony (Example 29.5). Then a sort of lullaby takes over, as if Roussel wanted to tell us that this mélodie is like a cure, an invitation to improve one's body and soul.

Example 29.5 Roussel, Albert: *La menace*. From *Douze mélodies*, Editions Salabert, 1910 and 1921 (ref. R.L. 11 273 & Cie), page 68, m. 64.

While the passage from the fourth to the fifth quatrain had been characterized by some tonal instability, the frequent presence of F♯ and B's in the bassline suggests movement toward B minor. The theme is extremely simple. The occasional orientalist touches that permeate the harmony are used frequently by Roussel, who made a thorough study of modes, and who had traveled to the Orient when he was a sailor.

At the same time, the vocal line returns on "Vous penserez à vous et à votre jeunesse" (measures 65–66, *dolce*) in a completely calmed atmosphere; the pitches are the same as those in the right hand of the accompaniment in measures 64–65, but set in subdivided rhythmic groupings to accommodate the text. Make sure to make little internal pauses between the three phrases "À la langueur, à la couleur, à la tendresse." Régnier wanted three connections of the groups of four feet (all three beginning with the sound [ala]), and even if Roussel's desire to maintain a *legato* line resulted in not setting them that way musically, the pauses, which should be executed very delicately, of course, are necessary to make the three "à la" 's audible.

The piano interlude between the fifth and sixth quatrains (measures 70–71) slides back into harmonic instability, but, at the *poco rit.* at the end of measure 71 ("À des pays lointains"), the repeated A♯'s lead—at long last!—to an arrival on B minor on measure 72 (common time, *très calme*).

The marking *très calme* begins the return to quadruple meter. Although the accompanying figures change to sixteenth-note subdivisions of the beat, the vocal line remains in triplets. This pattern is followed by the vocal peak of the mélodie— F♯—on "à des **fontaines**," in the middle of a new linking of four-foot fragments, beginning this time with four occurrences of "à des" [adɛ]. Roussel has marked them a little better than he did in measures 67–69 for the three occurrences of "à la." The triplet passage in measure 76 (*poco rit.*) is beautifully written, and the parallel with

Straussian writing—which includes a brief shift to G major (measures 77–78)—is striking. The *assez lent* (*poco lento*) that follows should in fact be understood as *un peu plus vite* (*poco più mosso*), since it came from a section marked *très calme*.

In the eighth quatrain (measures 79–86), the music returns to the dark drama of the beginning of the work. There are some notable moments, such as Roussel's treatment of the repetition of "plus doux" written by Régnier (rehearsal 9, measures 84–86): the composer followed the poet to the letter, since he recapitulates the very same motive on the same notes D–B♮—but these words are set to radically different harmonies: the first, an F diminished seventh chord (with the B of the vocal line forming a tritone with the F in the bass), the second, a luminous E dominant seventh chord that embodies the "softness" of the text (Example 29.6).

Example 29.6 Roussel, Albert: *La menace*. From *Douze mélodies*, Editions Salabert, 1910 and 1921 (ref. R.L. 11 273 & Cie), page 70, mm. 85–87.

Softness permeates the setting of the final quatrain (measures 86–92)—until the very last line of text: the words "couleur d'ambre" (measure 92, four measures after rehearsal 10) are set to an incomplete F♯ chord, in which the G natural of the vocal line rubs against the quintal harmony (including three F♯'s) in the accompaniment, adding some bitterness to the "honey." The F♯-G tension returns one last time, in measure 95, before fading away in the poignant last two measures: three soft B-minor chords.

For a lyric voice, *La menace* is a must: it pairs all the resources of well-controlled, full-throttle vocal power and musical intelligence with a gorgeous text that must be well assimilated to be effective. The reward will be the enthusiasm of the audience, which generally gives a warm reception to this beautiful but unknown vocal poem. If performers want to put together a brilliant and lyrical group of mélodies associating Roussel and Régnier, they can add to this one a work from 1907: *Les adieux*, which, like *La menace*, is also available in versions for voice and piano and voice and orchestra, and which lasts around six minutes.

30

Camille Saint-Saëns

Au cimetière (1870)

Music by Camille Saint-Saëns (1835–1921)
Poem by Armand Renaud (1836–1895)

Presentation

Au cimetière is the fifth of Saint-Saëns's MÉLODIES PERSANES, op. 26 (1870–1872) on poems of Armand Renaud, from the volume *Nuits persanes* (1870). In 1891, Saint-Saëns turned the cycle into a work with soloists, chorus, and orchestra and renamed it *Nuit persane*, dividing it into four parts with preludes. For the occasion, Saint-Saëns added the mélodie for tenor and chorus *La fuite*, based on Renaud's poem *Cavalcade*. The entire cycle is worth studying, given the quality of the musical writing (including contrasting accompaniments, which range from simple to virtuosic), and the admirable balance between the orientalism of the poems and the discreetly applied "exoticism" of the music.

I have chosen this song because it can be performed by a young singer without technical danger, and it's a good introduction to Saint-Saëns's vocal works. *Au cimetière* was originally published in two keys: A major for tenor and E major for baritone. It's worth noting that Saint-Saëns has chosen two sharp keys, with bright colors. Compared to the other songs in the cycle, which are sometimes highly dramatic and rhythmically turbulent, this is a very contemplative song. As is always the case with Saint-Saëns, it has a big, rich accompaniment, while the vocal part is rather restrained and devoid of gimmicks. The poem by Armand Renaud—a poet whose works I like very much and who was part of the first group of Parnassians—is absolutely beautiful. The volume from which it was taken was published at the same time as the songs and thus proves that she poet and the composer—like Gautier and Berlioz in LES NUITS D'ÉTÉ—worked in parallel.

As a whole, the mélodie is rather minimalist, in keeping with the text. It makes a good impression on the audience, if the interpretation is sufficiently evocative. The text is perfect for it, with as exactly as much illustration as necessary—without ever falling into pseudo-orientalism—and the language is beautifully crafted. The first

Le chant intime. François Le Roux and Romain Raynaldy, Oxford University Press. © Oxford University Press 2021.
DOI: 10.1093/oso/9780190884178.003.0031

quatrain in particular is exemplary, with an opposition between the nasal sounds of "Assis sur cette blanche **tom**be, / Ouvrons notre cœur!" and open [a] sounds in the line "Du **mar**bre, sous la nuit qui tombe / Le **char**me est vainqueur." The poem is certainly not exempt from a few coquetries ("Nous effeuillerons des corolles / Sur son Sahara")—but Saint-Saëns doesn't emphasize them.

One of the difficulties in the interpretation of this mélodie is to smoothly realize the quietude and bright color with which Saint-Saëns has infused the poem, which can be likened to the serenity of a graveyard. This graveyard, like Gautier's, set to music by Berlioz (see chapter 5 pages 53–58), is not lugubrious. It is rather the orientalist vision of a place where coolness reigns, tinged with a nocturnal atmosphere typical of the nineteenth century, which transformed the evil night into a consoling night, especially through the Romantic symbol of moonlight. There is no hidden religious motive. It is above all evocative of amorous serenity and benumbed lasciviousness, the idea that the graveyard is there only to allow the imagination to avoid thoughts of a hereafter that cannot be perceived clearly: it is an invitation to take advantage of a moment suspended in time that will fade into eternity.

Musically, another point to keep in mind is that the vocal works of Saint-Saëns always have an instrumental element—first because the composer was himself a great pianist, but also because his writing always surpasses the instrument to reach a larger, more symphonic vision. Even though Saint-Saëns wrote beautifully for the voice (he was also a singer), it remains an instrument like any other upon which he imposes his vocabulary. He is concerned with key and tessitura so that the voice will sound good, but he doesn't deny himself the opportunity to do things that other composers might not consider good vocal writing: Saint-Saëns is not a lover of the voice for its own sake, as Massenet can be. And he is not obsessed with stripping music down to its essence, like Reynaldo Hahn. Knowledgeable about Mozart, whose music he played frequently, and a great admirer of Liszt, whom he knew personally, he knew how to synthesize elements so as never to exceed a work's boundaries and how to use all the means of expression that seemed to him adequate.

In sum, *Au cimetière* has all the qualities to attract a singer, even a beginner. It requires serious vocal work, especially to find the right balance and the right color, but doesn't contain the same difficulties as others of the MÉLODIES PERSANES. As for me, I consider this cycle to be fundamental to the French vocal repertoire. It should find a similar place in vocal recitals as is held by Brahms's ZIGEUNERLIEDER. I intentionally make reference to this work, because I believe that Saint-Saëns's cycle is the equivalent, in the body of French mélodie, of German gypsy-inspired lieder. Additionally, there is much work to be done, on one hand, on the parallel between Gypsy and Italian influences in German music, and on the other hand, on Oriental and Spanish influences in the French repertoire. Music lovers, this is something to think about!

Analysis

Au cimetière	*In the graveyard*
Assis sur cette blanche tombe,	Seated on this white tomb,
Ouvrons notre cœur!	Let us open our hearts!
Du marbre, sous la nuit qui tombe	As night falls around us,
Le charme est vainqueur.	The marble's spell is irresistible.
Au murmure de nos paroles	At our whispered words
Le mort vibrera;	The dead man will quiver;
Nous effeuillerons des corolles	We will pull off petals of flowers
Sur son Sahara.	Over his Sahara.
S'il eut, avant sa dernière heure,	If, before his last hour,
L'amour de quelqu'un,	He enjoyed someone's love,
Il croira du passé qu'il pleure	He will think he smells the fragrance
Sentir le parfum.	Of the past he laments.
S'il vécut sans avoir envie	If he lived without wishing
D'un cœur pour le sien,	For a heart to accompany his,
Il dira: "J'ai perdu ma vie,	He will say: "I have wasted my life,
N'ayant aimé rien."	For I have loved nothing."
Toi, tu feras sonner, ma belle,	You, my lovely, will jingle
Tes ornements d'or,	Your gold ornaments,
Pour que mon désir ouvre l'aile	So that my desire may open its wings
Quand l'oiseau s'endort.	When the bird falls asleep.
Et sans nous tourmenter des choses	And without fretting over life
Pour mourir après,	Only to die afterwards,
Nous dirons: "Aujourd'hui les roses!	We will say: "Today we have roses,
Demain les cyprès!"	Tomorrow it will be cypresses!'

Unlike Massenet, Saint-Saëns always gives tempo markings—here *moderato assai*. In the orchestral version, he marks *très modéré sans lenteur* (very moderate without slowness) and even gives a rather quick metronome mark: dotted quarter note = 76. The mélodie contains practically no rhythmic interruptions: from the first note to the last, the tempo stays constant, with the exception of one *ritenuto* in the last system, before a reprise of the original tempo. The form is very simple, ABA'. Saint-Saëns, who was also a poet, created an interesting and very personal arrangement of the text: the first part (up until "Sur son Sahara") brings together the first two quatrains; the second part (up until "N'ayant aimé rien") joins the next two, while each of the last two verses is treated individually.

The brief introduction, consisting of A major block chords in the piano, continues into the second measure, where the voice enters. The harmony and texture remain static until the introduction of a beautiful variation: a gentle swaying figure (measures 9–10) over an ostinato A in the bass, which is present for the first thirty-seven measures (Example 30.1).

Example 30.1. Saint-Saëns, Camille: *Au cimetière.* From *Mélodies persanes*, Editions Durand, Schoenewerk & Cie, 1872 (ref. D. & F. 5065), page 3, mm. 14–20.

The second set of eight lines is an exact melodic and rhythmic reprise of the first, with the same rhythmic augmentation at the end of the eight lines: while the very regular rhythm is based on a short-long motive in each quatrain (Example 30.2a), Saint-Saëns writes long-note values of equal length at the end of the eight lines (Example 30.2b).

Example 30.2a and b

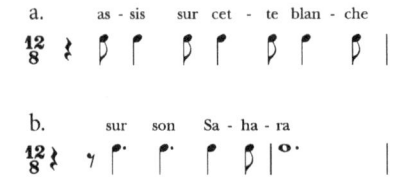

Harmonic changes arrive in the fifth quatrain, with a different accompaniment figure and a louder dynamic (*poco* forte). The lines "Toi, tu feras sonner, ma belle, / Tes ornements d'or," are now accompanied by rolled piano chords; it's as if the gold ornaments were a guitar or a lute. Here the harmony seems to be evolving towards D major—in any case, there is now a D ostinato in the bass of each harmony. All these changes, as modest as they may be, serve to illustrate the arrival, on "Toi, tu feras sonner," of another person in the graveyard: up until now, we've only had "nous" (we) and "him" (meaning "le mort", the dead person buried, a man). Is it a real woman, or a houri, one of the beautiful virgins in Allah's paradise? The D-centric harmonic interlude gives way to the gradual reestablishment of A major, via a reiteration of the swaying gesture from measures 9–10, and finally, to the block-chord accompaniment and the ostinato A in the bass. After this brief shift, Saint-Saëns returns to the last quatrain, *dolcissimo* and *pianissimo*; here, the tessitura, which ranges from E4 to A5, should be sung in a very delicate fashion.

I would like to call attention to a figure that is often encountered in this mélodie, but that is rarely found in French mélodie: the little descending melisma—the ornament in which several notes are sung on the same syllable—that occurs on "Ouvrons" and "envie," for example. Gounod uses the device—in *Sérénade*, for example—but these are Italianate ornaments. Here, the melisma is used to "orientalize" the music, as Fauré does in *Les roses d'Ispahan*. Singing it requires great precision, and the performer must be careful not to make an attack on each individual note, as, unfortunately, many singers do. Glottal stops or inopportune accents (or an [h] on each syllable beginning with a vowel) are completely irrelevant, and do not respect Saint-Saëns's writing, for melismas are instrumental ornaments, sung slurred. Now, no instrument reattacks slurred notes such as these. Moreover, Saint-Saëns chose this kind of writing in perfect knowledge of the facts: he knows what he is doing and always uses the appropriate vocabulary and grammar. On "Ouvrons notre cœur " (Example 30.3), the ornament is nothing but a prolongation of the tonic accent on "-vrons," so, obviously, it can't be sung [uvrõhõhõ].

Example 30.3 Saint-Saëns, Camille: *Au cimetière*. From *Mélodies persanes*, Editions Durand, Schoenewerk & Cie, 1872 (ref. D. & F. 5065), page 2, mm. 4–5.

Similarly, on the line "S'il vécut sans avoir envie," if Saint-Saëns puts an additional note on "-voir" (Example 30.4), it is obviously not supposed to be given the same value as the three triplet eighth notes on the beat: the "en-" of "envie" should be treated differently, because this note, set on its own syllable, is clearly placed on the upbeat. So, the second eighth note of [vwa-aʁ] should have less weight.

Example 30.4 Saint-Saëns, Camille: *Au cimetière*. From *Mélodies persanes*, Editions Durand, Schoenewerk & Cie, 1872 (ref. D. & F. 5065), page 4, mm. 29–30.

Notice that, on "Sahara," Saint-Saëns does not write a slur, because there is an [h], which should be made audible with a short breath. Although very rare a case in French, this pronunciation is allowed here because the word is of foreign origin. The second part (quatrains 3 and 4) is easy to perform and should be sung with a fuller sound.

The ending contains superb, expressive vocal writing. On the high A of "roses," find a vibrant, warm *piano* with which to sing it. A light rolling of the *r* could help to create this effect. But it should absolutely not be just a purely technical effect: roses are ambiguous flowers—they smell lovely, but they have thorns, and there is, perhaps, a small interior pain expressed by the poet and the musician: pleasure lasts for but a short time, but the eternity of death is long! The last phrase, "Demain les cyprès!"—the only phrase where the tempo slows down—should definitely not be sung more loudly than the preceeding *pianissimo* on "roses." Finally, the melismas "Demain les cyprès!" [dəmɛ̃ɛ̃ɛ̃lɛɛsiprɛ] should be handled like a stringed instrument, as a violist or cellist would do it, and let the piano create a sense of conclusion: the end of the vocal line is not the end of the song.

Si vous n'avez rien à me dire (1898)

Music by Camille Saint-Saëns (1835–1921)
Poem by Victor Hugo (1802–1885)

Presentation

Saint-Saëns set a good number of Victor Hugo's works to music: more than twenty mélodies on Hugo's poems were composed over a sixty-five-year span, from 1850 to 1915.[1] The composer chose poems from practically every volume,

---

[1] Other works by Saint-Saëns on poems of Hugo include *Les djinns* (1850), a choral work; *Moïse sauvé des eaux* (1851), an oratorio; *La lyre et la harpe* (1879), a cantata for soloists, chorus, and orchestra; and a *Hymne à Victor Hugo* for orchestra, op. 69 (1881).

although he seems not to have had a particular preference for any of them. That said, the most emblematic of these mélodies come from the early collections: the *Odes et ballades* (1826), *Les chants du crépuscule* (1835), *Les voix intérieures* (1837), and the *Contemplations* (1856), from which this poem is derived (it comes from Volume I, *Autrefois*, Book II, *L'âme en fleur*). The original title of the poem is *Chanson*. Composed in 1870 (but not published by Durand until 1896), the mélodie is a masterwork of elegance and simplicity that audiences really enjoy. It is in A major; its tessitura is medium range (from C#4 to F#5) and it is three minutes long.

Analysis

Si vous n'avez rien à me dire   *If you have nothing to tell me*

Si vous n'avez rien à me dire,   If you have nothing to tell me,
Pourquoi venir auprès de moi?   Why do you draw near?
Pourquoi me faire ce sourire   Why give me that smile
Qui tournerait la tête au roi?   That would turn a monarch's head?
Si vous n'avez rien à me dire,   If you have nothing to tell me,
Pourquoi venir auprès de moi?   Why do you draw near?

Si vous n'avez rien à m'apprendre,   If you have no news to tell me
Pourquoi me pressez-vous la main?   Why are you pressing my hand?
Sur le rêve angélique et tendre,   About this tender, angelic dream
Auquel vous songiez en chemin,   You dreamt on your journey here,
Si vous n'avez rien à m'apprendre,   If you have no news to tell me
Pourquoi me pressez-vous la main?   Why are you pressing my hand?

Si vous voulez que je m'en aille,   If you wish me to go away,
Pourquoi passez-vous par ici?   Why do you pass by here?
Lorsque je vous vois, je tressaille: When I catch sight of you, I tremble:
C'est ma joie et c'est mon souci.   That both gladdens and troubles me.
Si vous voulez que je m'en aille,   If you wish me to go away,
Pourquoi passez-vous par ici?   Why do you pass by here?

Although the composer changes the title, he retains the chanson's rather simple strophic character, making it similar to a romance: a main theme in the vocal part (which begins on the fifth scale degree, E, which sets up the questions) for lines 1–2 and 5–6 of the first verse (Example 30.5).

Following the poetic writing, this theme frames a counter-theme for the two central lines. But the two subsequent verses thwart the pattern, and give a greater depth to the amorous question endlessly repeated ("Si vous"). At the beginning of the second verse, the vocal line descends to the low part of the voice; after a reprise of the first theme on "Si vous voulez que je m'en aille, / Pourquoi passez-vous par ici?" the vocal line ends in a grand burst of lyricism on the two following lines,

Example 30.5 Saint-Saëns, Camille: *Si vous n'avez rien à me dire.* Editions Durand, Schoenewerk & Cie, 1896 (ref. D. & F. 5173), page 2, mm. 5–11.

which are quickly calmed for the last two. The opening tempo marking is *lento a capriccio*—which can be interpreted to mean "slow, according to the mood." One should use *rubato* here, something that is rarely asked for in French mélodie! But this capricious *rubato* should come from internal expression, not from unrestrained impulse. The phrasing and timbre of the vocal line should be that of a stringed instrument, and the phrases should be balanced according to what Saint-Saëns has clearly indicated. For example, all of the upbeats (an eighth note for "**Si** vous n'avez," a quarter note for "**Pour**quoi me faire") are different, and that indicates precise phrasing; therefore, in practice, a reading of the poem (without the melodic line) that follows Saint-Saëns's rhythmic patterns will help the performer to easily grasp what the composer had in mind: "Si" (If) is conditional, while "Pourquoi" (Why?) is more direct and more anxious. The *crescendo* on "auprès de **moi**?" is balanced by the *decrescendo* of "la tête au **roi**?" and requires a perfect, vibrant *filato di voce*: a whispered but not uncolored voice. The big outburst of "Lorsque je vous vois" can be, to follow the requested capricious side, *colla parte*: that is to say, lightly slowed down, but without excess, for the *ritenuto* of the last "Pourquoi" is the only true *rallentando* to execute, while maintaining right until the end of the long final *tenuto* of "d'ici" a beautiful, vibrant voice. This mélodie is ultimately a French version of bel canto writing.

Grasselette et maigrelette (1921–1922)

Music by Camille Saint-Saëns (1835–1921)
Poem by Pierre de Ronsard (1524–1585)

Presentation

It was at the end of his life, in 1920–1921, that Saint-Saëns, following the fashion of his time, set poems from the distant past to music, in this case CINQ POÈMES DE RONSARD. I have chosen the fourth mélodie of the cycle, whose original title was

Première folastrie or *Gayeté IV*. Like Saint-Saëns's *La cigale et la fourmi*, it can serve as a joyful encore, or a *scherzo* to get a laugh—both of which require sophisticated interpretative qualities: rapid and precise diction from the singer, the ability of the pianist to perform a virtuosic and precise accompaniment, and a talent by both performers for imparting humor. All that in two hectic minutes!

Analysis

Grasselette et maigrelette	*Fleshy and skinny*
Une jeune pucelette,	A young damsel,
Pucelette grasselette,	Young and fleshy,
Qu'esperdument j'aime mieux	Whom I love distractedly
Que mon cœur ni que mes yeux,	More than my heart and eyes,
À la moitié de ma vie	Half of my life
Esperdument asservie	Has distractedly enslaved
De son grasset en-bon-point:	With her fleshy perfection:
Mais fasché je ne suis point	But in no way am I sorry
D'estre serf pour l'amour d'elle,	To be enslaved by her,
Pour l'en-bon-point de la belle	By the fair damsel's fleshiness
Qu'esperdument j'aime mieux	Whom I love distractedly
Que mon cœur ny que mes yeux.	More than my heart and my eyes.
Las! une autre pucelette,	Alas! Another young damsel,
Pucelette maigrelette,	Young and skinny,
Qu'esperdument j'aime mieux	Whom I love distractedly
Que mon cœur ni que mes yeux,	More than my heart and eyes,
Esperdument a ravie	Has distractedly laid siege
L'autre moitié de ma vie	To the other half of my life
De son maigret en-bon-point:	With her skinny perfection:
Mais fasché je ne suis point	But in no way am I sorry
D'estre serf pour l'amour d'elle,	To be enslaved by her,
Pour la maigreur de la belle	By the fair damsel's skinniness
Qu'esperdument j'aime mieux	Whom I love distractedly
Que mon cœur ny que mes yeux.	More than my heart and eyes.
Autant me plaist la grassette	The fleshy one delights me
Comme me plaist la maigrette	As much as the skinny one,
Et l'une à son tour autant	And each in turn,
Que l'autre me rend contant.	Satisfies me as much as the other.

. . . .	. . . .
Ny le temps ny son effort,	Neither the ravages of time,
Ny violence de mort,	Nor violent death,
Ny les mutines injures,	Nor unruly abuse,
Ny les mesdisans parjures	Nor false oaths nor slander,
Ny les outrageux brocars	Nor insulting gibes
De vos voisins babillars,	From prating neighbours,

Ny la trop soigneuse garde	Nor an overzealous
D'une cousine bavarde,	Garrulous cousin,
Ny le soupçon des passans,	Nor suspicious passers-by,
Ny les maris menaçans,	Nor threatening husbands,
Ny les audaces des freres,	Nor fraternal audacity,
Ny les preschemens des meres,	Nor maternal homilies,
Ny les oncles sourcilleux,	Nor avuncular arrogance,
Ny les dangers perilleux	Nor perilous danger
Qui l'amour peuvent desfaire,	That can tear love asunder,
N'auront puissance de faire	Nothing will ever prevent me
Que tousjours je n'aime mieux	From always loving them
Que mon cœur ny que mes yeux	More than my heart and eyes:
L'une et l'autre pucelette,	Each of my young damsels,
Grasselette et maigrelette.	The fleshy and the skinny one.

Saint-Saëns chose to use a modernised version of the poem, which we have kept for this book and reproduced here:

Une jeune pucelette,
Pucelette grassouillette,
Qu'éperdument j'aime mieux
Que mon cœur ni que mes yeux,
À la moitié de ma vie
Éperdument asservie
À son grasset embonpoint.
Mais fâché je ne suis point
D'être serf pour l'amour d'elle,
Pour l'embonpoint de la belle,
Qu'éperdument j'aime mieux
Que mon cœur ni que mes yeux.
Las! Une autre pucelette,
Pucelette maigrelette,
Qu'éperdument j'aime mieux
Que mon cœur ni que mes yeux,
Éperdument a ravie
L'autre moitié de ma vie
De son maigret embonpoint.
Mais fâché je ne suis point
D'être serf pour l'amour d'elle,
Pour la maigreur de la belle
Qu'éperdument j'aime mieux
Que mon cœur ni que mes yeux.
Autant me plaît la grassette,
Autant me plaît la maigrette,
Et l'une à son tour autant
Que l'autre me rend content.

. . . .

Ni le Temps ni son effort,
Ni violence de mort,
Ni les mutines injures,
Ni les médisants parjures
Ni les courageux brocards
De vos voisins babillards,
Ni la trop soigneuse garde
D'une cousine bavarde,
Ni les soupçons des passants,
Ni les maris menaçants,
Ni les audaces des frères,
Ni les prêchements des mères,
Ni les oncles sourcilleux,
Ni les dangers périlleux
Qui l'amour peuvent défaire,
N'auront puissance de faire
Que jamais je n'aime mieux
Que mon cœur ni que mes yeux
L'une et l'autre pucelette,
Grasselette et maigrelette.

Of the 210 lines of this poetic work, the composer retained only the first twenty-eight and the last twenty. For the musical setting, as shown above, he divides the piece into verses of unequal length:

12 lines (4+3+2+3)—12 lines (4+3+2+3)—4 lines (2+2)—15 lines (4+4+4+2+1)—5 lines (3+2)

Written specially for baritone voice[2] in a cycle in which each mélodie is indicated for different singers, the range of this mélodie in D major goes from D4 to F5. The tempo marking is *vivamente*, which allows great latitude to the vocal-piano duo to find just the right tempo that will allow every word to be understood without having to strain the ear: a metronome marking of quarter note = 92 (we are in $\frac{2}{4}$) seems reasonable. The trap to avoid is a vocal *staccato* that would create a hopping effect in the piano's sixteenth notes; on the contrary, the performers must "globalize" through *legato* the complete phrase as Saint-Saëns indicates: the first, for example, goes from the beginning "Une jeune pucelette" to "grasset embonpoint." The *poco rit.* of this last allows the singer to savor the two words. The phrase that follows (Example 30.6) features staccatos marked over the eighth notes in the vocal line under a slur, and the singer must render this articulation as a *louré* (an articulated bow stroke separating slurred notes) rather than a hop.

---

[2] The song is dedicated to André Mauguière, a baritone.

Example 30.6 Saint-Saëns, Camille: *Grasselette et maigrelette*. From *Cinq poèmes de Ronsard*, Editions Durand & Cie., 1921 (ref. D. & F. 10,032), page 3, mm. 13–17.

And the waves of *crescendo* will thus be distinctly perceptible. The second musical strophe is very close to the first in the writing ("Las!" should be sung [lɑ], with a silent *s*), and the singer should all the same lead the vocal line up to the *poco rit.*, from "De son maigret embonpoint," another tasty treat! For the four lines of the third musical strophe ("Autant me plaît . . . me rend content"), be sure to sound the *t*'s in "grassette" and "maigrette," with no *e*'s at the end. The part with the "Ni"'s (Example 30.7) is rendered wonderfully precise by the composer's accents, which should be followed by a parallel *piano subito* in the accompaniment, then by the chattering trill in the left hand of the piano. It's suitable to remain *forte* from "Ni les maris menaçants" to "Qui l'amour peuvent défaire," taking care with the intervals between ornamented *staccato* notes in

Example 30.7 Saint-Saëns, Camille: *Grasselette et maigrelette*. From *Cinq poèmes de Ronsard*, Editions Durand & Cie., 1921 (ref. D. & F. 10,032), page 5, mm. 53–58.

order to differentiate the accents under "frères" [fʀɛɛʀə] and "mères" [mɛɛʀə]; for one should return to the *piano* for "N'auront puissance . . . que mes yeux," and end without slowing down with a *forte*, then a double *ff*. This *mélodie* is a good example of gourmet humor in music. It's a feast for the performers and the audience!

31

Déodat de Séverac

Paysages tristes–Soleils couchants (1898)

Music by Déodat de Séverac (1872–1921)
Poem by Paul Verlaine (1844–1896)

Presentation

This poem, taken from *Poèmes saturniens* (1866), Verlaine's first published collection, was the source of numerous musical settings; *Paysages tristes* is also the name of the part of the volume from which the eponymous poem was taken. Séverac's mélodie, which dates from 1898, remained unpublished for a long time; it was only in 2002 that the Presses de l'Université de Paris-Sorbonne included it in a volume entitled *Trois mélodies et quatre pages pianistiques inédites*, in the "Musique" series of the collection Musiques/Écritures, directed by Louis Jambou. The volume also contains two other previously unpublished mélodies by Séverac: a *Ritournelle* on a poem by François Coppée (probably from 1896) and *Renouveau* (1897), on a poem by Charles d'Orléans, which would also be set to music by Debussy in 1904 (it's the first of the TROIS CHANSONS DE FRANCE) and by Saint-Saëns (in 1921, with the title *Temps nouveau*).

The original 1898 version of *Paysages tristes* was revised for the first performance on May 11, 1901 (the 296th concert of the Société Nationale de Musique) at the Salle Pleyel by the baritone and friend of the composer Jean Balbous (aka Carlos Riddez), accompanied by the famous pianist Édouard Risler. This was the second musical setting of Verlaine by Séverac: the other mélodie, published by Salabert, is the well-known poem *Le ciel est, par-dessus le toit*. The only extant manuscript is not in Séverac's hand, but possibly was written out by his sister Alix. It is dedicated to "*mon cher maître Vincent d'Indy.*"

Analysis

Paysages tristes–Soleils couchants	*Sad landscapes–Setting suns*
Une aube affaiblie	A weak dawn
Verse par les champs	Pours across the fields
La mélancolie	The melancholy

Le chant intime. François Le Roux and Romain Raynaldy, Oxford University Press. © Oxford University Press 2021.
DOI: 10.1093/oso/9780190884178.003.0032

Des soleils couchants.	Of setting suns.
La mélancolie	Melancholy
Berce de doux chants	Cradles with sweet songs
Mon cœur qui s'oublie	My heart, which forgets itself
Aux soleils couchants.	Amid setting suns.
Et d'étranges rêves,	And strange dreams,
Comme des soleils	Like suns
Couchants sur les grèves,	Setting on shores,
Fantômes vermeils,	Ruby-colored spectres,
Défilent sans trêves,	Pass ceaselessly by,
Défilent, pareils	Pass, like
À de grands soleils	Great suns
Couchants sur les grèves.	Setting on shores.

Rarely has a poem given such a strong feeling of being isolated in the almost autistic melancholy of a sad landscape. And Séverac succeeds through simplicity in creating this sense of isolation. First of all, there is no time signature (a rarity for this period), which allows the singer great freedom in the framework of Séverac's marking *sans affectation et assez lent* (without affectation and rather slow), which applies both to the flow and to the articulation. Secondly, the range is narrow, from C4 to D5. The key is nominally D minor, but the overall sound is modal: for most of the song, the Aeolian mode is evoked through the frequent occurrence of C natural in the melody and the use of C-major triads at cadence points. The song has a kind of archaic atmosphere, maybe indicating the humility that must be retained in the face of such a masterful poetic achievement. And there are no dynamic markings: it seems that the volume should not exceed a gentle *mezzo-forte*. The great majority of the chords in the piano accompaniment are written in root position, and the writing suggests the sound of a positive organ (a small tabletop instrument) or a harmonium. The vocal line, in the style of a Gregorian chant, flows along through the first four lines, at which point (line 4) the "Soleils couchants" make their appearance. The last syllable ("cou**chants**") is elongated by a melismatic triplet tied to a quarter note held by a fermata. Thus, take a good breath before attacking this phrase, and sing it very "neutrally," very much like a cathedral singer. In the same way, the second phrase, from "La mélancolie" to "soleils couchants," should remain neutral and simple. It's only from "Et d'étranges rêves" that the phrasing is cut into smaller units: one line, then two lines grouped under a slur (Example 31.1), then another line, then a single word ("Défilent"), and finally a last long phrase; if necessary, a breath could be inserted just before the concluding "sur les grèves."

Example 31.1 De Séverac, Déodat: *Paysages tristes-Soleils couchants.* From *Trois Mélodies et quatre pages pianistiques inédites*, Editions Presses de l'Université de Paris-Sorbonne, Série "Musique," 2002 (ref. ISBN 2-84050-239-9), page 18, mm. 3–4.

Les hiboux (1898)

Music by Déodat de Séverac (1872–1921)
Poem by Charles Baudelaire (1821–1867)

Presentation

While it is fitting to assert that Duparc is the composer who made the greatest musical settings of Baudelaire's poetry with his two mélodies *L'invitation au voyage* and *La vie antérieure*, it is, on the other hand, unjust not to speak of other wonderful musical settings of the poetry by this great magician of the French language.[1] In this book, we have decided to study two of Baudelaire's poems. The first was d'Indy's *L'Amour et le crâne* (see Chapter 21 pages 186–189). The second is Séverac's magnificent mélodie, which dates from 1898.

The original key chosen by Séverac is D minor. Dedicated to Paul Payan, a bass at the Opéra-Comique, it is written for low voice (the range is G3 to D5). It is unfortunate that, in the volume published by Salabert that includes this mélodie, the song is in G minor—a key that, apparently, was chosen by Séverac for singers with

---

[1] Debussy's CINQ POÈMES DE CHARLES BAUDELAIRE (composed from 1887 to 1889) are not to be forgotten!

less "deep" voices. While this key signature allows a singer with a medium-range voice to perform the mélodie (if, indeed, the highest note, G5, is within the singer's range), much of the music's character is lost in this key. Fortunately, the song in the original key is reproduced on the website IMSLP.net

Analysis

Les hiboux	The owls
Sous les ifs noirs qui les abritent,	Beneath the shelter of black yews,
Les hiboux se tiennent rangés,	The owls perch in a row,
Ainsi que des dieux étrangers,	Like alien gods, whose
Dardant leur œil rouge. Ils méditent.	Red eyes flash. They meditate.
Sans remuer ils se tiendront	Motionless they will perch
Jusqu'à l'heure mélancolique	Till the melancholy hour
Où, poussant le soleil oblique,	When pushing aside the slanting sun,
Les ténèbres s'établiront.	The shadows will settle into place.
Leur attitude au sage enseigne	From their pose the wise man learns
Qu'il faut en ce monde qu'il craigne	That in this world he ought to fear
Le tumulte et le mouvement;	All movement and commotion;
L'homme ivre d'une ombre qui passe	The Man drunk on fleeting shadows
Porte toujours le châtiment	Will always pay the penalty
D'avoir voulu changer de place.	For having wished to roam.

The song ($\frac{4}{4}$ meter, *lento*) sets the emotional tone from the very first measure of the piano introduction. An ostinato half-note dyad (D2-A2) in the bass clef of the piano evokes tolling bells (albeit in bass register) on beats one and three (marked *ppp*), answered, in the treble clef, by another set of bells on beats two and four. The *meno lento* in measure 2 initiates a rocking motion, a sort of melancholy lullaby (I recommend a metronome marking of quarter note = 58). The vocal line begins in measure 7, and it would be ideal to perform it the way that Sévérac notated it: he strikes a balance between setting the poem line by line (with many changes in the punctuation, compared to the original poem), but also encompassing a complete quatrain, without overtly pointing out either the hemistiches or the rhyme scheme. Therefore, in order not to cut the quatrain into two parts, the singer should not take time after "se tiennent rangés," and should absolutely not slow down. The sung phrase should end only with the *sotto voce* of "ils méditent" (measures 13–14). The first quatrain is followed by the return of the "bells" motive, *pianissimo*. In the second quatrain, try to move forward without too many divisions of the long line, other than the slight *ritardando* on "oblique" and "s'établiront" (measures 21–24). Keep the line moving through "Les ténèbres s'établiront," for the piano is imperturbably playing the theme of the first quatrain in the accompaniment (Example 31.2). There is no disruption until then, since the bells are now set in syncopation before the first tercet.

Example 31.2 De Séverac, Déodat: *Les hiboux*. Editions S. Chapelier, 1913 (ref. S.C. 103), page 4, mm. 24–25.

Ideally, the tercet should be sung as one long phrase, moving the tempo forward ever so slightly toward the *meno lento* (measure 30) that reprises the tempo of the song's second measure. That doesn't mean, however, that the singer shouldn't take a breath!—a good place to breathe would be, for example, before "et le mouvement," lightly increasingly the speed up until the *meno lento*; in fact, this brief piano solo, inserted between the two tercets, should be played in the same subtle change of tempo that occurred at the beginning, in measure 2. The last tercet[2] (measure 32 to the end), very soft and slow, accompanied by a "celestial harp" pattern in *arpeggiando* sixteenth notes, is marked *mezza voce*; it should be sung with great warmth, but in a restrained manner, so as not to sound like "the moral of the story," or a boogeyman, but rather to evoke nostalgia for a paradise lost.

---

[2] The poem is a classical sonnet (see the Glossary page 267).

32

Germaine Tailleferre

Vrai Dieu, qui m'y confortera

Music by Germaine Tailleferre (1892–1983)
Anonymous fifteenth-century poem

Presentation

The only woman member of the Groupe des Six, Germaine Tailleferre had had, before World War II, an important place in the recital hall. A remarkable pianist, she was, between 1949 and 1957, the favorite accompanist of the baritone Bernard Lefort (1922–1999).[1] It was, however, mostly for female voices that she composed forty-some mélodies, on the poems of a wide range of authors, including Lord Byron, Guillaume Apollinaire, Robert Pinget, and Jean Tardieu. Her first, and, until recently, her only published collection was called SIX CHANSONS FRANÇAISES (Heugel, 1930), on fifteenth-, sixteenth-, and seventeenth-century texts.[2] In it we find three well-known poets: Jean-François Sarazin (1614–1654), Gabriel-Charles de Lattaignant (1697–1779), and Voltaire (1694–1778), and three fifteenth-century texts without an author's name. This cycle, composed in 1929, with an accompaniment either by piano or orchestra, is a kind of equivalent for female voice of Poulenc's famous cycle CHANSONS GAILLARDES (1925–1926), by virtue of its concision, the frank subject matter, the pastiche of early popular songs, and the refinement of the accompaniment. It lasts only six minutes (for six mélodies!). I have chosen the fourth of the cycle, relatively long: a whole 1 min 30 sec.

---

[1] He is better remembered as a former Artistic Director of the Marseilles Opera (1965–1968), of the Aix-en-Provence Opera Festival (1973–1982), and finally (1980 to 1982) of the Paris Opera. However, some of his recordings are available on YouTube (i.e., Ravel's *Chanson de Don Quichotte à Dulcinée*, with Germaine Tailleferre at the piano, recorded in 1953 during a recital in Bremen, Germany).

[2] The composer found these texts in an anthology entitled *La chanson française du XVe au XXe siècle* (Paris: Collection La Renaissance du Livre, Éditions J. Gillequin & Cie., 1909).

Le chant intime. François Le Roux and Romain Raynaldy, Oxford University Press. © Oxford University Press 2021.
DOI: 10.1093/oso/9780190884178.003.0033

Analysis

Vrai Dieu, qui m'y confortera

Vrai Dieu, qui m'y confortera
Quand ce faux jaloux me tiendra
En sa chambre seule enfermée?

Mon pèr'* m'a donné un vieillard
Qui tout l'† jour crie: Hélas! Hélas!‡
Et dort au long de la nuitée.
    * Tailleferre writes "père"
    † Tailleferre writes "le"
    ‡ In Tailleferre, the word is repeated six times

Il me faut un vert galant
Qui fût de l'âge de trente ans
Et qui dormît la matinée.

Rossignolet du bois plaisant,
Pourquoi me vas* ainsi chantant,
Puisqu'au vieillard suis mariée?†
    * Tailleferre writes "va"
    † In Tailleferre, the line is repeated

Ami tu sois le bienvenu;
Longtemps a que t'ai attendu
Au joli bois, sous la ramée.*
    * In Tailleferre, the line is repeated

True God, who will comfort me

True God, who will comfort me
When this deceitful, jealous man keeps me
Locked up all alone in his bedroom?

My father gave me an old man
Who shouts all day long: Alas! Alas!
And sleeps all night long.

I need a strapping young beau
About thirty years old
Who sleeps all morning.

Nightingale in the pleasant woods,
Why do you keep singing to me,
Since I am married to an old man?

Lover, I bid you welcome;
I've waited for you for a long time
In the pretty woods, under the boughs.

Written in the bright key of E major, the mélodie implies that the text is not meant to be tragic. The range (from E4 to G5) poses no difficulty for a medium soprano. Given the subject matter, the singer should "incarnate" a young woman married to an old fogey, and who nonchalantly sings the song at her window in order to attract a young man who would be "smitten" and ready to "abduct" her from her jailer. So, the voice should be beguiling, caressing, and even a bit plaintive in order to be convincing. As for the writing, the form is simply cyclical, varying only a little bit to follow the prosody, and each line encompasses two tercets—except for the last, which, made of only one tercet, is continued by a piano solo, in a sort of suspended waiting. The accompaniment is both simple and refined through these strange notes that give a backdrop as much of tender sensuality as sad reproach. All the expressive markings are clear and don't raise any questions. The prosody requires that the final *e* of "père" [ə] should be elided with the first line of the second tercet.

The singer can have fun with the six repetitions of "hélas," which descend sequentially in thirds, carrying the voice, as indicated, toward the low register each time in various comical ways, but without exaggeration (Example 32.1.).

Example 32.1 Tailleferre, Germaine: *Vrai Dieu, qui m'y confortera*. From *Chansons françaises*, Editions Heugel, 1930 (ref. H. 30,235), pages 11–12, mm. 7–15.

Similarly, the line "Et dort au long de la nuitée," (no liaison between the *t* of "dort" and "au"! One has to sing [dɔro]) accompanied by a B-major chord, is always sung on the same note (F♯) to evoke boredom, and can be performed intentionally "boringly"—especially on the word "long"; the pianist can help by leaning into the grinding dissonance created by the B-major chords with added D naturals. In the same spirit, the repetitions asked for by the composer on the line "Puisqu'au vieillard suis mariée?" allows for variety of expression: the first recalls, in a higher tessitura, the sequence of "hélas"'s (alas!); the second, continuing the descending thirds into a lower register, can be touching—or can be a way of touching the soft spot of a potential savior! The five-measure piano interlude that follows continues the descending third motive on the repeated pitches A and F♯; it can be interpreted as a waiting period or a hope when time seems interminable. And the song ends with a direct appeal to the rescuer, whose identity the young lady already seems to know—and who has already figured out a secret meeting place!

For lovers of historic recordings, there are two: the first, of the entire cycle, made in 1930, is sung by soprano Jane Bathori, accompanied by the composer (rereleased on CD by Marston Records in 1999)[3]; the second is a recording of excerpts (numbers 2, 4, and 6) by Irène Joachim accompanied by Maurice Franck, on a ten-inch vinyl disc entitled *Le Groupe des Six*, on the Le Chant du Monde label (out of print).

---

[3] *Jane Bathori: The Complete Solo Recordings*, Marston (Mis B00000JLKW), 1999.

33

Pauline Viardot

***Lamento* (ca. 1885)**

Music by Pauline Viardot (1821–1910)
Poem by Théophile Gautier (1811–1872)

Presentation

Pauline Viardot was not only the great singer lauded by Berlioz, Saint-Saëns, and many others: she also composed operas, chamber music, and mélodies in different languages (German, Spanish, French). A close friend of Russian novelist Ivan Turgenev, she also wrote mélodies on Russian poems translated into and adapted in French by her friend Louis Pomey (1835–1901). She also turned Chopin's waltzes into songs with texts by the same Louis Pomey. Over the course of her long life she wrote around 140 mélodies. Her first *Album de mélodies* was published in 1843, when she was twenty-two. We are happy to present here two late mélodies: *Lamento*,[1] on a poem by Théophile Gautier, published by Enoch & Costallat (Paris), and dedicated to Madame Evelyn Enoch, who was a contralto; and *Ici-bas tous les lilas meurent*, which will be discussed further on.

Pauline Viardot's setting of *Lamento* is a barcarolle with a dramatic touch. The cover of the score includes a beautiful blue illustration by an unidentified artist, in which a fisherman sails his boat on a sea that appears calm—but surging waves on the right side of the drawing seem to foreshadow a coming storm. However, the mélodie focuses only on the interior storm of the fisherman, who sings either of the lack of love in his life, or the loss of his beloved.

This mélodie (in B minor, with a meter signature of ⁶⁄₈), is marked by a sense of fluidity. The range is rather wide, from B3 to G5. For a baritone, the song could be transposed down a half step, to B♭ minor, without affecting the general color. The mélodie lasts about three minutes.

---

[1] *Lamento* was set to music by many other composers. Two of the best-known settings are by Berlioz, who gave his mélodie the title *Sur les lagunes* and included it in LES NUITS D'ÉTÉ, and by Gounod, who set it twice: first in 1841, for the mélodie intitled *La chanson du pêcheur*, and then again thirty years later, in 1872, for *Ma belle amie est morte (Lamento)*, a discussion of which is included in Chapter 16 of this book (pages 153–156).

Le chant intime. François Le Roux and Romain Raynaldy, Oxford University Press. © Oxford University Press 2021.
DOI: 10.1093/oso/9780190884178.003.0034

Analysis

Lamento

Ma belle amie est morte:
Je pleurerai toujours;
Sous* la tombe elle emporte
Mon âme† et mes amours.
Dans le ciel, sans m'attendre,
Elle s'en retourna;
L'ange qui l'emmena
Ne voulut pas me prendre.
Que mon sort est amer!
Ah! sans amour,‡ s'en aller sur la mer!

    * Viardot writes "Dans"

    † Viardot writes "Ma vie"

    ‡ Viardot writes "amours"

Sur moi la nuit* immense
S'étend comme un linceul;
Je chante ma romance
Que le ciel entend seul.
Ah! comme elle était belle
Et comme je l'aimais!
Je n'aimerai jamais
Une femme autant qu'elle.
Que mon sort est amer!
Ah! sans amour,† s'en aller sur la mer!

    * Viardot writes "mer"

    † Viardot writes "amours"

Lamento

My dearest love is dead;
I shall weep for evermore;
To the tomb she takes with her
My soul and all my love.
Without waiting for me
She has returned to Heaven;
The angel who took her away
Did not wish to take me.
How bitter is my fate!
Alas! To set sail loveless across the sea!

The immense sea above me
Is spread like a shroud;
I sing my song,
Which heaven alone can hear.
Ah! how beautiful she was
And how I loved her!
I shall never love a woman
As I loved her.
How bitter is my fate!
Alas! To set sail loveless across the sea!

Not all of the poem has been set to music: the middle verse ("La blanche crea-ture . . .") is omitted (see Chapter 16 for Gounod's setting). Additionally, several words have been changed. It's possible that these changes come from an edition of Gautier's poem other than the original *La comédie de la mort* (1838). (To my knowledge, these changes have not appeared in any of the fifty-odd other musical settings of the poem.) One particular change that I find interesting: at the end of both verses, Viardot writes "amours," plural, whereas in the original poem, the word "amour" is singular. It is difficult to draw any conclusion, but, for Gautier, the distinction is wanted, since "amours," plural, appears in the fourth line. The performer can choose to return to Gautier's original version or can use Viardot's changes: neither choice will upset the musical phrasing—the sole exception being the collision between the two vowels *i* and *e* in the fourth line, "Ma **vie et** mes amours" [maviemɛzamur], a problem that doesn't exist in the original "Mon **âme et** mes amours" [mõnamemɛzamur]. In the case in which the singer choses to retain the version in the score, I suggest making a tiny stop between "vie" and "et," without, of course, adding an [ə] to "vie"; adding a syllable to the line would transform the hexameter into a heptameter. This small stop will make the text clearer to a francophone ear.

To create a sense of flow, I would suggest a metronome marking of dotted quarter note = 64. All the thematic elements pass from the piano to the voice and vice versa. In strophic form, but printed as if there were two different forms, the mélodie has the same construction for each verse, a design that should be faithfully adhered to by the two performers. That said, there are slight differences from verse to verse: the first verse is preceded by a seven-measure piano introduction; the two sung lines that follow are subsequently repeated in the piano, then two joined lines are sung. Be careful: the printed comma after "emporte" is not a stopping point, but a *luftpause*. (Example 33.1.)

Example 33.1 Viardot, Pauline: *Lamento*. Editions Enoch Frères & Costallat, 1886 (ref. E.F. & C. 1248), pages 2–3, mm. 15–19.

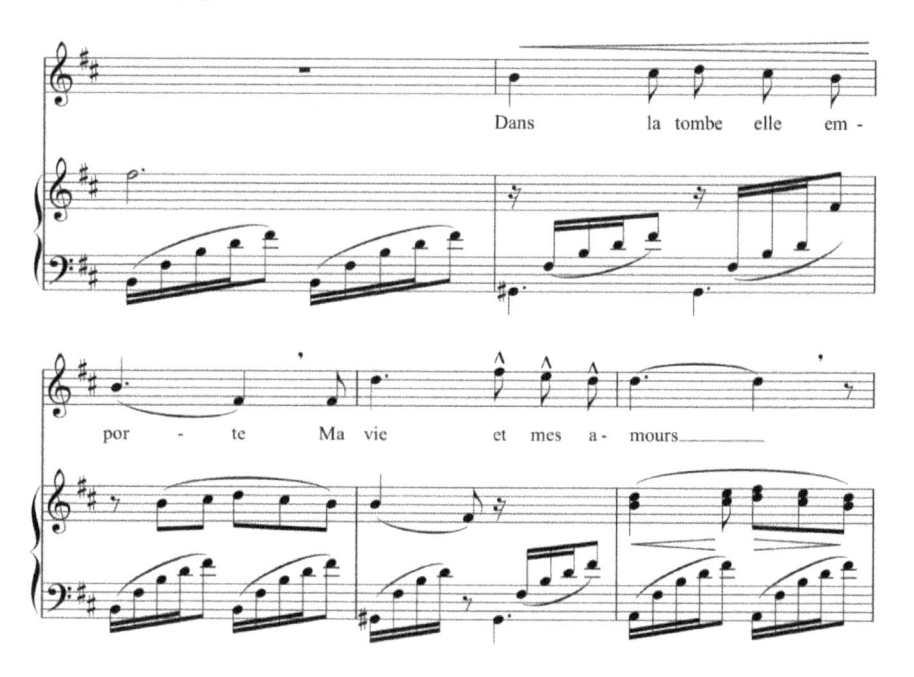

The second line contains dramatic accents on "**et mes** amours" (first verse) and "**ciel entend** seul" (second verse), which should be understood as signs of *non legato*—but not more. It is introduced by a big tremolo in the piano, beginning in measure 28 and going up to the *ff* in measure 30, and is followed by a big *crescendo* for the singer, going from the G5 of "sort" to "amer!" There is no tempo change indicated, but as the marking *1° Tempo* is written in measure 32 (after the voice has sung a *piano* "Ah!"), the *crescendo* and its dramatic peak could imply that the music could move forward a bit when the piano is playing the tremolo. The last line of each verse is divided into two phrases of four and six syllables, and should be sung *legato*. The second of these descends in dramatic manner by a full octave, and, here, the color should be the same throughout, with absolutely no change of timbre: it should be sung strictly *a tempo* for the first verse, and with a concluding *rallentando* at the very end of the song (Example 33.2).

Example 33.2 Viardot, Pauline: *Lamento*. Editions Enoch Frères & Costallat, 1886 (ref. E.F. & C. 1248): page 5, mm. 68–77.

To sum up, Viardot has written a beautiful musical setting of this poem—less well known than other versions, but one that deserves to be explored.

Ici-bas tous les lilas meurent (1888)

Music by Pauline Viardot (1821–1910)
Poem by Sully Prudhomme (1839–1907)

Presentation

The poems written by Sully Prudhomme, the first laureat of the Nobel Prize in Literature (1901), are among the favorites of composers of the nineteenth century. Pauline Viardot composed five mélodies on his verses, of which four—including this one—were taken from the collection *Stances et poèmes*, published by Alphonse Lemerre (Paris) in 1866—the same year and the same publisher as for Verlaine's *Poèmes saturniens*. The most famous of the musical versions among the thirty settings of this poem is certainly that of Fauré (op. 8, no. 3, composed in 1874). Pauline Viardot's own son, Paul (1857–1941), made his own musical setting, and his was published one year earlier than this one, in 1887, by Heugel, the same publisher as his mother's.

Published in two keys, D minor (the original key) for medium voice and F minor for high voice, this mélodie, beautifully melancholic, is the third of the collection of six published by Heugel in 1888. It is relatively short, lasting around two minutes.

Analysis

Ici-bas tous les lilas meurent	*In this world all lilacs die*

Ici-bas tous les lilas meurent,
Tous les chants des oiseaux sont courts;
Je rêve aux étés qui demeurent
   Toujours...

In this world all lilacs die,
All the songs of the birds are brief;
I dream of summers that endure
   Forever...

Ici-bas les lèvres effleurent
Sans rien laisser de leur velours;
Je rêve aux baisers qui demeurent
   Toujours...

In this world lips skim but lightly
And nothing of their velvet remains;
I dream of kisses that will last
   Forever...

Ici-bas tous les hommes pleurent
Leurs amitiés ou leurs amours;
Je rêve aux couples qui demeurent
   Toujours...

In this world all men weep
For their friendships or their love;
I dream of couples who remain together
   Forever...

Here, Pauline Viardot is absolutely faithful to the printed text: no verses are shortened or omitted, nor (as Fauré does) are any words repeated in the mélodie. In ¾ meter, the tempo marking is *andante*, and I suggest a metronome marking of quarter note = 92. The vocal range is exceedingly small, only spanning a perfect fifth (from D4 to A4 in the medium version in D minor, from F4 to C5 in the version in F minor). The piano part suggests a guitar *arpeggiando* for the first two lines of each quatrain (Example 33.3), and the dynamic for the voice in this spot is *mf*. For the two other lines of each quatrain, the piano part comprises a simple line of two "voices" played in a direct manner, in a major key, for the first verse, while the voice is marked *p*.

Example 33.3 Viardot, Pauline: *Ici-bas tous les lilas meurent*. From *Six mélodies*, Editions Henri Heugel, 1888 (ref. H. 6399), page 1, mm. 6–10.

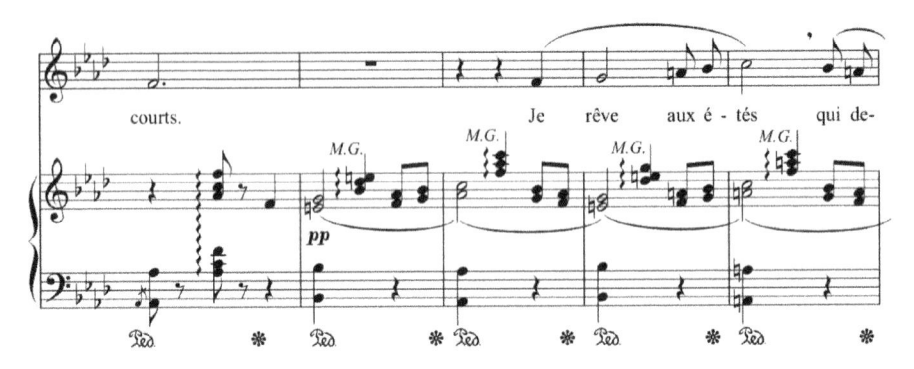

The second verse ends on a dominant seventh chord, which is connected immediately to the last verse, in which, on the word "pleurent," a new key appears: E♭ major for the medium-voice version, G♭ major for the high-voice version (in Example 33.4).

Example 33.4 Viardot, Pauline: *Ici-bas tous les lilas meurent*. From *Six mélodies*, Editions Henri Heugel, 1888 (ref. H. 6399), page 3–4, mm. 27–30.

Then, to conclude, it's the piano that has the melody, *pp*, for the thirteen final measures. During this section, the dreamy voice remains on the same note—the highest that it has to sing (either A4 or C5, depending on the key)—on "Je rêve aux couples qui demeurent / Toujours . . ."; the passage is set in F major, but the piano returns to the minor three measures before the end.

Compared with Fauré's mélodie, Viardot's version doesn't have any moments of brilliance or outburst: the only expressive markings are two pairs of *crescendi-decrescendi*, on "couples" and "demeurent." The mélodie maintains a sort of dreamy tenderness, evoking a simple, almost naïve sentiment of "if only it were possible . . . ."

For the simplicity of expression required by this mélodie, the singer must know how to perform undemonstratively, in a manner worthy of what the composer wrote. The last song of our book is a *chant intime* "par excellence"!

Glossary of Poetic Forms and Terms

Alexandrine a verse of twelve syllables, the quintessential form of a verse in classical French poetry.

Caesura a break or pause near the middle of a line.

Decasyllable a word or line of verse with ten syllables.

Enjambment the running of the sense and syntax of one line into the next; it isolates a particular word or phrase, encouraging the reader to give it both greater attention and extra stress. One of the most famous is set by Verlaine in "Clair de lune" from *Fêtes galantes* (set to music many times—for instance, by Fauré and Debussy), between the third and the fourth verse:

> "Jouant du luth et dansant et quasi
> Tristes sous leur déguisement fantasque."

The emphasis is there brought to the adjective "Tristes," set at the beginning of the fourth verse, although the vocal phrasing should give "et quasi tristes." It implies also that "quasi," the word ending the third verse, being the rime with "choisi" [ʃwazi] (end of the first verse), has to be normally sung [kwazi], in what is called a "rich rime," making not only the last syllable, but the two last syllables riming together.

Foot The basic unit of measurement of accentual-syllabic meter. A foot usually contains one stressed syllable and at least one unstressed syllable.

Hemistich a half-line of verse, followed and preceded by a caesura and making up a single overall prosodic or verse unit.

Octosyllable a word or line of verse with eight syllables.

Quatrain four lines of verse, usually with alternate rhymes.

Sestina a poem with six stanzas of six lines and a final triplet; all stanzas have the same six words at the line-ends in six different sequences that follow a fixed pattern.

Sonnet In French classical poetry, a sonnet is made of fourteen verses. Each verse should be either an alexandrine or a decasyllable. The fourteen verses are divided in four strophes, the first two of four verses, the last two of three verses.

Tercet a set or group of three lines of verse rhyming together or connected by rhyme with an adjacent tercet.

Bibliography

Interpretation of French Mélodie

Abraham, Hélène. *Un art de l'interprétation: Claire Croiza: Les Cahiers d'une auditrice*. Paris: Office de centralisation d'ouvrages, 1954. Reprinted in English as *The Singer as Interpreter: Claire Croiza's Master Classes*. Edited and translated by Betty Bannerman. London: Victor Gollancz, 1989.

Bathori, Jane. *Sur l'interprétation des mélodies de Claude Debussy*. Paris: Les Éditions ouvrières, 1953. Reprinted in English as *On the Interpretation of the Mélodies of Claude Debussy*. Annotated and translated by Linda Laurent. Hillsdale, NY: Pendragon Press, 1998.

Bergeron, Katherine. *Voice Lessons: French Mélodie in the Belle Epoque*. New York: Oxford University Press, 2010.

Bernac, Pierre. *The Interpretation of French Song*. New York: Norton Library, 1978.

Bernac, Pierre. *Francis Poulenc et ses mélodies*. Paris: Buchet Chastel, 2016. Reprinted in English as *Francis Poulenc: The Man and His Songs*. Edited and translated by Winifred Radford. London: Kahn & Averill, 2001.

Daykin, Frank. *The Encyclopedia of French Art Song*. Vox Musicae Series 10. Hillsdale, NY: Pendragon Press, 2013.

Gartside, Robert. *Interpreting the Songs of Maurice Ravel* (bilingual edition). Webster, NY: Leyerle Publications, 1992.

Gerar, Marcelle. *A la recherche du chant perdu*. Preface by Reynaldo Hahn. Paris: Alphonse Leduc, 1938.

Grubb, Thomas. *Singing in French: A Manual of French Diction and French Vocal Repertoire*. New York: Schirmer Books, 1979.

Hunter, David. *Understanding French Verse: A Guide for Singers*. New York: Oxford University Press, 2005.

Le Van, Timothy. *Masters of the French Art Song: Translations of the Complete Songs of Chausson, Debussy, Duparc, Fauré & Ravel*. Lanham, MD, and London: Scarecrow Press, 2001.

Nedecky, Jason. *French Diction for Singers: A Handbook of Pronunciation for French Opera and Mélodie*. Toronto: Jason Nedecky (University of Toronto Bookstore), 2011.

Panzéra, Charles. *50 mélodies françaises*. Mainz, Germany: Schott, 1964.

Patel, Aniruddh D. *Music, Language and the Brain*. New York: Oxford University Press, 2008.

Poulenc, Francis. *Journal de mes mélodies*. Paris: Cicero, 1993. Reprinted in English as *Francis Poulenc—Diary of My Songs*. Translations by Winifred Radford, with an introduction by Graham Johnson. London: Kahn & Averill, 2006.

Rohinsky, Marie-Claire. *The Singer's Debussy*. New York: Pelion Press, 1987.

History of French Mélodie

Adams, David. *A Handbook of Diction for Singers, Italian, German, French*. New York: Oxford University Press, 2008.

Barthes, Roland. *L'obvie et l'obtus*. Essais critiques III chapter "Le corps de la musique." Paris: Le Seuil, collection "Tel Quel," 1982. Reprinted as a pocket book in *Points Essais, 239*. Paris: Le Seuil (1992).

Chimènes, Myriam. *Mécènes et musiciens, du salon au concert à Paris sous la IIIème république*. Paris: Fayard, 2004.

Faure, Michel and Vincent Vivès. *Histoire et poétique de la mélodie française*. Preface by François Le Roux. Paris: CNRS Éditions, 2000.

Flothuis, Marius. "... *Exprimer l'inexprimable ...*": *Essai sur la mélodie française depuis Duparc*. Amsterdam: Rodopi, 1996. Contains five unpublished mélodies by Caplet, Chausson, and Roussel.

François-Sappey, Brigitte and Gilles Cantagrel. *Guide de la mélodie et du lied*. Paris: Fayard, "Les indispensables de la musique", 1994.

Johnson, Graham. *The Songmakers' Almanac: Twenty Years of Song Recitals in London; Reflections and Commentaries*. London: Thames Publishing, 1996.

Johnson, Graham and Richard Stokes. *A French Song Companion*. New York: Oxford University Press, 2000.

Meister, Barbara. *Nineteenth Century French Song: Fauré, Chausson, Duparc, Debussy*. Bloomington: Indiana University Press, 1998.

Miller, Catherine. *Cocteau, Apollinaire, Claudel et le Groupe des Six*. Sprimont, Belgium: Mardaga, 2003.

Noske, Frits. *La mélodie française de Berlioz à Duparc*. Paris: Presses Universitaires de France, 1954. Revised and translated into English by Rita Benton as *French Song from Berlioz to Duparc*. New York: Dover Publications, 1970; 2nd edition 2012.

Reuter, Evelyn. *La mélodie et le lied*. Paris: Presses Universitaires de France, "Que sais-je?", 1950.

Tunley, David. *Salons, Singers, and Songs: A Background to Romantic French Song*. Farnham, UK: Ashgate, 2002.

White, Ruth L. *Verlaine et les musiciens*. Paris: Minard, 1992.

Vocal Technique

Bourlet, Dominique. *Le Vlac! Approche napolitaine du chant lyrique*. Paris: Francis Van de Velde, 1978.

Davids, Julia and Stephen LaTour. *Vocal Technique: A Guide for Conductors, Teachers, and Singers*. Long Grove, IL: Waveland Press, 2012.

Miller, Richard. *On the Art of Singing*. New York and Oxford: Oxford University Press, 1996.

Panzéra, Charles. *L'amour de chanter*. Paris: Henry Lemoine, 1957.

Panzéra, Charles. *L'art de chanter*. Paris: Billaudot, 1972.

Panzéra, Charles. *L'art vocal, trente leçons de chant*. Paris: Librairie théâtrale, 1959.

Composers

Baker, Théodore and Nicolas Slonimsky. *Baker's Biographical Dictionary of Musicians*. New York: G. Schirmer, 1958.

Launey, Florence. *Les compositrices en France au XIXe siècle*. Paris : Fayard, 2006.

Georges Auric

Auric, Georges. *Quand j'étais là*. Paris: Grasset, 1979.

Mas, Josiane (sous la direction de). *Centenaire Georges Auric-Francis Poulenc*. Montpellier: Centre d'études du XXᵉ siècle, Université de Montpellier II, 2001.

Roust, Colin. *Georges Auric, a Life in Music and Politics*. New York: Oxford University Press, 2020.

Hector Berlioz

Berlioz, Hector. *The Memoirs of Hector Berlioz*. Translated by David Cairns. Everyman's Library Series. New York: Knopf Doubleday Publishing Group, 2002.

Cairns, David. *Hector Berlioz*. Paris: Fayard, 2002.

Holoman, D. Kern. *Berlioz: A Musical Biography of the Creative Genius of the Romantic Era*. Cambridge, MA: Harvard University Press, 1989.

Macdonald, Hugh. *Berlioz*. Master Musician Series. New York: Oxford University Press, 2001.

Lili Boulanger

Laederich, Alexandra (editor). *Nadia et Lili Boulanger, témoignages et études*. Lyon, France: Symétrie, 2007.
Potter, Caroline. *Nadia and Lili Boulanger*. New York: Routledge, 2016.
Spycket, Jérôme. *À la recherche de Lili Boulanger*. Paris: Fayard, 2004.

Emmanuel Chabrier

Chabrier, Emmanuel. *Correspondance*. Edited by Roger Delage. Paris: Klincksieck, 1994.
Delage, Roger. *Emmanuel Chabrier*. Paris: Fayard, 1999.

Cécile Chaminade

Citron, Marcia J. *Cécile Chaminade: A Bio-Bibliography*. Westport, CA: Greenwood Press, 1988.
Tardif, Cécile. *Portrait de Cécile Chaminade*. Montreal: Louise Courteau, 1993.

Ernest Chausson

Brétaudeau, Isabelle. *Les mélodies de Chausson—Un parcours de l'intime*. Arles, France: Actes Sud, 1999.
Chausson, Ernest. *Écrits inédits—Correspondance, Roman de jeunesse*. Edited by Jean Gallois. Monaco: Éditions du Rocher, 1999.
Gallois, Jean. *Ernest Chausson*. Paris: Fayard, 1994.

Claude Debussy

Bathori, Jane. *On the Interpretation of the Mélodies of Claude Debussy*. Hillsdale, NY: Pendragon Press, 1998.
Briscoe, James R. (editor). *Debussy in Performance*. New Haven, CT: Yale University, 1999.
Cobb, Margaret G. (editor). *The Poetic Debussy: A Collection of His Song Texts and Selected Letters*. Boston: Northeastern University Press, 1982; revised second edition (Richard Miller, with Margaret G. Cobb, editor). Rochester, NY: University of Rochester Press, 1994.
Debussy, Claude. *Correspondance*. Par François Lesure et Denis Herlin. Paris: Éditions Gallimard, 2005.
Debussy, Claude. *Monsieur Croche et autres écrits*. Paris: Éditions Gallimard, 1971.
Lesure, François. *Claude Debussy*. Paris: Fayard, 2003. Reprinted in English as *Claude Debussy*. Rochester, NY: University of Rochester Press, 2019. Translation and revised edition by Marie Rolf.
Nichols, Roger. *The Life of Debussy*. Cambridge, UK: Cambridge University Press, 1998.

Henri Duparc

Northcote, Sydney. *The Songs of Henri Duparc*. New York: Roy Publishers, 1950.
Stricker, Rémy. *Les mélodies de Duparc*. Arles, France: Actes Sud, 1996.

Louis Durey

Robert, Frédéric. *Durey, l'aîné des six*. Paris: Éditeurs français réunis, 1968.

Henri Dutilleux

Gervasoni, Pierre. *Henri Dutilleux*. Arles, France: Actes Sud, 2016.

Glayman, Claude. *Henri Dutilleux, Mystère et mémoire des sons, entretiens*. Arles, France: Actes Sud, 1997. Translated in English by Roger Nichols as *Henri Dutilleux: Music—Mystery and Memory: Conversations with Claude Glayman*. New York: Routledge, 2003.

Gabriel Fauré

Caballero, Carlo. *Fauré and French Musical Esthetics*. Cambridge, UK: Cambridge University Press, 2003.

Caballero, Carlo and Stephen Rumph, editors. *Fauré Studies*. Cambridge, UK: Cambridge University Press, 2021.

Duchen, Jessica. *Gabriel Fauré*. London: Phaidon, 2000.

Fauré, Gabriel. *Correspondance*. Edited by Jean-Michel Nectoux. Paris: Fayard, 1990. Reprinted in English and translated by J. A. Underwood, as *Gabriel Fauré: His Life through His Letters*. New York: Marion Boyars, 1984.

Fauré, Gabriel. *Correspondance, suivie de Lettres à Madame H*. Edited by Jean-Michel Nectoux. Paris: Fayard, 2015.

Fauré, Gabriel and Camille Saint-Saëns. *Correspondance: Soixante ans d'amitié*. Edited by Jean-Michel Nectoux. Paris: Société française de musicologie, 1975.

Gordon, Tom (editor and translator). *Regarding Fauré*. Newark, NJ: Overseas Publishers Association, Gordon & Breach Publishers, 1999.

Jankelévitch, Vladimir. *Fauré et ses mélodies*. Paris: Plon, 1938.

Johnson, Graham. *Gabriel Fauré: The Songs and Their Poets*. Farnham, UK: Ashgate, 2014.

Nectoux, Jean-Michel. *Gabriel Fauré ou les voix du clair-obscur*. Paris: Flammarion, 1990. Reprinted in English as *Gabriel Fauré: A Musical Life*. Translated by Roger Nichols. Cambridge: Cambridge University Press, 1991.

Charles Gounod

Condé, Gérard. *Charles Gounod: Biographie et catalogue*. Paris: Fayard, 2009.

Flynn, Timothy. *Charles François Gounod: A Research and Information Guide*. New York: Routledge, 2016.

Reynaldo Hahn

Blay, Philippe (editor). *Reynaldo Hahn, un éclectique en musique*. Arles, France: Actes Sud/Palazzetto Bru Zane, 2015.

Depaulis, Jacques. *Reynaldo Hahn*. Empreinte Series. Paris: Éditions Séguier, 2007.

Gavoty, Bernard. *Reynaldo Hahn: Le musicien de la Belle Époque*. Paris: Buchet Chastel, 1997.

Hahn, Reynaldo. *Du chant*. Paris: Gallimard, 1957. Reprinted in English as *On Singers and Singing*. Translation by Leopold Simoneau. Portland, OR: Amadeus Press, 2003.

Hahn, Reynaldo. *Journal d'un musician*. Paris: Plon, 1933.

Hahn, Reynaldo. *L'Oreille au guet*. Paris: Gallimard, 1937.

Hahn, Reynaldo. *Thèmes variés*. Paris: J.-B. Janin, 1946.

Philippe Hersant

Hersant, Philippe. *Le filtre du souvenir, entretiens*. Edited by Jean-Marc Bardot. Paris: Cig'Art, 2003.

Augusta Holmès

Friang, Michèle. *Augusta Holmès ou la gloire interdite*. Mémoires Collection. Paris: Autrement, 2002.
Géfen, Gérard. *Augusta Holmès l'outrancière*. Paris: Belfond, 1987.
Olivier, Brigitte. *Les mélodies d'Augusta Holmès, essai*. Arles, France: Actes Sud, 2003.
Passler, Jann. "The Ironies of Gender, or Virility and Politics in the Music of Augusta Holmès." *Women and Music* 2 (Fall 1998): 1–25.

Arthur Honegger

Halbreich, Harry. *Arthur Honegger*. Paris: Fayard, 1992. Translated in English by Roger Nichols. Portland, OR: Amadeus Press, 2003.

Vincent d'Indy

d'Indy, Vincent. *Ma vie*. Selection, presentation, and annotations by Marie d'Indy. Paris: Séguier, 2001.
Schwartz, Manuela (editor). *Vincent d'Indy et son temps*. Sprimont, Belgium: Mardaga, 2006.

Marie Jaëll

Hurpeau, Laurent (editor). *Marie Jaëll, monographie*. Lyon, France: Symétrie, 2004.

Thierry Lancino

Lancino, Thierry. Personal website of the composer of *L'Amour par terre*. http://www.thierrylancino.org.

Jules Massenet

Dibbern, Mary and Hervé Oléon. *Massenet: General Catalogue of Works*. Hillsdale, NY: Pendragon Press, 2016.
Irvine, Demar. *Massenet: A Chronicle of His Life and Times*. Pompton Plains, NJ: Amadeus Press, 1997.
Massenet, Anne. *Jules Massenet en toutes lettres*. Paris: Éditions de Fallois, 2001.

Olivier Messiaen

Boivin, Jean. *La classe de Messiaen*. Paris: Christian Bourgois, 1995.
Hill, Peter and Nigel Simeone. *Olivier Messiaen*. New Haven, CT: Yale University Press, 2005. Reprinted in French translation as *Olivier Messiaen*. Translated by Lucie Kayas. Paris: Fayard, 2008.
Massin, Brigitte. *Olivier Messiaen: Une poétique du merveilleux*. Aix-en-Provence, France: Alinea, 1989.
Samuel, Claude. *Permanences d'Olivier Messiaen*. Arles, France: Actes Sud, 1999.

Darius Milhaud

Milhaud, Darius. *Entretiens avec Claude Rostand*. Paris: Belfond, 1992.

Milhaud, Darius. *Ma vie heureuse*. Paris: Belfond, 1974. Reprinted in English as *My Happy Life: An Autobiography*. Translated by Donald Evans and Christopher Palmer. London: Marion Boyars, 1995.

Francis Poulenc

Buckland, Sidney and Myriam Chimènes. *Poulenc, Music, Art and Literature*. Farnham, UK: Ashgate, 1999.

Johnson, Graham. *Poulenc: The Life in the Songs*. New York and London: Liveright, 2020.

Lacombe, Hervé, *Poulenc*. Paris: Fayard, 2013.

Machart, Renaud. *Poulenc*. Paris: Le Seuil, 1995.

Nichols, Roger. *Poulenc: A Biography*. New Haven, CT, and London: Yale University Press, 2020.

Poulenc, Francis. *Correspondance 1910–1963*. Edited by Myriam Chimènes. Paris: Fayard, 1994.

Poulenc, Francis. *"Echo and Source": Selected Correspondance 1915–1963*. Edited by Sidney Buckland. London: Victor Gollancz, 1991.

Poulenc, Francis. *J'écris ce qui me chante*. Edited by Nicolas Southon. Paris: Fayard, 2011.

Poulenc, Francis. *Journal de mes mélodies*. New edition by Renaud Machart. Paris: Cicero/Salabert, 1993. Reprinted in English as *Diary of My Songs* (bilingual edition). Translated by Winifred Radford, foreword by Graham Johnson. London: Kahn & Averill, 2006.

Ramaut, Alban. *Francis Poulenc et la voix*. Lyon, France: Symétrie, 2002.

Maurice Ravel

Marnat, Marcel. *Maurice Ravel*. Paris: Fayard, 1986.

Orenstein, Arbie. *Ravel: Man and Musician*. Mineola, NY: Dover Publications, 2014.

Ravel, Maurice. *Lettres, écrits et entretiens*. Edited by Arbie Orenstein. Paris: Flammarion, 1989. Reprinted in English as *A Ravel Reader: Correspondance, Articles, Interviews*. Compiled and edited by Arbie Orenstein. New York: Dover Publications, 2003.

Albert Roussel

Follet, Robert. *Albert Roussel: A Bio-Bibliography*. Westport, CA: Greenwood, 1988.

Roussel, Albert. *Lettres et écrits*. Paris: Flammarion, 1987.

Top, Damien. *Albert Roussel*. "Carré musique" Collection. Paris: Séguier, 2000.

Camille Saint-Saëns

Gallois, Jean. *Camille Saint-Saëns*. Sprimont, Belgium: Mardaga, 2004.

Passler, Jann (editor). *Saint-Saëns and His World*. Princeton, NJ: Princeton University Press, 2012.

Rees, Brian. *Camille Saint-Saëns: A Life*. London: Faber and Faber, 1999.

Saint-Saëns, Camille. *Au courant de la vie*. Paris: Dorbon-Aîné, 1914.

Saint-Saëns, Camille. *Divagations sérieuses*. Paris: Flammarion, 1922.

Saint-Saëns, Camille. *École buissonnière*. Paris: Pierre Lafitte, 1913.

Saint-Saëns, Camille. *Harmonie et mélodie*. Paris: Calmann-Lévy, 1885.

Saint-Saëns, Camille. *Portraits et souvenirs*. Paris: La Société d'édition artistique, 1899.

Saint-Saëns, Camille. *Rimes familières*. Paris: Calmann-Lévy, 1891.

Studd, Stephen, *Saint-Saëns*. Vancouver, Canada: Fairleigh Dickinson University Press, 1999.

Déodat de Séverac

Séverac, Déodat de. *Écrits sur la musique*. Edited by Pierre Billot. Sprimont, Belgium: Mardaga, 1993.
Séverac, Déodat de. *La Musique et les lettres—Correspondance, 1873–1921*. Sprimont, Belgium: Mardaga, 2002.
Waters, Robert F. *Déodat de Séverac: Musical Identity in Fin de Siècle France*. Farnham, UK: Ashgate, 2008.

Germaine Tailleferre

Hacquard, Georges. *Germaine Tailleferre, la dame des Six*. Paris: L'Harmattan, 1998.

Pauline Viardot

Friang, Michèle. *Pauline Viardot au miroir de sa correspondance, biographie*. Collection "Points d'orgue." Paris: Hermann, 2008.
Kendall-Davies, Barbara. *The Life and Work of Pauline Viardot Garcia* (2 vols.). Volume I: *The Years of Fame, 1836–1863*. Cambridge, UK: Cambridge Scholars Press, revised edition 2004. Volume II: *The Years of Grace, 1863–1910*. Cambridge, UK: Cambridge Scholars Publishing, 2012.

French language

Dictionnaire de la langue française, par É. Littré, Reprinted in seven volumes by the *Encyclopaedia Britannica*. Versailles, France: 1999. The application for smartphone can be downloaded at no cost.
Abbott, Helen. *Baudelaire in Song 1880–1930*. New York: Oxford University Press, 2017.
Gravollet, Paul. *Déclamation, école de mécanisme*. Paris: Albin Michel, 1930.
Jouvet, Louis. *Le Comédien désincarné*. Paris: Flammarion, 1954.
Jouvet, Louis. *Écoute, mon ami*. Paris: Librairie Théâtrale, 1952.
Jouvet, Louis. *Réflexions de comédien*. Paris: Librairie Théâtrale, 1941.
Le Roy, Georges. *Grammaire de la diction française*. Paris: Éditions de la pensée moderne, 1967.
Le Roy, Georges. *Traité pratique de la diction française*. Paris: Jacques Grancher, 1968.
Martens, Paul. *Nouveau solfège de la diction*. Paris: Librairie Théâtrale, 1986.

Websites

http://www.melodiefrancaise.com: Centre International de la Mélodie Française / Académie Francis Poulenc. In the "Repertoire" there are more than 30,000 French songs listed. In French and English.
http://www.francoisleroux.net: Personal website of one of the authors. Many recordings are present, and can be heard (pages: Audio & Video). In French and English.
http://www.musimem.com: only in French. A lot of information on lesser-known French composers.
http://www.charles-gounod.com: a lot about the composer.
https://www.wisemusicclassical.com: website of the French publisher Leduc, but also of Hamelle, Heugel, etc.
http://www.durand-salabert-eschig.com/en-gb/: where to find information on scores published by main French publishers: Durand, Max Eschig, Salabert, etc.
http://www.bnf.fr: website of the Bibliothèque nationale de France. The Gallica catalogue from which to download scores is available at http://www.bnf.fr/en/collections_and_services/digital_libraries_gallica/a.gallica_digital_library.html.

Credits

The musical examples were produced by Laurence Ardouin and Christophe Arfan.

***

The authors would like to thank Richard Stokes for permission to reproduce his English translations of the following poems:

Jean-Antoine de Baïf: *Ô ma belle rebelle*. Théodore de Banville: *Pierrot*. Charles Baudelaire: *Les hiboux*. Baronne de Brimont: *Cygne sur l'eau*. Théophile Gautier: *Au cimetière*; *Lamento-La chanson du pêcheur*. Johann Wolfgang von Goethe: *Romance de Mignon*. Victor Hugo: *L'absent*; *Si vous n'avez rien à me dire*. Stéphane Mallarmé: *Apparition*; *Soupir*; *Placet futile*; *Éventail*; *Sainte*. Gabriel Marc: *Sérénade*. Clément Marot: *D'anne, qui luy jecta de la neige*; *D'anne*. Olivier Messiaen: *Pourquoi?*; *La fiancée perdue*. Sully Prudhomme: *Le galop*. Henri de Régnier: *Les grands vents venus d'outre-mer*. Armand Renaud: *Au cimetière*. Jean Richepin: *Larmes*. Pierre de Ronsard: *Grasselette et Maigrelette*. Edmond Rostand: *Pastorale des cochons roses*. Cécile Sauvage: *Le sourire*. Paul Verlaine: *Sur un vieil air*; *La chanson bien douce*; *En sourdine*; *Paysages tristes-Soleils couchants*.

***

The authors would like to thank the following for permission to reproduce published material:

© Alphonse Leduc—Henri Dutilleux: *San Francisco Night*.

© Durand—Claude Debussy: *Nuits blanches*. Louis Durey: *Trois poèmes de Pétrone*. Philippe Hersant: *Paroles peintes*. Olivier Messiaen: *Trois mélodies*.

© Flammarion—Paul Fort: *Le chasseur perdu en forêt*, *Cloche du soir*, *Chanson de fol* from *Complaintes et dits*.

© Gallimard—Paul Éluard: *Paroles peintes* from *Cours naturel*. Max Jacob: *Passé et présent* (renamed *Poète et ténor* by Francis Poulenc) from *Laboratoire central*. Jules Supervielle: *Le petit bois* from *Poèmes de la France malheureuse*.

© Heugel—Germaine Tailleferre: *Vrai Dieu, qui m'y confortera* from *Six chansons françaises*.

© Salabert—Georges Auric: *Le petit bois* from *Quatre chants de la France malheureuse*. Arthur Honegger: *Trois poèmes de Paul Fort*. Darius Milhaud: *L'innocence* from *Trois poèmes en prose de Lucile de Chateaubriand*. Francis Poulenc: *Poète et ténor* from *Quatre poèmes de Max Jacob*; *Pierrot*.

© Seghers—Paul Gilson: *San Francisco Night* from *Au rendez-vous des solitaires*.

© Thierry Lancino—Thierry Lancino: *L'Amour par terre*.

***

Index

Aesop, 26
Albani, Emma, 75
Alençon, Anne d', 227, 227n3
Alliot-Lugaz, Colette, 201
Anacréon, 20
Apollinaire, Guillaume, 7, 22, 26, 41, 42, 215, 255
Aragon, Louis, 21, 49
Armandie, Rose, 179n2
Arrieu, Claude, 27
Audran, Edmond, 21
Augier, Émile, 25, 138, 149
Auric, Georges, 21, 26, 43, 44, 49–52, 219
Azraël, 165n4

Bach, Johann Sebastian, 179, 217
Bagès Jacobé de Trigny, Maurice, 28
Baïf, Jean Antoine de, 149
Balbous, Jean, 249
Banville, Théodore de, 15, 215, 218, 219
Barbier, Georges, 141
Barbier, Jules, 114, 149
Barrault, Jean-Louis, 219n4
Barrès, Maurice, 24
Barthes, Roland, 17
Bartók, Béla, 18n2
Bathori, Jane, 1, 29, 258, 258n4
Baudelaire, Charles, 6, 15, 22, 36, 37, 73, 108, 186, 190, 252
Béclard d'Harcourt, Marguerite, 194n2
Beethoven, Ludwig van, 114
Bergeron, Katherine, 144n3
Berlioz, Hector, 2, 12, 13, 14, 25, 28, 31, 53–58, 59, 117n4, 118, 127, 153, 174, 237, 238, 259, 259n1
Bernac, Pierre (Pierre Bertin), 1, 2, 8, 22, 29, 34, 35, 36, 38, 39, 41, 42, 43, 43n8, 214
Bertin, Louise, 53
Bizet, Georges, 33, 34, 103n3
Bloom, Peter, 53
Bodin, Thierry, 135n1
Bonis Mel (Mélanie), 27
Bordes, Charles, 59–62
Bordèse, Stephan, 175
Borel, Pétrus, 59
Bouchor, Maurice, 59
Boulanger, Lili, 23, 32n3, 63–69
Boulanger, Nadia, 27, 63, 66n4, 82, 82n2, 91n1

Bourget, Paul, 14, 23
Brahms, Johannes, 16, 23, 32, 181, 202, 238
Brassens, Georges, 180, 180n3
Brecht, Bertold, 18n2
Breton, Geneviève, 175, 175n4
Bréville, Pierre de, 59
Brimont, Baroness Antoine de, 30, 141, 142, 148
Britten, Benjamin, 21
Brizeux, Auguste, 175
Brousse, Marie, 78
Büsser, Henri, 64n2, 127
Bussine, Romain, 19, 131
Byron, George Gordon, Lord, 255

Calypso (Homer), 67
Canal, Marguerite, 82, 82n6
Caplet, André, 21, 179n1, 218n3
Carné, Marcel, 18n2, 50n1, 219n4
Carré, Michel, 114
Carter, Elliott, 91n1
Caruso, Enrico, 103n3
Casella, Alfredo, 19
Cassou, Jean, 127
Castellane, Boniface (Boni) de, Comte, 141
Cazalis, Henri. *See* Lahor, Jean
Cecrops, King of Athens, 126
Chabrier, Emmanuel, 70–74, 75
Chalupt, René, 49
Chaminade, Cécile, 75–80
Char, René, 20, 20n5, 25
Charpentier, Gustave, 103n3
Chateaubriand, Lucile de, 211
Chausson, Ernest, 15, 16, 37, 40, 41, 46, 63, 65, 81–90, 180
Chausson, Étiennette, 82
Chopin, Frédéric, 192, 258
Claudel, Paul, 21, 22, 194, 211
Cocteau, Jean, 9, 26, 104n4, 122, 123, 211, 215
Cohen, Jeff, 39, 194, 201
Cole, Nat King, 18
Conneau, Madame Henri, 75n2
Coppée, François, 250
Costeley, Guillaume, 78
Croiza, Claire, 64n2, 179, 179n1
Cros, Charles, 14
Cui, César, 191

Damase, Jean-Michel, 129
David, Félicien, 163
Deburau, Jean-Gaspard, 219n4
Debussy, Claude, 1, 7, 8, 11, 14, 15, 16, 19, 20,
    22, 23, 23n8, 25, 28, 29, 30, 31, 33, 36, 37, 38,
    40, 41, 41n7, 44, 46, 59, 63, 64, 65, 66, 75, 85,
    86, 91–107, 127, 158, 158n1, 159, 179, 180,
    184, 186, 195, 202, 208, 210, 212, 219, 220,
    222, 224, 231, 250, 252n1
Dehmel, Richard, 16
Delafosse, Léon, 16
Delage, Maurice, 15, 26
Delage, Roger, 70
Delannoy, Marcel, 27
Delaquys, Georges, 66, 66n4
Delibes, Léo, 163, 175n2
DeMille, Cecil B., 21
Desbordes-Valmore, Marceline, 13n1, 30
Dessau, Paul, 82, 82n7
Devoyon, Patrick, 167
Devriès, David, 64n2
Diepenbrock, Alphonse, 82, 82n3
Dietsch, Louis, 138
Disney, Walt, 72
Dubois, Théodore, 118
Duchambge, Pauline, 13n1
Ducros, Jérôme, 128
Dufranne, Hector, 66
Dukas, Paul, 46
Duparc, Henri, 6, 16, 17, 18, 28, 31, 37, 42, 46,
    53, 59, 63, 73, 74, 87, 93, 95, 108–121, 153,
    186, 188, 202, 252
Durand, Jacques, 122, 221
Durey, Louis, 25, 26, 122–126, 227
Dutilleux, Henri, 29, 91n1, 117n4, 127–130
Dutoit, Charles, 214
Duval, Denise, 35

Eisler, Hanns, 18n2
Éluard, Paul, 22, 25, 49, 167, 172, 215
Enesco, Georges, 118, 227
Enoch, Evelyn, 259
Essarts, Emmanuel des, 175
Esty, Alice, 127, 128

Fabre, Gabriel, 16
Falk, Lina, 179
Falla, Manuel de, 103n3
Fargue, Léon-Paul, 221
Fauré, Gabriel, 7, 14, 16, 17, 19, 22, 23, 25, 28,
    29, 37, 40, 41, 41n7, 42, 43, 44, 45, 53, 59,
    69, 75, 81, 117n4, 131–148, 153, 155, 158,
    158n1, 179, 191, 191n1, 193, 202, 212, 241,
    263, 265

Faure, Jean-Baptiste, 28
Faure, Michel, 14
Ferré, Léo, 82
Fischer-Dieskau, Dietrich, 31, 34, 38
Flégier, Ange, 180, 180n4, 191, 191n1
Florian, Jean-Pierre Claris de, 59
Fort, Paul, 179, 180, 185
Fournier, Paul, 24
Franck, César, 40, 135
Franck, Maurice, 258
Francis I (King of France), 227n3
Fugère, Lucien, 70

Gabory, Georges, 49
Gallet, Louis, 114
García Lorca, Federico, 19
Garden, Mary, 30n1
Gargenville, 66, 66n3
Gartside, Robert, 1
Gaubert, Philippe, 127
Gautier, Théophile, 13, 15, 25, 31, 33, 37, 45,
    53, 109n1, 153, 154, 168, 237, 238, 259,
    259n1, 260
George, Stefan, 16
Gérard, Rosemonde, 75, 75n1
Gide, André, 211
Gilson, Paul, 127, 128, 128n3, 129
Gluck, Christoph Willibald, 29
Goethe, Johann Wilhelm von, 16, 108,
    114, 168
Goltzius, Hendrick, 186
Gounod, Charles, 13, 19, 25, 28, 30, 37, 42,
    45, 103n3, 114, 138, 149–156, 202, 241,
    259n1, 260
Gouvy, Théodore, 78
Gréco, Juliette, 18, 49
Grovlez, Gabriel, 82, 82n4
Grümmer, Elisabeth, 76
Guilbert, Yvette, 50, 51
Guiraud, Ernest, 78
Gutmann, René-Albert, 225

Hachette, Louis, 175
Hafiz, 175
Hahn, Reynaldo, 16, 19, 20, 81, 135, 157–166, 238
Hameau, Louise, 75n1
Haraucourt, Edmond, 19
Hardy-Thé, Lucien, 226
Haydn, Joseph, 45
Héguin de Guerle, Charles, 122
Heine, Heinrich, 23, 24, 32, 44
Heredia, José-Maria de, 230n1
Hermant, Pierre, 82, 82n5
Hersant, Philippe, 167–173

Hillemacher, Pierre & Paul, 78
Hindemith, Paul, 21, 217
Hoerner, Germaine, 127
Hoffman, Gary, 167
Holmès, Augusta, 174–178
Homer, 67
Honegger, Arthur, 91, 117n4, 179–185
Horne, Marilyn, 38
Houville, Gérard d', 230n1. *See* Régnier, Marie de
Howat, Roy, 135
Hugo, Victor, 14, 15, 16, 22, 23, 25, 42, 43, 45, 78, 131–140, 175, 190, 215, 218n3, 242, 242n1, 243
Huston, John, 49

Ibert, Jacques, 15
Indy, Vincent d', 186–189, 250, 252

Jacob, Max, 43, 213, 215, 216, 217
Jaëll, Alfred, 190
Jaëll-Trautmann, Marie, 190–193
Jammes, Francis, 23, 59, 63, 211
Janequin, Clément, 227n2
Joachim, Irène, 127, 258
Johnson, Graham, 1, 17, 39
Jolivet, André, 167
Joncières, Victorin de, 175n1
Jouvet, Louis, 24, 24n10

Katz, Martin, 38
Kilpatrick, Emily, 135
Klingsor, Tristan (Léon Leclère), 17, 221
Koechlin, Charles, 29
Kosma, Joseph, 18, 18n2

La Fontaine, Jean de, 7, 20, 21, 26
Lahor, Jean (Henri Cazalis), 37, 59, 73, 105, 108, 175, 186
Lamartine, Alphonse de, 45, 141
Lancino, Thierry, 2, 194–200
Laparra, Raoul, 194n2
Lattaignant, Gabriel-Charles de, 255
Latil, Léo, 211
Laussel, Adam, 138
Leblanc, Georgette, 16
Lecocq, Charles, 21
Leconte de Lisle, Charles-Marie, 14, 15, 20, 42, 93
Lee, Noël, 38, 91, 91n1, 167, 201, 217
Lefort, Bernard, 255, 255n1
Leguerney, Jacques, 27
Lehmann, Liza, 75
L'Hermite, Tristan, 20

Liszt, Franz, 114, 190, 193, 238
Lott, Felicity, 26
Louis XV (King of France), 106
Louÿs, Pierre, 33, 92, 230, 230n1
Lucas, Hippolyte, 78
Lully, Jean-Baptiste, 29
Luquiens, Hélène, 221
Lyvron, Louis de, 175

Maeterlinck, Maurice, 16, 63
Magnard, Albéric, 24
Mahler, Gustav, 33
Mallarmé, Geneviève, 106, 224
Mallarmé, Stéphane, 9, 15, 16, 22, 25, 31, 37, 63, 101, 102, 103, 104n4, 105, 106, 107, 130, 221, 224, 225
Maquet, Thérèse, 75n1
Marc, Gabriel, 108, 113
Marot, Clément, 26, 221, 226, 227, 228
Martini, Jean (Johann Paul-Egide Schwarzendorf), 59
Massé, Victor, 78
Massenet, Jules, 14, 15, 16, 28, 35, 44, 103n3, 201–205, 238, 239
Matha, Louise, 206
Mauclair, Camille (Camille Laurent Célestin Faust), 59
Mauguière, André, 247n2
Mendelssohn, Felix, 149
Mendès, Catulle, 174, 175
Mercey, Suzanne, 75n1
Messiaen, Olivier, 29, 36, 206–210
Mesureur, Amélie, 75n1
Milhaud, Darius, 128, 179n1, 211–213, 214, 215
Milhaud, Madeleine, 214
Minne, Georges, 64
Mirbeau, Octave, 175n1
Molière (Jean-Baptiste Poquelin), 19
Montand, Yves, 18
Monteverdi, Claudio, 33, 148n4, 164, 164n3
Moore, Gerald, 38
Moore, Thomas, 13
Moréas, Jean (Ioannis Papadiamantopoulos), 22, 22n6, 22n7, 59, 81
Moscheles, Ignaz, 190
Mozart, Wolfgang Amadeus, 20, 29, 42, 43, 63, 103n3, 155, 238
Müller, Wilhelm, 10
Musset, Alfred de, 23, 24, 45, 78, 175

Navarre, Marguerite de, 227n3
Nectoux, Jean-Michel, 135
Nerval, Gérard de, 32
Nichols, Roger, 108, 115n3

Noailles, Anna de, 30
Noailles, Marie-Laure de, 218
Noske, Fritz, 131
Nuitter, Charles, 114n2

Ochsé, Fernand, 194n2
Offenbach, Jacques, 21
Orléans, Charles d', 20, 227, 250
Ottenfels, Baroness Cécile d', 75n1

Pahud, Emmanuel, 167
Paliard, Camille, 211
Panzéra, Charles, 1, 9, 28, 29, 117, 117n4,
    127, 127n1
Parny, Évariste-Désiré de Forges de, 221
Pasqualini, Juliette. *See* Conneau,
    Madame Henri
Passerat, Jean, 149
Pavarotti, Luciano, 8
Payan, Paul, 252
Péguy, Charles, 24
Peignot, Suzanne, 29, 35
Penelope (Homer), 67
Perny, Louise, 75n1
Petrone (Petronius), 26, 122, 123, 227
Picasso, Pablo, 43
Piccioni, Beatrix. *See* Rochaïd, Countess Joseph
Pinget, Robert, 255
Plançon, Pol, 75
Poe, Edgar Allan, 22, 221
Pomey, Louis, 259
Ponge, Francis, 25
Poulenc, Francis, 7, 21, 22, 25, 26, 29, 35, 35n4,
    36–37, 38, 41, 42, 43, 104n4, 110, 128, 167,
    214–220, 255
Prévert, Jacques, 18, 18n2, 50n1
Proust, Marcel, 16, 141
Pugno, Raoul, 66n4
Puig-Roget, Henriette, 27

Raalte, Albert van, 179
Radiguet, Raymond, 49, 104n4
Rameau, Jean-Philippe, 127
Ravel, Maurice, 1, 16, 17, 23, 26, 29, 31, 36, 37,
    38, 122, 123, 130, 149, 167, 183, 184, 202,
    221–229, 255n1
Regnault, Henri, 175n4
Régnier, Henri de, 162–164, 221, 230, 235, 236
Régnier, Marie de, 230, 230n1
Remacle, Jeanne, 81
Renard, Jules, 148, 221
Renaud, Armand, 23, 53, 237
Respighi, Ottorino, 19
Reyniel, Pierre. *See* Perny, Louise

Richepin, Jean, 33, 53, 190, 191
Riddez, Carlos. *See* Balbous, Jean
Rienzi, Emma di, 75n1
Riese, Alexander, 123
Rieti, Vittorio, 128
Rilke, Rainer Maria, 16
Rimbaud, Jean Arthur, 21, 211
Risler, Édouard, 249
Robin, Mado, 175, 175n2
Rochaïd, Countess Joseph, 75n1
Rogé, Pascal, 38
Rohinsky, Marie-Claire, 1
Rollinat, Maurice, 73
Ronsard, Pierre de, 16, 19, 22, 43, 77, 78, 149,
    211, 215, 215n1, 221, 227, 244, 245
Ropartz, Joseph Guy, 32, 44
Rorem, Ned, 91n1
Rosenthal, Manuel, 128
Rossi, Tino, 175, 175n3
Rossini, Gioacchino, 29
Rostand, Edmond, 70, 72, 75
Roussel, Albert, 37, 179n1, 230–236

Saint-John Perse (Alexis Saint Léger-
    Léger), 21, 26
Saint-Marceaux, Marguerite de, 226
Saint-Saëns, Camille, 14, 17, 24, 25, 28, 30, 37,
    44, 53, 59, 135, 186, 190, 202, 218n3, 237–249,
    250, 259
Samain, Albert, 23
Samazeuilh, Madame Gustave, 230
Sand, George, 174
Sanderson, Sybil, 28
Sarazin, Jean-François, 255
Satie, Erik, 24, 122, 123
Sauguet, Henri, 128
Sauvage, Cécile, 206
Schiller, Friedrich von, 16
Schmitt, Florent, 27
Schoenberg, Arnold, 16, 24, 32, 215
Schubert, Franz, 10, 15, 16, 18, 32, 33, 39, 46,
    63, 114, 118, 138
Schumann, Robert, 15, 16, 23, 32, 44, 114, 202
Selva, Blanche, 81
Sermisy, Claudin de, 227n2
Séverac, Déodat de, 50, 182, 250–254
Silvestre, Armand, 22, 23, 44, 45, 203
Sinatra, Frank, 18
Singher, Martial, 36
Souzay, Gérard (Gérard Tisserand), 179n1
Stimer, David, 128
Stokes, Richard, 1, 150
Strauss, Richard, 16, 17, 43, 231
Stravinsky, Igor, 43, 215, 217

Stricker, Rémy, 31n2, 109
Sully Prudhomme (René François Armand
  Prudhomme), 108, 116, 262–263
Supervielle, Jules, 49, 211

Tagore, Rabindranath, 141
Tailleferre, Germaine, 128, 255–258
Tardieu, Jean, 255
Thénard, Jenny, 75n1
Theocrite, 122
Thill, Georges, 103n3
Thiriet, Maurice, 27
Thomas, Ambroise, 114
Tosti, Francesco Paolo, Sir, 19
Trélat, Marie, 28
Turgenev, Ivan, 259

Ulysses (Homer), 67
Upshaw, Dawn, 128

Vallin, Ninon, 103, 103n3
Van Lerberghe, Charles, 23
Varèse, Edgar, 46
Vasnier, Marie, 14, 28, 29, 30, 31, 91, 101, 102
Verdi, Giuseppe, 29, 35

Verhaeren, Émile, 66n4
Verlaine, Paul, 7, 15, 16, 21, 23, 25, 26, 30,
  41, 59, 61, 63, 81, 81n1, 84, 85, 86, 87, 88,
  89, 90, 157, 181, 194, 194n2, 211, 222, 224,
  250, 263
Viardot, Paul, 263
Viardot, Pauline, 28, 259–265
Viau, Théophile de, 20
Vigny, Alfred de, 180n4
Villon, François, 20, 104, 174, 176, 177,
  206, 228
Vilmorin, Louise de, 215
Vinci, Leonardo da, 12
Vivès, Vincent, 14
Voltaire (François-Marie Arouet), 255

Wagner, Richard, 16, 17, 24n9, 70, 73, 73n1,
  78, 114n2, 202
Watteau, Antoine, 12, 194, 195
Weber, Carl Maria von, 181
White, Ruth L.: 82
Wilder, Victor, 108, 114
Wolf, Hugo, 16, 17, 114

Zenta, Hermann, 174. See Holmès, Augusta